BOOK DESIGN: Systematic Aspects

abcdefgghijklmnopqrstuvw
DEFGHIJKKLMNOPQQRRS
1 2 1 2 1 2
1234567890
‚‘’’——!?¢%/*)

BOOK DESIGN
SYSTEMATIC ASPECTS

Stanley Rice

R. R. BOWKER COMPANY
New York & London

[For Joel and Leslie]

ACKNOWLEDGEMENTS

The author is grateful for permission to reprint material that appears on the following pages (as indicated):

p. 9 (12 lines beginning "That is finished . . . ") from Silence *by John Cage (Cambridge, Mass.: MIT Press, 1966, p. 124);*
p. 35 (two line graphs at page bottom) from How to Live With Statistics *by Darrell Huff & Irving Geis (New York: W. W. Norton, 1954, pp. 61 & 63);*
pp. 64 & 65 (adapted automatic paging rules) and p. 209 (information sheet) from Computerized Typesetting *(Allentown, Pa.: ComCom, 1977, pp. 10 & 16);*
p.67 (flow chart) adapted from Computer Compostion Using PAGE-1 *by John Pierson (New York: John Wiley & Sons, 1972, p. 54);*
p. 68 (automatic paging rules for floating illustrations) adapted from Textran-2 Extended Language Capabilities *(Lake Success, N.Y.: Alphanumeric, 1969, pp. 54–55);*
p. 95 (table of castoff results) from Format Notes *(Medford, N.Y.: Science Typographers, 1976, p. 6);*
p. 116 (example of mathematical compostion) from documentation of the Quinn & Boden Company (Rahway, N.J.);
pp. 216–217 from Pricing and Ethical Guidelines *(New York: Graphic Artist Guild, 1975, pp. 38–39);*
p. 218 (opposite Chapter 12 opening) and p. 232 (two posterized photos) from Metacolor, Inc. (San Francisco);
pp. 228–229 (suggestions for coding) adapted from the Seybold Report *(Media, Pa.: Seybold Pubs., Vol. 6. No. 4, Oct. 25, 1976, pp. 4–13 & 4–14);*
pp. 251–261, adapted from Special Libraries *(New York: Special Libraries Assn., Vol. 60, No. 12, Dec. 1969, pp. 627–634).*

Published by R. R. Bowker Company
1180 Avenue of the Americas, New York, N.Y. 10036

Library of Congress Cataloging in Publication Data

Rice, Stanley.
Book design—systematic aspects.
Bibliography: p.
Includes index.
1. Book design. I. Title.
Z116.A3R5   070.5'3   77–28186
ISBN 0–8352–1044–8

Contents

Preface xi

1 *The Designer as Go-Between 1*

Publisher to printer 2
The design process as a sequence of events 4

2 *Design and Editorial Processes—Words 7*

Editorial structures: what are they? 8
Complexity and flexibility of editorial structures 10
  Mathematical displays 10
Specification of editorial structures 11
  Lists 12
The keying of complex manuscripts 14

3 *Design and Editorial Processes—Images 21*

Finding the right artist 23
Providing photographs 27
  Checklist for location photography 29
Charts and graphs 31
Maps 33
Diagrams: information and distortion 38
Design specifications for science drawings and diagrams 40
Design specifications for charts and graphs 41
Design specifications for maps 42

4 *Typesetting Options: Documentation and Specification 45*

Documentation from the typesetter 46
  Vertical and horizontal spacing 47
  Word spacing 47
Typographic planning 49
Specification of editorial structures 50
  The decision-making process 50
  Display composition 53

The composition order 56
"The invisible book" 57

5 *The Making of Pages 63*

General paging instructions 63
Typical rules for automatic paging 64
The dummy 66
Illustrations 66
Floating illustrations in multicolumn format 68
The concept of the modular text 70

6 *The Adjustment of Book Length 75*

Character count: the general method 75
Castoff using a pocket calculator 77
Castoff and text fitting 80
Tables of castoff results 82
Text makeup in relation to even press forms 86
The book length optimization form 88
Individual book castoff adjustment 91
The programmable calculator 91
Three aids to castoff 94
Conclusion 94

7 *Difficult Composition 99*

The traditional Monotype system 99
Special characters 102
Basic information relating to difficult book design 106
Capabilities of the compositor 107
Sources of information about technical style 109
Tables 110
Mathematics 114
Foreign languages 117
Chemistry 118
Other difficult composition 118

8 *Design Processing of Complex Texts 121*

Responsibilities of the art director 122
The delegation of design work 123
Functions of the art editor 125
Planning the illustration program 125
An essential information folder 126
Predummy planning for nontechnical books 127
The dummy 129
The master illustration list 131
Illustrations not supplied by the author 133

Picture research 133
An illustration file for nondummied books 136
Legends (captions) and credits 136
Sending the dummy to the compositor 138
Final steps in the art-editing function 138
Checklist of art-editor/assistant-designer functions 139
Art and design pricing 140
In summary 141

9 *Scheduling Art Activities 143*

Scheduling simple books 143
Scheduling multiple large design/art projects 145
Using the "Critical Path Method" to schedule books 147
A "Books-in-Work" chart 156
Weekly job-status report 158
Work standards file 158

10 *Paper, Printing, and Binding: The Design Aspects 163*

Text paper 163
Printing 166
Color planning for press forms 167
Four-color process printing 170
Correcting color proofs 173
Rules of thumb for color copy 176
Bindings 177
Preprinted paper 177
Preprinted cloth or nonwoven synthetic material 177
Stamped covers 180
BMI specifications 186

11 *The Processing of Illustrations 189*

Artists and artwork 189
Illustrations in the offset process 191
Further notes on the handling of illustrations 194
Scaling and cropping 195
Bleed allowances 197
Mounting and retouching photos 198
Handling photographic prints 199
Handling color transparencies 199
Reproduction quality photostats and Veloxes 200
Handling of late illustrations 201
Handling letterpress illustrations 203
Forms useful in dealing with illustration processing 204
Forms for artists 210
Code of ethics and standards of fair practice 216

12 *New Directions in Design 219*

Designing by exception 220
Computer control and composition 222
  Stored control formats 223
Catalogs of designed formats 225
The text structure matrix 226
A publisher-compositor interface for noncomplex work 227
Automatic electronic page makeup and layout 229
Electronically generated color 231

APPENDIX A: Legal aspects of illustration and design use 235
APPENDIX B: The attributes of pictures 251

Selected Bibliography 262
Glossary 264
Index 271

Forms, charts & tables

Specification options for lists 15
Artist record sheet 25
Artist information card 26
Free-lance book design handling 51
Basic compositor information sheet, for designers 54–55
Composition specifications (trade books) 58
Composition order (technical books) 59
Summary castoff form 78
Separate castoff of selections 79
Castoff results for 6″ × 9″ trimmed size 83–84
Page makeup adjustments 87
Book-length estimate form and page makeup guide 89–90
Castoff "plus" 92
Castoff results per 100,000 characters of manuscript (6″ × 9″) 95
Characters per line from characters per pica 96
Book pages per thousands of characters in manuscript 97
Government Printing Office list of signs and symbols 103
Accented characters, mathematical symbols and Greek 104
Accented characters, arranged by language 105
Definition and parts of a table 112–113
Illustration list 132
Picture research transmittal slip 134
Art and design activities, and preceding events 146
A CPM graph of a model book 148
Art department scheduling chart 153–154
Books-in-work chart: art department 157

Art department weekly job status report 159
Work rate experience sheet 160
Some trimmed sizes, from standard sheet sizes 166
Web offset and converting rolls and trimmed sizes 166
Press form plan 168
Press forms (pages) 170
Appearance of colors under flourescent lamps 174
Smyth-sewn books, cover sizing guide 178
McCain side-stitched books, cover sizing guide 179
Relation of maximum spine width to bulk (Smyth-sewn books) 184
Binding specifications for hardbound stamped covers 185
Standard instructions for handling picture sections and mechanicals 205
Checklist for offset dummies 206
Illustrations to offset camera 207
Art/photo transmittal 208
Illustration information sheet 209
Artist contract 211
Photographer contract 212
Map specifications 213
Chart notes 214
Art department work sheet 215
Text structure matrix form 227
Standard model release form 247
Art classification card for the humanities 256

Preface

The aim of this study is to help the book designer with the nonartistic or "systematic" aspects of the design function. Traditionally there has been little help available in this area, one on which designers themselves usually lavish scant attention or affection.

This, then, might seem to be a rather unsolicited and, perhaps, thankless labor. Why was it undertaken? In response to a serious and growing need. In the last few years book designers have been so mercilessly assaulted by technology and other winds of complication and change that, in fact, they do require help, in the form of some usable strategies and weapons.

More specifically, we shall attempt to: (1) concentrate on the essential, systematic, and permanent aspects of the design of books, rather than on the changing stylistic and mechanical aspects; (2) treat the designer as a professional or, more modestly, as a craftsman, who must find professional solutions to a great variety of everyday publishing problems, rather than as an artist, who may pick and choose the right conditions in which to display artistry; (3) simplify and clarify the various systems with which the book designer works, in order that design may be seen in practical relation to present or future editorial and technological problems; (4) present everyday design problems as practical adjustments to current conditions rather than as aesthetic solutions to past problems; (5) make clear to beginning designers and those who work with designers how it is that designers function, especially in larger publishing companies, and what information they need in order to work successfully; and (6) analyze tools and methods that may now be appropriate to various phases of the designer's job, even though they may not be traditional ones.

It is not the author's intent to belittle aesthetics, which is the heart of the designer's job, but aesthetics has had a great deal of exposition, while systematics has had almost none. Furthermore, books about aesthetics or mechanics in relation to book design have tended to be out of date even before readers have had a chance to consider them—design styles and machines are constantly changing, and changes have been so swift.

This book will not go out of date. The systematic aspects of putting together complex packages of words and images do not change very much regardless of styles and machines. The intention is to offer only the kinds of practical analysis of design problems that can be applied with equal success no matter what style is desired or what technology is employed, whether the latest or the most traditional. New methods are suggested only when they can supply information that is useful in relation to the designer's job today, and/or be significantly simpler and less tedious than traditional ways of doing things.

Complex books, especially textbooks in larger companies, receive a good deal of attention here. (Methods suitable for complex books are more easily adaptable to simpler books than the other way around.) With respect to the internal processing of complex texts, the author does not wish to suggest that design departments should all conduct their affairs in the same manner. However, supply services are the same for all, and end products are very similar, so that all publishers take similar steps for the same kinds of books. They differ most with regard to job titles and the exact division of tasks.

Although there is no practical advantage to uniformity in job titles, a clarification of the terminology used in this study may be useful to the reader. The term "designer" has been used to signify a trained person exercising the functions of design and typographic specification; "art director" to imply the more supervisory, managerial, and purchasing aspects of the design function; and "assistant designer" to designate a responsible designer operating under the general supervision of another designer or art director.

The less general term "art editor" has been adopted for a person functioning under the general direction of a designer, in many ways as a quasi-designer, but without specific typographic or graphic-design training. Jobs assigned to the art editor in this study are: (a) dummying, (b) dealing with artists after they are chosen, (c) picture research, and (d) art and research traffic records and payments. These are all design-related tasks, of course, and may be divided in many ways among many people with different job titles. The exact divisions and titles are relatively unimportant and will vary, depending on the size and organization of the publisher, but the actual tasks and their requirements will remain essentially the same.

S.R.

BOOK DESIGN: Systematic Aspects

new st nd posi

[u2] 2.5 Text ations. Th

of ce o.

is n from a

basis order" pu

as shing for

[u2 .5 Illu program

siz ges. [u4]

Th ans by hich

on the part

c g ats built

by which

mo ning by the pu

CHAPTER 1
The Designer as Go-Between

A large part of the reading public is unaware of the complex series of decisions required to transform a manuscript into a well-designed book. While many people are aware that styles change, many others believe that a book evolves from its manuscript with the inevitability of an oak from an acorn. To those who are actually involved in publishing, however, it is apparent that the designer plays a key role in determining the final form of the book. It is the purpose of this book, therefore, to help designers understand the systematic aspects of their jobs.

The designer helps coordinate two separate systems by considering two sets of conditions and requirements: first, the editing, sales, production, and all other relevant aspects of the publishing process (including the production of images, such as art and photography, as well as words); and second, the manufacturing processes that produce the physical book: the typesetting, the printing, and the binding. Design specifications are the link between manuscript and physical product.

Only occasionally, even in art and photography, is the designer required to decide what is to go into a book, and on the other hand no one else is required to decide *how* anything is to appear in a book, except in the case of another person functioning as the designer. The designer is, therefore, the main specifications connection or bridge between the publisher, who produces the manuscript with its accompanying visual material, and the manufacturers, who produce the physical book. By means of specifications, the designer forms the connection between the two systems, and is, in the language of the systems analyst, the "interface" between them. Book manufacturing renders information into a new format. Nothing else takes place except the duplication of the new format, which is the complete physical product of the book publisher.

For this reason, the designer would do well to understand as much as possible about the publishing process, as well as the manufacturing process. But since, today, one cannot know it all, one has to decide what it is most profitable to know and then try to understand, at least, that much. For simpler types of books, one can get along knowing a little about a few things.

A rather common method of designing a book is simply to "look at the competition" and then design it in basically the same way, but with different details. No one boasts much about this approach, since it is assumed to be rather uncreative. If various problems turn out to have no counterpart in the competition, then there is always *A Manual of Style* (University of Chicago) to suggest an industry standard of acceptability and enable the designer to make a professional choice.

There are, of course, some tricks of the trade about just how to specify this derivative product, so that what is expected is actually what is produced, but for simple books this is not so tricky after all. If a copy of a book to be matched "as closely as possible" is sent to the compositor with the manuscript, the resulting book is likely to be quite presentable—which illustrates the well-known point that the designer does not need to specify everything in detail and the not-so-well-publicized point that the designer who leaves a lot up to the compositor may seem very competent, without having much right to.

This description of the basics of derivative design, while scarcely an in-depth discussion, can be put in storage for an emergency and may serve to compensate for any self-importance the designer may acquire through being so indispensable an interface. Imitation is still the way many designers learn their craft. William Blake observed that copying is the mother of originality, yet there is more to the craft than that.

Publisher to printer

The central position that the designer's specifications occupy as interface between the publishing and manufacturing systems is shown in the circle diagram (Figure 1–1).

To provide more detail, we may enlarge the central circle representing design and add some specific functions (Figure 1–2). We subdivide design into the areas of typography, art, research, paper, printing, binding, and scheduling, and add arrows to show movement of product or information. Solid arrows indicate the movement of product or service, with a bullet to show where control rests, and dashed lines represent movement of information.

Let us consider the "Art" function in relation to the publisher's own processes, as an example of how to read the diagram.

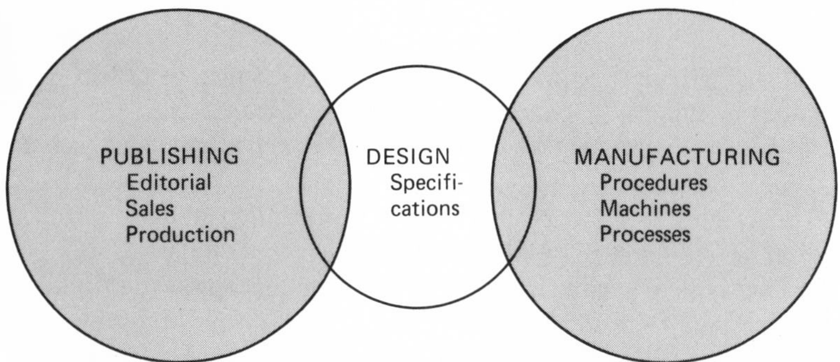

1-1 *Design specifications form the main connecting link between the publishing and manufacturing systems.*

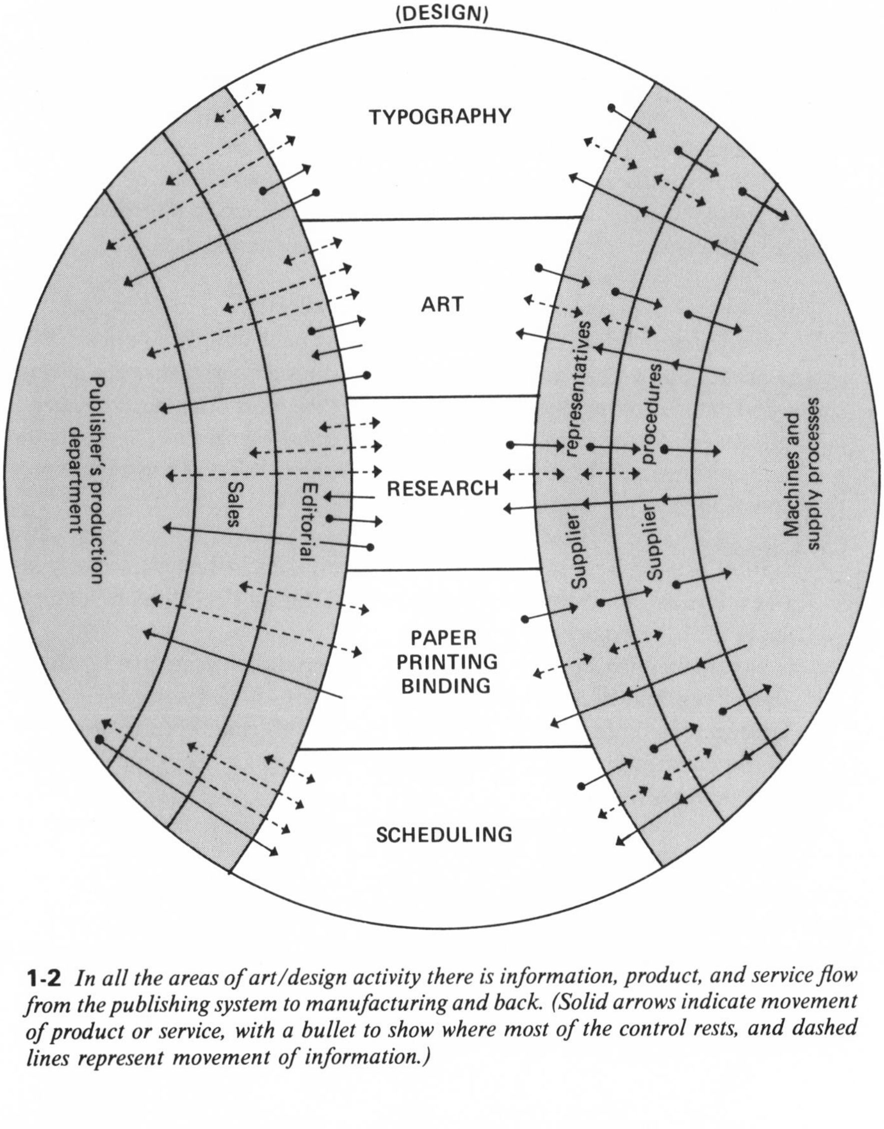

(DESIGN)

TYPOGRAPHY

ART

RESEARCH

PAPER
PRINTING
BINDING

SCHEDULING

Publisher's production department

Sales

Editorial

Supplier representatives

Supplier procedures

Machines and supply processes

1-2 *In all the areas of art/design activity there is information, product, and service flow from the publishing system to manufacturing and back. (Solid arrows indicate movement of product or service, with a bullet to show where most of the control rests, and dashed lines represent movement of information.)*

1. Editorial product (requirements for artwork) comes to design—control resides in editorial
2. Information is exchanged with editorial, sales, and production departments of the publisher
3. Product goes to editorial from design (proofs, etc.)—but control is not stated to reside chiefly in design
4. Product goes to production from design (camera copy)—in this case, control is stated to reside in design.

Note that in respect to design interaction with manufacturers, the diagram represents the designer as dealing directly with supply representatives but indirectly with procedures and machines. This is so represented because the designer must take all these things into account, but in large publishers, especially, the formal details of dealing with manufacturers and suppliers even on design requirements may well all be handled through the publisher's production department. In any case, with respect to these outside suppliers, information is exchanged in both directions. Product goes to, and comes from, the suppliers, but design control rests with design. There is information exchange with respect to procedures and methods of specification.

The design process as a sequence of events

We can represent the design function within the publishing house in another more "linear" and verbal way, by listing the various activities that are part of the design process in the general order in which they most often occur, remembering that: (1) not all the activities occur for every book; and (2) events do not happen necessarily in sequence, but instead can overlap in ways that vary, depending on the type of book.

1. Start of project: Transmittal of the manuscript, and all relevant materials and information, to the design and manufacturing departments for production of the book
2. General planning for the book (conference, etc.); design study of the manuscript and illustrations
3. Typographic design of text and working out of general illustration plan
4. Layout, markup, and specification of sample page material; obtaining sample pages and OKs
5. Castoff of manuscript based on sample page design (with adjustments to samples or book plan?)
6. Design markup of the manuscript
7. *Typesetting of galleys**
8. Design corrections for the galley stage

*Italicized activities are production-oriented activities.

9. Castoff of galleys (as a check on book length) and subsequent required adjustments for length
10. Predummy plan and review of picture specifications (if complex dummy is required)
11. Dummying the book (or any necessary part of it)
12. Art sketches (for art not supplied in reproducible form by author or editor)
13. Correction of art sketches
14. Art finishes
15. Correction of art finishes
16. *Art camera work and blues or proofs*
17. Picture research and photography (for materials not provided in reproducible form by author or editor)
18. Decisions on the uses of researched pictures
19. Cropping, retouching, and mechanicals for researched pictures
20. *Camera work and blues or proofs of researched pictures*
21. Adjustment of dummy, if any, for text changes and final requirements of illustration program
22. *Page makeup*
23. Design review and correction of pages
24. Design of cover (sketch, OK, and mechanical)
25. Proper listing of illustration program credits and captions
26. Design of back matter, index, etc.
27. Design of front matter, OK, and mechanicals
28. Payment of art bills and storage of artwork
29. Payment of illustration research bills, return and filing of photos, etc.
30. Final design check on page corrections, front and back matter, cover proofs, camera work, etc.

It is often helpful to refer to a list such as this one for art department job status reports and scheduling. The numbers can be referred to, rather than having to describe the various stages. These are the events in the design of complex books, a kind of checklist of system structure that will be used later in connection with scheduling and reporting of art and design functions (see Figure 9–4 and the Art Department Weekly Job Status Report form in Chapter 9).

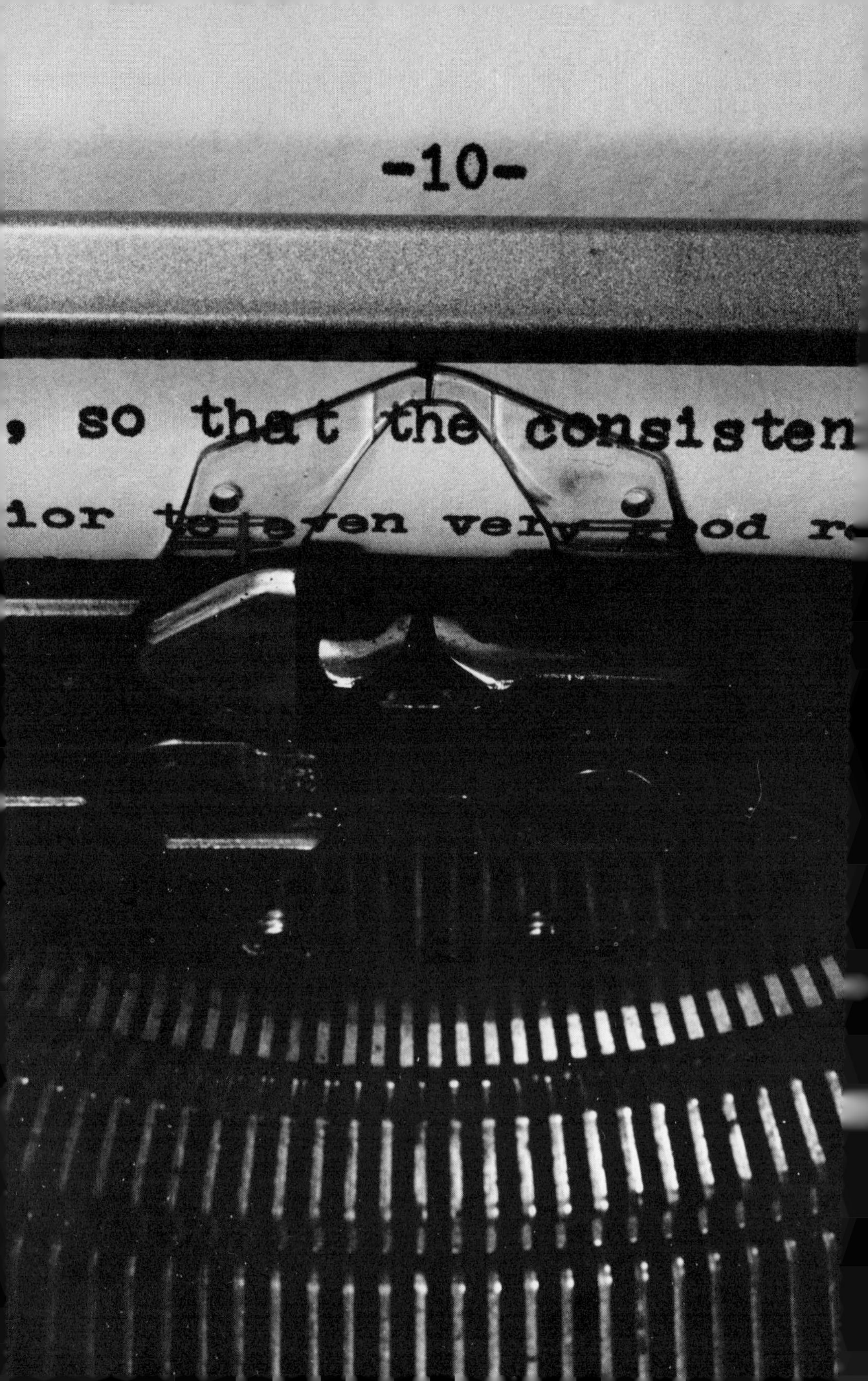

-10-

, so that the consisten

ior to even very good r

CHAPTER 2
Design and Editorial Processes—Words

The book designer, through his or her work, gives form to the work of another, the author. As a professional, the designer does not have to be in sympathy with the author, or with the author's point of view, but simply should try to do a professional job in each case. The experienced designer knows that constantly indulging feelings of sympathy or antagonism towards book content is not only unprofessional but is self-destructive and unproductive of good design. Even when the feelings are positive, the results in design are often inexplicably negative.

Each book has chiefly two aspects that concern the designer, an emotional tone and a detailed editorial structure. Both must be understood and dealt with in a professional way. Much thought is usually lavished on emotional tone, and this is obviously warranted. The tone, point of view, bias, personality, specialness, involvement, or whatever it may be, is probably more important to the author than anything else. This is true even if the special tone is to prove that the author is entirely objective.

The range of tone in books is as broad as the range in author personality. This presents a challenge to designers, who are restricted by their own personality or style. Some very excellent designers design every book as though it were essentially the same book, the tone always being their own. If this is a handsome reflection of current style, then it may be quite sufficient to please editor and publisher. Nevertheless, since books are essentially the careful products of authors, there is much to be said for real understanding and accommodation on the part of design to the author's product. Designers, like everyone else, could benefit from less self-absorption, an attitude sometimes fostered by the emphasis on self-expression, not to say solipsism, in the study of art and design.

In any case, nothing further will be said here about emotional tone. There is a good deal that can be said, with more profit, about editorial structures in books. It is probably more advantageous for the designer to be involved attentively with the structures of a book, than to agonize about tone. Such involvement may accomplish more in the way of unique design, as well.

Editorial structures: what are they?

The basic editorial structure is the sentence. Apart from any meaning they may possess, sentences are so completely structured that they may be described by formal means—grammar; a knowledge of grammar enables us to know that "all topled foibles can fly" is a sentence, even though it is not particularly sensible. Authors and editors attempt to clarify thought, beyond the level of word and sentence, by the arrangement of these into other traditional editorial structures, such as paragraphs, main text, headings, footnotes, lists, bibliographies, legends, tables, and formulas. These are the editorial structures that concern the designer of books. The same words can have quite different meanings depending on whether they occur as chapter title or table footnote. All of this seems rather obvious—so obvious that we seldom think about it.

The problem is that people in publishing, designers included, know the editorial structures of books so well that we cannot see them. Like constant sounds, constant visual features tend to disappear from consciousness, becoming unavailable to thought and design. For this reason, and because designers often slide over the words and editorial aspects of books, some analysis may be worthwhile. Words are, after all, the very stuff of the design of books. Without real attentiveness to words and editorial structures, book design becomes uninteresting and difficult. Given real attentiveness to words and their meanings, book design is full of life, suggestive of infinite interesting solutions that require only to be worked out in visual detail.

The essence of good typographic design of text is fidelity to editorial meaning, form following function—but not blindly or without thought. A fruitful design-test question often has the form: "Who says this structure has to look like the usual model? In this case wouldn't *this* modification have more consistency, relation, clarity, or whatever?" All solutions are permissible, except those that obscure. Consider the examples shown in Figure 2–1 of rather unusual editorial structures. The structure is part of the meaning in every case.

2-1 *Editorial structures have many forms for many purposes. The visual form is the expression of editorial intent as well as content. (Imagine these structures set in run-on sentences.)*

REFERENCES

1. K. G. Birch, A spatial frequency filter to remove zero frequency, *Optica Acta* **15**, 113–127 (March-April 1967).
2. L. S. G. Kovasznay and H. M. Joseph, Image processing, *Proc. IRE* **43**, 560–570 (May 1955).
3. J. J. Kulikowski, Adaptive visual signal preprocessor with a finite number of states, *IEEE Trans. Systems Science and Cybernetics* **SSC-2**, 96–101 (December 1966).
4. W. K. Taylor, Pattern recognition by means of automatic analogue apparatus, *Proc. IEE* **106B**, 198–209 (March 1959).
5. G. Nagy, Preliminary investigation of techniques for automated reading of unformatted test, *Comm. ACM* **11**, 480–487 (July 1968).

Solution

$$\underset{\substack{2(23\,+\,35.5)\text{ g}\\117\text{ g}}}{\overset{234\text{ g}}{2\,NaCl}} + H_2SO_4 \longrightarrow \underset{\substack{2(1\,+\,35.5)\text{ g}\\73\text{ g}}}{\overset{x}{2\,HCl\uparrow}} + Na_2SO_4$$

♍

That is finished now. It was a pleasure .
And now , this is a pleasure.
"Read me that part a–gain where I disin–herit everybody ."
The twelve–tone row is a method; a
method is a control of each single
note. There is too much there there .
There is not enough of nothing in it . A structure is
like a bridge from nowhere to nowhere and
anyone may go on it : noises or tones
, corn or wheat . Does it matter which
? I thought there were eighty–eight tones .
You can quarter them too .

A

Acoustic Coagulation and Precipitation of Aerosols, Mednikov 161
Acoustical Holography, Series 136
Acta Astronomica Sinica (J) 261
Acta Botanica Sinica (J) 261
Acta Entomologica Sinica (J) 261
Acta Genetica Sinica (J) 261
Acta Geologica Sinica (J) 261
Acta Geophysica Sinica (J) 261
Acta Mathematica Sinica (J) 261
Acta Microbiologica Sinica (J) 261
Acta Phytotaxonomica Sinica (J) 261
Acta Zoologica Sinica (J) 261
Actual Contact Area Between Touching Surfaces, The, Dyachenko et al. 204

To see that this is true we substitute into Eq. 8-82 and take the differential operators inside the integral since they do not operate on the primed variables. Thus we obtain

$$\left(\nabla^2-\frac{1}{c^2}\frac{\partial^2}{\partial t^2}\right)\mathbf{A}(\mathbf{x},t)=\frac{1}{c}\int d^3x'\int dt'\left(\nabla^2-\frac{1}{c^2}\frac{\partial^2}{\partial t^2}\right)G(\mathbf{x}-\mathbf{x}',t-t')\mathbf{J}(\mathbf{x}',t')$$

$$=\frac{4\pi}{c}\int d^3x'\int dt'\,\delta(\mathbf{x}-\mathbf{x}')\,\delta(t-t')\mathbf{J}(\mathbf{x}',t')$$

$$=-\frac{4\pi}{c}\mathbf{J}(\mathbf{x},t) \qquad (8\text{-}85)$$

SIGHTSEEING

GIRO TURISTICO

1213. Where can I rent [a car]?
Dove posso noleggiare [una macchina]?
DOH-vay PAWS-so no-layj-JAH-ray [OO-nah MAHK-kee-nah]?

1214. —— a bicycle.
una bicicletta.
OO-nah bee-chee-KLAYT-tah.

1215. —— a horse and carriage.
una carrozza.
OO-nah kahr-RAWT-tsah.

1216. I want a licensed guide who speaks English.
Vorrei una guida patentata che parli l'inglese.
vohr-REH_ee OO-nah GWEE-dah pah-tayn-TAH-tah kay PAHR-lee leen-glay-say.

1217. What is the charge [per hour] per day?
Quanto si paga [all'ora] al giorno?
KWAHN-toh see PAH-gah [ahl-LO-rah] ahl JOHR-no?

FEDERAL RESERVE SYSTEM BANK RESERVE REQUIREMENTS

Percent of deposits.

	Net demand deposits				Time deposits (all classes of banks)		
	Reserve city banks		Country banks			Other time deposits	
Effective date of change [1]	Under $5 mil.	$5 mil. and over	Under $5 mil.	$5 mil. and over	Savings deposits	Under $5 mil.	$5 mil. and over
1966—July 14, 21	16½		12		4	4	5
Sept. 8, 15	16½		12		4	4	6
1967—Mar. 2	16½		12		3½	3½	6
Mar. 16	16½		12		3	3	6
1968—Jan. 11, 18	16½	17	12	12½	3	3	6
In effect Sept. 30, 1968	16½	17	12	12½	3	3	6
Present legal requirements:							
Minimum	10		7		3	3	3
Maximum	22		14		10	10	10

[1] When two dates shown, first applies to reserve city banks, second to country banks.

Source, tables 439 and 440: Board of Governors of the Federal Reserve System.

On the other hand, most common and relatively simple editorial structures have standard forms to which the designer makes only a few minor modifications. Text design is a matter of adjusting and adding up trifles, but as Michelangelo observed, "Trifles make for perfection, and perfection is no trifle." The designer adjusts and adds up, when required, by arranging for: (a) consistency (not having a lot of conflicting and meaningless indentions or alignments, for example), or (b) contrast (making a hierarchy of heads easily distinguishable by contrasting settings, for example). Consistency and contrast are achieved by the use of available typographic parameters, such as size, indention, boldness, spacing, position, mode, alignment, and color when available.

Complexity and flexibility of editorial structures

Editorial structures may be simple or complex, and flexible or inflexible. They can be simple and flexible (chapter openings), simple and inflexible (footnotes), complex and flexible (tables), and complex and inflexible (mathematical displays). Most structures have well recognized traditional forms, such as those found in *A Manual of Style* (University of Chicago) or the U.S. Government Printing Office *Style Manual,* but sometimes they are invented by authors to express some relationship of text elements that is novel or difficult. Teacher's editions of student texts often have unusual structures.

Mathematical displays

It is worthwhile considering the case of relatively inflexible and complex structures, because it is common practice for beginning designers, unsure of what is required, to slide over them and to concentrate only on obvious display. To take an extreme example of this, the display structures of mathematical typesetting are seldom specified in any detail by designers. We have already noted that these displays are "complex and inflexible," even though they are, in fact, structured to be read as sentences and are broken and punctuated accordingly. They are not sentences that make much sense to nonmathematical readers, but the designer can make as much sense of them as the mathematical typesetter usually does, simply by knowing the general rules of syntax as they apply to mathematical displays. The question is whether, and to what degree, this is necessary for the designer.

Most mathematics is "designed" by sending it to a compositor specialized in mathematical composition, with very little marking by the designer for any design considerations. The compositor just sets the work in a form consistent with traditional usages. But since the term "relatively inflexible" does not mean rigor mortis, the designer may specify certain details, such as spaces above and below equations and whether displays are to be centered or otherwise. This minimal specification is often the wisest course, unless the designer is very familiar with the design of mathematical texts and with the capabilities of the composition house. On the other hand, the designer who thinks that the setting of mathematical displays is cut and dried has only to discuss the matter with a mathematician, who is likely to propose something akin to hand setting to obtain niceties of spatial relationships.

At the other extreme, the designer usually takes great care to specify every detail of the chapter opening or contents page, structures that are both flexible and simple. In between these extremes there are obviously many mixed cases. In fact, one of the problems facing new designers is that of knowing when they are expected to specify and when they are not. It should always be remembered that whatever is specified in a *non*standard way should be followed up through editing, copy editing, typesetting, and all stages of proof, for all instances of the specification. In other words, nonstandard ways of handling design problems can be sources of misunderstanding and error that are the designer's responsibility.

Specification of editorial structures

The general rule as to what text should be most "designed," then, seems clear enough and there is nothing unexpected about it:

1. Simple-flexible structures are the main area for design.
2. Simple-inflexible structures need to be tended to, but require little specification.
3. Complex-flexible structures are design-optional, but should not be designed in more special detail than the designer is willing to follow up.
4. Complex-inflexible structures should be left almost entirely to traditional solutions, unless there is real reason for modification, or the designer is experienced and knows what can profitably and safely be modified, and the typesetter is known and capable.

For the experienced designer the burden of follow-up is a great incentive to avoid specifying needless modifications in complex structures. In general, the safest rule is this: If what the typesetter will do when you do *not* specify a certain detail is acceptable for the book in question, do not give a different specification, unless you are prepared to follow through. Simply confirm the compositor's usage in your specifications, or even specify nothing if you are sure of what to expect (as you may be if the compositor has a style sheet or standard samples). For example, the designer will think twice before specifying many spacing and alignment details for tabular composition.

Most of this knowledge about what *not* to design becomes habit in experienced designers. In fact, they seldom think about the wealth of detail that must be decided by someone, until this lack of attention creates problems. Such problems often can occur with new compositors, or those inexperienced in a certain kind of work (such as mathematics or chemistry), or perhaps with new systems, such as computer-controlled systems, which do not always have experienced workers to overlook every stage of the job and call the publisher if something doesn't look right. The computer is marvelously consistent but not very good at knowing whether something looks right or not.

Lists

It may be useful to take one example of an editorial structure of medium complexity, consider how it is usually specified, and then estimate how many format decisions might actually be involved in full specification. The list, a common structure in the text of many kinds of books, is most often specified simply as "hanging style" or "paragraph style." But it is not always specified even to this extent by the designer, who often assumes: (1) that it will be set in the style of the material in which it occurs, or (2) that the editor will decide whether it is to be hanging or paragraph style. Even the principles on which that second decision is to be made are often obscure.

But the list is not always such a simple problem. A glance at tables of contents in highly designed books will show the many forms that just one type of list can have, if the designer takes pains with it. A list may require a design to contrast with the text. It may or may not have item identifiers, such as arabic or roman numerals, letters, or ornaments, such as bullets. Item identifiers may be of only one level, or they may be of several levels like an outline (which is a specialized form of list). A list may also be set in several columns variously related to each other.

An analysis of what a systematic specification of lists might entail follows. It appears formidable because it makes some attempt at being exhaustive and logical in a way that might be appropriate for an automatic system. But in fact, any part of this decision-making process may crop up in almost any manuscript. Some hints may be gained from a study of this systematic approach, which can make it less necessary for the designer to reinvent the wheel every time an unusual list presents itself.

Simplified hanging indent lists

In general, set the list hanging style only when: (a) there are five or fewer items in the list, or (b) when the list items average three or fewer lines in the manuscript. Set all other lists paragraph style. The following are simplified choices that accord with general practice but that do not allow for many options that can be exercised:

1. A list may have these list item identifiers: (a) numerals, (b) letters, (c) ornaments, or (d) no symbol. For all hanging indent lists, except (d), all lines of item text align with each other to the right of item identifiers. All item identifiers start flush left on the page, except those that clear for another wider item identifier.

2. The following specifications for list setting are assumed to be the same for both list items and identifiers as for the text in which the list occurs (e.g., main text, extract, etc.).

Typeface	Measure
Type size	Justification-hyphenation
Type body	Quadding (left, right, center)
Set size	Indent left or right
Mode (roman, bold, etc.)	Numerical style (lining or old style)

3. If the list-item identifiers are numerals, they align at the right, with the widest one aligning flush left on the measure. If there are more than nine items, the first nine numerals are cleared for ten. Since arabic numerals are centered on an en escapement, or width, they automatically align vertically.

4. If the list item identifiers are alphabetic (any style, including roman numerals), they align on the right, with the widest one aligning flush left on the measure. Letters of the alphabet have various widths of escapement and, therefore, do not align on the left. The designer should be aware that the right alignment of alphabetic list identifier elements is not practical for some composition systems, because the width of the widest identifier cannot be established before the list is started.

5. Where the list identifiers are either numeric or alphabetic [except where parentheses are used, as (a)], they are followed by a period and an en space, not an em space.

6. If the list item identifier is one type of ornament, such as a bullet, the ornaments align vertically flush left on the measure, and are followed by 1-en space only. If the identifiers include more than one type of ornament, follow the rule in Item 4 above.

7. If there is no list identifier at all, a hanging list is set, indenting all lines after the first in each list item by 1 em. The first line of each item starts flush left.

8. Extra space above and below the list should be 1 line. In paging, lists may be broken at any point that does not create widows or leave less than 2 lines on the first or the last page. No extra space is added between list items.

9. Any subitems in the list will have the same characteristics listed above for the list items. They align at left with the text of the main items, as in outline style, except for a list with no identifier, as noted in Item 7 above.

10. If all items are less than full measure, but more than ½ measure,* the entire list may be centered on the measure when there is a compelling reason to do so. But this is usually avoided, because it almost always involves a hand operation.

11. If almost all items are less than ½ measure,* the list may become a 2-column list. Columns are ½ × (measure minus 1 pica). If almost all items

*More exactly, measure minus 1 pica, divided by 2.

are less than 1/3 measure, the list may become a 3-column list. All columns are 1/3 × (measure minus 2 picas). A 1-pica space is assumed between all columns.

12. In a multicolumn list, the last column may be short when total items are not evenly divisible by the number of columns.

A generalized picture of the hanging indent list will look like this:

9. XXXXXXXXXXXXXXXXXXXXXXXXXXXXXXXXXXXXX
XXXXXXXXXXXXXXXXXXXXXXXXXXXXXXXXXXXXX
XXXXXX.

10. XXXXXXXXXXXXXXXXXXXXXXXXXXXXXXXXXXXXX
XXXXXXXXXXXXXXXXXXXXXXXX.
a. XXXXXXXXXXXXXXXXXXXXXXXXXXXXXXXXXXX
XXXXXXXXXXX.
b. XXXXXXXXXXXXXXXXXXXXXXXXXXXXXXXXXXX
XXXXXXXXXXXXXXXXXX.

11. XXXXXXXXXXXXXXXXXXXXXXXXXXXXXXXXXXXXX
XXXXXXXXXXXXXX.

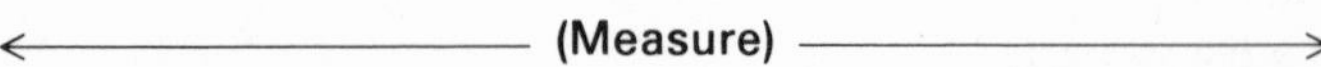

Obviously the above specifications eliminate a great many possible options. To give an idea of some of the options actually available to the designer we list them in the table opposite rather systematically, providing a kind of checklist for ordinary list setting. There are roughly 40 possible design options that can be exercised by writing a specification in the blank provided. For the designer who does not wish to exercise any of the 40 options, a full set of specifications is given for a centered list, and another is given for an off-center list. Either one of these may be chosen, in which case a specification is made only when the one given in the column is not wanted. The entire table may be used as a checklist.

The reader familiar with the lists in school workbooks and various kinds of catalogs will recognize that many types of lists have not even been considered here, such as true-false lists, outlines (hierarchical lists), and key lists. The designer should consider the list as one of the most basic and flexible modes of the organized presentation of verbalized thought. Authors sometimes have their own methods of utilizing list structures; these are well worthy of attention.

The keying of complex manuscripts

In a composition order all the hanging indent list specifications could be referred to by the tag or key "L2." The symbol L2 would then be allowed to stand for all the specifications related to the hanging indent structure, wherever one might occur, for use in manuscript marking. It is the aim of manu-

SPECIFICATION OPTIONS FOR LISTS
(with centered and off-center solutions)

Option	*Specification*		*Centered list* ☐	*Off-center list* ☐
Typeface	Name/#	____	Same as text	Same as text
Type size	Points	____	"	"
Type body	Points	____	"	"
Set size	Points	____	"	"
Mode (roman, bf, etc.)	Name	____	Roman	Roman
Width (list only)	Pi/points	____	Text measure	Text measure
Justify & hyphenate	Yes/No	____	Y	Y
or quad to . . .	L/R/C	____	–	–
Indent list left	Points	____	0	0
Indent list right	Points	____	0	0
Center on long line	Yes/No	____	N	N
Paragraph style*	Yes/No	____	–	–
Hanging style*	Yes/No	____	–	–
Space above list	Points	____	Text body	Text body
Variable in paging +	%	____	100	100
Variable in paging –	%	____	30	30
Space below list	Points	____	Text body	Text body
Variable in paging +	%	____	100	100
Variable in paging –	%	____	30	30
Item identifiers	Per ms.	____		
Typeface	Name/#	____	Same as text	Same as text
Type size	Points	____	"	"
Set size	Points	____	"	"
Punctuation after	. : none	____	Period	Period
Space after punctuation	Points	____	Text en #	Text en #
Space between items	Points	____	0	0
Variable in paging +	%	____	0	0
Variable in paging –	%	____	0	0
Subitem typeface	Name/#	____	Same as item	Same as item
" type size	Points	____	"	"
" body size	Points	____	"	"
" set size	Points	____	"	"
" mode	Name	____	"	"
" indent from item text	Points	____	0	0
Title of list (if any)	Head #	____	–	–
Break list only at:				
1. End of list				
2. End of item or subitem				
3. Marked breaks				
4. Any non-widow break	1234	____	4	4
Consider multicolumn**	Yes/No	____	Y	Y
Center the multicolumn	Yes/No	____	N	N
Space between columns	Points	____	12	12

*Set hanging when there are fewer than five items in the list, or when list items average fewer than three lines in manuscript. Otherwise set paragraph style.

**Make multicolumn only if almost all items will fit proposed column width without breaking over.

script keying of this kind to relate the necessary specifications of the composition-specification order to the specific editorial structures of the manuscript on a one-to-one basis. This method requires little marking and provides as much flexibility as possible. Flexibility means that any or all specifications can be subject to changes without having to re-mark the manuscript to accommodate them; and it also means that the manuscript can be keyed without knowing what the design will turn out to be.

To relate a specific manuscript to a completed composition order, every editorial structure or element that is separately specified on the order should be keyed in the manuscript, whenever it occurs. If no composition order yet exists, then every editorial structure that is thought *likely* to receive separate typographic treatment should be keyed. There is, in fact, no accepted practice as to whether the copy editor, editor, or designer originates the keying scheme. There are advantages to each. The designer is more familiar with the design and composition order and knows which structures can be handled separately in design, but the copy editor or editor is more familiar with the manuscript.

For a simple manuscript without many editorial structures, a few letter keys will do, and all that is required is the recognition of signals. For complex text, more care is required. (The tagging of structures for automatic retrieval or handling by computerized typesetting systems is not considered here, since that is almost entirely an editorial matter.)

Text. The main text mode of the book is seldom keyed at all. "Main text" is what is assumed, unless something else is indicated. In a complex book there may be more than one class of main text, however, and in this case these must be separated by keying all but one of them.

Secondary text. This is often referred to as "extract" on the assumption that all secondary text is quoted from other sources. However, modern texts may have several kinds of secondary text, all subordinate in some way to the main text. Secondary passages may be so long that they illustrate a problem that comes up in connection with a number of other editorial structures: Sometimes it is necessary to mark the end of a structure as well as its beginning. This is often done by drawing colored lines in the margins of the manuscript beside the entire structure for every instance. This is awkward, not only because it clutters up the manuscript, but because there are color-blind compositors. An alternative is to modify the beginning key to form an end key. If [A] begins a structure, [$\bar{A}$] (with a bar over it, the logic symbol for "not A") can end the structure.

Headings. The heading scheme of a book is its hierarchical skeleton, proceeding logically from book title to part or section title, to chapter title, and through all the text heads. By tradition, the text heads often are considered to be a separate group, starting with "A" for the first text head under the chapter title. In complex manuscripts there may be a problem in that there may be several hierarchies; for example, one for text, one for secondary, one for appendixes, and one for commentary. Unless there is some reason to convey the hierarchical structure of the book to persons unfamiliar with it, there is no reason that keying schemes need be consistent as to the order of inclusiveness or importance, as long as the keys are unique. In fact, the designer should not assume that a head keyed "D" is necessarily subordinate to a head keyed "C" without inquiry, although such is likely to be the case.

Structures that *always* appear together in a given manuscript (for example, the word "chapter," the chapter number, and the chapter title, or the word "table," table number, and table title) should be given one key. This key will then be associated with all the specifications for the group of structures as they are given in the composition order, thus saving manuscript marking. A useful extension of letter keying is to add numerals for parts of the same general structure, where the manuscript may be ambiguous, e.g., P1 for the word "part" and the number, P2 for part title, P3 for subtitle, P4 for part-title page introductory paragraph.

It is not always clearly understood by copy editors or editors that the usefulness of keying is not confined to headings and that anything that may be repeatedly associated with the same specifications may most conveniently and efficiently be keyed. Conversely, anything that does not repeat itself in respect to specifications should not be keyed but should be separately marked.

It should be clear that it is not necessary to key substructures separately when they are recognizable parts of larger structures, even if they may receive separate typographic treatment. For example, parts of tables, table number, title, column heads, and footnotes may all be given separate typographic treatment, but they are all unambiguous parts of the editorial structure "table," and need not be separately keyed, unless they may be in some way ambiguous (for example, values of heads within a table).

Occasionally it may be worthwhile for a company or department to adopt a consistent keying scheme appropriate to the kind of work usually done. In this case the keys can be worked out with some care to be hierarchically representative and mnemonically convenient. Such a scheme is proposed below for moderately complex text or trade books. It would allow a number of people to work on various manuscripts with a minimum of confusion, permitting some job interchangeability, as necessary, and simplifying communications with compositors. As in all keying, where no ambiguity exists, no key need be used; where more than one variety of a structure exists, these can be numbered (e.g., if L is list, L1 can be paragraph style, and L2 hanging indent, etc.).

PA	Part title group
CH	Chapter title group
A	First head under chapter title
B	Second head under chapter title

C Third head under chapter title
D Fourth head under chapter title
E Fifth head under chapter title
F Footnote
G Glossary (or gloss)
H Heading not in main text (H1, H2, etc.)
I Bibliography (written with a stroke above and below)
J Personal letter
K Credit
L List
M Math structure
N Legend
O (not used)
P Play (drama)
Q Equation or formula
R Problem or example
S Study material
T Table
U Appendix
V Verse (poetry)
W Workbook structure (fill in, etc.)
X Extract (secondary)
Y Special floating feature
Z (not used)

The use of numerals with the letters (A1, A2, etc.) gives considerable flexibility, no matter what scheme of letters may be adopted.

It is obvious that the editorial structures of books vary tremendously and that the overall structure (except for novels and such) is likely to be in some sense hierarchical. It is the well-recognized job of the book designer to make these relationships obvious. The overall shape of the book is easily seen in the table of contents, but in the text of the complex book the organizational work of the designer is somewhat obscured. The reader can only see two pages at a time and, hence, is most of the time only vaguely aware, for example, of the subordination of the D heading and its text to the C heading and its text. This can seldom be helped, but still it is something for which authors often propose solutions, some of them rather bizarre and impractical (such as rules up and down the margins to indicate certain kinds of material).

Editorial structures, like the features of language, display a consistency within their possible variety and can be standardized in many ways. They function as a kind of higher-level language that must be understood by the designer to be reflected accurately (as well as imaginatively) in the design treatment. The full specification of non-main-text structures, even when, apparently, they are as common and simple as lists, may require considerable thought. We seldom appreciate what a mature, not to say ancient, craft the arranging of text is until we discover how much we take for granted.

It has not been the intention of this chapter to analyze editorial structures in detail, and still less to suggest design solutions for the many variations. The matter of acquiring experience in design is to construct a set of general principles, rules of thumb, general working methods, and so on, that enable the designer to deal intelligently with an ever widening scope of graphic problems.

The designer who wishes to approach a text with a fresh eye, taking nothing for granted, can scarcely do better than to consider carefully the actual relationships that exist in the book as a whole and among the various editorial structures—as well as the meaning and tone. An understanding of these relationships is, in fact, the real basis for many of the best design ideas for books.

On the other hand, there is no reason why several sets of good solutions to common problems should not be described in detail for use in automatic systems, for the benefit of those who do not need to be original all the time.

CHAPTER 3
Design and Editorial Processes—Images

Most of the images in book illustration programs fall into several familiar categories: photographs, drawings and paintings, charts and graphs, and maps. The varieties and combinations of these are enormous, from the simple and pedestrian to the complex and innovative. In this chapter we shall be concerned with the editorial/design approach to these, rather than the mechanical, artistic, or reproductive aspects.

Images, or illustrations, are symbols, and in that respect they are a great deal like words. They can be used, modified, combined, abused, conceived with great or little imagination—but they can perhaps never be wholly invented. Imagination and innovation in visual images is a matter of modification, combination, extrapolation, elimination, appropriateness, timing, and relationship. Like words, images may be denotative and more or less "literal" (charts, graphs, maps, realistic drawings, pictograms, most photographs, etc.). Or they may be connotative, more suggestive than literal (impressionist or expressionist or abstract art, some photographs, decorations, and in fact a great many charts, graphs, and even maps that are used not to present facts but to create an impression, as in so much of advertising).

Images are the concern of the designer, but they are also the concern of the editor. The illustration program for a book may come as a complete package from the author, with nothing to decide except how it is to be presented. Or, as in the case of many textbooks, only suggestions may come from the author, and the illustration program may be worked out almost entirely by the publisher. Between these two extremes are many variations, but it is in general true that for trade (bookstore) books and for books of more advanced subject matter the illustration programs come predominantly from the authors. The lower the grade level and the more authors and advisors there are for a book, the more the illustration program tends to be worked out by the publisher. Visual modes of expression are not the specialty of most authors, and they are, in general, very glad of assistance in this area, only reserving to themselves the right to object if their intentions or facts are distorted.

As was emphasized at the beginning of the last chapter, book designers give form to the work of another in all aspects of their job. Illustrations are all extensions of text, extensions of its tone and intention. The designer who takes little responsibility in this area or who assumes an unthinking stance (such as insisting that it is the designer's responsibility to make everything more connotative and less denotative, more suggestive and less literal, or the other way around) is not doing a good job. It is not the job of designers always to be "far out," but rather to be on target with the specific visual problems of the book in hand. In order to do this, it is necessary that the designer and the artists, photographers, and others with whom the designer works actually do *desire* to communicate with the prospective reader. This is a question of motivation. If it is the real desire of the designer to be in a class apart from the reader, above the reader, at a more sophisticated level, perhaps, then this will be what is expressed in the illustration program.

Still, it is true that in certain respects this is what is required in the design of all graphics, books included. "The word" and the image are being published by the more knowledgeable for the less knowledgeable. The illustration program, like the book as a whole, is intended to create the impression of perfection. If the impression of remote perfection is carried to an extreme, however, the reader may be initially impressed but will not relate to the book and will seldom read it, or, possibly, even buy it in the first place.

Images require analysis in relation to their text. How, then, is this done? The designer, in consultation with the editor or author, must ask questions. Usually these questions are asked in specific relation to a preliminary set of illustration specifications drawn up by the author or editor. The answers arrived at affect such things as the choice of artist, the choice of medium, the amount of space given to the illustrations, the use of color, the amount of money and time to be spent on the illustration program, and the changes to be made in the original specifications. Typical questions are:

Exactly what is the focus of the illustration?
What effect is the illustration intended to produce?
What does the text have to say about the subject of the illustration?
Is the problem really visual in nature, or can it be made so?
Can the main elements be visualized?

If the problem is not visual, can it be symbolized?
Who can best deal with the problem (artist, photographer, etc.)?
Are special techniques or combination processes called for?
Should the illustration be combined with another?
How much space should be devoted to it?
Is it properly conceived for the readership intended?
Is it offensive to any part of the readership?
Is it legal? Is it infringing copyrighted material? (See Appendix A.)
Is it worth what it will cost?
Can it be well reproduced?
Can author, editor, and designer agree on what is needed?
Can it be understood without reference to the text?
Does it try to do too much, or not enough?
Would it be better to make more than one illustration of it?

It should not be assumed that the artist or photographer will ask all these questions before producing an illustration. The success of an illustration program depends to a very large extent on the care with which it is specified, and it is this care that allows the artists to make their maximum contribution. This does not mean overspecification, especially not careless overspecification, but rather giving the artist the thoughtful orientation really required to do the best work. First, of course, having chosen the proper medium, it is necessary to choose the right artist.

Finding the right artist

Choosing the right artist is a matter of finding an artist (or photographer, map maker, chart maker, or whatever) who is free to undertake the job, who is right for it artistically, who can understand it, who will do it for a reasonable price, and who can be *remembered* or otherwise contacted by the art director or designer.

One easy way to go about this is to get in touch with artists' agents, explain the job carefully, and let them come around with suggestions and samples. There is much to be said for this approach when the designer is not sure or is not able to recall anyone who would be just right. In fact, for important jobs it is a good idea anyhow, because the artists that are available are a very changing population and the designer's knowledge of available people is limited and probably out of date, unless there has been a similar project recently. New people are constantly coming into the art market, many of them very talented, and many of the old friends move away or otherwise become unavailable. Agents can be found in the yellow pages of the telephone book, and their services are free to the publisher. Little more need be said about this approach, except to note the fact that agents may be specialized in certain areas, and to add that more samples are better than fewer. In spite of protests to the contrary, artists cannot always do well the kinds of art they have seldom or never tried before.

At the start of any new project, the designer must have a way of finding an artist, or several possible artists, to match a certain set of requirements. Chances are that the designer will have a file of names of artists who are particularly appropriate for the usual kinds of work. Artists may even be interviewed on a regular basis. The problem is that the *requirements* cannot be looked up in a name file or in a media file, and unless the designer has a phenomenal memory, important details about an artist's work will soon be forgotten.

What the designer must do is find a way of recording information at the time the artist is interviewed that allows the designer to look up requirements rather than artists' names. This is not a difficult problem, but it does require a method, such as the one suggested below, and a little care. The designer in a large publishing house may be able to get someone else to help with this file, and, in fact, designers and editors can collaborate on it. The file can be rather simple, but, like all files, it is no better than the information put into it, and it must be kept reasonably up to date.

An artist record sheet, such as the one shown opposite, is the first requirement. This one could be modified in many ways to suit other needs. (Photographers are not represented, although they could be.) The problem with such a sheet is that it is filed alphabetically by the artist's name, and many sheets need to be laboriously read to find any combination of requirements. There is a far easier and better way. In addition to the artist record sheet, it involves an inverted index, which can be put in the form of edge-notched cards very quickly. This enables the searcher to look for only the desired combination of requirements without having to read and compare the original sheets.

When the artist is interviewed, information is filled out on the top of the artist record sheet. Then checks are made opposite only those categories for which the artist is especially well suited and professionally competent, and a general excellence grade of A, B, or C is given. (It would not be worth keeping a record for those below C.) The information on these artist record sheets is transferred to cards on which an edge notch is made opposite each area of professional competence that has been checked (see Figure 3–1).*

The cards are put in a file that can, in fact, be in any order at all. To this file the designer comes with a set of requirements for, let us say, an artist to work in pen and ink and to draw teenagers in a humorous way. A special needle is passed through all the cards, opposite "ink," and the cards are lifted. The ones that drop represent artists that do professional pen and ink especially well. Then, the needle is passed through the dropped cards, opposite "teenagers," and the cards

*Note that if the interviewer wishes, the information sheet may be dispensed with, and the cards may be punched and annotated directly.

ARTIST RECORD SHEET

ARTIST ______________________ AGENT ______________________

ADDRESS ______________________ ADDRESS ______________________

______________________ ______________________

ARTIST PHONE ______________________ AGENT PHONE ______________________

DATE INTERVIEWED ______________________ INTERVIEWER ______________________

NOTE: All checks indicate a recommended professional competence.

OVERALL ARTISTIC GRADE: A B C

People Specialties

- ☐ Caricatures
- ☐ Non-white
- ☐ Poor
- ☐ Rich
- ☐ Sports
- ☐ Social (genre)
- ☐ Faces & Hands
- ☐ 4–12 Years
- ☐ Teen-agers
- ☐ Adults
- ☐ Famous Portraits

Animals, etc.

- ☐ Fish
- ☐ Insects
- ☐ Birds
- ☐ Wild Animals
- ☐ Domestic Animals

Subject Specialties

- ☐ Math
- ☐ Medical
- ☐ Physics & Chemistry
- ☐ Biology & Botany
- ☐ Social Studies
- ☐ Literary
- ☐ Religious
- ☐ Science (general)
- ☐ Historical
- ☐ Charts & Graphs
- ☐ Cartography
- ☐ Costume
- ☐ Still Life
- ☐ Air & Space
- ☐ Industrial
- ☐ Architecture
- ☐ Ships & Sea

Style

- ☐ Linear
- ☐ Painterly
- ☐ Realistic
- ☐ Expressionistic
- ☐ Abstract
- ☐ Decorative
- ☐ Cartoon
- ☐ Stylized
- ☐ Diagrammatic
- ☐ Humorous
- ☐ Most Styles

Media

- ☐ Full Color
- ☐ Preseparated
- ☐ Oil/Acrylic
- ☐ Watercolor
- ☐ Ink
- ☐ Airbrush
- ☐ Woodcut
- ☐ Scratch Board
- ☐ Most Media

Audience

- ☐ K–Grade 2
- ☐ 3–6
- ☐ 7–9
- ☐ 10–12
- ☐ College
- ☐ General

- ☐ Retouching
- ☐ Mechanicals
- ☐ Music Notation
- ☐ Pictograms
- ☐ Calligraphy

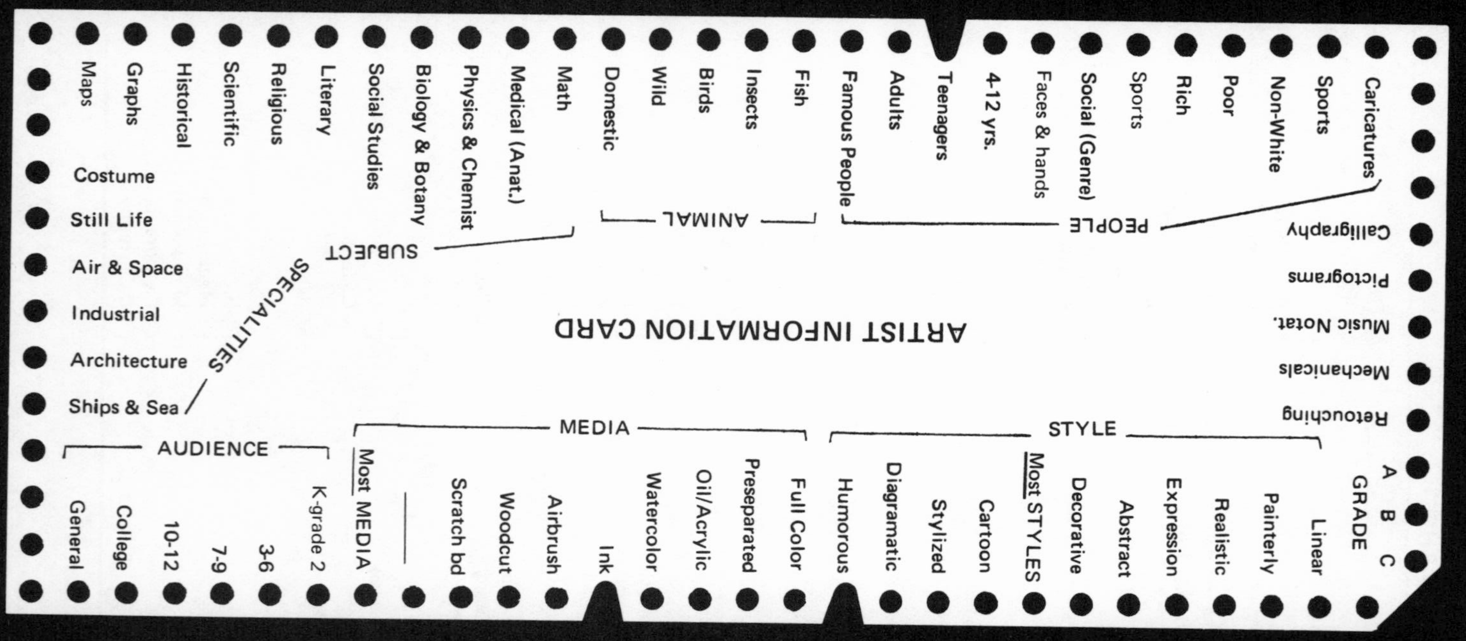

3-1 *Edge-notched cards permit the art director to search for artists by looking for specific combinations of abilities, rather than by trying to remember names. One card represents all relevant information for one artist. (The card shown is the McBee Keysort card #KS-371B.)*

are lifted again. The ones that drop represent artists that work well in pen and ink *and also* draw teenagers well. If there is still a fair number of artists (cards) to consider, the designer may stick the needle through the cards opposite "humorous," again lift, and those that drop will be only those artists who do professional work in ink, of teenagers, and in a humorous vein. The designer only has to turn the cards over to get names, addresses, telephone numbers, agents, and so on. *If* the file is reasonably up to date, the designer can do rather well. And there is no other way to do the same thing with regular indexes or files, even though they are extensively cross-indexed. This method is, in reality, very easy to manage and use; the fact that it may be unfamiliar to designers or art directors should not deter them from trying it, for it is exceptionally well adapted to their needs. (Commercial edge-notched cards are available, such as the McBee Keysort card illustrated, KS–371B.)

Providing photographs

Photographs are, of course, found or made—researched or taken. The author may supply them as part of the illustration program package, picture editors or researchers may help, or a photographic studio may be available. Both picture agencies with extensive files and photographers are abundant, and there are many free sources of pictures, especially those related to large businesses. Standard source books of picture research are *Picture Sources* (Special Libraries Assn.), now in its third edition, and *Stock Photo and Assignment Source Book* (Bowker).

However, since photography is so simple, it is hard to understand why designers do not more often take photographs for their books. All the sources of photographs notwithstanding, a designer who does not learn to use a camera rather professionally is overlooking a great means of expression and a convenient and inexpensive way to work out many ideas ("rather professionally" because the essence of real professionalism is the ability to create good pictures under adverse conditions, which is not required of designers). In fact, designers start any photographic job with a great advantage over any photographer they may hire—they know what they want and are intimately acquainted with the requirements of each book, the format, the reproductive processes, and the other elements of design that surround the needed photograph.

Designers do not need to have extensive training and equipment. The modern 35mm single lens reflex camera with automatic exposure control does almost everything for the photographer, and with a couple of auxiliary lenses (say 35mm and 135mm), a tripod, and a cable release, many kinds of photographs can be taken. A professional darkroom takes care of the processing (although some darkroom experience is very valuable for a designer). It is true that a certain amount of familiarity with the camera and the photographic process has to be acquired to do a great variety of jobs, but designers who have an art school background have generally had at least one course in photography as a start, and such courses are available to others.

Whether or not the designer uses a camera, he or she, on occasion, will have to direct other photographers. In a large publishing house, there may be a professional photographer on staff. It is especially economical in terms of money and time for educational publishers to have a staff photographer, for there are many kinds of photographs impossible to research but easy to take. Great savings can be realized, especially when color is involved. Quality and design cohesiveness are more easily realized if the designer is knowledgeable and plays an active part in the direction of the photography.

Effective specification of photography requires just as much care as that of artwork, and just as much attention must be paid to the specific problem to be illustrated. In artwork by one artist, unity of approach can usually be taken for granted, but unity in the photographic program is often overlooked because the means to attain it is not available through the traditional picture research method, which might be likened to writing an essay by using nothing but quotations. The photographic program in a book should, whenever possible, possess its own unity, coherence, and style. Usually this is possible only when a reasonable proportion of the photographs are taken under the same creative direction, and usually this direction must come from the designer.

Here are a few points for the designer to keep in mind when directing original photography:

1. Do as much photography as possible with a few important locales and models, choosing carefully those that can provide the most pictures. People dashing unnecessarily from one place to the other are not getting much done.

2. Cover each subject thoroughly before leaving it. This means considerable overshooting. Two or three good shots can justify the shooting of a roll. Film and processing are relatively inexpensive compared to the expenditure of time of everyone involved. If there is any chance that a shot may be useful, take it. Nothing is more wasteful than having to go back again because you undershot the subject.

3. Help the photographer, directly or indirectly, to stage the action or the subject imaginatively. You will regret it if, through diffidence, you neglect to explain exactly what you want. Don't be afraid to look through the viewer sometimes yourself. If the photographer wants to do it a certain way, that is fine, too. This is only to be expected, but make sure that you get what you think is necessary. And remember not to frame too tightly. You can crop later.

4. Brief the photographer thoroughly, giving detailed directions. Keep analyzing the subject for the photographer, not in an arbitrary or pompous way, but as a mutual investigation in which you are each playing a professional part.

5. If you cannot be present during the shooting, put as much as you can in writing. There must be specific instructions, such as "a picture of this" or "some shots of that," but it is important to give additional information, as well, such as "try to cover this situation from this point of view . . . the important aspect is this . . . so and so can act as model . . . enclosed is a copy of the text being illustrated . . . make sure to get as close in on this as you can . . . keep the background as plain as possible . . . allow the upper third of the frame blue sky for superimposed type . . . make these all horizontal frame . . . ."

6. Always be sure to take a number of "establishing" shots of a situation as a whole before starting detailed coverage. Take close-ups of significant details whenever possible. If there are many people in the picture, take many more shots, because many of the shots will be spoiled by at least one person.

7. Hiring a photographer is likely to mean a full day's cost, as a minimum, so plan carefully to take full advantage of it. Group smaller projects and ask editors or other designers whether they need anything with related locales or models.

The above suggestions are only a start, for as the publisher's use of photography matures, the staff and studio may grow, with increased economy and quality of product. This is especially true of educational publishers. Editors and authors should be made aware of the current capabilities.

Aside from the general considerations noted above, it is useful to have a checklist of practical details that must be taken care of when extensive shooting is contemplated. Such a list is given below for a house in which art editors work with designers on projects involving coherent sets of pictures or "picture stories."

Checklist for location photography

The photography could be anything from Dick and Jane at play, to the work of a scientific laboratory under the direction of the author, to photography of museum specimens or fine art. Such photography can often be used in sales features for a book, especially a textbook, but it is usually up to the designer to propose these features since editors do not usually know when they can be produced with reasonable expenditure of time and money.

The designer or art editor usually will be responsible for arrangements prior to photography, but the editor should approve the plan before any specific arrangements are made. The following should be done before the day on which the photography is scheduled:

1. Arrange time and place and find a responsible person at the site who can give permissions, provide background information, and so on. Decide what the weather requirements are, and make any alternate arrangements that may be necessary on account of weather.

2. Find models, if needed, and show the editor pictures, if that is necessary. Arrange for appropriate releases and have parents of minors agree to the release before shooting, but releases should actually be signed after the shooting. Check legal aspects (see Appendix A).

3. Inform all necessary people of the arrangements and make sure of the editor's cooperation. The people involved are the photographer, model, designer, art editor, editor, and contact person.

4. Prepare background research and tentative shooting notes. An outline should be drawn up to brief all concerned, especially the photographer.

5. Arrange with the model for proper clothes. Make a list of necessary props and arrange to have them available. Plan transportation, meals, and the time schedule. Have enough cash to cover transport, meals, fees, tips, etc. Settle ahead of time the fee models are to be paid (usually nothing for nonprofessional adults; a small amount, such as $15 per day, for minors).

6. Get the photographer's contract signed ahead of time.

On the day of shooting be sure to get necessary model releases signed.* Also get the names and addresses of all persons who may possibly be useful later. Take notes on all activity significant to the photography. Research done ahead of time, supplemented by notes taken on the spot, is the basis for legends and other text material to be written later.

As the photography is being done, check the shooting notes to make sure that necessary work is not omitted and give the photographer a helping hand when possible. The designer also may wish to take some photographs, or do some of the black and white work while the photographer is shooting color. This can sometimes save a day.

After the photography is completed, either the photographer or the art editor may handle the film processing. The designer and art editor should go over the contact prints and the transparencies with a 5x glass, date, identify, and annotate them, as necessary, and mark the most promising exposures while the subject matter is still fresh in mind. Notes should be delivered to the editor, and prints that have been promised to others should be ordered with any other enlargements. Details of the photographer's contract should be followed up (e.g., return of unwanted color transparencies, negatives, etc.) and color and contact sheets filed in proper and safe places.

Drawings and photographs may sometimes be alternative solutions for the

*For more details concerning the legal aspects of photography see Appendix A. In general, model releases for principal subjects should be obtained even when they are not strictly necessary. They are especially important when any invasion of privacy might be claimed or libel interpreted, or when any situation being photographed might be interpreted as derogatory or ridiculing. It is most necessary when any advertising use, or use with fiction, is contemplated, or when minor children are involved. On the other hand, people in public places and "public people" cannot claim rights of privacy except in very unusual cases, although their pictures may usually not be used in advertising without consent. No payment is necessary to make a photographic release binding.

same problem. When this is the case, it is good to remember that a photograph seldom will have the analytical clarity of a drawing, where detail or precision is wanted, but the drawing will seldom have the solidity or actuality of the photograph.

Charts and graphs

It is obvious that bar charts, pie charts, area graphs, line graphs, pictorial charts, and so on, all have to do with the presentation of comparative quantities, no matter what the subject of the chart or graph may be. They present statistics in a pictorial or graphic way. Therefore, it is equally obvious that in order to judge anything except how pretty the graph or chart is the designer will have to know something about statistics—not much, but something. It is not the business of the book designer to check on the statistics of the book being designed, but if the object is to improve or change the visual presentation of the statistics, there are some pitfalls of which the designer should be aware.

Often the only improvement to be made on artwork submitted by the author is to have the figures redrawn or relabeled, with color added in appropriate ways when it is available. An artist or studio specialized in this type of work may be engaged to do this. Be wary of those who are not specialized, however, or are inexperienced, especially where the visual presentation is to be worked up from raw statistics. In any case, the designer should always cast a critical eye on art received from the author (or even from an experienced studio). Here are some fairly elementary things to look for:

1. If pictographic symbols are used, they should be clear and self-explanatory and the statistical unit they represent clearly indicated.
2. Larger quantities should be shown by a larger *number* of symbols, not by larger symbols. If each small ship symbol represents 10 million tons of shipping, 100 million tons should be represented by 10 small ship symbols, *not* by a bigger ship ten times as long as the smaller symbol. As may be obvious, a ship ten times as long may well be a hundred times (at least) the *volume* of the smaller ship, and this creates an entirely false impression of the quantities involved.
3. Pictorial charts compare only approximate quantities, not detailed quantities. The degree of detail in the statistics presented on the graph should be reasonable for the number of symbols used to represent it.
4. Mixed scales of representation should not be employed without adequate explanation.
5. Arithmetic changes (2–4–6–8) must not be represented visually as geometric changes (2–4–8–16).
6. Charts should not be truncated in a way that distorts the proportions represented (e.g. see Figure 3–3, bottom).

7. Trivial relationships should not be visually featured at the expense of important relationships.

The basic form of most charts and graphs, except "pie" charts and flow charts, is the "histogram" or bar graph. Line graphs are basically lines drawn through the mid-points of the ends of bars in the bar graph. Pictograms are most often bars divided up into little pictures. So-called "frequency polygons" and "band graphs" are made by connecting the mid-points of histogram bars and filling in the area below the lines (see Figure 3–2). Band graphs are really multiple frequency polygons.

There often appears to be an ambiguity in interpreting band graphs, based on the illusion that each lower band may appear to be in front of those behind, all of them being seen as extending to the lower boundary of the chart. This is not correct. If it is kept in mind that band graphs are developed from divided histogram bars, this difficulty will not arise. Band graphs are more sophisticated than the divided-bar graphs that serve the same function, and they should not be used for unsophisticated readers.

In general, designers should not encourage those who have no conscience about lying with statistics and who present them in misleading visual forms. To discourage lying and carelessness, designers have to be willing sometimes to give up fancy effects for honesty. Certainly they should not themselves introduce distortion by ignorantly applying perspective, color, and so on. *How to Lie with Statistics* by Darrell Huff (see Bibliography) is a classic book on pitfalls and is funny as well.

By clear labeling and titling, the reader should always be able to determine at a glance the aspects, attributes, units, time spans, and so on, that are being compared on charts and graphs.

In addition to the charts briefly dealt with above, there are pie charts, flow charts, area charts, and a tremendous variety of diagrammatic techniques, scientific and otherwise (see Figure 3–3). Certainly the designer is not expected to become an expert in all these techniques. On the other hand, the attitude should not be one of unquestioning acceptance of whatever comes along. Simply to understand that distortion and untruth are very common in visual statistics, particularly when the source of the statistics is self-interested (as is usually the case with advertisers), is sufficient to put the designer on guard. Care should be taken by the designer to avoid introducing distortion when redesigning a graph, although any distortion is less likely to result from self-interest than from carelessness, ignorance, or the desire to create an effect.

For all charts and graphs, it is primarily the designer's responsibility to see that they are as consistent in style and make as effective use of the reproduction process as is possible. This may mean redrawing, relabeling only, the addition of color or art, or the entire replanning of the chart. The requirements of time

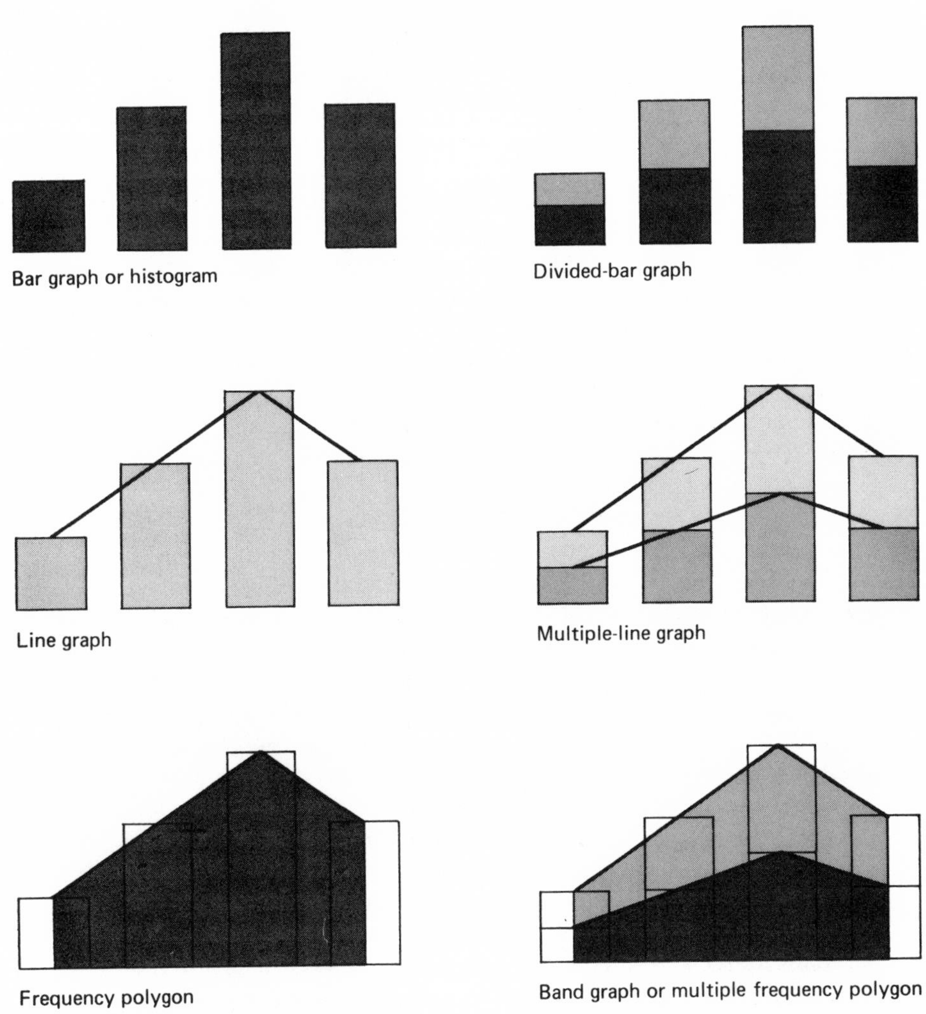

3-2 *These figures show the derivation of several types of graphs from the basic bar chart or histogram.*

and money may make it necessary to do a minimal job, but of course this is not always the case.

Maps

Maps are a specialized branch of graphics and one that few designers need concern themselves with very often. Perhaps the most important decision required of the designer is in choosing a cartographer. The obvious choice would be someone who had done good work before on maps of at least the same degree of complexity as the job at hand. Many artists who advertise themselves as cartographers have, in fact, no competence beyond being able to trace source maps and invent new color schemes or decorative lettering. Sometimes this is all that is required, but even here it is necessary to show some judgment as to which maps to trace and how to represent various elements that may be required besides place locations and boundaries.

Readers and artists alike often consider themselves quite familiar with maps and yet know very little of their basic nature. The assumption is not uncommon, for instance, that a flat map can somehow be a "correct" representation of the round earth or even of a reasonable part of it. It cannot. Still, it is well worth knowing what things can be shown "correctly" on the various available map projections, even though the projections are not correct in every respect. One important question a designer should consider, especially if the artist who will do the maps is not a very experienced map maker, is what special property of correctness is required for the map.

No flat map of a round surface can be correct in all respects. Attempting to make a projection with one kind of correctness fulfill the requirement for another kind of correctness introduces error and distortion. The map may be correct in *area* and thus be an "equal area" map—one on which the areas that are equal on the earth are represented as equal areas on the map. Or it may be correct in *distances* from one point, or in *directions* from many points, or the *shapes* may be approximately correct (see Figures 3–4 and 3–5). But no more than one of these properties can be better than approximately true on the same map projection. (For this reason, however, there are many compromise projections that render specific compromises approximately true.)

Most of the maps that concern the unspecialized book designer are *not* of the reference type, such as are found in atlases. They are, for the most part, either special purpose analytical maps for social studies texts or essentially decorative maps for trade books concerned with politics, wars, history, and so on. Maps for social studies texts are a problem of some complexity. It is true that many authors of such books with sizable map programs specify their own projections, but it is the books with only a few maps that become the concern of the designer.

Certainly the most common error in map work is the plotting of geographic

3-3 *Note the following in the graphs on the opposite page. In the pie graph* (top left) *the size of each segment is determined by multiplying the percent distribution times 360 (the total number of degrees in a circle). The two blast furnaces* (top right) *misleadingly imply a volumetric comparison—the graph is in fact based only on height of each overall drawing. The pictogram graph* (center left) *illustrates that cutting up the pictogram units to show fractional units is not always a happy solution. The use of electrical transmission poles in the spot drawing adds something to the otherwise very stark bar graph* (center right). *The two line graphs of the same statistics* (bottom) *clearly and humorously show that the emotional impact of a graph may depend greatly on how the ranges are chosen and also on how the grid is drawn.*

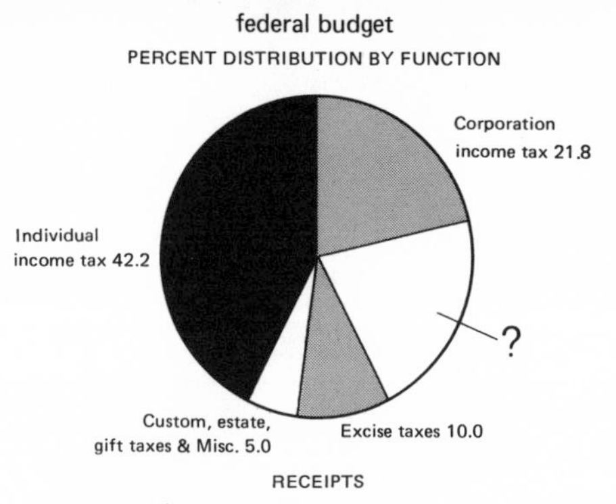

(Pie graph)

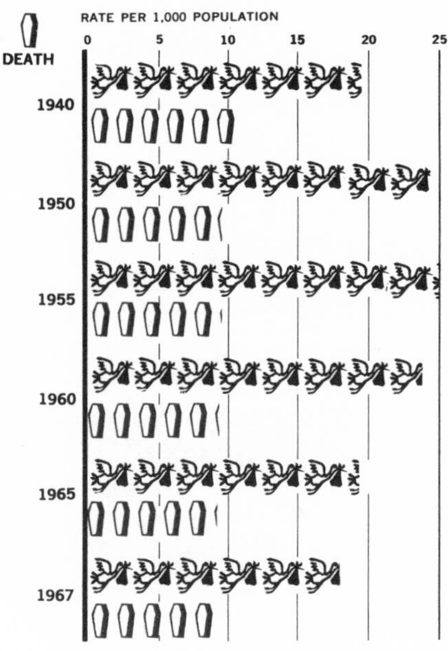

(Pictogram graph)

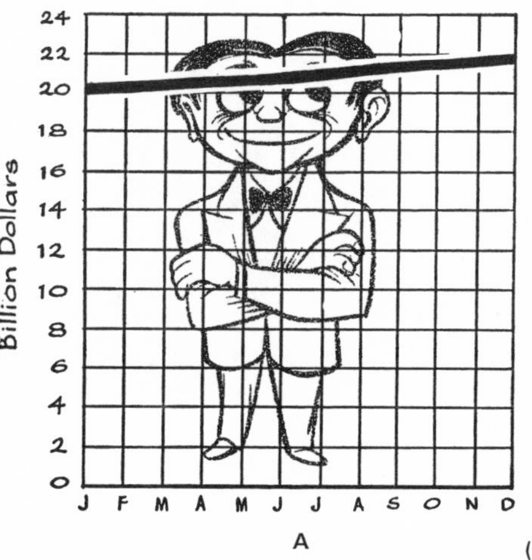

A

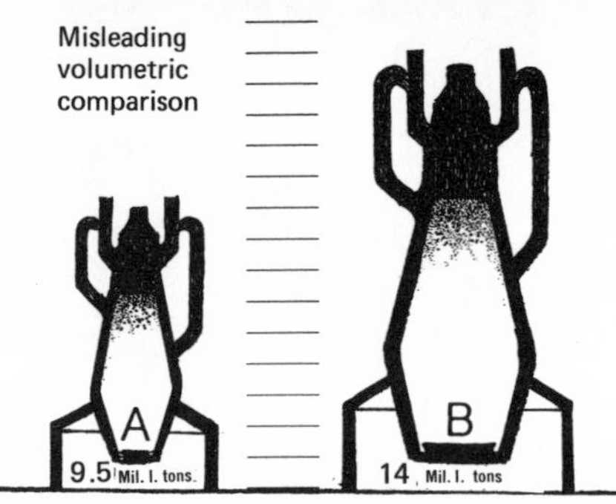

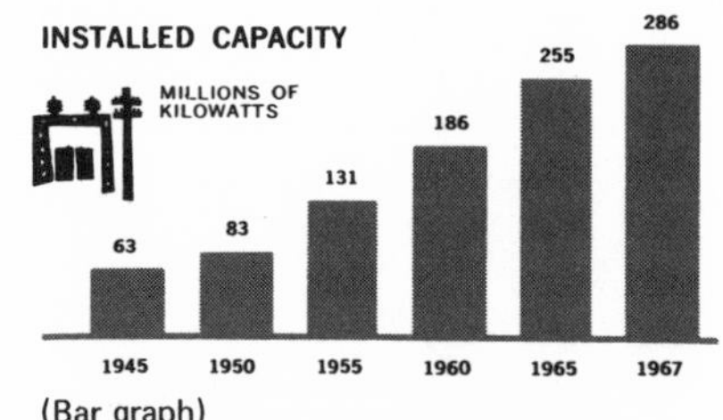

(Bar graph)

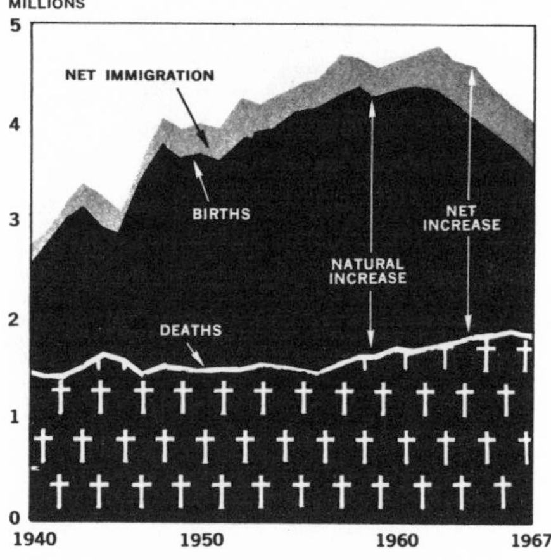

(Frequency polygons or band graph)

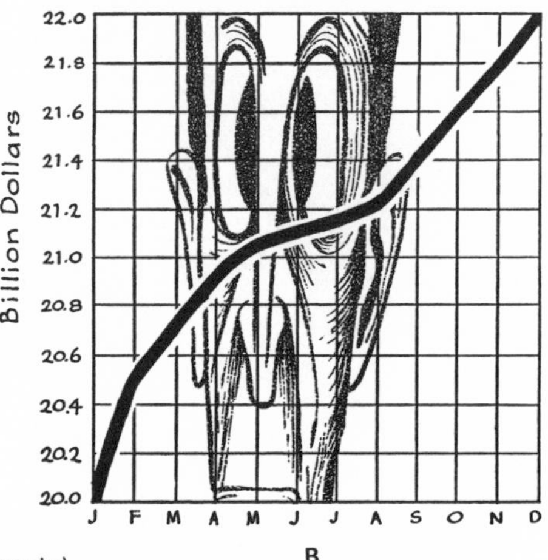

B

(Line graphs)

3-4 *Three "perspective projections"*

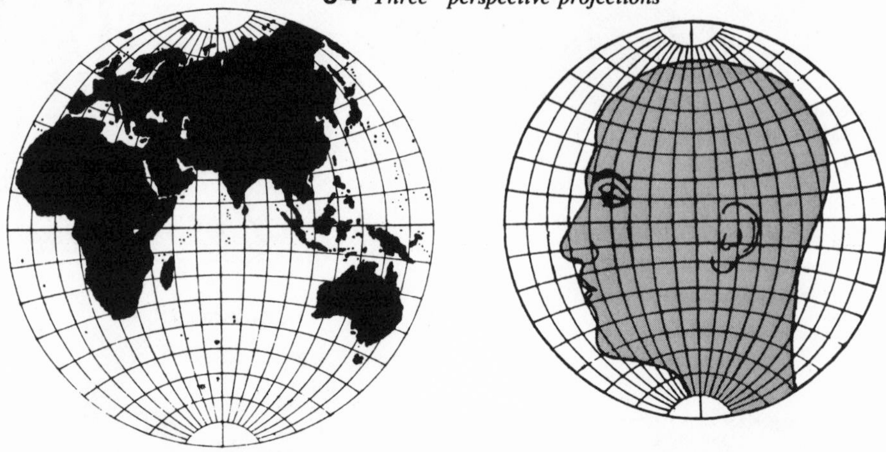

Equidistant or globular projection

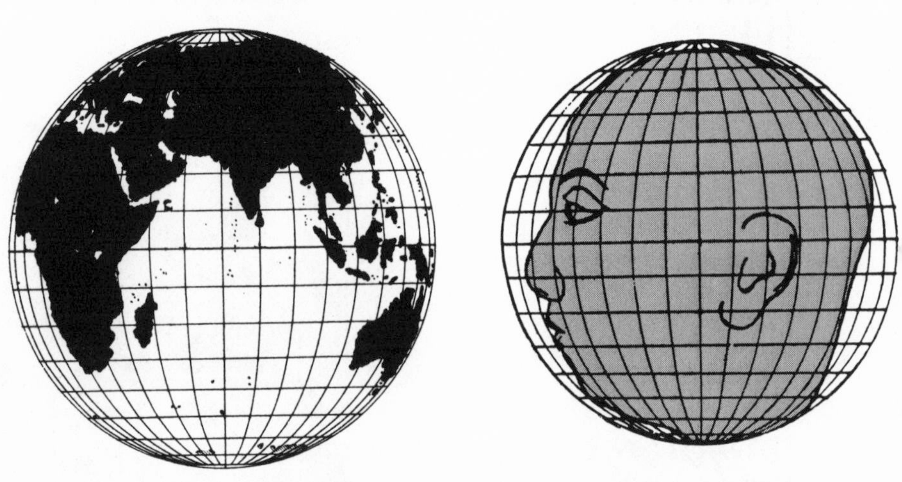

Orthographic projection

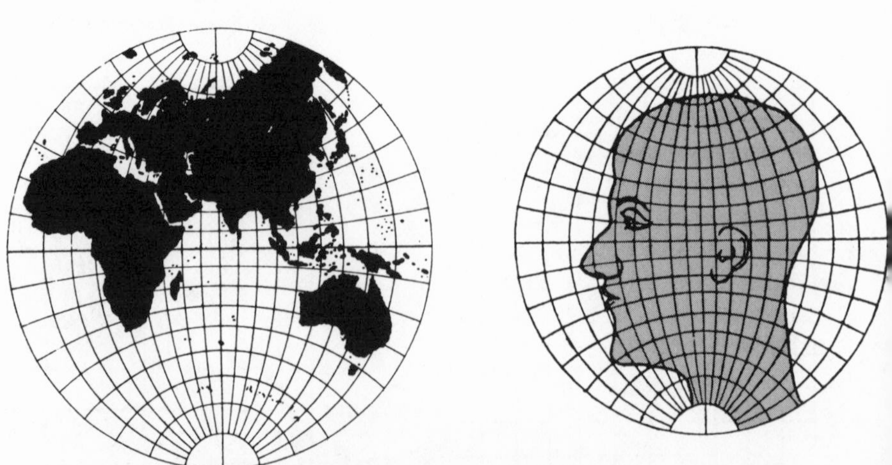

Stereographic projection

The head shown at the top has been plotted on the other projections (from *Elements of Map Projection* by C. Deetz and O.S. Adams [Washington, D.C.: U.S. Government Printing Office, 1945]).

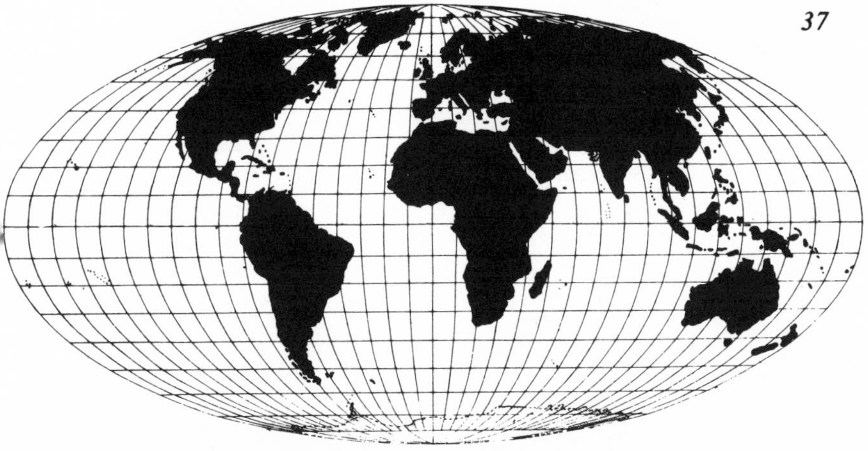

Mollweide projection (areas are correctly proportional, i.e., the map is "equal area").

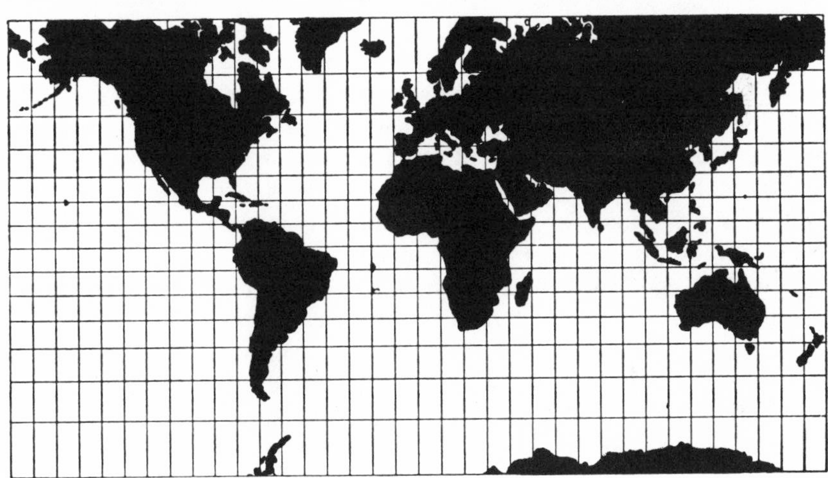

Mercator projection (compass directions correct at any point, but areas not correctly proportional, i.e., not "equal area").

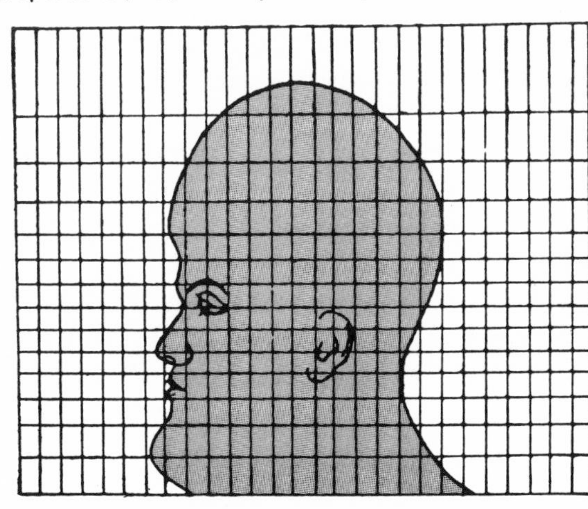

The head at the top of Figure 3-4 has been plotted on the Mercator projection.

3-5 *World maps showing contrasting treatment of area and direction.*

distributions over large areas on maps that are not of the equal-area type. If the map shows population density by one dot per 100,000 persons, it makes a great deal of difference if Greenland appears twice as large, or more than twice as large, as the United States (as it does on the very common Mercator projection), when it is only about half as large in reality. The population dots on the Mercator map are spread over a much greater area than they should be and consequently give a very false impression. This is a rather extreme example, however, for, in fact, the difference between projections becomes less and less apparent as the area covered by the map becomes smaller and smaller, so that maps of areas smaller than the United States are not very obviously different from one projection to another.

The idea, then, is not for the designer to become an expert in map projections, but for the designer to know enough to ask questions of the map maker. Knowing that map projections are not interchangeable and that each tends to be good only for a certain class of problem, the designer should have the map maker explain which projection is being proposed for use and why, whenever the map covers an area, for example, bigger than the United States. This will ensure that the map maker will not simply take the first solution at hand but will have to think about it first. In any case, do not allow statistical distributions to be plotted on any except an equal area projection. The uses of other projections for particular purposes can be roughly checked in reputable atlases.

As book designers will almost always be concerned with analytical maps, they should see to it that each map does not have too much information but rather carries out its analytical function with clarity. This judgment is a function of (1) the relatedness of the several kinds of analysis assigned to one map, (2) the size of the map, (3) the availability and use of color(s), (4) the degree of crowdedness of the map, and so on. The designer should review the work of the map maker at sketch stage with these things in mind.

Diagrams: information and distortion

We may consider one example, out of the myriad that could be used, to illustrate the amount of information that should be presented in a diagram and the kinds of seemingly innocent distortion that can creep into simple subjects. The diagram in Figure 3–6 illustrates the orbit of the moon around the earth. To show that distortions in simple diagrams do not always go unnoticed in academic circles, we quote some remarks about the diagram by the dean of the College of Education at Pennsylvania State University.*

*Dr. A. W. VanderMeer, "An Investigation of the Improvement of Educational Filmstrips and a Derivation of Principles relating to the Effectiveness of the Media," in *Educational Screen and Audiovisual Guide* (June 1967).

Obviously, the artist intended to show that (1) the moon is 238,000 miles from the earth. He also shows, stylistically, that (2) the moon revolves around the earth. He gives ambiguous information about (3) the direction of the moon's revolution. In addition, something of the (4) shape of the earth's and (5) moon's silhouette is told. If the viewer assumes that the path of the orbit is "to scale" with respect to the diameters of the earth and moon, he may make an inference (erroneous) regarding (6) the size of the earth and (7) moon.

If he assumes that only the diameters of the earth and moon are on the same scale, while the orbit is on a different scale, he may make an inference on (6a) the relative size of the earth and (7a) moon. If he observes that the diagram shows (8) the moon's orbit to be slightly elliptical, he will not only have this fact but also may infer something concerning the (9) constancy and (10) range of distances from the earth to the moon.

To continue the illustration, it is clear that if the dotted line representing the moon's orbit were removed from the frame, the bits of information numbered (2), (3), (9) and (10) will be deleted, and a different construct relating to information bits (7) and (8) will appear. It does not seem possible to reduce the size of step further while retaining the diagrammatic form, but it could easily be increased.

These remarks very definitely assume that the diagram is intended for analysis and not for reference, as was certainly the case. The example is artificially simple for the purpose of showing how much specific information

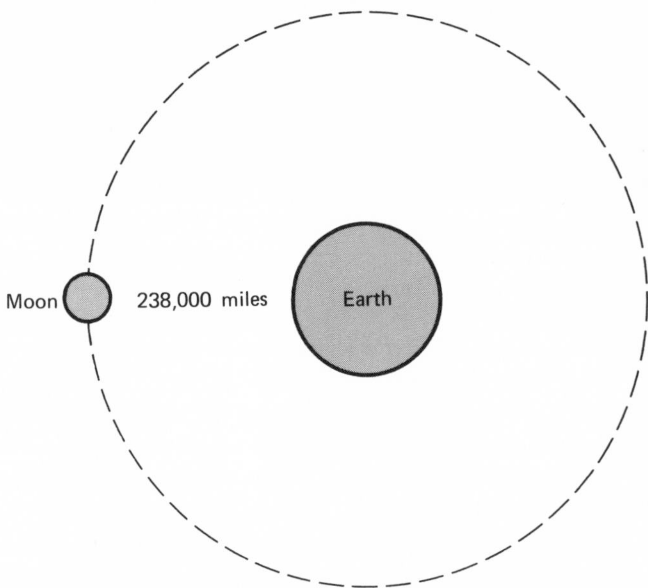

3-6 *A simple diagram of the moon's orbit around the earth.*

can be contained in even an extremely uncomplicated visual. It also shows how easy it is to distort visual presentation in supposedly acceptable ways, which are assumed (by those sophisticated in visual presentation) to be so easily understood that they are seldom mentioned.

It is important for the designer to be aware that if an analytical diagram carries too much information the central analysis may well be missed, and that it is sometimes only through rather careful thought that one can discover whether the diagram is distorting the facts (without any clue being given) in ways that may be unfair to the reader.

On the other hand, a reference diagram, like a reference map, may be expected to carry a great deal of varied information. The point here is not to limit the information arbitrarily but to make it possible for the reader to *find* the various kinds of information that may be required. (Indexes, if necessary, are generally outside the duties of the designer. But the designer should use well all the analytical graphic means available.)

Design specifications for science drawings and diagrams

Diagrams, charts, graphs, and maps are parts of the illustration program that require close coordination with the design plan and typography of the book. To maintain appropriate and consistent design throughout a program of science drawings, careful planning by designer, editor, and copy editor is required before work is assigned to artists. The editor supplies necessary references and research materials and, if necessary, fills out an editorial specification form for each illustration. The copy editor draws up a labeling style sheet covering the problems to be encountered in the special field of the book —standard spellings, abbreviations, exceptions, uses of caps, lowercase, bold, italic, and so on. Initial cap and lowercase is quite standard for diagram labels, except for heads, titles, and the like. (The author's figure number should not be used in the labels, since the number may very well be changed.) Legends are set whenever they are available; in the case of the scientific book, this is sometimes as early as galley stage. Figure numbers in scientific books very often adopt the usage of numbering within chapters (e.g., 12–7 means "Chapter 12, Illustration 7").

The designer should go over the illustration requirements carefully and decide which elements should actually be specified in order best to integrate the illustrations with the design and typography of the book as a whole. Some elements should be distinctly specified, while others should be discussed with the artist. Most of the following elements should be specified.

1. *Size.* This may be specified in fractions of a page, by width only, by modular units, by width and depth, or by relative importance, or it may be left to the discretion of the artist after general specifications are agreed upon. It is most important that full-page or full-column illustrations fit

properly. All such illustrations should be identified and legend length should be decided upon, so that awkward spaces are not left when finishes are made. Also, the necessity of similar scale should be considered for more that one picture of comparable subject matter (particularly when presented in close proximity).

2. *Titles and subtitles.* If these are to be used, they require consistent design and placement. They may relate to book display type.

3. *Typography of labeling.* This may relate to the text typeface, sometimes to a display face, or sometimes to both (but traditionally, at least, to one of the two). Different typography may relate to different categories of information.

4. *The uses of color.* The numbers and types of colors available make it possible for color to be used for various kinds of analysis or contrast. But, whenever appropriate, color should be used to fulfill specific functions, rather than simply for miscellaneous decoration.

5. *Limiting outlines or borders for illustrations* (or partial outlines in the form of base lines). These may or may not be used. The function of such borders or outlines is to protect the area of the illustration from the distracting visual elements that often surround it. Outlines or borders may be utilized in different weights and styles, and titles may be incorporated into them.

6. *Label styling* (decided in collaboration with the editor). This may involve various uses of roman, bold, italic, caps, lowercase, letter key style, such as: a, b, c; A, B, C; (A), (B), (C); and arrows or lead-in lines to elements identified by labels. Generally speaking, arrows should not be used on lead-in lines.

7. *The uses of perspective and cross section.* These should be reasonably consistent throughout the program.

8. *Standard models for any equipment to be shown.* Beakers, microscopes, clamps, and so on, should also be consistent in appearance. An equipment catalog may be chosen and appropriate items marked for standard use as models.

Design specifications for charts and graphs

The same general considerations that apply to scientific drawings also apply to charts and graphs. Again the designer should decide which items will be specified and which will simply be discussed with the artist. Visually speaking, charts and graphs are closely related to the typeset editorial structures of the book.

The editorial department provides complete chart specifications, including: (a) necessary statistics, (b) reference materials, and (c) copy edited labels. The completeness of the data to be presented is the responsibility of the editor, not that of the designer or art editor, and normally not that of the artist. It is not unusual for inexperienced authors or editors to request charts on subjects for which no statistics are even known to exist. In most cases, such requests should be returned for clarification. However, it should be noted that some specialized chart and graph artists and studios will provide research and other specialized services. These may be useful, on occasion, but naturally such services increase the costs of the program. Prepared stock charts on various types of common statistics are available, especially of the pictographic variety. These may be investigated when there is likelihood that they might prove useful.

Most of the following elements should be specified: (1) size,* (2) titles and subtitles,* (3) typography,* (4) the type of chart (general considerations relating to bar, pie, frequency polygon, pictograph, three-dimensional projection, and so on, were discussed earlier in this chapter), (5) the uses of color,* and (6) uses of tints and Benday screens.

Drawings, symbols, and photographs may be added for both decorative and functional reasons. If color and artwork are considered together, the potential for enlivening charts and graphs is considerable. It should be kept in mind, however, that a chart program should have a fair degree of internal consistency, and that charts in books are intended to be studied for the information they impart. (Advertising really carries no such burden and hence can afford charts that "wow" rather than present information in a truly palatable style.)

Design specifications for maps

In designing a map program for a book it is very important that all editorial, design, and production specifications be worked out thoroughly before the cartographer starts work. A full-color map program can be one of the most complicated, time-consuming, and expensive art projects handled by the art department. A change in production specifications can be very costly in time and money.

The editor provides complete editorial specifications for each map (see the Map Specifications form in Chapter 11), but these should be checked by designer or art editor for clarity and completeness. Editing a complex map program is a specialized job for which considerable experience is required. Some points have already been mentioned in relation to projections. The designer should especially consider whether the subject matter might better be presented in either a more analytical fashion or a more condensed fashion—whether one map might better be presented as two or more owing to the nature of the analysis, or whether several maps might better be consolidated into one. Difficulties in relation to a one-map representation of timed stages of a process in space (the stages of a battle, westward expansion, and so on) require special analysis.It may be worthwhile to discuss such matters with the editor.

Most of the following factors should be discussed with the cartographer. For actual specifications refer to the Map Specifications form at the end of Chapter 11.

*The same considerations apply as do for scientific drawings above.

1. *Size.* (Same considerations as for scientific drawings above.)

2. *Projection.* Some considerations have been suggested in the discussion of maps earlier in this chapter. Editor and cartographer should agree on projections for world maps and large sectional maps. If the type of projection is important to a knowledgeable reader, it should in most cases be identified on the map, in small type.

3. *Typography.* For maps showing many kinds of distinct information, the typographic distinctions can become very detailed both as to style and size (and, when color is available, as to color too). Land labels, sea labels, physical features, historical information, cultural information, place names of varying degrees of importance and size, and so on, all need to be distinguished. The hierarchical problems of labeling may be quite distinct for each map program, and they should be worked out consistently within each program.

4. *Color.* Available colors, including black, should be used imaginatively, but with consistency and in accordance with normal cartographic usage.

5. *Titles and subtitles.* (Same considerations as for scientific drawings above.)

6. *Optional elements.* Outside borders, cartouches, scales of miles, legend boxes, north indicators, textures, spot illustrations, decorative shorelines, and so on.

7. *Line weights.* For boundaries (international and internal), for rivers, roads, map boundaries, and so on.

8. *Grid lines and grid numbers, explicit labeling of tropics, circles, and so on.*

9. *Simplification.* The degree of simplification (for example, of the shorelines) is one that should be generally appropriate to the kind of map in question, its purpose, its audience, and the general design of the book. All maps are, essentially, simplifications, and artists often have styles of simplification with which they work most easily.

After the specifications have been discussed with the cartographer, several sample maps should be prepared that are representative of the problems in the total program. Final specifications should be put down in writing only when these samples have been thoroughly considered by editor, designer, cartographer, author, and production control.

CHAPTER 4
Typesetting Options: Documentation and Specification

Manufacturers of composition systems and typesetters are proud of the "zippy" new systems that have evolved, and indeed they should be. But in order to use these complex typesetting systems, differing one from another in ways that affect design specification, designers need accurate and current information about them, in a form that can be easily referred to. Such information is all too seldom made available.

There was a time when books on typography attempted to document the particulars of various typesetting systems, but the time for that is past. The new systems are rapidly changing and have too many details. (In fact, it never did make much sense, since the designer needs to know the details for the particular installation being used, and too much other information leads only to confusion.) Furthermore, the compositor is the only reliable source of information on the current capabilities of a system. Few systems are completely standard; each system is adaptable, and local adaptations are constantly made. This is especially true in the case of computer-controlled systems.

The designer cannot be expected to guess or make endless phone calls, taking notes over the phone, in order to find out the details of each system. If much of this is required, the manuscript may be sent to the compositor designed for the "nothing-in-particular" machine. Little may be done to adapt the design to the needs of the particular system or to take advantage of the special features, except perhaps by accident. As a result, most of the new machines are incompletely and even badly used, and many end up functioning like the old Linotype machine (out of production for years now), because that was the last machine most designers thought they could understand without help.

The designer should, as much as possible, insist that each composition source provide adequate documentation. To be useful, this information must be at the designer's disposal before the design is started.

Documentation from the typesetter

The compositor should provide the designer with a list of all available machine set typefaces, giving sizes, styles, and alphabet length or characters-per-pica information. Special fonts and universal characters, fractions, ligatures, and accents should be listed, with their size ranges, as well as foreign alphabets such as Greek, phonetic, and so on. It is unreasonable to expect complete samples of all sizes and faces now that faces and sizes and their variations are so numerous, but at least sample alphabets in one size should be provided. If the system condenses, expands, and obliques the normal alphabet, this should be indicated exactly. It should also be made clear how and under what conditions the mixing of faces and sizes is permitted in the system.

The maximum utilizable text width (measure) should be stated, as should the minimum keyboard space, what kind of letterspacing is permitted, and whether letterspacing can be negative (kerning) as well as positive. If the "set" width (horizontal escapement factor) of the normal typeface design can be altered electronically, this should be stated in terms of its limits and some representative expansions and condensations shown. (It is not reasonable to expect that all of them should be shown because they are often too numerous.)

The kinds and weights of rules and leaders that can be set on the machine should be stated, as well as how these are specified, what the limits are to weight, how vertical rules are handled, and so on. All machine ornaments should be shown, since they cannot be described in any other way, and available sizes stated.

Certain classes of difficult composition handled by the system should be described in appropriate detail, such as tabular, mathematical, chemical, and foreign language work. It is important for the publisher to know what kinds of such material (and what degree of complexity) the typesetter is ready to undertake.

Display typography should also be described, and the way in which it is to be specified should be made clear. Since the advent of the Typositor and similar film display systems, the range of display faces has become so great that showing of even one sample size of each face has become a large project. Also faces are so generally available in samples that it is unnecessary for every typesetter to show them. It is enough that compositors list which faces of the hundreds available they have conveniently at hand.

Different systems set up the basic type page in different ways, in addition to using different minimum measurement units. Some will set material in the margins at no extra cost and some will not; some can even set type (as well as rules) vertically on the page—running titles, for example. Who knows what may be available by the time the reader sees these words.

Vertical and horizontal spacing

The matter of spacing is handled differently by different systems, and since designers often must specify spacings, both horizontal and vertical, they must know what is available and how it is specified. They must know whether they are to specify in picas, in points, 1/18-em units, ½ points, 1/10 points, "vids," or whatever.

As to vertical spacing, two varieties may be specified in some cases: spaces that are fixed in relation to paging and those that can be varied in paging. The adjustment of leading in order to equalize facing pages, when other adjustments are not available or are insufficient, is traditionally referred to as "carding," from the old practice of inserting paper strips between the lines. Designers need to know if this practice may be used (they may wish to permit it or prevent it, depending on the book). In some systems vertical spacing may be added negatively, that is, the type size may be larger than the body size, permitting the close setting of capitals, for instance. Vertical spacing and leading may always be specified in points. In some systems it can also be less than a point: ¼, ½, or 1/10 point. This can be very useful to the designer in adjusting the number of lines on a page. With one point leadings the least that can be added to or subtracted from a page without changing its dimensions is 3–4 lines. With ½-point leadings, this is reduced to 2 lines, and with 1/10-point leadings, to one line.

As to horizontal spacing, we may distinguish three kinds: (1) measure setting and other width specifications, such as tabs, (2) fixed spaces specifiable as various width quads, thin spaces, points, and so on, and (3) justification spaces, whose operating parameters may or may not be susceptible to design control. The word space for nonjustifiable material is also of interest (poetry, paragraph line ends, etc.). If the width-of-setting specifications can be made in points, there is no reason why measures need be set to even picas or half picas. This may be of great use in multicolumn work.

Word spacing

The best trade practice requires close and even word spacing as the standard. This means that all word spaces should be less than 1/3 em, with the minimum about 1/5 em. But even in careful composition 1/3 em is not always practical. The narrower the type measure and the larger the type the more impossible good spacing becomes. Most bad spacing is the result of bad design rather than bad typesetting.

The analysis of word spacing options in justified setting is very complex and relates to the mechanical or logical options and to the hyphenation procedures of the composition system. Automatic systems have logical word-break operations and exception dictionaries that may consist of thousands of words. All this is not the concern of the designer, except that in any composition system the designer should avoid posing really difficult hyphenation problems if they can be avoided. In justified setting, any unspecified letterspacing of words, and word spaces over 1 en, are normally not allowed.

When bad spacing will result from justification of lines set to narrow measures (e.g., in word tables, indexes, etc.), the lines should be set unjustified (ragged right). A rule of thumb is: When text line width is less than 18 ems of any size, do not justify. Do not justify 10-point type less than 15 picas, or 8-point type less than 12 picas, for instance.

The word space for unjustified material (also paragraph end lines, poetry, etc.) may be differently defined for each typesetting system, but usually it is between ¼ and 1/3 em. The term "thin space" has no definable meaning in most systems. Designers should avoid it and find out what keyboard spaces are available in the target system and how these can be unambiguously specified. (They also should know what may be involved if they specify nonkeyboardable spaces, as, for example, points.)

Two kinds of sentence spacing are traditional: (1) normal close sentence spacing in which only the word space for the line is used after the sentence-ending period (sometimes called "French" spacing), and (2) "sentence spacing," which uses a quad, usually an em, after the period instead of the line word space (sometimes called "standard" spacing by publishers of technical books, dictionaries, bibliographies, and classical texts, where such spacing is common).

Heads set in caps, caps and small caps, small caps, boldface, or extended face are usually word spaced more than for normal sentence style in order not to appear too closely set. An en space is most often used.

There is a relatively new spacing feature on many modern typesetting devices, including some cathode ray tube (CRT) systems and almost all of the inexpensive electronic machines. It is still unfamiliar to many designers and typographers even though it is of specific interest to them. The essence of it is the ability to make small subtractions from or additions to the horizontal escapement value of all characters equally, thus modifying the normal character escapements or "side-bearings." This makes tighter or looser letter fitting possible and subject to design control, without affecting the "set" or shape of the letters. The actual design of the typeface determines the extent to which it can reasonably be tightened up (or loosened up), but the amount of tightening will seldom exceed ¼ of one point of set size. The eye is, of course, the only reliable judge. Word spaces are also affected.

This line has been set with 2/9 of one point letterspacing subtracted.

This line has been set with 1/9 of one point letterspacing subtracted.

This line has normal letterspacing (none added or subtracted).
This line has been set with 1/9 of one point letterspacing added.
This line has been set with 2/9 of one point letterspacing added.

This universal escapement-adjustment feature is carried out in slightly different increments in the various composition systems. The designer is advised to find out whether the adjustment is available, and if it is to describe the general results wanted in terms of what the system offers—and then to see sufficient samples in the adjusted sizes and measures required. The character count, of course, will be affected. If the compositor does not supply modified character counts the designer can have necessary lowercase alphabets set and divide the length of these, in points, into 342 to obtain characters per pica.

The design uses of small text setting modifications, both of set size and escapement values, have not yet been much explored by designers. They provide opportunities to change emphasis and to make minor distinctions—without changing size or typeface.

Typographic planning

Ordinarily design starts more or less all at once, as the designer first considers the whole project. Certain information is necessary to an orderly beginning, and the transmission of this information may require that all the parties concerned get together and have a start-up discussion, often referred to as a "transmittal meeting." The editor, the designer, the copy editor, production control, and perhaps a department head may typically all attend the transmittal of a complex project to design and production. For a simple project the designer may get only the manuscript and various forms containing information. In any case, this minimum information must include:

Compositor	Pages planned
Printing process	Illustration program (if any)
Trimmed size	Schedule
Color (if any)	Missing elements (if any)

and notes concerning any special problems (editorial or production). Various other details of the project also may need to be discussed, such as the general sales and editorial expectations for the book or the wishes or peculiarities of the author. The standard editorial question is "When can we have books?" The standard production control response is "When do we get the completed manuscript?" (Usually the meeting is held before everything is quite settled with the manuscript.)

Pretty much the same information is given to free-lance designers but in somewhat fuller detail, especially in regard to various procedures the art director may want to have followed. These special instructions may be given verbally, but a checklist form is a great aid.

Design processing of really complex texts is taken up in Chapter 8. Here we consider texts of lesser degrees of complexity that can be handled at one go. The designer's instruction sheet shown here (Free-lance Book Design Handling form) was evolved for a general trade publisher with a considerable variety of books and was intended for use by free-lance designers, but it can also serve in job training. Most of the considerations apply most closely to trade books and simple to medium-complex educational books. Details such as the specific composition order to be used can be only illustrative. (The composition order referred to is shown in Figure 4–1, and the Book Length Estimate form referred to in the text-fitting procedure is the same one that appears in Chapter 6.) The form provides for a minimum information context within which the designer can start work. Because the form makes sure that all necessary information is accounted for, it saves time; it also enables the designer to consider the book plan as a whole during the initial phases of design.

Specification of editorial structures

Editorial structures, discussed in Chapter 2, generally can be classified under about two dozen headings, but the possible variation within these classifications is quite beyond calculation. It is the elements of this mixture that the book designer must put into visually presentable and clarified form. The specifications involved fall into two categories: general specifications for the more regular examples of editorial structures, and detailed specifications for individual, less regular examples.

It is quite wasteful of effort and productive of error and inconsistency to mark all editorial structures as though they were unique problems. They benefit by being treated as consistently as possible within any one manuscript. Conversely, problems occur if exceptions are not recognized and dealt with at the time the manuscript is designed. When the general rule does not apply, the typesetter must get in touch with the designer, who, while on the phone and without having the manuscript at hand, must try to remember the job and come up with a decision. This is not productive of good design.

In this chapter only regular editorial structures are considered: how to specify them in orderly and intelligible form and also how to document, integrate, and modify the specifications easily and efficiently when necessary. But if we analyze exceptions carefully, we find that they contain the same elements and entail the same considerations and decision-making processes as the regular structures.

The decision-making process

The text designer's work always follows one general pattern, whether conscious or not: "(1) This is the editorial structure appearing in the manuscript;

FREE-LANCE BOOK DESIGN HANDLING

Designer: ______________________________ **Phone**________________

Title: ____________________ **Date assigned**__/__/__**To complete**__/__/__

Text compositor: _______________ **Output device**____________________

The object of these instructions is to make the problem as clear as possible, and to enable the designer to design the complete book at one time (as far as possible).

COMPOSITION: Please use the composition order* supplied, and write so that it can be photocopied. Put spaces above and below elements under "Sink." (Index will be specified by us.) Typositor is available from text compositor (yes) (no). See "Special Composition," below.

TEXT FITTING: Manuscript character count (is) (is not) necessary. Please complete the "Book Length Estimate Form" supplied, as far as necessary. This is provided as an aid. If you want to do it another way, OK, but please enter the relevant figures and return to us. Book should be planned to come out slightly less than an even 32 page unit, unless character count is not requested.

LAYOUTS: Supply for full page spreads, part openings, chapter openings, and others you may think necessary.

SPECIAL COMPOSITION: For display, mechanicals, picture sections, etc., when it cannot be set practically at text compositor. Send marked copy to us, and we will get repros, read, and return to you as rapidly as possible.

COPY MARKUP: Please spare us a lot of compositor queries by solving and marking all typographic problems in ms. (OK to leave the fitting of large tables to the compositor, subject to general instructions).

BINDING: To be designed with book, even though some specifications may have to be changed later (such as cloth color). Binding specification form is supplied. Please fill out completely, submit rough sketch with colors noted, and then marked mechanical. Cloth grades and number of hits maximum are to be noted.

PICTURE SECTIONS: Please size all illustrations by percent of original, or by one dimension. We will return two sets of untrimmed blues for mechanical or dummy. Please supply mechanicals for all full page illustration groups. Use Letrafilm opaque #151M over blues, or red ink outline, with captions & credits in position. If you wish to bleed call us for gripper restrictions. To save time in emergency size both dimensions to fit mechanical ( ), or use stats ( ), which we will order. On all mechanicals use registry corner marks in black. (Book prints offset unless noted.)†

DUMMIES: If a book will require dummying please indicate this on composition order. Supply a reproducible dummy form, and dummy sheets will be printed for you. In dummying, short pages are OK, long only in emergency, widows over 2/3 line OK.

Size all text illustrations, check the galley references, and mark captions for measure. Check photos for spotting and mark retouching you can't do to our attention. Same for other artwork.

Last minute corrections will be done by us; or you can stop by and make them in work space available (tools also available). We expect good work, and we will do anything we can to help you. Please call on all traffic questions, or technical questions.

---

*See Figure 4-1. †Printing process, if not offset: ____________________

(2) this is the generally expected form for the structure in question; (3) this is the typesetting system being used; (4) *now* what choices or options do I have, which are feasible from the point of view of time, money, and my own energy and imagination?"

The generally expected form for any editorial structure is peculiar to itself. Every reader knows, in general, what most of them are, and designers know more of them and in more detail. But when considering options, the designer may wish to distinguish between an editorial structure and a substructure, because every substructure is a new typographic option. A table is a structure, while a column head is a substructure; a chapter title is a structure, but it may be useful to consider the word "chapter," or the number, as substructures. The usual presumption is that the substructure will inherit most of its characteristics from the structure of which it is a part. For example, the numbers that identify list items, although a separable substructure of the list, are usually set in the style of the list. Table footnotes (substructure) are often set table size as well as table face and table width—but not always.

So whenever a change is to be made, the designer must first notice whether the change involves a structure or substructure. If it is a substructure, what characteristics should it inherit from its main structure, and which should be specified differently? If it is a structure, then is it of a type that has already been designed or a new one? (The designer should obviously avoid specifying conflicting designs for the same general structure, unless there is a reason for an exception.) If it is a new structure, what options are available? The following are almost always available, within the restrictions imposed by the typesetting system:

A change of typeface
- type size
- type body
- type set width
- type mode (roman, italic, or bold)
  - caps
  - caps and lowercase
  - initial cap and lowercase
  - lowercase only
  - even small caps
  - caps and small caps

A change to justify and hyphenate
- neither justify nor hyphenate
- hyphenate without justifying
- justify without hyphenating
- change the measure of setting
- set more than one column

center on the regular measure
center on another measure
quad left flush (with or without indention)
quad right flush (with or without idention)
begin a new page (right or left)
begin a new right-hand page (or left-hand page)
start a new line
run in with whatever preceded
set an initial letter, word, or words differently
set an initial line or lines differently
set a certain space before starting the structure
allow the space to vary or not vary in paging
set a decoration or rule before the structure
use an illustration before the structure

(Give a rule for when the structure accidentally starts a page)
(Give a rule for when the structure is broken in paging)

Not all of these options are applicable to all structures, nor are they available in all composition systems. Furthermore, the list is by no means exhaustive, but hopefully it will be suggestive.

"*When in doubt, set it a little smaller*" This is the typographer's golden rule, traditionally the best way to avoid unexpected and awkward turnover lines or too-tight lines. It is always easier to adjust when you have a little white space to play with. The situation is most critical, of course, with respect to complex composition such as tables.

In automatic composition this rule can sometimes be relaxed because specifications can be changed at "galley" stage without penalty for the reset. No lead is involved, and the output is usually rerun through the system for editorial corrections anyhow. The designer can thus afford some trial sets that don't quite work, without paying the traditional penalty. The situation in this regard should be checked, however, because systems may charge more than just the basic keystrokes for changing the output controls.

Display composition

Not all machines used for text composition can set large type sizes too. There is some tendency to interpret the word "display" to mean anything that cannot be set with the text. If such display involves many words, then economics is involved, for extensive hand composition is much more expensive than keyboarded composition. Two factors are involved: sizes available and typefaces available. Hundreds more faces and sizes are available for hand composition. Where no more than a few dozen words are required, design flexibility is usually sufficient to decide the matter in favor of hand composition, in spite of the fact that this probably makes more work for the designer and involves

BASIC COMPOSITOR INFORMATION SHEET (FOR DESIGNERS)

Compositor ____________ Contact ____________ Date ____________

Address ______________________________ Phone ____________

Typesetting device ______________________________ Paper/film/non-CRT/CRT

Point size range ____________ Number of sizes in the range ________

Characters in a font ____________ Number faces on-line ________

Number sizes on-line ________

Smallest leading increment specifiable ________ Negative leading? ________

Maximum text measure ____________ Minimum unit of measure definition ________

Automatic base-alignment of sizes and faces mixed in one line? ________

Restrictions on mixing of faces and sizes ______________________

Will set vertical tabular rules as well as horizontal? ________

Rule weights specifiable in ____________ increments, from ________ to ________

Quadding: ragged right text? ________ ragged left? ________ center all? ________

Can hyphenation be used with ragged settings? ________ not used? ________

Accents floating or integral? ____________ Automatic kerning: ____________

Does display type appear in position in galleys (or "first pass")? ________

Spacing: System divides the square em into minimum units of ____________

Minimum horizontal spacing unit specifiable ____________

Minimum horizontal spacing unit on keyboard ____________

Hyphenation normally defined to occur between max ________

and min ________ word #s.

Basic interword space (nonjustified) is ____________ (e.g., poetry)

Letterspacing adjustment available for all text ________ by increments of ________

Most practical units for designer-specified occasional letterspacing ____________

Mathematics: Built-up math of 2 levels? ________ more than 2 levels ________

Case fractions (en piece) available? ________ Special fractions (em piece)? ________

Displays may be left-indented as well as centered? ________

Equation numbers may be at left as well as at right? ________

Tabular: Standard intercolumn space for tables not filling measure_________

Limit on number of columns?_________Restrictions on word tables? _________

____

Can word tables be set unjustified?_________Math in tables OK?_________

Paging: Documentation of typesetter's makeup rules provided herewith?_________

Paging rules permit (unless otherwise specified): "carding"?_________

long pages?_________short pages?_________widow lines over _________ %

Variable and fixed spaces are specifiable by customer for paging?_________

Page makeup is manual/semiautomatic/automatic/interactive _________

CRT systems additional information: Is the first pass (galley) rough-paged?______

Electronic typeface expansion?_________condensation?_________limits?_________

____

Electronic obliquing?_________Degrees of oblique slant_________2-column OK?______

Footnotes by symbol?_________Illustration space allowances in paging? _________

Any penalty for size, leading, and measure specification changes at first pass, for text?_________for tables?_________

Are lines letterspaced for justification automatically noted?_________

Are any automatic character counts provided the customer?_________

What are the size limits on repeating texts assigned macro calls? _________

Is there a defined "scan-and-replace" capability? _________

Cost and time for digitization of new characters? _________

Hyphenation exception dictionary?_________size? _________

Are standard "flag characters" used for format control routines or for special character identification?_________which? _________

DOCUMENTATION IS REQUESTED FOR THE FOLLOWING:

1. Machine-set faces (please note original or most common names also)
   A. Styles and sizes available (roman, italic, bold, small caps, weights, types of figures available). 10 point alphabets are useful.
   B. Characters per pica or alphabet lengths (at least for text sizes)
2. Special characters that are part of font design.
3. Universal special characters, math characters, special alphabets, accents, superiors, inferiors, etc.
4. List of handset display faces (with sizes for metal faces).
5. Rules and ornaments (machine and handset).
6. Typesetter's normal rules for page makeup.

a system of composition often incompatible with the text composition, making it necessary to correlate the output at every proof stage, to paste up, and sometimes to buy the display type at another source than the basic text compositor.

Because of the economics and the trouble involved (especially if the book is to be a permanent machine readable file), the designer should consider carefully whether the hand-set display is really necessary. There are, of course, some advantages in the consistency obtained by setting the display in the same face or family as the text. In this case, where the sizes involved are not too big for the system, display can usually be set best with the text. The designer must check the typesetter's list of machine sizes available.

Hand composition by the Typositor system (or similar systems) involves a gain in flexibility, but also entails a loss of consistency. The spacing of letters and words is usually by eye and is dependent upon the experience and habits of the operator and the way instructions for letter fitting are interpreted. (In general, the tendency is to set Typositor letters and words much closer than similar foundry or machine-set faces.) Sizes are specified by the height of the cap letter in inches. It makes no sense to specify in traditional point sizes, because this would impose artificial restrictions where none exist in the system. In fact, there are no real size restrictions at all, since sources specializing in such composition will photostat to any desired size. Problems arise mainly in small sizes, where the usual tight spacing may appear a little too tight.

Typositor and similar systems can kern, overlap, set spacing to such specifications as "very tight," "tight," "normal," "TV" (wide), and so on. Each system uses its own terminology. They can also condense, expand, italicize, and backslant. The limits imposed on these operations vary somewhat with the individual systems and their optical lenses. The designer should check with the supplier. The thing that these flexible systems often cannot do is to produce consistent spacing, especially letterspacing. To add a consistent letterspace between letters, a fixed space, such as the side bearings of metal display types, must be assumed to begin with. Typositor has no side bearings, of course, so the best way to specify letterspacing is to make one basic spacing specification and then to state that a certain amount of spacing is to be added to that. The result cannot be guaranteed, but this seems a small price to pay for such flexible options.

The composition order

The document used to specify typesetting, whether it is handwritten or a standard form, is generally called a composition order. In either case it is not an easy document to prepare for the complex book. If it is written to fit each book individually, the designer may forget to specify various details listed on a standard form. A standard form, however, does not fit any individual book very well, unless the publisher is engaged in producing books having similar sets of editorial structures.

When there are few problems, the standard form is indicated. It can also be helpful when there are many problems, as is usually the case with educational publishers. If it does not fit the book in hand it can always be supplemented or replaced with other specifications, and it can be used as a checklist in any case. Usually it is evolved by the publishers for their own use, but sometimes the typesetter provides one.

Shown below is a simple form for general trade books, filled out for a specific title (Figure 4–1), and another one, specialized for mathematics, filled out as a standardized order (Figure 4–2).

These forms are basically similar even though they are designed for very different classes of composition. In part, this is because all books have similar specifications, and in part, because many details of mathematics composition are left unspecified. It would be tedious to analyze these forms in detail, but the reader may wish to give them rather careful consideration. Certain conventions are used here to abbreviate specifications—such as A/17, B/6 to mean "space above 17 points, and space below 6 points." The trade order is for Linotype setting, and the mathematical text order is for Harris Fototronic CRT setting. In this CRT application, ½-point type sizes and ½-point leadings and measures are used, although the Harris CRT can work with 1/10-point spacing increments. (The typeface called Vega is the CRT version of Helvetica.)

"The invisible book"

All innovation and originality implies a departure from a norm. We have quoted William Blake's observation that originality depends on copying. If there is nothing from which to depart, it makes it hard to depart. What is it, then, *from* which the innovative book designer departs, in search of the stars? The designer departs, of course, from the book that looks like every other book, "the invisible book," the book that the reading public assumes does not need to be designed, the book that looks just like "a book." It is not a beautiful book, and it is not an ugly book. It does not look cheap or expensive, big or small, plain or fancy. It is completely invisible as a graphic arrangement; nothing comes through but the words and pictures, the author and the images. In fact, when it is described in these terms there will be those who say that this is the ideal book. The most evolved book, like the most evolved Zen master, is perhaps not to be distinguished from the most ordinary. That is one point of view, but not one that is universally shared by designers. In any case, it would seem worthwhile to know more of this ordinary and invisible book, this norm, if only to depart from it as rapidly as possible. The trimmed size, the display pages, the text pages, the way illustrations are handled, all contribute in their own way to its consummate ordinariness. There will be differences of opinion

COMPOSITION SPECIFICATIONS

Title BOOK TITLE

To COMPOSITOR

Order No.

Date

Author JOHN AUTHOR

Pub. Date

Editor

Imprint

Designer

Illustrations: Line 1 (MAP, 2 PP., FM.)

Binding CLOTH

Halftone —

End Sheets MAP (TO COME)

Color —

Trim Style FLUSH

Char. Per Line 64 Char. Per Page 2304 Total FM XXii Total Pages 185 FOR 192

Lines Per Page 36 Total Char. 313,000 Total Text 143 + 20 BACK MATTER

Trim Size 5½ x x 8¼. Type Page Size 24 x 40½ Picas. Margins, Head 5/8" Gutter 3/4"

Body Matter	Type Face	Size	Sink	Indent
Text	TIMES ROMAN	10/13		¶ INDENT 1 EM
Left R.H.	TIMES ROMAN, EVEN S.C.	10		1 EM FROM FLUSH IN
Copy	BOOK TITLE			
Right R.H.	TIMES ROMAN C+LC ITALIC	10		1 EM FROM FLUSH IN
Copy	CHAPTER TITLE			
Folios	TIMES ROMAN ITALIC	10		1 EM FROM FLUSH OUT
Part Nos.	—			
Part Titles	—			
Chap Nos. (N)	GOUDY O.S. ROM. #394 ARABIC LIN.	24	6 PI. (1½ PI/B)	CTR. ABOVE #996 ^ RULE SUNK 9 PI.
Chap Titles (T)	GOUDY O.S. ITALIC #3941 C+LC	24/30	11 PI. (4 PI/B)	CTR.
Sub Titles				
(A)	TIMES ROMAN C+LC ITALIC	10/13	1½ L./A, ½ L./B	CTR.
(B)	TIMES ROMAN EVEN S.C.	11/13	2 L./A, 1 L./B	CTR.
(C)	TIMES ROMAN BOLD C+LC	10/13	1 L/A	FL.L. (RUN IN OR ^ SEP. LINE)
Opening Style	REGULAR 1 EM ¶ INDENT		16 PI. ON 1 LINE OPENER	
Extract				
Poetry				
Footnotes				
Index	TO COME	7/8 (?)		

Remarks DISPLAY MONO GOUDY O.S. #394 AND 3941, ON HALF TITLES, TITLE, PP. 2, 4, CONTENTS AND FORWARD, CHAPTER OPENINGS. USE SWASH CAPS AS SHOWN ON LAYOUTS AND MARKED IN MS. FOR CHAPTER TITLES USE ALL AVAILABLE SWASHES. WORD SPACE FOR CHAPTER TITLES 8 PTS (NOT EN).

4-1 *A typical trade book composition order filled out for a specific title. Note that the book is fitted conservatively (185 first-pass pages) into 6 forms of 32 pages (192 pages). It is easier to add pages than to subtract them.*

PUBLISHER *Any* | **Production** | **Design** *S. Rice*
TITLE *Default format specifications—#1* | **Author** | **Edition** *1st*
ILLUSTRATIONS *Line 00, halftone 00, captions with ms.* | **PROOF (Galley)** *2* | **(Page)** *2*

TEXT SPECIFICATIONS (Text runs with assigned sans serif. Text has 10 forms, sans serif 6. All figures lining.)

Trim *6 × 9"* | **Type page** *27 × 45 picas* | **Text area** *27 × 43* | **Lines pg.** *43*
Text type *Times Roman* | **(Assigned sans serif)** *Vega + med.**** | **Size/body** *10/12* | **Parag. ind.** *15 pts for all*
Secondary *[EX] Times* | **Size/body** *9/10* | **Spaces A/B** *A/6 pts, B/6 pts* | **Indent** *15 pts left*
Legends *[LE] Times 8.5/9.5 × 27, 15 pts ind. L&R* | **Fig. No.** *Vega Med: "Fig.00"* | **Start** *FL.L.*
Footnotes (text) *[FN] Times 7.5/8, 5 pi FL.L. rule over* | **Start** *FL.L., all* | ☒ **Symbol** ☐ **Number**
Bibliographies *[BB] Times 8/9 × 27, 15 pts hanging indent*
Appendixes *[AP] Times 8.5/9.5 × 27 (head: same as contents, index, etc.**)*
Index *Times 8/9 × 13 (42 chars), subs sep. line, ☐ ind.* | **Letter breaks** *1 line space* | **Turnovers** *1 EM*
Problems/examples *[PR] Times 10/12, indent L&R 15 pts*

TABLES: Face *Times* | **Size (or to fit)** *8/9 (min. 6/7)* | **Table No. & title** *[TB] 8.5/9 Vega med. caps FL.L.*
Boxheads *Init. c&lc Italic* | **Rules** *1 pt top, bottom & below box hds, rest ½ pt* | **Ftnts.** *Table size*
Table subtitles 8.5/9 Vega c&lc, FL.L. internal heads 8/9 Vega med. c&lc. Tables not 'spread'

MATH DISPLAYS: ☒ **center** ☐ **flush left** *Times 10/12, equation numbers FL.R.* | **#A turnovers** *10 pts* | **#A&B** *A/12 pts B/12*
Numerical text fractions ☐ **case** ☐ **shilling 2/3. Subscripts** ☒ **align with superscripts** ☐ **precede supers** ☐ **follow supers**
Space around math operators: "med. tight"—#3

HEADINGS (Face, size, body, style, sinkage, spaces A/B, indents, alignments, breaks, runovers, next line)

[*PA*] **Part** *Vega med. obliq. caps 16/20, 15 pts ind., starts new RHP, A/6 picas, B/6. See samples**
[*CH*] **Chapter** *Vega med. c&lc 14/18, 15 pts ind. starts new R or L, A/6 picas, B/12. See Samples**
[*A*] **Head** *Vega med. caps 9/12, 15 pts ind., sep. line, A/18, pts, B/6. See Samples**
[*B*] **Head** *Vega (reg.) caps 9/12, 15 pts ind., sep. line, A/18 pts, B/6. See Samples**
[*C*] **Head** *Vega med. init. c&lc 10/12, 15 pts ind., sep. line, A/8 pts, B/4. See Samples**
[*D*] **Head** *Vega med. init. c&lc 10/12, 15 pts ind., run-in period☐, A/12 pts.*
[*E*] **Head** *(References, etc.) 8.5 Vega caps, FL.L., Ltr #1 pt, underlined, sep. line A/12, B/6*
[*M1*] **Head** *(Theorem, Lemma) 10 Vega med. init. c&lc, FL.L. (run-in period☐ to italic) A/12*
[*M2*] **Head** *(Proof, etc.) 10 Times bold italic init. c&lc, ind. 15 pts (run-in period☐ to roman) A/12*

RUNNING TITLES: Copy, left *'Part' title* | **Copy, right** *Chapter title*
Style, left *7.5 Vega oblique caps, Ltr #1 pt, ☐☐ to folio* | **Style, right** *Same as left*
Folios *8.5 Vega med. obliq. ltr #1 pt flush out* | **Drop folios** *Same as reg. folios, 6 pts below page*

NOTES **All separate line text heads: 15 pts indent, turns flush, max 85% of line, non-justif, ⅓ em word #, next text is ¶ indent. If not caps then initial C&LC (principal words not capped).*
***Contents, index & other new-page FM & BM heads 16 Vega (reg.) c&lc, 15 pts ind. A/6 pi B/6*
****Note: Vega 'medium' is the bold version of Vega (as with Helvetica). There is no 'bold.'*

4-2 *A composition order for a specialized mathematics typesetter, filled out for a standard format in the common 6" × 9" trimmed size. Half-point type sizes and leadings are used. The typesetting device is the Harris Fototronic CRT.*

on details, of course, but "the book" will probably have specifications similar to those given below.

Trimmed size: 6″ × 9″
Arrangement: Probably centered, but possibly flush left for all separate line elements.
"Text" type: Caledonia, Times Roman, or other common face, with bold
"Display" type: Same as text face, or same family (or sans serif)
Text page: 26 × 43 picas, text only; 26 × 44½ with running title
Main text: 10/12 (for text counts see tables in Chapter 6)
Margins: Head ⅝″, gutter 13/16″
Paragraph indent: 1 em.
Figures: Lining (throughout)
Running titles (heads): Text size, small caps, centered (2 ems from folios for flush books). Book title on the left; chapter title on right
Part numbers: 36-point caps, sink 8 picas, centered (or flush) 2 picas space below
Part titles: 24/36 display, c&lc, 2 picas below part numbers
Chapter numbers: 24-point display (arabic, omit word "chapter"), sink 6 picas
Chapter titles: 18/24 display, c&lc, roman, 2 picas below chapter numbers
Chapter subtitles: 12/14 text c&lc, 2 picas above, 4 picas below (i.e., A/2 pi, B/4 pi)
Chapter opening text: Starts flush left, sentence style, 4 picas below chapter title, or subtitle
First separate line text head: 9/12 text, caps, A/18 pts, B/6 pts, centered (or 1-em indent for flush books)
Second separate line text head: 11/12 text, small caps, A/10, B/2, centered (or 1-em indent for flush books)
Run in head: Text size, bold, initial cap and lowercase, 1-line space above, 1-em indent, run in, with period and em quad after
Extract: 9/11 text, indented 1 em at left, ½ pica above and below
Poetry: Text size, center long line, 1-line space above and below; titles: 12/15 text, italic, c&lc, center, 6 points below (flush left for flush books)
Footnotes: 8/9 text, paragraph style, superior numerals, by page, ½ pica minimum space above
Tables: 8/9 text, 1½ picas above and below (9/10 if tables are small)
Table number: 10-point text, bold, caps, run into table title
Table title: 10-point text, bold, c&lc, ½ pica below, center with number (flush left for flush books)
Column heads: 8/9, initial c&lc, italic, center, align bottom
Table body: 8/9 (9/10 for small tables) or smaller to fit, tables not spread, no stub leaders, center on page
Footnotes: Table size, paragraph style, by symbol
Rules: 1 point top and bottom, rest ¼ point, no down rules

Front matter: (Separate line elements consistently center or flush)
Half title: 12-point text, italic caps, sink 12 picas
Card page: Authors: 9/12 text, cap and small cap, run into titles; titles: 9/12 text, c&lc, italic (series title, if any, 10 text caps, 1 pica below), sink same as title-page title

Title page: Book title 24/36 display, c&lc, broken for sense (if 1 line, sink 8 picas; 2 lines, 6 picas; 3 lines, 4 picas) 4 picas below, or 3 picas to a subtitle
Subtitle: 14/20 display, c&lc, italic, 4 picas below
Author(s): 12/18 text, caps, space below to fill page (or 6 points to affiliations), 1 pica between authors
Authors' affiliations: 9/11 text, c&lc, italic
Imprint: 12-point text, c&lc, 4 picas above bottom of text page
Copyright page: 8/10 text, broken for sense, 4 picas above bottom of text page. If credits are on copyright page, sink 4 picas, 8/9 text, full measure
Dedication: 12/16 text, italic, c&lc, broken for sense, sink 12 picas
Contents: Head: 18-point display, c&lc, sink 6 picas, 4 picas below
Body of contents: 10/14 text, center long line (unless display is flush, then flush left)
Style: Number, em quad, title, em quad, folio
Foreword, list of illustrations, preface, etc.: Head: same as contents; text: same as text of book; author line: c&lc, italic, flush right

This is an example of "the basic invisible book" and as a very experienced designer once said, "If you are going to change it in some way, you'd better know what you are doing, because it's not so bad."

CHAPTER 5
The Making of Pages

Pages are not logical units of a book; they are mechanical units. Books have been made, and are still made in some places, in ways that do not involve pages. The scroll or volumen form has characteristics to recommend it and reminds the designer that the necessities of paging, as we commonly practice it, are not divine injunctions but conventions that should be examined occasionally. There may be times when the logical divisions of the book take precedence over the mechanical divisions, and in such cases the running of short or uneven pages should be permissible.

General paging instructions

The mechanical rules of makeup are, in their rudimentary forms, fairly simple and well-known, although even here there are differences in practice. But as we go on into the logic of exactly what is to be done in each paging situation, the countless decisions that must be made, the logic becomes very complex indeed. In fact, no one but computer programmers trying to evolve automatic paging logic seems ever to have reduced much of this mare's nest to regularity.

When the publisher returns corrected galleys to the compositor for paging, certain instructions that govern the paging operation are given, or verified, and other general rules are assumed. The specific instructions are generally similar to those following:

Verification of page depth, number of lines per text page, and white space between text and running title
Verification of lines per chapter opening (normal)
Front and back matter running heads
Edited copy (if necessary) for text running heads
Part or chapter-opening decisions as to L or R, L only, R only
Margins (if necessary to makeup)
Special instructions for illustrations and legends
Any sections dummied by the publisher
Any other special instructions or clarifications of the general paging rules under which the compositor works

What, then, are the general rules of paging with which the compositor works? *A Manual of Style* (University of Chicago) says almost nothing on the subject, which is perhaps natural since it is primarily for editors and authors. The Oxford University Press, with centuries of experience, has a basic booklet, *Rules for Composition and Make-up* (1971), with a few rules, most of which relate to the placement of illustrations. These include the doubtful injunctions that all pages are to be of the same depth, except in the case of verse, and that no widow is to be tolerated, even when it is a full line.

Most experienced compositors have, it seems, sets of rules that are seldom published because it is suspected that they are neither complete nor really consistent and logical. It is certainly almost impossible to make them complete and logical, but attempts are sometimes made. A typical set of rules would resemble the following set, which are for a computer-controlled composition system. (Automatic composition rules provide a better example than those for manual makeup, because they are more specific.*)

Typical rules for automatic paging†

1. Facing pages are equal in length. Long and short spreads are allowed, but one may not follow the other. (Long or short pages are automatically noted.)
2. Widows over 2/3 line are permitted at top of page, below illustrations, and below tables.
3. Spaces above all separate line text heads, but not below, may be increased in paging. Spaces around extracts, mathematics, lists, illustrations, set-off material, and above footnotes may also be increased in paging but may be decreased only in emergency. Space below chapter titles may be varied

*Those who are interested in automatic electronic page makeup and layout will find some discussion of these topics in Chapter 12.

†Adapted from Stanley Rice, *Computerized Typesetting* (Allentown, Pa.: ComCom, Haddon Craftsmen, 1977).

if necessary in paging (space above is varied only in emergency).

4. Space above separate line heads and space-break indicators (such as asterisks) is retained at the top of a new page only if requested. A blank line used as a space break is not retained. Space above run-in heads, illustrations, tables, math, extracts, lists, etc. is not retained.
5. No less than two lines of text are permitted below separate line subheads at foot of page. A minimum of four lines of text is required on any page with illustration(s) or table(s), at the end of a chapter, or above a run-in chapter title.
6. If a run-in chapter title falls at the top of a page with no text above it, the running head and the normal space above the title is retained. If there is text above it, the running head copy will be from the previous chapter.
7. Illustrations in automatic page makeup are placed at the foot of the page on which they are referenced, if possible; otherwise at the top of the page following, aligning with the first line of text. The running head is retained, unless the illustration is larger than the normal text page. If the placement specification reads "directly after reference," it is so placed in the "first pass" paging run, even if the resulting space breaks over to the next page, making subsequent adjustment necessary. (Illustration space is allowed on first-pass pages, the normal galley stage, when information on depth is supplied in time.)
8. If tables are set separately from text, only reference numbers are set in first pass, unless tables have been set ahead of time and can be treated as illustration space. When an illustration depth is not specified, only a reference number is set for that illustration in first pass.
9. Running feet maintain constant position, that is, they do not move up with short pages. Long pages are permitted in books with running feet only if the running feet are allowed to move down.
10. Index lines are not justified when abnormally large word spacing will result. Index continued-line notices are not set on the following page, unless requested, but are set on the previous page only.
11. Electronic "carding" is allowed as a last option in page makeup, unless the customer specifies otherwise.
12. Runover footnotes take a ½-point rule × 6 picas, flush left.
13. Pagination of front matter is by lowercase roman numerals.
14. Maximum number of consecutive line-end hyphens is three.
15. Turned-page tables and illustrations read correctly when the book is turned to the right.

If the publisher wishes to change any of the above specifications, notice of such modifications should be included in the composition order.

The dummy

In situations where paging decisions are complex, the designer decides that a dummy must be made; and when made by an experienced person, the book plan will come out in a presentable and, more or less, optimum form. In other words, all the decisions will have been made in an acceptable way. But aside from repeating a few very simple rules, the dummier, who usually works intuitively, will have no idea exactly how this was accomplished.

The rules evolved by experienced publishers to guide those who make dummies follow, in general, the kind of rules stated above for automatic paging, sometimes adding such items as:

Widows are allowed in the right-hand column of a 2-column book.

Space between illustration and caption is 6 points.

Minimum space between caption and text is 1 pica.

Text lines in 2-column books should align across.

A folio must appear somewhere on every double-page spread, even if running titles are dropped.

An illustration should not come before its reference.

For a more detailed discussion of dummying see Chapter 8.

There are many conflicting demands in the actual practice of making a dummy. It is, of course, sometimes necessary to adjust the text or illustration specifications, run short or long pages, or even bend some of the paging rules in order to arrive at a sensible solution. But these are last resorts, and the dummier makes every effort to live up to the rules without drastic compromise.

Illustrations

Certainly the greatest problem in page makeup is the accommodation of illustrations. This is natural because illustrations cannot normally be broken to meet the needs of paging. It may be useful to consider the strictly logical decisions involved in setting up an automatic paging system for illustration space allowance. The flow chart on the next page (Figure 5-1) illustrates the logic implied by the following rules:*

1. If the illustration space will fit on the current page, following its reference, then allow the space on the current page. ("Space" includes picture depth, caption, and vertical spaces around these.)
2. If, at the reference, there is not sufficient space for the illustration to appear on the same page, allow the space at the top of the following page.
3. If the space to be allowed is less than half the text-page (or column) depth, allow the space at the top of the page (or column).

*Decisions about widows and short or long pages are not part of this decision process.

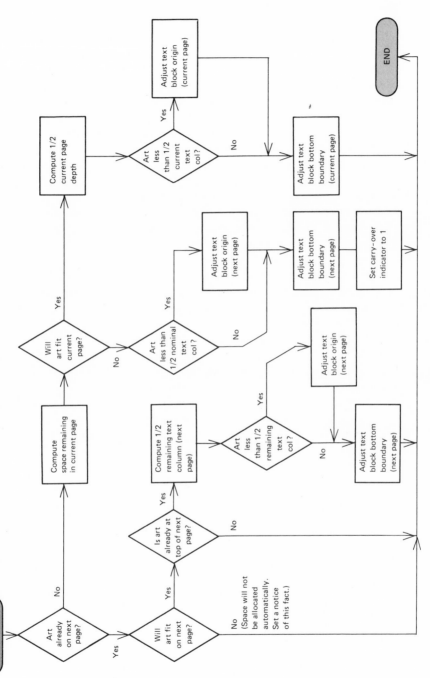

5-1 *A flow chart showing the logical procedures for allocating illustration spaces on single-column pages, for an automatic typesetting system (VideoComp) operating with rules as described in the text.*

4. If the space to be allowed is over half the text-page (or column) depth, allow the space at the bottom of the page (or column), but above any footnotes.
5. If the space is to be allowed on the next page, the same top and bottom rules apply as in #3 and #4.

Reading the labels in a sequential way will be enough to indicate the kinds of decisions that must be made by the person who dummies even a simple illustrated book. Happily, these decisions are made, for the most part, without knowing how it is done. Lest the working out of even such relatively simple paging logic as this be assumed to be trivial, we may imagine the chart futher complicated by all the paging rules mentioned above.

Floating illustrations in multicolumn format

General rules may sometimes be given by the designer for handling illustrations of miscellaneous sizes in multicolumn format, the most difficult of dummying problems. The solution of such a problem was perhaps never reduced to logic before the advent of automatic handling, but an analysis of automatic rules can sometimes serve manual methods, as well as the other way around.

The following automatic rules are formulated for books with any number of columns and with illustrations of varying sizes, as long as the illustrations can be allowed to float (i.e., they need not follow the reference directly).* The rules do not allow for multicolumn heads, but any designer who would design a multicolumn book of this nature with multicolumn heads should be willing to dummy it personally! The logic places the illustrations around the perimeter of the page and puts each illustration in the *first* of the following locations in which it will fit without changing the page dimensions:

1. At the bottom of the column where the reference occurs
2. The top of the next column, which may be on the next page if necessary
3. The bottom of the next column, after that in #2
4. The next top . . . next bottom . . . next top . . . next bottom, etc.

The illustration space includes the spaces around the illustration and optionally includes legend. An illustration previously positioned at the bottom of the first or last column on a page will be moved up to make space for another that is of equal or greater width. Also, an illustration will be placed below one previously positioned at the top of the first or last column, if it is the same width or narrower than the first. Figure 5–2 shows the general result of these paging rules.

*Adapted from *Textran-2 Extended Language Capabilities* (Lake Success, N.Y.: Alphanumeric, Inc., 1969), pp. 54–55.

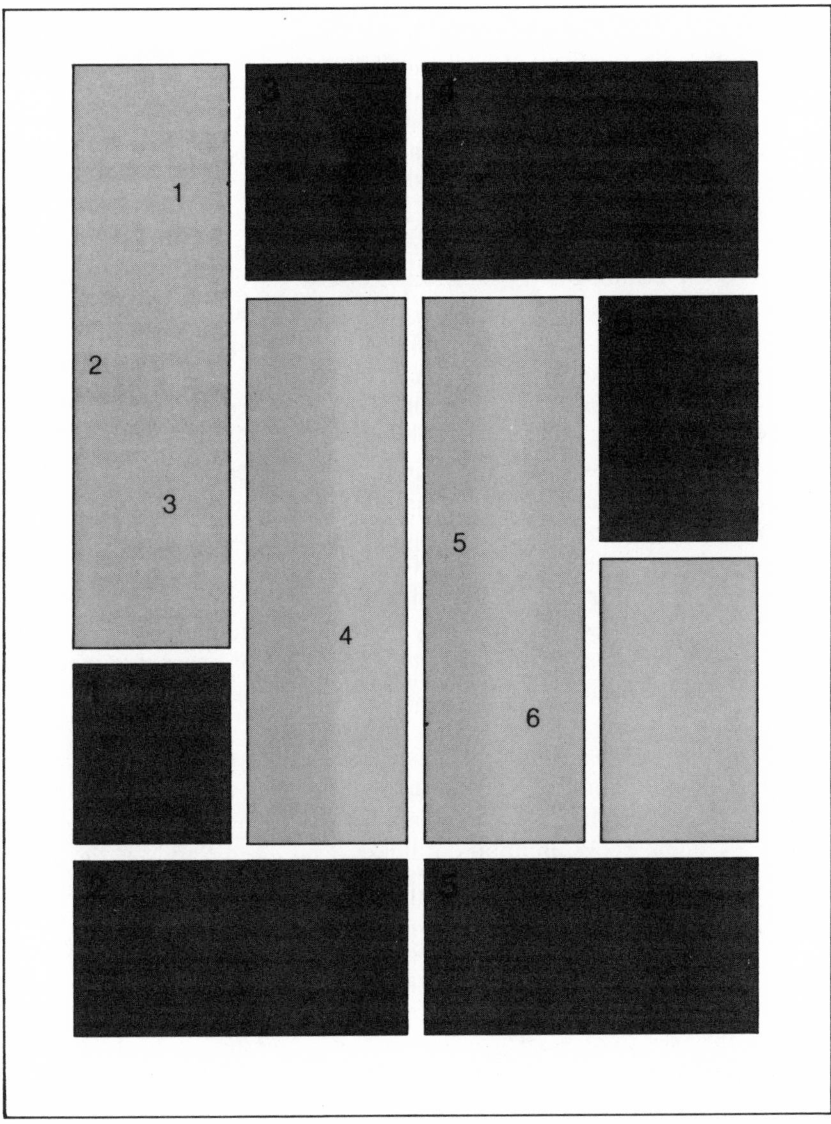

5-2 *Diagram of a multicolumn page with typical illustration spaces allowed by automatic paging procedures designed to place the spaces around the perimeter of the page.*

The concept of the modular text

A "module" is a unit of structural planning or building, and a "modular text" is one that is built with the help of such a planning unit. In the case of books, the structure or layout of pages is planned, and the modular unit is an even subdivision of a page; the book page is itself too large a unit to be really efficient for detailed planning.

When text is relatively continuous, with few illustrations, there is no real need for the modular unit. Also, when few illustrations are smaller than ¼ page, modular planning is probably unnecessary. But the more complex the text becomes, and the more illustrations there are of miscellaneous sizes, the more useful the modular unit can be. When many things have to fit together on crowded pages, modular planning makes it possible for them to fit harmoniously. Both purely illustration pages and pages of mixed illustration and text are easily and flexibly planned.

The modular unit is useful not only in design execution but in editorial preplanning as well. The number of characters of text, extract, study materials, etc. per modular unit can be calculated. This enables the editor to plan editorial features to fit desirable subdivisions of the page.

How is the modular unit chosen? In general, it approximates the smallest even division of the text page that may be useful in planning. Often it relates to the smallest common picture size and shape. There is no need to make the unit very small, because it can be subdivided easily for the unusually small illustration.

Six, eight, or ten units per page are likely to be most useful, but this depends a good deal on the trimmed size and the shape of the book, as well as on the common illustration size. For a 2-column book, multiples of two are needed, and for 3-column books, multiples of three. It may be helpful for the depth of the unit to be close to an even multiple of text lines, but this is not usually crucial.

The modular unit should be chosen by the designer in consultation with the editor, and dummy sheets should be made to show modular division, making sure that the units are divisions of the normal text page, not the trimmed size, and that they are all of equal size. The units can be extended to the trim for bleeds, allowing units of different sizes and shapes (see Figure 5–3). Also, in drawing up the dummy sheets, allowance should be made for the intercolumn space, if any, as well as for the space between modular units, so that illustrations can be sized directly from the dummy.

Through modular planning a great variety of design is attainable, with the book still retaining an impression of unity. On a page with six modular units, about 20 different illustration shapes are possible, and text and pictures can be combined in over 60 different ways, not counting bleeds. There is no reason at all for the modular text to look monotonous. On the other hand, it will look well planned, even when it is dummied by an inexperienced person.

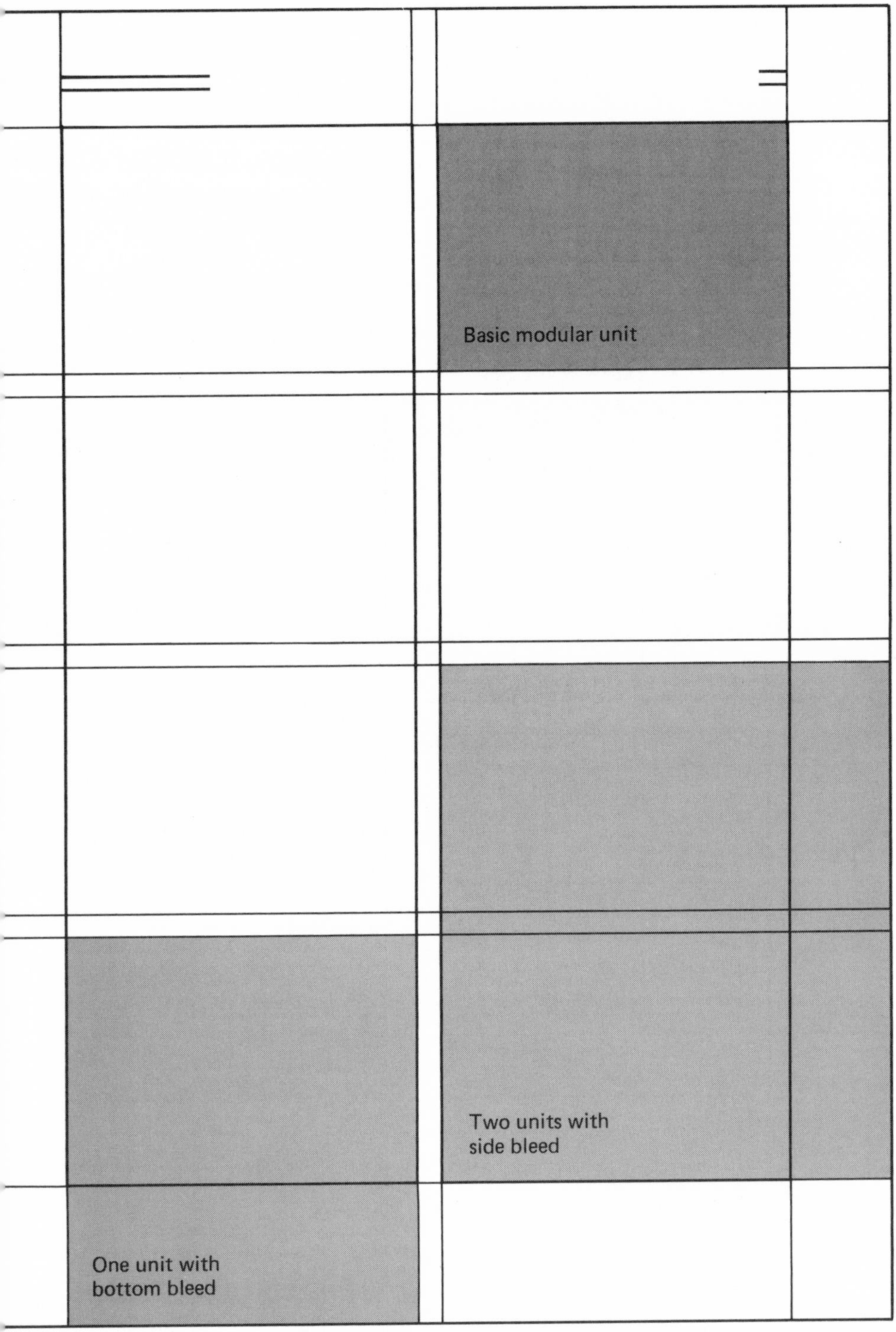

Basic modular unit

Two units with
side bleed

One unit with
bottom bleed

5-3 *A modular page plan for a two-column book of 6 3/8″ × 9″ proportions. Running heads are assumed, and spacing between pictures (i.e., modules) equals the intercolumn space. Note that while modular units themselves are equal, their bleed variations are not.*

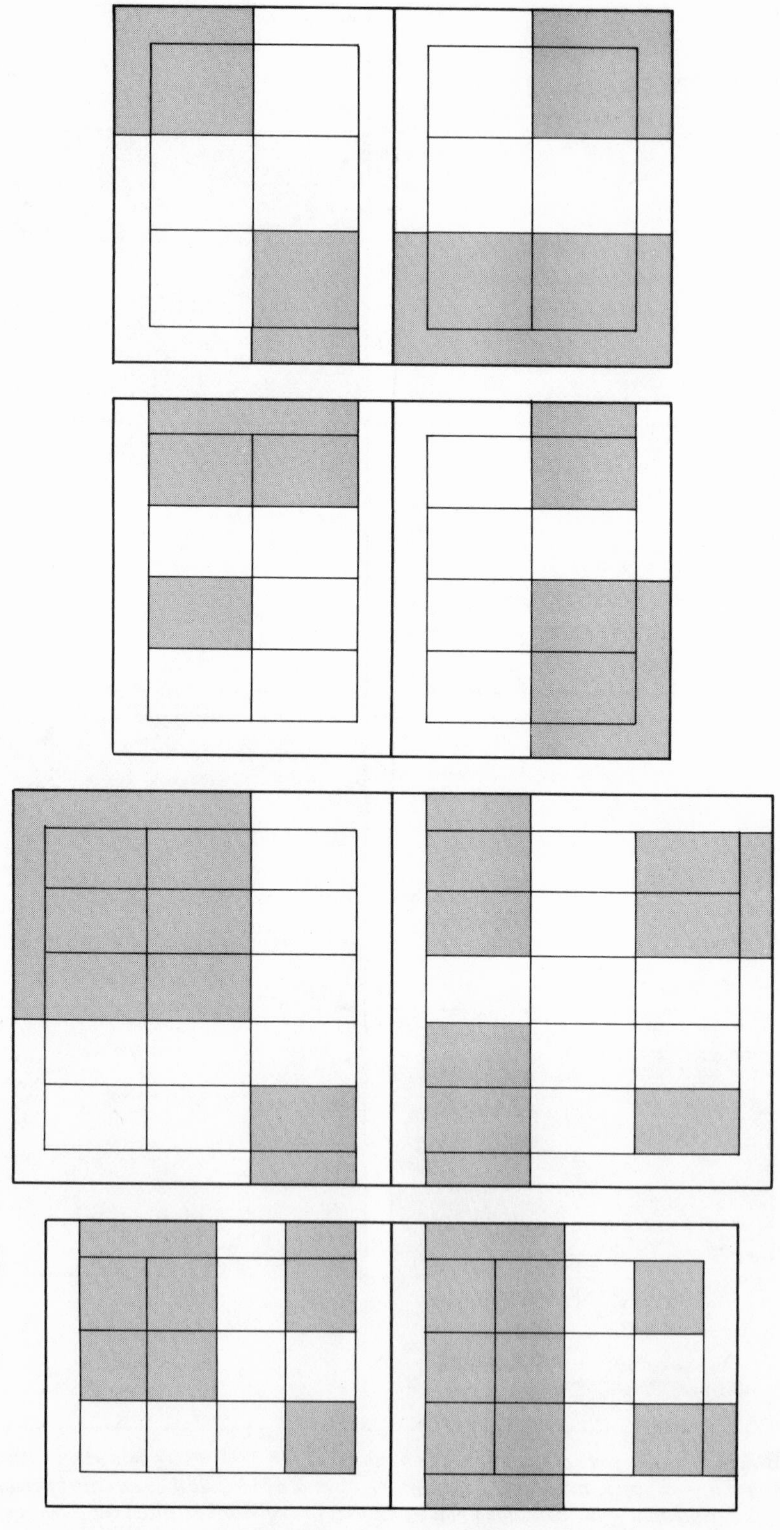

The maverick element in the modular text is sometimes the legend. Legends should not be subtracted from the modular illustration spaces. That is, they should not be treated as part of the illustration, because this interferes with visual unity by creating odd sizes. Illustrations should occupy the full modular spaces, and legends should occupy text space. It is preferable for legends to be set with galleys. If this is not possible, then they may be set before the dummy is made, or estimated and then written to fit.

The designer who has not worked with modular planning is apt to presume that it would make the sizing of photographs very difficult. This is almost never the case. The considerable variety of shapes possible allows for a broad design scope in handling most photos and commissioned art. A photograph that cannot be cropped or pre-existing art in an odd shape simply should be treated as exceptions. Where even 80 percent of the illustrations are in modular units, the effect on overall design unity is one of startling purposefulness.

Probably the greatest usefulness of modular units is in double-column or other multicolumn books, and for illustration sections or pages in single-column books. For illustration sections it is, of course, not necessary to use the off-center placement of the text page on the paper page. An arrangement centered on the paper page may be preferable.

Modular planning is not at all an attempt to put the designer in a strait-jacket. But it can give the entire book a look of organization, unity, purpose, and clarity that the complex nonmodular book, with its miscellany of picture sizes and shapes, and its irregular fitting of the various elements on the page, can almost never attain.

Any modular scheme that fits the nature of the illustration problem may be considered (see Figure 5–4).

The modular concept has been used in various other types of design planning (architecture and magazine design, for example), but thus far, although the modular concept has been proposed, it has not been used as much as it could profitably be for book planning.

5-4 *These are generalized typical modular page plans for differing trimmed sizes and shapes. The details would be worked out similarly to the details of Figure 5-3.*

SST
RCL
SUM
NOP
fix
R/S
RST
EE
CP
subr
pause
CE
(
÷
π
7
8
×
Σ+
Σ−
RAD
4
5
−
Mean
P→R
1
2
+
S. Dev.
prt
list
0
•
+/−
=
Palatino Bold
Permanent Headline Italic

CHAPTER 6
The Adjustment of Book Length

The adjustment of book length depends, in part, upon calculations that enable the designer to relate the number of characters in the manuscript (the character count) to book pages. Such calculations (castoff) can be simple and rough or they can be of varying degrees of exactness, depending on the exactness of the character count, the condition of the manuscript, and the complexity of editorial text structures.

Character count: the general method

1. Determine the average number of characters in the manuscript line, counting both spaces and characters. If there are significant numbers of pages with different line counts these must be counted separately. The best method is to select several pages that seem most typical of each typing and draw light pencil lines at the right showing what seems to be the end of the average line. Elite typewriter is 12 characters to the inch, pica typewriter 10 characters to the inch. Others must be counted.

2. Determine the average number of lines on the average manuscript page and multiply this figure by the average number of characters per line to obtain the average number of characters per manuscript page. Paragraph endings, spaces above headings, space breaks in the manuscript, short pages before subdivisions that start a new book page, and so on, are to be counted as full lines and pages. This is true of all spaces in the manuscript that also require similar spaces in the book, except when it is anticipated that the book space

will be proportionately much larger or smaller than the same space in the manuscript. Then an adjustment may be called for, which should be handled as a separate adjustment apart from character count.

3. Identify the parts of the manuscript that are not part of the main text and that may require a separate character count. Some structures will occupy about the same proportional space in the book as they do in the manuscript. For example, since extracts and footnotes are usually set smaller in the book but typed the same size in manuscript, it might be assumed that they should be counted separately. However, they also take extra spaces in the book that may not be allowed in proportion in the manuscript (1-em indent and spaces above and below in the case of most extracts, and at least ½ pica above in the case of footnotes). Typically, extracts must average over 8 lines per extract to save space. (If over 10 percent of the manuscript is made up of extracts averaging over 10 lines, it might be worth counting the extracts separately. This would depend on how they are typed in the manuscript.)

On the other hand, tables usually require considerably less space in the book than in the manuscript. These should be estimated separately, even though it may take time to do a careful job. Some tables can be estimated in tenths of pages, like illustrations, but others should be counted by line, according to the line depth of the table design, added up, and translated into pages.

Poetry, of course, runs line for line both in the manuscript and the book, and unless a special design, such as one poem per page, is called for, it is probable that poetry will occupy proportional spaces in the manuscript and book. Short poems, when they occur in groups, as in anthology sections, may sometimes be treated as illustrations. This is because they cannot be run-on or broken arbitrarily and must be shown to good advantage. All judgments for such irregular text structures are quite arbitrary, but the designer should try to anticipate special design requirements. However, for complex books it is quite unrealistic to expect that all the various structural settings will be correctly anticipated in character count and castoff.

4. Identify the "special" elements in the manuscript that may need a separate count. Check for pages that have been added (10a, 10b) or skipped in consecutive numbering, and for short pages other than those that end a subdivision. It may be desirable to count manuscript subdivisions such as chapters individually, especially if these must start right-hand pages in the book, in which case blank left-hand pages may need to be added to the count. Books consisting of selections may have the selections juggled in editing, and a separate count saves recounting when changes are made.

Illustrations are always counted separately from text, of course. It is usually convenient to estimate these to the nearest 1/10 page, including captions and spaces around the illustrations. This makes for easy calculations.

Front- and back-matter pages, of course, must be handled separately in castoff and length estimating. Indexes should be typed with the same average number of characters per line as is anticipated for a line of book type, or accurate fitting is rendered very difficult. Contents must be counted by line in relation to the proposed design. Introductions and prefaces, if lengthy, should be counted like text.

All things considered, the counting of a complex manuscript, when done by the traditional method just described, can produce only approximate results. It is theoretically possible to make automatic counts of various classes of fairly simple text when it is keyboarded for computer-controlled composition, but this is seldom done because the counts cannot be made available during the planning stages of the book when they are needed.

In making the traditional character count, by the mathematical rules of accuracy used for calculating with approximate numbers, the result of multiplication or division should be rounded to the same number of significant digits as shown in the less accurate of the original factors. Since the manuscript-page character count is almost always four significant digits (the last of which is of doubtful significance) this means that a manuscript character count of more than three or four unrounded-off digits is claiming more accuracy than it actually possesses. A count of 1,763,328 might actually be more justly rounded to 1,763,000 (or even 1,760,000). No great harm is done if the digits are retained, but they can be dropped legitimately for purposes of hand calculation.

Two typical forms that may aid in character counting are shown on the next two pages: summary castoff form for textbooks and a form for the separate counting of selections.

Castoff using a pocket calculator

With the help of even a simple pocket calculator, all castoff calculations become trivial, despite the fact that decimal fractions and some large numbers are often involved. Besides the always available add, subtract, multiply, and divide, all that is needed is a single memory location that can be added to and subtracted from. Sometimes a percent key also may be useful. A little practice then suffices for the designer to dispense with calculation worries.

The most common castoff problem involves dividing the total number of manuscript characters by (characters per pica × measure × lines per page). Let us say, 1,870,000 divided by (2.83 × 26.5 × 47). This is the sort of thing that designers working with pencil and paper have no desire to do any more often than necessary. But on a $10–$15 calculator the answer can be arrived at in 30 seconds with virtually no chance of error and no mental strain.

The keying of the sample problem is: 2.83 × 26.5 × 47 = M+ 1870000 ÷ MR = (answer), where M+ means "add to memory" and MR means "recall from memory." That takes about thirty seconds. The answer is 530.5.

SUMMARY CASTOFF FORM

Date ________

Title ______________________ **Author** ________

DATA USED TO MAKE CASTOFF:

Text settings

Typeface________________ Characters per pica ________

Measure______ Characters per line ________

Lines per page______ Characters per page ________

Other (editorial use ________________________

Typeface________________ Characters per pica ________

Measure______ Characters per line ________

Lines per page______ Characters per page ________

Other (use________________) Characters per page ________

Other (use________________) Characters per page ________

TOTALS (To nearest tenth of a page)

______Pages text

______Secondary (separate if over 10%, averaging over 10 lines ms)

______Text footnotes (if extensive)

______End-of-chapter or study material

______Illustrations ( ) estimate is before sizing ( ) after sizing

______Legends (averaging____lines)

______Front matter

______Back matter, except index

______Index

______Tables

______Chapter opening adjustment (for______chapters)

______Unit opening adjustment (for______units)

______Text headings allowance (approx.______heads)

______Feature material not part of text

______**Total pages in book. Press forms:**____64s____32s

Castoff by__________**Checked by**________

SEPARATE CASTOFF OF SELECTIONS THAT ARE IN VARIOUS MANUSCRIPT FORMS

Characters per book page______(= P in form below).
Estimate pages to nearest tenth. Use a pocket calculator.

Selection title ________________________________

Ms. characters/line ________

× ms. lines/page (______) = ________

× ms. pages/selection (______) = ________ /P = book pages text ________

+ heads, etc. ________

= selection total ________

Selection title ________________________________

Ms. characters/line ________

× ms. lines/page (______) = ________

× ms. pages/selection (______) = ________ /P = book pages text ________

+ heads, etc. ________

= selection total ________

Selection title ________________________________

Ms. characters/line ________

× ms. lines/page (______) = ________

× ms. pages/selection (______) = ________ /P = book pages text ________

+ heads, etc. ________

= selection total ________

Selection title ________________________________

Ms. characters/line ________

× ms. lines/page (______) = ________

× ms. pages/selection (______) = ________ /P = book pages text ________

+ heads, etc. ________

= selection total ________

Page______of______ Subtotal pages______

The simple calculator can often be used as a counter. To count by ones, the keying would usually be something like: 0 + 1 = = = =, etc. But if you want to count by the number of characters per manuscript page, say 2025, that is just as easy: 0 + 2025 = = = =, etc. At each equals sign 2025 is added to the display.

Many inexpensive calculators provide an automatic "constant," which can be used to repeat an operation without having to rekey it. For example, such a constant often is obtained automatically as the result of any multiplication operation. It is the first factor entered. Thus the first factor keyed can be used again without having to reenter it. Let us say that there are 2025 characters per manuscript page. You wish to multiply this times the manuscript pages in each of a number of chapters to obtain characters per chapter, and you also want the total characters in the whole manuscript.

If the first chapter has 16 manuscript pages, you key 2025 × 16 =. This gives both an answer and a constant, 2025. Thereafter the constant need not be entered, and if you key 29 = you get 58725 (2025 × 29), or 42 = you get 85050 (2025 × 42), and so on indefinitely. You can add up all the separate answers, if you wish, by adding them all to memory (M+).

To get separate answers and also a total, multiplying 2025 characters times chapter lengths of 16, 29, 42, and 38 pages:

Key	*Answer*	*Comments*
0 M+	(0)	Starts memory at 0
2025 × 16=	32400	2025 is now the constant
M+		32400 added to memory
29=	58725	2025 × 29
M+		58725 added to memory
42=	85050	2025 × 42
M+		85050 added to memory
38=	76950	2025 × 38
M+		76950 added to memory
MR	253125	Recalls memory total

This might take about thirty seconds, and very little mental strain. With 55 chapters the benefits are even more obvious. (The calculator used for the above samples was the inexpensive Texas Instruments TI–1250, but many other calculators operate similarly.)

Castoff and text fitting

The fitting of a manuscript and any accompanying illustration program to the most acceptable format, in the most economical trimmed size and number of press forms, is a matter of considerable economic importance. It is also, in practice, a matter of considerable complexity, even if only a few of the possible solutions are actually evaluated. In spite of the rather common assumption that there is not much choice, there is often a practical 20–40 percent variability in book length that can be effected through typographic adjustment alone, using only one size of type and without the ordinary reader being aware of anything unusual in the typography.

An illustration program of any scope, of course, can provide considerable additional flexibility. But illustrations cannot be assumed for most books, and there is no way to anticipate the increased flexibility when a book does have them. For these reasons illustrations will not be considered here in relation to the fitting of a book to format.

It is up to the designer to fit the book and to propose options in relation to trimmed size and market. Assuming for the moment that only text typography is to be involved, how does the designer go about this job? Without changing the trimmed size there are only five adjustments possible: (1) an increase or decrease of the type body, by leading, which decreases or increases the number of lines in a given page depth, (2) the use of a more condensed or a more expanded type or "set," (3) letterspacing (positive or negative), (4) increase or decrease in the type-page width (measure), and (5) increase or decrease in type-page depth. These can be changed one at a time or in any combination. In the past, the increments by which variables could be adjusted were not as refined as they are today. Leading used to be variable only in points, whereas now it is often variable in ½, ¼, or 1/10 points. Measure used to be variable in picas and is now often variable in points. Positive or negative letterspacing in very small increments is now possible. Condensation and expansion used to be built into typefaces so that the designer who wanted to change the set width had to change face or change size; now it is often possible to change the width of the type electronically, without changing the face or its size.

If, as is commonly done, page width and page depth can be varied by 2 picas, in ½ pica increments, and leading can be varied by 2 points, in ¼ point increments, and 10-point type setting width can be varied in four ranges of characters per pica, say 2.50–2.59, 2.60–2.69, 2.70–2.79, and 2.80–2.89 (the range from 10-point VIP Baskerville to 10-point VIP Times Roman), there are then four variable factors with four choices each. This would provide $4 \times 4 \times 4 \times 4$ or 256 methods of varying book length by the text setting, using only one trimmed size, one size of type, and a modest range of width, depth, and leading. Naturally we shall want no part of such a mess of options, but they exist, so what is the best sense we can make of them?

When considering adjustment of book length, a manuscript character count of reasonable accuracy must be assumed, of course. Then, between the two limits of the manuscript count and a chosen trimmed size the designer seeks the most acceptable and, at the same time, the most economical solution. In the traditional typesetting systems the designer had no second chance. The first design was set in lead. In electronic composition, for example, there is a second chance to fit the book, without penalty, at galley or "first pass" stage. But with either method of composition, the designer needs a good method for adjusting book length.

In general, the matter proceeds in one of three ways: (1) a suitable type page and trimmed size can be decided upon and its effect on book length accepted, with minor adjustments expected at galley and page stages by the addition or subtraction of optional pages, the decision on how to open chapters, and the addition or subtraction of lines or points of leading, (2) a specified book length can sometimes dictate the typographic format, though this is not practical as a general method (in any case it also poses a fitting problem that must be solved), and (3) the desired book length may be allowed to influence the typography within certain judgmental limits, and vice versa. This last method is a compromise that requires the ideal type page and the desired number of pages to influence each other. It is the solution most often aimed at, but also the type of optimization most difficult to achieve without considerable calculation.

There are two general methods by which to approach such optimization: (1) an investigation of options for each individual manuscript, or (2) the use of generalized tables that present an appropriate range of options, making it unnecessary to calculate. Tables can be very useful, but for modern composition, tables of options and trimmed sizes are impractical unless the choices are narrowed down to the common sizes and page arrangements most needed by the individual publisher. Unrestricted tables would be too unwieldy to consult. Tailored tables can easily be produced by a data-processing department or supplier, if the requirements are made clear. Or modest tables can be calculated on a programmable pocket calculator.

Tables of castoff results

Four tables have been computed (using a calculator) as samples, for the common 6″ × 9″ trimmed size. These are rather modest in scope. The leading is varied only in full points, and the measure and depth in full picas (three steps each). The characters per pica is varied in four steps as described above, each step being an individual table. Each of the four tables has 3 × 3 × 3 or 27 choices of body + measure + characters per pica, giving 108 choices for this 6″ × 9″ trimmed size. However, even such modest tables give rather considerable and useful information, and even more importantly they give it in a form that permits easy comparisons. To use the tables proceed as follows:

1. Start with an ideal typeface, leading, and page size. (Almost always what is wanted is a set of options to *compare* with an ideal planned solution, so start with the ideal.) Include *only* the text area for the width and depth, not the running titles, etc.

2. Determine the characters per pica for the face and size chosen (or for the set, if different from size), and turn to the table for that figure.

CASTOFF RESULTS: FOR 6″ × 9″ TRIMMED SIZE (Per 100,000 Characters ms)

A. For typefaces with 2.50 to 2.59 characters per pica (e.g., 10 pt VIP Baskerville)

Type Body	*Width (measure)*	*Depth*	*Lines/pg*	*Chars/pg*	*Elite* Factor*	*Pica* Factor*	*Words** book pg*	*Text pp/ 100M chars*
11	26	43	47	**3104**	.65	.54	564	**32.22**
		44	48	**3170**	.64	.53	576	**31.55**
		45	49	**3236**	.63	.52	588	**30.90**
	27	43	47	**3223**	.63	.52	586	**31.02**
		44	48	**3292**	.62	.51	599	**30.38**
		45	49	**3360**	.60	.50	611	**29.76**
	28	43	47	**3343**	.61	.50	608	**29.92**
		44	48	**3414**	.59	.49	621	**29.29**
		45	49	**3485**	.58	.48	634	**28.70**
12	26	43	43	**2840**	.71	.59	516	**35.21**
		44	44	**2906**	.70	.58	528	**34.41**
		45	45	**2972**	.68	.56	540	**33.65**
	27	43	43	**2949**	.69	.57	536	**33.91**
		44	44	**3018**	.67	.56	549	**33.14**
		45	45	**3086**	.66	.54	561	**32.40**
	28	43	43	**3058**	.66	.55	556	**32.70**
		44	44	**3129**	.65	.54	569	**31.96**
		45	45	**3200**	.63	.52	582	**31.25**
13	26	43	39	**2576**	.79	.65	468	**38.83**
		44	40	**2642**	.77	.63	480	**37.86**
		45	41	**2708**	.75	.62	492	**36.93**
	27	43	39	**2675**	.76	.63	486	**37.39**
		44	40	**2743**	.74	.61	499	**36.45**
		45	41	**2812**	.72	.60	511	**35.56**
	28	43	39	**2774**	.73	.60	504	**36.05**
		44	40	**2845**	.71	.59	517	**35.15**
		45	41	**2916**	.69	.57	530	**34.29**

*Factor × typewritten pages = book pages **Word = 5.5 characters

CASTOFF RESULTS: FOR 6″ × 9″ TRIMMED SIZE (Per 100,000 Characters ms)

B. For typefaces with 2.60 to 2.69 characters per pica (e.g., 10 pt VIP Janson)

Type Body	*Width (measure)*	*Depth*	*Lines/pg*	*Chars/pg*	*Elite* Factor*	*Pica* Factor*	*Words** book pg*	*Text pp/ 100M chars*
11	26	43	47	**3226**	.63	.52	587	**31.00**
		44	48	**3295**	.61	.51	599	**30.35**
		45	49	**3363**	.60	.50	612	**29.73**
	27	43	47	**3350**	.60	.50	609	**29.85**
		44	48	**3421**	.59	.49	622	**29.23**
		45	49	**3493**	.58	.48	635	**28.63**
	28	43	47	**3474**	.58	.48	632	**28.78**
		44	48	**3548**	.57	.47	645	**28.18**
		45	49	**3622**	.56	.46	659	**27.61**
12	26	43	43	**2952**	.69	.57	537	**33.88**
		44	44	**3020**	.67	.55	549	**33.11**
		45	45	**3089**	.66	.54	562	**32.38**
	27	43	43	**3065**	.66	.55	557	**32.63**
		44	44	**3136**	.65	.53	570	**31.88**
		45	45	**3208**	.63	.52	583	**31.18**
	28	43	43	**3179**	.64	.53	578	**31.46**
		44	44	**3252**	.62	.51	591	**30.75**
		45	45	**3326**	.61	.50	605	**30.06**
13	26	43	39	**2677**	.76	.63	487	**37.36**
		44	40	**2746**	.74	.61	499	**36.42**
		45	41	**2814**	.72	.60	512	**35.53**
	27	43	39	**2780**	.73	.60	505	**35.97**
		44	40	**2851**	.71	.59	518	**35.07**
		45	41	**2922**	.69	.57	531	**34.22**
	28	43	39	**2883**	.70	.58	524	**34.69**
		44	40	**2957**	.68	.57	538	**33.82**
		45	41	**3031**	.67	.55	551	**33.00**

*Factor × typewritten pages = book pages **Word = 5.5 characters

CASTOFF RESULTS: FOR 6″ × 9″ TRIMMED SIZE (Per 100,000 Characters ms)

C. For typefaces with 2.70 to 2.79 characters per pica (e.g., 10 pt VIP Caledonia)

Type Body	*Width (measure)*	*Depth*	*Lines/pg*	*Chars/pg*	*Elite* Factor*	*Pica* Factor*	*Words** book pg*	*Text pp/ 100M chars*
11	26	43	47	**3348**	.60	.50	609	**29.87**
		44	48	**3420**	.59	.49	622	**29.24**
		45	49	**3491**	.58	.48	635	**28.65**
	27	43	47	**3477**	.58	.48	632	**28.76**
		44	48	**3551**	.57	.47	646	**28.16**
		45	49	**3625**	.56	.46	659	**27.59**
	28	43	47	**3606**	.56	.46	656	**27.73**
		44	48	**3683**	.55	.45	670	**27.16**
		45	49	**3759**	.54	.45	684	**26.60**
12	26	43	43	**3063**	.66	.55	557	**32.64**
		44	44	**3135**	.65	.53	570	**31.90**
		45	45	**3206**	.63	.52	583	**31.19**
	27	43	43	**3181**	.64	.53	578	**31.44**
		44	44	**3255**	.62	.51	592	**30.72**
		45	45	**3329**	.61	.50	605	**30.04**
	28	43	43	**3299**	.61	.51	600	**30.31**
		44	44	**3376**	.60	.50	614	**29.62**
		45	45	**3452**	.59	.49	628	**28.97**
13	26	43	39	**2778**	.73	.60	505	**35.99**
		44	40	**2850**	.71	.59	518	**35.09**
		45	41	**2921**	.69	.57	531	**34.24**
	27	43	39	**2885**	.70	.58	524	**34.66**
		44	40	**2959**	.68	.57	538	**33.79**
		45	41	**3033**	.67	.55	551	**32.97**
	28	43	39	**2992**	.68	.56	544	**33.42**
		44	40	**3069**	.66	.55	558	**32.59**
		45	41	**3146**	.64	.53	572	**31.79**

*Factor × typewritten pages = book pages **Word = 5.5 characters

CASTOFF RESULTS: FOR 6″ × 9″ TRIMMED SIZE (Per 100,000 Characters ms)

D. For typefaces with 2.80 to 2.89 characters per pica (e.g., 10 pt VIP Times Roman)

Type Body	*Width (measure)*	*Depth*	*Lines/pg*	*Chars/pg*	*Elite* Factor*	*Pica* Factor*	*Words** book pg*	*Text pp/ 100M chars*
11	26	43	47	**3470**	.58	.48	631	**28.81**
		44	48	**3544**	.57	.47	644	**28.21**
		45	49	**3618**	.56	.46	658	**27.64**
	27	43	47	**3604**	.56	.46	655	**27.75**
		44	48	**3681**	.55	.46	669	**27.17**
		45	49	**3757**	.54	.45	683	**26.61**
	28	43	47	**3737**	.54	.45	680	**26.76**
		44	48	**3817**	.53	.44	694	**26.20**
		45	49	**3896**	.52	.43	708	**25.66**
12	26	43	43	**3175**	.64	.53	577	**31.49**
		44	44	**3249**	.62	.52	591	**30.78**
		45	45	**3323**	.61	.50	604	**30.10**
	27	43	43	**3297**	.61	.51	599	**30.33**
		44	44	**3374**	.60	.50	613	**29.64**
		45	45	**3451**	.59	.49	627	**28.98**
	28	43	43	**3419**	.59	.49	622	**29.25**
		44	44	**3499**	.58	.48	636	**28.58**
		45	45	**3578**	.57	.47	651	**27.95**
13	26	43	39	**2880**	.70	.58	524	**34.73**
		44	40	**2954**	.69	.57	537	**33.86**
		45	41	**3027**	.67	.55	550	**33.03**
	27	43	39	**2991**	.68	.56	544	**33.44**
		44	40	**3067**	.66	.55	558	**32.60**
		45	41	**3144**	.64	.53	572	**31.81**
	28	43	39	**3101**	.65	.54	564	**32.24**
		44	40	**3181**	.64	.53	578	**31.44**
		45	41	**3260**	.62	.51	593	**30.67**

*Factor × typewritten pages = book pages **Word = 5.5 characters

3. Find the line that corresponds to the chosen ideal type body, measure, and page depth. This one line will give all the information necessary to relate book page to manuscript page.

The information in the tables that is most commonly sought in copy fitting is the number of characters per book page. But probably the most useful figure is the one in the last column, which gives text pages per 100,000 characters of manuscript. One first divides the total number of characters estimated in a manuscript by 100,000. Taking that answer, one multiplies by the figure in the last column to obtain the estimated number of text pages. For example, with a factor of 31.55, and 1,765,000 characters in the manuscript count, divide 1,765,000 by 100,000 (move the decimal 5 places to the left). Multiply the result (17.65) by 31.55, giving 557 text pages. This takes only a moment with a simple calculator.

In addition to lines per book page, the tables also give words per book page (since some authors and editors prefer to think in words), and multiplier factors for pages of elite and pica typewriter. When multiplied by manuscript pages, these factors will give the number of corresponding book pages for the chosen format.

If the resulting number of text pages is as ideal as the format no more need be done, but since this is seldom the case, the designer may question whether the book needs to be longer (or shorter), and *which* combination of the five variable factors (leading, characters per pica [including letterspacing], measure, page depth) would be best to try to adjust. One order in which the options may be considered is: (a) page depth, (b) measure, (c) leading, (d) characters per pica. But as we have seen there are many possibilities, and the choice is up to the designer. No final choice need be made until several options have been investigated. Using the tables and a calculator, this is not so difficult and might result in many dollars saved on press.

The differences between the various alternatives (all in common use) may appear small from a casual glance at the tables shown, for just one trimmed size and one type size. The average reader would be unlikely to see much unusual in any of the settings. Solid setting is not even considered. Yet for each characters-per-pica figure, the most expanded version will require about 35 percent more pages than the most condensed. If we consider all four characters-per-pica figures (say, 10-point VIP Baskerville, Janson, Caledonia, and Times Roman), the most expanded version will require 46 percent more pages than the most condensed. This is not a trivial difference and is well worth some investigation, for economic reasons, if not for reasons such as salability or portability.

Some notes on the sample tables. The way in which lines per page are calculated reflects a common practice among designers. If a chosen even-pica depth will "almost" allow one more line, then the tables allow for the extra line (if it will fit with the addition of no more than 2 points to the stated page depth). The stated depth can be checked easily by the designer, if for some reason it is critical to do so.

The words per page are calculated on the basis of 5.5 characters per word. This includes one word space. The average English word is close to 4.5 characters, which is more accurate than is generally realized for a wide diversity of English writing styles, subject matter, and age groups, though not as accurate as a good character count.

Elite and pica manuscript page multipliers are based upon 8½″ × 11″ paper with 1⅛″ margins average all around, double-spaced. The counts allow 2025 characters for elite and 1675 characters for pica typewriters. As mentioned, manuscript pages times the factor will give book pages; book pages divided by the factor will, of course, give manuscript pages (though that would normally be much less useful to the designer). It would be best if manuscripts were always typed in one of these two styles, but that can no longer be counted on.

Characters per pica is the basic factor necessary to estimate the way a given face will compose. Alphabet length simply serves to enable the designer to enter a table to find characters per pica. The great bulk of modern text composition is done with fewer than a dozen text faces. However, these faces may be available from several sources, some of which use the same name for different designs, with different characters per pica—or different names for essentially the same design. Obviously we do not need a typeface name at all for castoff purposes, but only the proper alphabet length or characters per pica figure. The name may even be more confusing than clarifying.

In the sample tables, characters-per-pica values are given as a range of values, each of which is accurate to the equivalent of one decimal place. This is the traditional degree of accuracy. Using a second decimal place, the results would differ by between 0 and 8 pages for a 500-page novel with a normal text face. This is well within the normal standard of accuracy imposed by most manual character counts for manuscripts. When options are to be calculated separately (rather than using tables), two decimal places are worthwhile. But a second decimal place would double the length of the tables.

The author has written a book of castoff tables (*Typecaster: Universal Copy Fitting*) that depend only on alphabet length to provide the characters per pica figure. This figure is combined with a specified body to give characters per square pica (or per square inch or per square centimeter). These tables enable the user to dispense with the confusion of names and go directly to factors that will give (1) characters to fit in a given area, or (2) area required for a given number of characters, or (3) type specifications, given the area and number of characters.

Text makeup in relation to even press forms

Calculations based on approximations, such as manuscript counts, are *only* estimates. Thus, when they prove to be in error, the conclusions concerning

PAGE MAKEUP ADJUSTMENTS

TITLE: ______________________ DESIGNER: ______________________

AUTHOR: ______________________ BOOK TRIM: ______________________

PRELIMINARY LAYOUT

Text lines per page: ______________

Running heads: ☐ yes ☐ no

Folios: ☐ at head ☐ at foot

Margins: ______" head; ______" gutter

REVISED LAYOUT

Text lines per page: ______________

Running heads: ☐ yes ☐ no

Folios: ☐ at head ☐ at foot

Margins: ______" head; ______" gutter

· **Original text makeup specifications:**

Text face: ______________________ set ______ / ______

Type page, including running head and folio: ______ x ______ Chapters start ☐ new left and right ☐ new right ☐ part titles ☐ none ☐ new right, backed blank ☐ run in.

______ Full page linecuts in text ☐ backed blank ☐ backed with text.

______ linecuts in text, less than full page, equaling ______ pages.

	PRELIMINARY LAYOUT				REVISED LAYOUT				SECOND REVISED LAYOUT				OKAYED LAYOUT FOR MFG.		
	Designer's estimate Date:		Compositor's Cast-off Date:		Designer's layout Date:		Compositor's paging Date:		Designer's layout Date:		Compositor's paging Date:		Margins: ______" head; ______" gutter Date:		
Element	Pages	Total	Pages	Total	Pages	Total	Pages	Total	Pages	Total	Pages	Total	Element	Pages	Total
1st halftitle													1st halftitle		
Card Plate													Card Plate		
Title													Title		
Copyright													Copyright		
Contents													Contents		
Foreword/Pref.													Foreword/Pref.		
Introduction													Introduction		
2nd halftitle													2nd halftitle		
Text													Text		
Bibliography													Bibliography		
Index													Index		
	Total		Total		Total		Total		Total		Total		Total		
Separate Illustrations:	Pages		To position		Pages		To position		Pages		To position		Pages	To position	

book length based on them need to be revised—usually at galley and page stages. The overall length of the book is of prime editorial and economic importance, but the fitting of the book to even press forms (usually some multiple of 32 pages) is an added mechanical consideration. This fit is usually made and adjusted by minor alterations to lines per page, by the exercise of front and back matter paging options, and perhaps by permitting up to four blank pages at the back of the book.

Consider the Page Makeup Adjustments form on the preceding page, which records estimates for fitting and the subsequent revisions. It shows four stages: (a) the preliminary plan, (b) the revised plan, at galley stage, (c) the second revised plan, at page stage or revised galleys, and (d) the final plan approved for manufacturing. Estimates for the first three stages include a designer's estimate and the compositor's castoff based on work actually done. Thus, even if the designer's estimates are not entirely accurate, the next set of adjustments are based on actual results. In each case it is up to the designer to adjust, and up to the compositor to show the actual result of the adjustment.

The book length optimization form

Book length optimization is not simply a matter of keeping track of minor adjustments for even press forms or looking up options in tables. It is desirable to get all design adjustments into proper perspective at the design stage. This involves a regular and documented procedure of adjustment—of optimization suited to the problem. The form shown on the next two pages standardizes this procedure and also allows for practical application of the typographic options we have discussed. It can be used in a number of ways.

If the typographic plan is to be allowed to dictate the number of text pages, with very little adjustment, then steps 5 through 10 of the form may be omitted. The typography is specified, calculated, or looked up in tables to find text pages, and the items in step 11 are filled in. If necessary, adjustments are made in steps 2–4 and carried forward again to step 11, until a satisfactory fit is found. This is the traditional method of fitting a book to even press forms, without adjustment to main text length.

If, on the other hand, a given number of book pages is to dictate the typographic plan (assuming that this is really practical), then steps 8 and 10 will not be used. The target will be solved for in steps 7 and 9 and entered in step 11. But both this method and the one previously described are somewhat static and cannot be said to be optimization procedures at all.

The form is designed, and is most useful, for guiding systematically a compromise or optimization procedure in which the typographic page and the length of the book are allowed to influence each other. It represents a sequence of steps by which the designer attempts to fit the book to a target number of pages. But if the result is unacceptable typography, then the number of target

BOOK-LENGTH ESTIMATE FORM AND PAGE MAKEUP GUIDE

Date ___/___/___

Designer ________

Title ________ Author ________ Editor ________

1. Trimmed size ______×______. Target total pages, excepting inserts (if any) ______

Ms. pages (text setting)______× average chars. per ms. page______= total chars. (text) ______

Total ms. characters secondary setting______*or* estimate % of ms: ______ % (See note, #9)

(Textheads, poetry, equations, outlines, etc. are counted in full pages of text, but see under #4 below.)

Editing complete?______Illustrations total______Half tone______Line. Complete?______

No. "PARTS"______"CHAPTERS"______

Elements to come ________

2. FRONT MATTER (circle blank pages)

PAGE	TO PAGE		NO. PGS.
___	___	Half title	___
___	___	Card	___
___	___	Frontisp.	___
___	___	Title	___
___	___	Copyright	___
___	___	Dedication	___
___	___	Epigraph	___
___	___	Contents	___
___	___	List of pix	___
___	___	Foreword	___
___	___	Preface	___
___	___	Introduct.	___
___	___	2nd Half T.	___
___	___	___	___
___	___	___	___
Total front matter			___

3. BACK MATTER (estimated pages)

PAGE	TO PAGE		NO. PGS.
___	___	Appendix	___
___	___	Notes	___
___	___	Glossary	___
___	___	Bibliography	___
___	___	Index (1/30 Text)	___
___	___	___	___
___	___	___	___
Total back matter___			___

4. MISCELLANEOUS (estimated pages)

	Pages
___Halftones in text @___/10 page =	___
___Linecuts in text @___/10 page =	___
Captions and spaces around pix, total	___
Tables and footnotes (if subtracted in #1)	___
Display space adjustment (space needed in book compared to what is allowed in ms.) Total	___
Total miscellaneous	___

5. TOTAL NON-TEXT PAGES (front matter, back matter, and miscellaneous) ________

6. LENGTH ADJUSTMENT: If *no target* total length has been set for the book go to #9. Start with the most desirable typographic solution and modify as necessary for even forms in #11. But if a target has been set, in even signatures, adjust to it as follows:

		Revise 1	Revise 2	Revise 3	Revise 4
TARGET PAGES (per #1)	___	___	___	___	___
Non Text pages (subtract)	___	___	___	___	___
Target *text pages only*	___	___	___	___	___

7. TARGET. Divide target *text* pages into characters in total text only (in #1) giving target characters per **text** page:

TARGET CHARS.	Revise 1	Revise 2	Revise 3	Revise 4
___	___	___	___	___

8. Determine text settings having the target characters (or slightly more) per text page—*and* having acceptable combinations of typeface, leading, page width, and page depth. Note the acceptable options, available at compositor, in the form under #9. If **no** solutions are available or acceptable for the target characters per page (in #7) then go to #10 to adjust the target pages.

NOTE: Compositor is ________ Output device ________

(Continued on next page)

9. OPTIONS ACCEPTABLE AND AVAILABLE (Circle the option used on composition order)

	Option 1	Option 2	Option 3	Option 4	Option 5	Option 6
Characters per pica						
Typeface and/or no.						
Size and body						
Page width (text only)						
Page depth **(text only)**						
Characters per line						
Lines per page						
Characters per page						
Resulting **text** pages						
Adjustment for secondary*						
ADD: Total non-text pp. (#5)						
TOTAL PAGES EXCEPT INSERTS						

*If secondary was separately counted in #1 above, then add actual pages of secondary. If the secondary was estimated as percent of ms. text: (1) ignore if less than 10% (2) if more than 10% adjust by subtracting from "resulting text pages" of line above (1/5 × the percent secondary × resulting text pages).

10. If target characters per text page (in #7) are too *many* for any acceptable typographic solution then **increase** the target pages by adding one signature of minimum size (for this book, ____pp.). Then start again at #6. If target characters are too few for a good solution then **subtract** one signature.

11. ADJUSTMENT TO EVEN FORMS______32s______24s______16s   OTHER:______

	1st ESTIMATE	Revise-1	Revise-2	Revise-3	Revise-4	*FINAL*
DATE:	/ /	/ /	/ /	/ /	/ /	/ /
Front Matter						
Text & Secondary						
Misc. non-text (#4)						
Back matter (except index)						
Index						
Blanks						
TOTAL (EVEN SIGNATURES)						

12. INSERTS:____groups of____pages. Placement follows pages: ______
For inserts without folios, sequence identification must be clear. **REVIEW PLACEMENT AT FINAL PAGING.**

13. TYPE PAGE AND MARGINS: Type page overall____×____picas. Space between text & running title____
Margins: head____gutter____. **NOT FINAL UNTIL CHECKED AT FINAL PAGING** (cf. lines per page + head margin).

14. EDITORIAL STRUCTURES PRESENT IN MS. (list separately)

pages is modified (step 10) in single-signature increments, until an acceptable solution becomes possible. The method is outlined by the steps in the sample form.

Individual book castoff adjustment

Though the usefulness of tables has been demonstrated, it is obvious that they can cover only a small part of the text-setting variations that the designer may have to investigate. With the aid of a programmable calculator, the form Castoff "Plus" (Figure 6–1) presents a practical alternative method for investigating options. Using this method, much more tailored options are possible than those that can be accommodated in standard tables. Two decimals can be used for characters per pica, the body can be variable in any fraction allowable by the composition system, and measure and depth can be set to any desirable fraction. Most important of all, the designer can decide just *which* options to investigate without having to consult extensive tables. (In order to accommodate such finesse, these tables would have to be quite impractical in their length.)

This Castoff "Plus" form assumes that the number of variations of an ideal format envisioned by the designer will usually be quite limited if they are to be acceptable. It also assumes that designers know what factors they are most willing to vary, the direction in which they will most probably need to be varied, and by what increments they *can* be varied in the composition system to be used for the book. It assumes that all designers faced with a fitting problem, or a direction that needs to be investigated, will ask certain questions, such as, how many pages will be saved if ½ point is taken off the body; or would increasing the measure by ½ pica *and* adding 2 lines to the page save 40 pages; or would it be better to go to another signature and increase the leading just enough to decrease the lines per page by 1; and what would these changes do to the text length? There are a great number of such questions possible, but only designers know which ones they *want* to ask. This castoff form assumes that they may wish to ask half a dozen such questions, anyhow, and gives room to answer them in detail.

The programmable calculator

In current practice designers are not accustomed to investigate many options of book fitting because a great deal of calculation would be involved in obtaining the answers. Editors do not ask questions for the same reason, but in fact a reasonable number of such options should often be investigated, provided a practical means is available to work out the answers. Pencil and paper is not suitable, and neither is the ordinary pocket calculator, because there are too many steps and too many chances for error, even though all the calculations are mathematically trivial. While computers are very practical for generating useful reference tables, it is not practical for designers to get in and

Castoff "Plus"

FOR DESIGNERS AND EDITORS:

CAST OFF "PLUS" INCLUDES RESULTS OF DESIGN ADJUSTMENTS TOWARDS DESIRABLE BOOK LENGTH ALTERNATIVES, OR EVEN FORMS

Publisher ANY

Book title or number SAMPLE

Author

Client

Phone Date

The purpose of this form is to enable you to evaluate possible alternative text settings of your choosing, in relation to book length and even forms. Text length, of course, is adjusted in four ways:

1. Increase type body by leading
   Decrease type body by leading*
2. Use a more condensed type (with increased characters per pica)*
   Use a more expanded type (with decreased characters per pica)
3. Increase the measure (width)*
   Decrease the measure
4. Increase the page depth*
   Decrease the page depth (Starred factors save pages)

Different combinations of these factors represent a tremendous number of book length alternatives. Needless to say, under ordinar conditions time is not available to calculate results for more than one or two of these. But it might often be desirable to have result for more combinations – which you can easily specify. You know the alternatives that are mechanically available at your composition source. And more importantly you know which variations are acceptable and possibly useful to you. This form can show the results, quickly, accurately, and cheaply.

Fill in the basic design elements in the blanks below. Then specify up to six sets of "DESIRED ADJUSTMENTS", A to F. If there is no change **from the original basic design** just leave the box blank. You will receive, by return mail computer evaluated results cor plete on this sheet. In a rush, results can be given over the telephone. Note that "chapter by chapter" treatment is available.

BASIC DESIGN SPECIFICATIONS, AND CHARACTER COUNT OF MANUSCRIPT:

1. Type body (include "lead") 13
2. Text type 10 TIMES ROMAN (CRT) (LEADING OK IN 1/10 PTS.)
   Characters per pica 2.71
3. Type measure (___cols) 26
4. Page depth (picas) 44
5. Characters in Ms. (text) 550,000
   If "by chapter," list over:
6. Total non-text pages: 47
   Front matter pp 16
   Back matter pp 14
   Number of pictures 20
   Size of pix (1/10 pg) avg. .5
   Captions 1
   Extra display in book 6

	DESIRED ADJUSTMENTS				(Leave blank)						
	BODY	CH/PI	MEAS.	DEPTH	Lines per page	Chars. per page	Text only	Total pages	32s	Blank	% Text + or –
	(None – basic design)				40	2818	196	243	8	13	—
A	12.5	2.71	26	44.5	42	2959	186	233	8	23	–5
B	12.2	2.71	26.5	45	44	3159	175	222	7	2	–11
C	12	2.79	26.5	45.5	45	3327	166	213	7	11	–15
D	13.4	2.71	25.5	43.5	39	2695	205	252	8	4	+5
E	13.8	2.74	25	43	37	2534	218	265	9	23	+11
F	12	2.74	27	45	45	3329	166	213	7	11	–15

Typeface for CH/PI used above: (2.79) 10 CALEDONIA (LAUREL) (2.74) 10 ELECTRA

6-1 *After manuscript character counts have been made, this form can be used to evaluate possible design adjustments to book length.*

out of most computer systems to investigate individual book options.

The programmable pocket calculator, while it is more expensive than the garden variety calculator and requires someone willing to work out the initial program for applications such as these castoff forms, is a very suitable and practical solution to problems. The four tables of options on pages 83 and 84 were computed on a calculator that may seem both old-fashioned and expensive by the time this book is out.* They were calculated about as fast as the numbers could be written down by hand.

The advantage of the programmable calculator is that it can be programmed by the inexperienced user to solve many kinds of problems that only the user is in a good position to define. (If the designer does not wish to program repetitive problems of calculation, there is often someone else available who can do it.) Various problems in book fitting and business arithmetic are examples, and useful specialized tables can often be written easily.

The program for the sample tables has only 57 steps. It is so simple that the author (no programmer) wrote it in a few minutes, and after testing it, found that it required no revision. So that its essential simplicity can be appreciated, it is given below. For any similar calculator, the program would be almost the same, and could be used to calculate the tables for any similar set of options.

A "register" is a storage location. "Store" and "recall" mean simply to press a key that stores the displayed value in the named storage register or recalls to the display whatever value is currently in the storage register. While a bit of translation has been used to make reading the program easier, anyone familiar with the calculator could write the program from these notes:

Register 1 = type body (decimals acceptable)
Register 2 = characters per pica (decimals acceptable)
Register 3 = measure in picas (decimals acceptable)
Register 4 = depth in picas (decimals acceptable)
Register 5 = 100,000
Register 6 = 2025 (elite characters per page)
Register 7 = (used for characters per page)
Register 8 = 1675 (pica characters per page)
Register 9 = (used for lines per page)

THE PROGRAM:

Fix two decimal places.
Recall-4 × 12, divide by recall-1 = stop (lines per page), store 9.
Recall-2 × recall-3 × recall-9 = store 7, stop (characters per page).
Recall-7 divide by recall-6 = make reciprocal, stop (elite factor).
Recall-7 divide by recall-8 = make reciprocal, stop (pica factor).

*The Texas Instruments Programmable SR56, costing less than $100.

Recall-7 divide by 5.5 = stop (words per page).
Recall-5 divide by recall-7 = stop (text pages per 100M characters).
(Enter new data.) Program resets to the beginning.

Three aids to castoff

In spite of the refinements possible in book fitting, simpler methods are often sufficient and therefore appropriate. Figures 6–2, 6–3, and 6–4 present aids that often can be helpful at a glance and also can suggest variations the designer may wish to construct.

Conclusion

In summary, it may be said that adjustments to book length are a rather messy business and that regular procedures are a great help to designers who want to do a good job in this area. This should include the use of forms to optimize and keep track of the work, tables of information relative to common trimmed sizes and page dimensions with which they commonly work, an inexpensive simple calculator for ordinary calculations, and possibly a programmable calculator that has been programmed to solve quickly for various options a designer may wish to consider.

Only when procedures are regular and well established will proper optimization be undertaken, and only then can the flexibility in book length possible in modern composition be appreciated. Such options may often permit making books of specified lengths, the saving of press forms, or the adjustment of some manuscripts so that they can be priced for more profitable publication—at no loss or inconvenience to the reader and with better control and less trouble for the designer.

6-2 *The left side of the table gives small variations of standard 6" × 9" pages, composed with Harris CRT Times Roman. The right side shows relevant castoff data, including a multiplier, which, when multiplied by 100,000s of characters in the manuscript, gives book text pages (e.g., given 2,569,000 characters, the calculation would be 25.69 × 30.44 (multiplier) = 782 pages, text only).*

ASTOFF RESULTS PER 100,000 CHARACTERS OF MANUSCRIPT

or small variations of standard 6×9″ Times Roman text page of 27×43 picas—not including running title.

Type body	*Times Roman chars/pi, size*	*Measure*	*Depth*	*Lines per page*	*Characters per page*	*Multiplier (text pages)*	*Percent of standard pages*
12.0	**2.71 (10 pt)**	**27**	**43**	**43**	**3146**	**31.78**	**(standard)**
			42	42	3073	32.54	102
			44	44	3219	31.06	98
		26	43	43	3029	33.01	104
			42	42	2959	33.79	106
			44	44	3100	32.26	101
		28	43	43	3262	30.65	96
			42	42	3186	31.38	99
			44	44	3338	29.95	94
	2.58 (10.5 pt)	27	43	43	2995	33.38	105
			42	42	2925	34.18	108
			44	44	3065	32.63	103
		26	43	43	2884	34.67	109
			42	42	2817	35.49	112
			44	44	2951	33.88	107
		28	43	43	3106	32.19	101
			42	42	3034	32.96	104
			44	44	3178	31.46	99
	2.83 (9.5 pt)	27	43	43	3285	30.44	96
			42	42	3209	31.16	98
			44	44	3362	29.74	94
		26	43	43	3163	31.61	99
			42	42	3090	32.36	102
			44	44	3237	30.89	97
		28	43	43	3407	29.35	92
			42	42	3328	30.05	95
			44	44	3486	28.68	90
12.5	2.71 (10 pt)	27	42.7	41	3000	33.33	105
			41.7	40	2926	34.17	108
			43.7	42	3073	32.54	102
		26	42.7	41	2889	34.62	109
			41.7	40	2818	35.48	112
			43.7	42	2959	33.79	106
		28	42.7	41	3111	32.14	101
			41.7	40	3035	32.95	104
			43.7	42	3186	31.38	99
	2.58 (10.5 pt)	27	42.7	41	2856	35.01	110
			41.7	40	2786	35.89	113
			43.7	42	2925	34.18	108
		26	42.7	41	2750	36.36	114
			41.7	40	2683	37.27	117
			43.7	42	2817	35.49	112
		28	42.7	41	2961	33.76	106
			41.7	40	2889	34.61	109
			43.7	42	3034	32.96	104
	2.83 (9.5 pt)	27	42.7	41	3132	31.92	100
			41.7	40	3056	32.72	103
			43.7	42	3209	31.16	98
		26	42.7	41	3016	33.15	104
			41.7	40	2943	33.98	107
			43.7	42	3090	32.36	102
		28	42.7	41	3249	30.78	97
			41.7	40	3169	31.55	99
			43.7	42	3328	30.05	94
11.5	2.71 (10 pt)	27	43.2	45	3293	30.37	96
			42.2	44	3219	31.06	98
			44.0	46	3365	29.71	93
		26	43.1	45	3170	31.54	99
			42.2	44	3100	32.26	101
			44.0	46	3241	30.85	97
		28	43.1	45	3415	29.29	92
			42.2	44	3338	29.95	94
			44.0	46	3490	28.65	90
	2.58 (10.5 pt)	27	43.1	45	3134	31.90	100
			42.2	44	3065	32.63	103
			44.0	46	3204	31.21	98
		26	43.1	45	3018	33.13	104
			42.2	44	2952	33.88	106
			44.0	46	3085	32.41	102
		28	43.1	45	3250	30.76	97
			42.2	44	3179	31.46	99
			44.0	46	3323	30.09	95
	2.83 (9.5 pt)	27	43.1	45	3438	29.08	91
			42.2	44	3362	29.74	94
			44.0	46	3514	28.45	89
		26	43.1	45	3311	30.20	95
			42.2	44	3238	30.89	97
			44.0	46	3384	29.54	93
		28	43.1	45	3565	28.04	88
			42.2	44	3486	28.68	90
			44.0	46	3645	27.43	86
Baskerville 12 pt body	2.78 (10 pt)	27	43.2	43	3227	30.98	97
Caledonia 12 pt body	2.79 (10 pt)	27	43.2	43	3239	30.87	97
Century Exp. 12 pt body	2.56 (10 pt)	27	43.2	43	2972	33.65	106

Note: This assumes that display math and display typography require about the same proportionate space in type as in manuscript. The page depths are given only to one decimal place. To obtain text multipliers for Baskerville, Caledonia, and Century find first for Times, then multiply by "percent of standard pages" for the face in question.

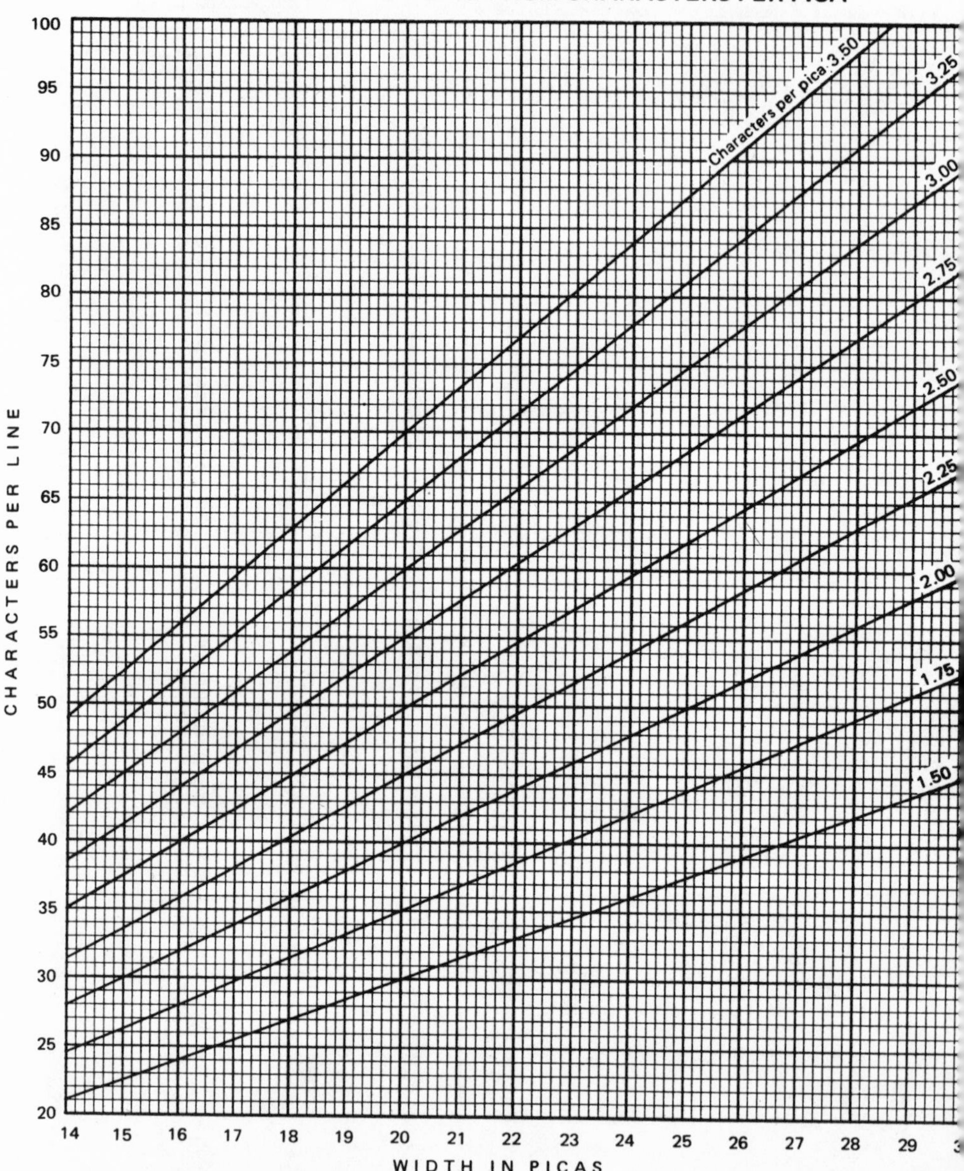

6-3 *This chart of characters per line is entered at the bottom with the proposed measure. Follow the line up to the characters per pica for the proposed typeface.*

6-4 *The chart opposite can be used to obtain a rough number of pages (text only) using defined formats and the thousands of characters in manuscript. Format 1, shown as a sample, represents: 10/12 Times Roman (or other 2.7-characters-per-pica type) and a 27 × 43 pica text page (not counting running titles). The reader may wish to plot lines for any format that may be useful.*

BOOK PAGES PER THOUSANDS OF CHARACTERS IN MANUSCRIPT

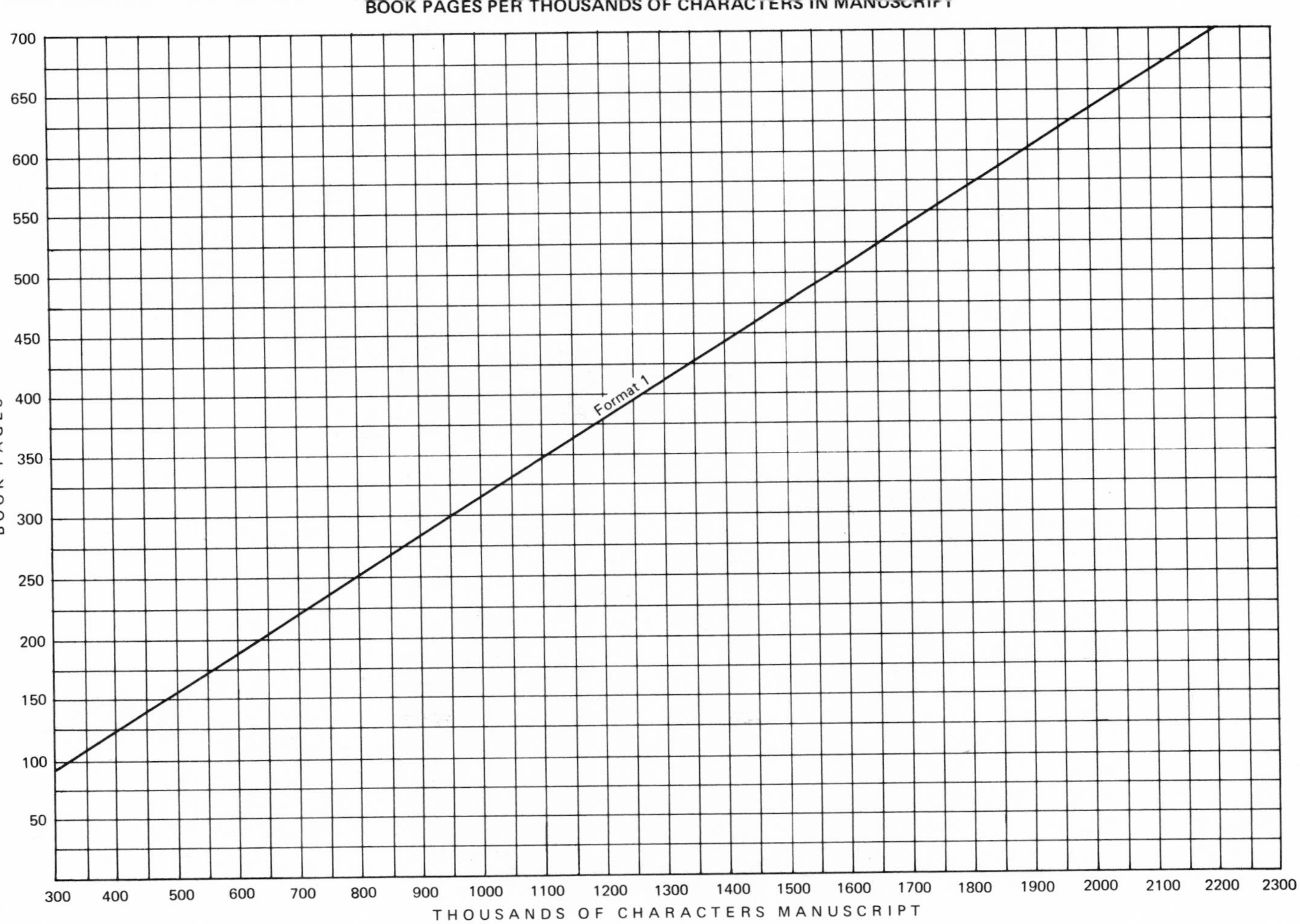

and *r* to refer to the fluid on the left and on
of the discontinuity.

rvation of mass equation can be written as

$$\int_{a_0(t)}^{a_1(t)} dx\,\rho(x,t) = \frac{d}{dt}\int_{a_0(t)}^{\xi(t)} dx\,\rho(x,t) + \frac{d}{dt}\int_{\xi(t)}^{a_1(t)} dx\,\rho(x,$$

$$= \int \ldots \rho + \rho_l(\xi,t)\dot{\xi} - \rho(a_0,t)\dot{a}_0$$

$$+ \rho \ldots - \rho_r(\xi,t)\dot{\xi} = 0$$

ve applied the well-k... rule for differentia...
... limits. ... th... no discontinuity, ... t
... cancel and ...

$$\int_{a_0} \ldots \Big]_{a_0}^{a_1} = \int \ldots \rho + \frac{\partial}{\partial x}\rho v\Big) =$$

$_0$ are ... of the f... $= a_1$ and ... $= a_0$.
prev... ved Eq. 6-6, ... ized to one dime
nd, ... a discontinu... may ta... the
that $a_0 < \xi <$ ... m of

ρ_l ... $(V -$

rite the conservation ... on as

$$\frac{d}{dt}\int_{a_0(t)}^{a_1(t)} dx\,\rho v = P(\ldots t) - P(\ldots$$

CHAPTER 7
Difficult Composition

The largest categories of difficult composition that the designer is likely to encounter are those involving tabular material and mathematical, chemical, and foreign-language work. Most book compositors make an effort to handle a certain amount of such work, especially of the simpler sorts. If they cannot set a few complex tables or formulas or equations themselves, they will obtain the composition elsewhere, either in type or in reproduction proofs, and treat it as illustration material.

Often it is difficult to determine the exact complexity of the work a given compositor can realistically and economically handle with normal schedules. But, if a compositor cannot show, in quantity, work that is a little more complex than the corresponding manuscript, there may be some doubt of the compositor's ability to give good service, especially with a tight schedule. The safest sources are well-established composition houses that specialize in complex typesetting. But new processes, machines, methods of control, and specialized sources are constantly emerging and should be evaluated (though this is not at all easy, considering their complexity).

The traditional Monotype system

Ever since the demise of hand composition, the traditional composition method for difficult materials has been the Monotype system. It is important for the designer to keep this fact in mind for two reasons. First, the system is still in general use for such composition, especially abroad (where much complex composition is bought), and second, the knowledge, experience, and even the notation habits of most editors and authors of difficult composition derive from the Monotype system. All new methods must stand comparison with Monotype editorially and economically. No matter what else a new method can do, if it cannot match the results of the Monotype machine, it may receive demerits. If its characters are not in every detail the same as the traditional Monotype characters, then they may not look quite right to some authors.

In the Monotype system the difficulties of providing special accented characters—mathematical and foreign language—were so great that these were provided for only a few typefaces, which became known as "well-equipped faces," for technical work. Two Monotype faces captured much of the complex work, especially in the United States: Modern #8 (traditionally used with Cushing 25J boldface) and, more recently, Times New Roman (with its bold), which has replaced Modern #8 as the most favored face for complex and technical work. It is worth noting that the text-design expectations of even the most unconventional technical editor and author almost certainly have been formed primarily through reading books set in Modern #8 and Times Roman. These are still the norms from which technical-book designers depart, when they depart.

Thus, the influence of the Monotype method continues, in spite of the often remarkable progress made by other systems in setting difficult composition. Its 4-line mathematical system, its extensive list of special characters, its flexibility in tabular work, its long establishment in the composition houses most specialized in difficult composition, and its new Monophoto system, all combine to make the Monotype system, even now, a great force in complex composition. This is not to suggest that the Monotype system is the way of the future, but to remind designers that it has helped to shape many of the traditions with which they must deal and is therefore well worth understanding.

Briefly stated, the Monotype system operates on the basis of a 15 × 15 character matrix case and a square em divided into 18 units. As shown in the illustration of the matrix case design (Figure 7–1), the characters of each horizontal row have one assigned unit value. There are three 9-unit rows, two 10-unit rows, and one row each of 5, 6, 7, 8, 11, 12, 13, 14, 15, and 18 units. What is known as the normal book or "C" arrangement of the matrix case (shown) contains roman and italic caps, lowercase, numerals, small caps (roman), ½, ¼, ¾, and a variety of punctuation and signs (about 35). This normal book arrangement is by no means the only arrangement available. There are many special arrangements of the matrix case for different purposes and types of specialized composition. This enables the matrix to hold various sets of characters appropriate to specialized needs.

Technical designers will undoubtedly work with the Monotype system, and it is suggested that they consult descriptive literature that is available. But they

MONOTYPE MATRIX CASE WITH NORMAL "C" BOOK ARRANGEMENT

A	B	C	D	E	F	G	H	I	J	K	L	M	N	O	
▮ 123	▮ 124	*l* 226	*t* 211	‘ 28	’ 31	. 109-237	, 108-236	▮ 23	l 98	i 86	] 9	[8	' 2	| 3	5 Unit
j 224	*f* 221	*i* 214	! 33	: 65	; 66	- 64-192	j 96	f 93	r 137	*!* 161	*:* 193	*;* 194	▮ 12	6 unit & justifying spaces. See Note.	6 Unit
c 231	*r* 210	*s* 219	*e* 209	) 11	(10	’ 30	‘ 29	r 82	s 91	t 83	J 147	*v* 232	° 1-25-243	*z* 229	7 Unit
‡ 6-26	*q* 207	* 4	*b* 233	*g* 222	*o* 215	? 32	I 42	z 101	c 103	e 81	Z 152	S 142	† 5-227-99	*?* 160	8 Unit
I 170	▮ 125	*9* 204	*7* 202	*5* 200	*3* 198	*1* 196	*0* 205	. 113-241	9 76	7 74	5 72	3 70	1 68	0 77	9 Unit
C 154	▮ 126	▮ 127	*8* 203	*6* 201	*4* 199	*2* 197	*$* 195	– 21	$ 67	8 75	6 73	4 71	2 69	▮ 111-239	9 Unit
x 230	*k* 225	*y* 212	*d* 220	*h* 223	*a* 218	x 102	J 52	g 94	o 87	a 90	P 139	F 144	L 149	T 134	9 Unit
A 141	*fi* 206	*u* 213	*n* 234	. 110	S 47	v 104	y 84	p 88	u 85	n 106	Q 130	B 156	O 138	E 132	10 Unit
D 143	▮ 27	*fl* 173	*p* 216	fl 45	fi 78	q 79	k 97	b 105	h 95	d 92	V 155	Y 135	G 145	R 133	10 Unit
H 146	& 150	*J* 180	*S* 175	*œ* 118	*æ* 117	*ff* 184	▮ 128	Z 57	▮ 121	ff 56	X 153	U 136	K 148	N 157	11 Unit
O 171	*L* 182	*C* 187	*F* 177	*w* 208	£ 159	æ 19	L 54	P 44	F 49	¶ 7	M 158	*Z* 185	*Q* 183	*G* 178	12 Unit
E 165	*&* 55	Q 35	V 60	C 59	B 61	T 39	O 43	E 37	A 46	w 80	*P* 172	*T* 167	*R* 166	*B* 189	13 Unit
D 176	*A* 174	*Y* 168	*ffl* 217	*ffi* 228	*m* 235	œ 20	Y 40	U 41	G 50	R 38	Œ 120	Æ 119	W 131	*V* 188	14 Unit
K 181	*N* 190	*H* 179	ffl 89	ffi 100	X 58	D 48	N 62	K 53	H 51	m 107	*&* 183	℔ 34	*X* 186	*U* 169	15 Unit
Œ 18	Æ 17	¾ 140-122	¼ 151-16	½ 162-15	*W* 164	*M* 191	— 22	.. 114-242	M 63	W 36	% 129	*Œ* 116-13	*Æ* 115-14	▮ 112-240	18 Unit

Characters in Matrix Case.

ABCDEFGHIJKLMNOPQRSTUVWXYZ&ÆŒ

ABCDEFGHIJKLMNOPQRSTUVWXYZ&ÆŒ

abcdefghijklmnopqrstuvwxyzæœfiflffffiffl

ABCDEFGHIJKLMNOPQRSTUVWXYZ&ÆŒ

abcdefghijklmnopqrstuvwxyzæœfiflffffiffl

- ; : ‘ ’ ’ ! ? ( ) [ ] ° * † ‡ ¶ – — . . . | % £ ℔ *; : ! ?* ‘ ’ .

$1234567890½¼¾*$1234567890*

Note: Both the Justifying-space Bars and Key 24 produce Matrix Case position 2-O. The Space Bars also bring up the Justifying-space Punch and consequently produce Justifying spaces. Key 24 produces 6 unit spaces because it does not bring up the Justifying-space Punch.

The numbers in the squares with the characters indicate the Keys that produce these characters.

See Keyboard Arrangement.

¼ 151-16	**Two or more numbers in the same square with a character indicate the different Keys that will produce this character; for example ¼ will be produced by either Key 151 or Key 16.**

special work these extra Keys are used for additional characters: Thus, Key 16 might be capped with any desired character of same th body as ¼, for which this extra character would be substituted, without affecting the justification, when the matter is corrected.

7-1 *The traditional Monotype normal "C" matrix case arrangement for book work. Many other arrangements have been used.*

will also work with other newer and different systems, and in all cases there are specific system details they will need to consider, different sets of options, different strengths, and different weaknesses or constraints.

Special characters

The only useful basis for defining a special character is in terms of its relative inaccessibility in a given composition system. A special character is one that does not occur on the normal typewriter keyboard, or in the normal book matrix case described above, or in the Linotype 90 channel magazine, or in whatever other set of characters one may be accustomed to. Often "special characters" are equated with "universal characters," which are those designed to go with any text face design, rather than with a specific one.

In the past, one of the greatest deterrents to complex composition has been the necessity for extended character sets in systems having rather limited storage of characters. In order to produce special characters, it has, until recently, been necessary to fit physical analogs in a physical casting or exposing mechanism, then cast or expose them in various sizes, designs, and positions in relation to each other, with various accents, cancels, over and under bars, etc. (then find ways to access them all efficiently). All of this can be a strain on ingenuity, to put it mildly. The number of combinations to be produced is enormous and still growing.

As an example, the English Monotype Company listed for their improved 4-line mathematics nearly 800 separate characters for setting one style of mathematical Greek usage, for one size of mathematics only, even though the same characters could be used for both superior and inferior positionings. In Times Roman #569 (mathematical), Monotype lists 5,815 special characters and 750 auxiliary mathematical characters. Of miscellaneous special signs, they list some 18,000.

Particularly when foreign languages and alphabets are involved, there is no limit to the special characters needed. If accents are "floating," meaning that they can be combined with any character—roman or italic, cap, lowercase, or small-cap form—with nine accents it is possible to compose in 11 European languages (Danish, Dutch, English, French, Flemish, German, Italian, Spanish, Swedish, Norwegian, and Portuguese). But there is no telling when a language like Vietnamese may be required, to say nothing of Russian, Arabic, or Chinese, or any one of the other non-European languages or alphabets. Special characters and accents are shown in Figures 7–2, 7–3, and 7–4.

Mathematics regularly uses accents of its own devising, as well as the Greek alphabet, German (fraktur), fancy script, sans serif, and an entire array of special mathematical signs. Even the manuscript identification of many special characters is difficult, since they are not on the normal "qwert" typewriter keyboard, and many are difficult to write clearly by hand.

Since the advent of the changeable typewriter ball, special-character balls

GOVERNMENT PRINTING OFFICE LIST OF SIGNS AND SYMBOLS

This list contains the signs and symbols frequently used in printing by this Office.

+ plus
− minus
± plus or minus
∓ minus or plus
× multiplied by
÷ divided by
= equal to
≠ or ≠ not equal to
≈ or ≒ nearly equal to
≡ identical with
≢ not identical with
≎ equivalent
∼ difference
≅ congruent to
> greater than
≯ not greater than
< less than
≮ not less than
≧ or ≥ greater than or equal to
≦ or ≤ less than or equal to
| | absolute value
∪ logical sum or union
∩ logical product or intersection
⊂ is contained in
∊ is a member of; dielectric constant; mean error
: is to; ratio
∷ as; proportion
≐ approaches
→ approaches limit of
∝ varies as
∥ parallel
⊥ perpendicular
∠ angle
∟ right angle
△ triangle
□ square
▭ rectangle
▱ parallelogram
○ circle
⌒ arc of circle
⊥ equilateral
≙ equiangular
√ radical; root; square root
∛ cube root
∜ fourth root
Σ sum
! or ∟ factorial product
∞ infinity
∫ integral
ƒ function
∂ or δ differential; variation
π pi
∴ therefore
∵ because
— vinculum (above letter)
( ) parentheses
[ ] brackets
{ } braces
° degree
′ minute
″ second
HP horsepower
Δ increment
ω angular frequency, solid angle
Ω ohm
μΩ microhm
MΩ megohm
Φ magnetic flux; farad
Ψ dielectric flux; electrostatic flux
ρ resistivity
γ conductivity
Λ equivalent conductivity
ℛ reluctance
→ direction of flow
⇆ electrical current
⌬ benzene ring
→ yields
⇄ reversible reaction
↓ precipitate
↑ gas
‰ salinity
☉ or ☉ Sun
● or ● New Moon
☽ First Quarter
○ or ○ Full Moon
☾ Last Quarter
☿ Mercury
♀ Venus
⊖ or ⊕ Earth
♂ Mars
♃ Jupiter
♄ Saturn
♅ Uranus
♆ or ♆ Neptune
♇ Pluto
♈ Aries
♉ Taurus
♊ Gemini
♋ Cancer
♌ Leo
♍ Virgo
♎ Libra
♏ Scorpio
♐ Sagittarius
♑ Capricornus
♒ Aquarius
♓ Pisces
☌ conjunction
☍ opposition
△ trine
□ quadrature
⚹ sextile
☊ dragon's head, ascending node
☋ dragon's tail, descending node
① Ceres
② Pallas
③ Juno
④ Vesta
● rain
⚹ snow
⊠ snow on ground
← floating ice crystals
▲ hail
△ sleet
∨ frostwork
⊔ hoarfrost
≡ fog
∞ haze; dust haze
⊤ thunder
⧼ sheet lightning
⦶ solar corona
⊕ solar halo
⊏ thunderstorm
↖ direction
○ or ⊙ or ① annual
⊙⊙ or ② biennial
♃ perennial
♂ or ♂ male
♀ female
□ male, in charts
○ female, in charts
℞ take (from Latin *Recipe*)
ĀĀ or Ā or āā of each (doctor's prescription)
℔ pound
℥ ounce
ʒ dram
℈ scruple
O pint
ƒ℥ fluid ounce
ƒʒ fluid dram
♏ minim
& or & and; ampersand
℘ per
number
/ virgule; solidus; separatrix; shilling
% percent
© copyright
℅ care of
℀ account of
@ at
¢ cent
* asterisk
† dagger
‡ double dagger
§ section
☞ index
´ acute
` grave
~ tilde
^ circumflex
¯ macron
˘ breve
¨ dieresis
¸ cedilla
‸ caret
ˇ caron

TITLE ________________________________ AUTHOR ________________________________

ACCENTED CHARACTERS, MATHEMATICAL SYMBOLS AND GREEK

Some special characters and symbols available for composition must be specially ordered. Please be sure to indicate on this sheet any special characters which may appear in the manuscript. The accented letters in the top portion of this list are repeated on the back of this sheet, grouped according to language.

Á À Â Ä Ã Ā Ă Å Ą Ä Â Ă Ă Á Ạ Ą́
Ā̧ A̵ Ǽ Ǣ á à â ä ã ā ă å ǻ ą ǟ ǡ â ă á ǟ ǡ
ạ ą̄ ạ̄ ạ ậ ạ ậ à a̵ ą ǟ ǣ ǽ æ

Ć Č Ç Ĉ Є C̲H̲ C̲h̲
ç ć č ĉ ĉ č ɛ c̲h̲

Ď D̄ Ḋ D̆ Đ Ḍ Ḏ D' D̲H̲ D̲h̲
d' d̄ ḋ d̆ d́ đ ḍ ḏ d̲h̲

É È Ê Ë Ẽ Ē Ĕ Ę Ê Ė Ë Ê É Ě Ę̄ Ę Ẹ
é è ê ë ẽ ē ĕ ę ê ė ë ė ê é ě ę̄ ę ę̄ ę ē ẹ
ê̌ ę̆ ẹ

Ǵ Ĝ G̃ Ġ Ģ Ģ Ğ Ǧ G̲N̲ G̲h̲ G̲n̲
ǵ ĝ g̃ ġ ģ ģ ğ ǧ g̑ ǧ g̲n̲ g̲h̲

Ĥ Ḥ Ḫ Ḫ Ħ Ḣ
ḣ ḥ ḫ ḫ ħ ḩ ẖ

Í Ì Î Ï Ĩ Ī Į Ĭ Î Ī Î Ị Í Ì Ɨ Ī
í ì î ï ĩ ī ī î ĭ í î í ị į ī ị ị į ì ị î į ı ị ĭ

Ĵ J̌
ĵ ǰ

Ķ Ḱ Ḳ K̲H̲ K̲h̲
ḱ ḳ ķ ḵ ǩ k̲h̲

Ł Ľ Ĺ Ḷ Ľ L̃ Ḻ Ḹ Ļ Ļ̌ L̲L̲
ł l' ĺ ḷ ḹ l̃ ḻ ļ ḹ ḻ ḷ ł ł

Ṁ Ṃ M̶
m̄ ḿ ṃ m̃g m̶ m̄ ḿ

Ń Ň Ñ Ṅ Ṇ Ṉ N̲ Ṇ
ń ň ñ ṅ ṇ ṉ ṅ ṇ n̄g ñ

Ó Ò Ô Ö Õ Ō Ŏ Ő Ø Ô Õ Ö Ő Ô Ọ Ǿ Ọ́
Ọ̄ Ọ Œ́ Œ̄ ó ò ô ö õ ō ŏ ő ø ô õ ö ő ô ọ ǿ ọ́
ọ̄ ọ ọ oo̅ oó ô ọ́ ọ ò ö œ́ œ̄

Þ Þ́

Ŕ Ř Ȑ Ȓ Ř Ȓ R̈ Ṟ Ṙ Ṛ
ŕ ř ȑ r̄ ř ȓ r̂ r̈ ṟ ṟ ṙ ṛ ṛ ꞧ

Ś Š Ş Ŝ Ŝ Š Ṣ Ṣ Ṣ Ṣ Ṣ S̵ S̲H̲ S̲h̲
ś š ş ŝ ŝ š ṣ ṣ ṣ ṣ ṡ ṣ ṣ s̲h̲

Ť Ţ Ť T̂ T̄ T̆ Ṭ T̆ T' T̲H̲ T̲h̲
t' ţ t̂ t̄ t̂ ť t̆ ṭ ŧ t̲h̲

Ú Ù Û Ü Ũ Ū Ŭ Ů Ű Ų Ū Ũ Ü Ú Ű
ú ù û ü ũ ū ŭ ů ű ū ü ú ǘ ű ů ų ṳ ų ụ
ụ ŭ ʉ ụ

Ŵ W̶ Ẉ
ŵ ẅ ẃ w̄ ẅ w̆ w̵

Ẋ

Ý Ỳ Ŷ Ÿ Ȳ Ỹ
ý ỳ ŷ ÿ ȳ ỹ ẏ ỵ ɏ

Ź Ž Ż Ż Ẕ Z̤ Ẓ Ẓ Ž Z̲H̲ Z̲h̲
ź ž ż ż ẕ.z̤ ẓ ẓ ž ž z̲h̲

Є Ȝ Þ Ƿ
ε έ ð ȝ þ þ ŋ ʒ є ij ᴙ

No.	Symbol	Name	No.	Symbol	Name	No.	Symbol	Name	No.	Symbol	Name	No.	Symbol	Name
1	+	Plus	18	:	Ratio	29	△	Triangle	63	⊢	Assertion sign	90	⌣	Arc
2	−	Minus	19	::	Proportion	74	◬	Triangles	82	‴	Triple prime	40	▽	Sector
3	×	Multiplied by	20	∺	Geometrical proportion	111	≚	Equal angles	96	$\underline{\underline{m}}$	Is measured by	79	⌓	Segment
4	÷	Divided by	21	<	Less than	30	∴	Hence, therefore	97	Σ	Summation of	41	▭	Rectangle
5	=	Equal to	58	⫟	Less than	31	∵	Because	98	π	Pi, 3.1416	95	[S]	Rectangles
6	±	Plus or minus	22	>	Greater than	32	′	Minute	99	ε	Base (2.718) of natural system of logarithms	42	▱	Rhomboid
7	∓	Minus or plus	57	⊏	Greater than	33	″	Second				62	[S]	Rhomboids
56	⩲	Plus or equal	125	⋛	Greater than or less than	34	°	Degree	113	θ	Theta	100	⬠	Pentagon
73	⧺	Double plus	23	≮	Not less than	67	′̣	Dotted minute	114	ϕ	Phi	101	⬯	Ellipse
8	∝	Variation	24	≯	Not greater than	64	″̣	Dotted second	115	Δ	Delta	83	∅	Diameter
9	∞	Infinity	88	⩽	Less than or equal to	65	°̣	Dotted degree	85	«		43	⊞	Cube
10	∫	Integral	81	≦	Less than or equal to	71	″̸	Cancelled second	86	»		122	√	Radical
11	∼	Difference	17	≤	Less than or equal to	36	⊥	Perpendicular to	117	c̄	Mean value of c	44	√	Root
112	∽	Difference	124	≶	Less than or greater than	68	⊥s	Perpendiculars	55	╱	Rising diagonal	45	$\sqrt[1]{}$	Root
12	≏	Difference between	91	⩾	Greater than or equal to	37	∥	Parallel	54	╲	Falling diagonal	46	$\sqrt[2]{}$	Root
60	∹	Difference excess	77	≧	Greater than or equal to	78	∥s	Parallels	69	⫽	Parallel rising diagonal	47	$\sqrt[3]{}$	Cube root
92	∂	Differential	84	≥	Greater than or equal to	38	⋕	Equal and parallel	70	⑊	Parallel falling diagonal	48	$\sqrt[4]{}$	Fourth root
13	≡	Identical with; congruent	25	≎	Equivalent to	121	∦	Not parallels	102	///	Rising Parallels	49	$\sqrt[5]{}$	Fifth root
87	≢	Not identical with	106	≭	Not equivalent	39	≐	Approaches a limit	103	\\\\\\	Falling parallels	50	$\sqrt[6]{}$	Sixth root
14	≠	Not equal to	107	≢	Not equivalent	26	○	Circle	104	⦀	Triple vertical	51	$\sqrt[7]{}$	Seventh root
15	≈	Nearly equal to	28	∠	Angle	75	ⓢ	Circles	108	≣		52	$\sqrt[8]{}$	Eighth root
61	≅	Equals approximately	72	⦣	Angle	27	□	Square	94	[S]	Squares	53	$\sqrt[9]{}$	Ninth root
93	≊	Equals approximately	76	∡	Angles	110	$\sqrt[2n]{}$	2nth root	89	⌢	Arc	109	$\sqrt[n]{}$	Nth root
16	⋝	Equal to or greater than	35	∟	Right angle	59	∫	Horizontal integral						
120	⋜	Equal to or less than				66	√	Horizontal radical						
80	·	Multiplied by												

1	Α	14	Ξ	26	β	39	ο	51	ά	333	ἆ	84	ί	282	ἶ	123	ή	405	ῆ	151	ὐ	199	ῶ	180	̏	292	Ω̣
2	Β	15	Ο	27	γ	40	π	52	ὰ	399	ᾆ	85	ὶ	104	ό	124	ἥ	406	ἧ	152	ὔ	408	ὤ	181	̑	293	ς
3	Γ	16	Π	28	δ	41	ρ	54	ἀ	63	ᾱ	87	ἰ	105	ὸ	125	ἢ	334	ἦ	275	ὖ	407	ὦ	182	̌	294	ϡ
4	Δ	17	Ρ	29	ε	42	σ	55	ἁ	68	έ	88	ἱ	106	ὀ	126	ἣ	137	ύ	400	ὗ	409	ῷ	183	̂	295	ϟ
5	Ε	18	Σ	30	ζ	43	ς	56	ἄ	69	ὲ	89	ἴ	107	ὁ	127	ἡ	138	ὺ	401	ὕ	412	ᾧ	193	`	414	κς
6	Ζ	19	Τ	31	η	44	τ	57	ἂ	70	ἐ	90	ἵ	108	ὄ	208	ἤ	139	ὑ	153	ὥ	196	ῳ	194	´	415	κῦ
7	Η	20	Υ	32	θ	45	υ	58	ἅ	71	ἑ	91	ἲ	109	ὅ	404	ἥ	140	ὒ	154	ὢ	316	ῴ	296	,	416	θς
8	Θ	21	Φ	33	ι	46	φ	59	ἃ	72	ἔ	92	ἳ	110	ὂ	403	ἡ	141	ὓ	155	ὣ	318	ῴ	325	”	417	θυ
9	Ι	22	Χ	34	κ	47	χ	62	ᾳ	73	ἕ	97	ΐ	111	ὃ	131	ῃ	142	ὓ	156	ὤ	169	ῥ	327	‟		
10	Κ	23	Ψ	35	λ	48	ψ	286	ᾴ	74	ἒ	98	ἰ	120	ή	353	ἥ	143	ὕ	157	ὧ	170	ῤ	410	ˮ		
11	Λ	24	Ω	36	μ	49	ω	204	ᾲ	75	ἓ	99	ἱ	121	ὴ	206	ἣ	144	ὗ	158	ὦ	178	ʽ	411	ˮ		
12	Μ	25	α	37	ν	50	ϝ	279	ᾶ	413	ἒ	280	ἶ	122	ἠ	313	ῇ	150	ϋ	159	ὥ	179	ʼ	290	Ą		
13	Ν			38	ξ			398	ἇ			402	ἷ			299	ή			160	ὧ			291	Ḥ		

ACCENTED CHARACTERS

(Arranged by language)

ALBANIAN
Á Ç É Ë Ë̋ Í Ó Ú Ý
á ç é ë ë̋ ɛ ɛ́ í ó ú ý

ANGLO-SAXON
Ā Ǣ Đ Ē Ę̄ Ʒ Ī Ō Þ Ǭ Ū Ȳ
ā ǣ ð ē ę̄ ʒ ī ō þ ǭ ū ȳ

BASQUE
Ç D̄ L̄ N̄ Ŕ S̄ T̄ Ü
ç d̄ l̄ n̄ ŕ s̄ t̄ ü

BASQUE-SPANISH
D̄ L̄ N̄ Ŕ S̄ T̄ Ü
d̄ l̄ n̄ ŕ s̄ t̄ ü

BASQUE-FRENCH
Ç D̄ L̄ N̄ Ŕ S̄ T̄ Ü
ç d̄ l̄ n̄ ŕ s̄ t̄ ü

BOHEMIAN ***(Czech)***
Á Č Ď É Ě Í Ň Ó Ř Š Ť
Ú Ů Ý Ž á č ď é ě í ň ó ř
š ť ú ů ý ž

CATALAN
À Ç É È Í Ï Ó Ú Ü L·L
à ç é è í ï ó ò ú ü l·l

DANISH
Å Ø å é ø

DUTCH
â ä à ë é è ê ì ï ó ò ô ö
ù û ü ij

ESPERANTO
Ĉ Ĝ Ĥ Ĵ Ŝ Ŭ ĉ ĝ ĥ ĵ ŝ ŭ

ESTONIAN
Ä Ö Õ Ü ä ö õ ü

FINNISH
Ä Å Ö ä å ö

FLEMISH
â ä à ë é è ê ì ï ó ò ô ö
ù û ü ij

FRENCH
À Â Ç É È Ê Ë Î Ï Ô
Ù Û Ü
à â ç é è ê ë î ï ô ù û ü

FRISIAN
Â É Ê Ô Ú Û â é ê ô ú û

GERMAN
Ä Ö Ü ä ö ü

HUNGARIAN
Á É Í Ó Ö Ő Ú Ü Ű
á é í ó ö ő ú ü ű

ICELANDIC ***(Modern)***
Á Đ É Í Ó Ö Þ Ú Ý
á ð é í ó ö þ ú ý

ICELANDIC ***(Old)***
Á Ǽ Đ É Í Ó Ǫ Ǫ́ Ø Ǿ Þ
Ú Ý á ǽ ð é í ó ǫ ǫ́ ø ǿ þ ú ý

ITALIAN
À È Ì Î Ò Ù à è ì î ò ù

LATIN TURKISH
Ğ İ Ş Ö ğ ı ş ö

LETTISH
Ā Č Ē Ģ Ī Ķ Ļ Ņ Ŗ Š Ū Ž
ā č ē ģ ī ķ ļ ņ ŗ š ū ž

LITHUANIAN
Ą Č Ė Ē Ę Į Š Ū Ų Ž
ą č ė ē ę į š ū ų ž

NORWEGIAN
Å Ø å á é ǫ ø

POLISH
Ą Ć Ę Ł Ń Ó Ś Ź Ż
ą ć ę ł ń ó ś ź ż

PORTUGUESE
Á Ã Ç É Ê Í Ó Ô Õ Ú
á ã ç é ê í ó ô õ ú

ROMANSH
Â Ā Ê Ē É Î Ô Ö Ü
â ā ê ē é î ô ö ü

ROUMANIAN
Â Ă À È Î Ì Ò Ș Ț Ù
â ă à è î ì ò ș ț ù

RUSSIAN
İ Ë Ў ë ў

SERBO-CROATIAN
(Yugo-Slav)
Ć Č Đ Š Ž ć č đ š ž

SLOVAKIAN
Á Ä Č Ď É Í Ľ Ĺ Ň Ô Ŕ
Š Ť Ú Ý Ž á ä č ď é í ľ ĺ
ň ô ŕ š ť ú ý ž

SLOVENIAN
Č Š Ž č š ž

SPANISH
Á É Í Ñ Ó Ú Ü
á é í ñ ó ú ü

SWEDISH
Å Ä Ö å ä ö

TAGALOG
Á É G̃ Í Ñ Ó Ú á à â é è ê
g̃ í ì î ñ ó ò ô ú ù û

TAMIL ***(Roman)***
Ḥ Ḵ Ḷ Ḻ L̥ Ṃ Ṁ Ṇ Ṅ Ṉ
Ṟ Ṣ ḥ ḵ ḷ ḻ l̥ ṃ ṁ ṇ ṅ ṉ ṟ ṣ

URDU ***(Roman)***
Ā Ạ̄ C̲H̲ Ḍ D̲H̲ Ē G̲N̲ Ḥ H̤
Ī Ḳ K̲H̲ Ṅ Ṉ Ō Ṛ Ṣ S̤ S̲H̲
Ṭ T̤ T̲H̲ Ū Ẕ Ẓ Z̤ Z̲H̲ ā ạ̄
c̲h̲ ḍ d̲h̲ ē g̲n̲ ḥ h̤ ẖ ī ḳ k̲h̲ ṅ
ṉ ō ṛ ṣ s̤ s̲h̲ ṭ ṭ̈ t̲h̲ ū ẕ ẓ z̤ z̲h̲

WELSH
Â Ê Î Ô Ŵ Ŷ â à è ê ë
î ï ì ô ö ò û ŵ ŷ ỳ

WELTEVREDEN, JAVA
(Dutch East Indies)
á à â ä ç é è ê ë í ì î ï ñ
ó ò ô ö ú ù û ü ij

YUGO-SLAV
(See Serbo-Croatian)

have become available in such sets as Cyrillic (Russian alphabet), Greek, international language (accents and alphabet capable of typing some 88 languages), the Klerer-May system of mathematical notation, Vietnamese, etc. Even normal correspondence typewriters are now sometimes made with some changeable keys to accommodate special characters. This development does make manuscript preparation a little easier.

In computer-controlled electronic composition, the storage available at reasonable cost for accessing special characters has been steadily and dramatically increasing, so that it now far outstrips other methods of character storage. As with all systems, it is necessary to ascertain the availability of specific special characters from the individual compositor. In electronic composition, character availability may be given as an arbitrary sounding figure, such as 768 characters, but the essential information is exactly *which* characters they are. Characters in electronic storage are usually all equally accessible, unlike those in traditional systems, which required auxiliary magazines, "pi" sorts, supplementary hand composition, etc.

In electronically controlled CRT (cathode ray tube) composition with floating accents, all the typefaces offered for text composition are, in effect, equally well equipped for technical composition. Different systems offer different combinations of the basic controls: positioning, mixing, sizing, accenting, sloping or italicizing, bold, super-impositioning, set-width changes, and combinations of these.

The potential control with CRT output is virtually unlimited, and the fact that most faces are equally equipped for technical composition will eventually give considerably more variety to technical book design.

Basic information relating to difficult book design

What information does the designer need in order to proceed with type specification for the technical book in any given area of complex composition?

The designer needs to be mindful of the author and the editor. A technical author may have very definite opinions about style and typography. Often an author is a leader in his or her own field, and, in any case, is a person whose opinions are to be respected. This is especially true of the experienced author. Look at the author's other books, and talk with the editor.

Designers need to be aware of the conventions of typography in the field represented by the book. In the most obvious terms, they need to look at similar books, such as the competition and other books by the same author, noting, in particular, the way in which various editorial structures are handled. The conventions of technical composition are almost all significant editorially, and they cannot be arbitrarily changed. In fact, conventions are so well defined in the treatment of most technical editorial structures that arbitrary design is not only unnecessary but often creates real problems.

Thus the designer's first decisions concern what elements should be designed or specified *at all.* Aside from the obvious display matter and heads, the same elements of some editorial structures can be observed to vary in most technical books, and these are the elements that appear on standard specification orders for composition. The designer usually has small wish to get into the really fine points, for example, of spacing around mathematical operators, the spaces around internal table rules, and an almost infinite list of spatial relationships in complex equation settings. On the other hand, some points must be considered, such as whether equation numbers can be set on either side of the page or whether tables can be indented instead of centered. The answers to such questions can only be obtained from the particular composition system.

Capabilities of the compositor

Compositors seldom inform customers about what they *cannot* do, or cannot do efficiently. This is a holdover from the days of combined hand and machine composition when anything could be done, pretty much, because handwork always could and did supplement machine setting. This supplementation will always be the case to some degree, but the extent of handwork is a great variable element in costs, and publishers generally try to eliminate handwork as much as possible, while compositors simply charge for it. Therefore, unless publishers (designers) inquire closely, they may not know what a composition system does *not* do efficiently.

Owners of computer-controlled systems often do not take the traditional attitude about handwork. Their system cannot process information most efficiently if it is constantly interfered with by the need for hand operations. They may be more likely to list what they do not do efficiently, in the hopes of persuading publishers to adopt usages that can be efficiently handled. The list of program limitations given on the next page is adapted from one provided by a computer typesetter specializing in mathematics, and applies only to that installation several years ago. By the time this book comes out, many of these limitations may well have been overcome. It is given here simply to illustrate the kinds of limitations that may be present in a system that does not wish to rely on handwork. Virtually anything can be done by hand, but at a cost in money and often in quality and consistency.

As may be seen, system limitations are not easy to communicate to editors and authors. Therefore, in all likelihood there never will be a perfectly satisfactory method of eliminating the exceptions that must be handled manually. But with the refinement of automatic systems, and better documentation of them, these exceptions should be reduced rather dramatically. This will be to the advantage of author, publisher, and compositor.

AN EXAMPLE OF PROGRAM LIMITATIONS FOR AUTOMATIC MATHEMATICAL COMPOSITION

(If required by specifications—the following elements will require hand time and will incur extra charge.)

Multiple weight rules (not including fraction bars) in tables or displayed equations.

Rules that extend only part of the height or width of tables or arrays.

Boxes around multi-line equations (not including built up fractions or multi-line arrays—which may be considered as part of a single line of math).

Flush left equation numbers or flush left text together with centered equations. (Flush left numbers with equations at standard indent is possible.)

Diagonal rules and arrows; chemical bond notation (except linear).

If all Σ $\int$ π or similar signs in an equation must be the same size, they must be approximately 14 point.

Characters are not set CRT above 18 pt. except for ( ) { } $< >$ $\int$ $\surd$ all of which are limited to 30 pt. [ ] are not limited to size.

Numerals or characters in circles. ⑦

Horizontal braces. $\underbrace{\hspace{6cm}}$

Tables which contain built-up math.

Alignment of groups of equations that are separated by text set flush left.

Accent marks, except overbars, set over more than one character, or accents above accents (i.e. $\hat{\hat{a}}$, $\check{\check{b}}$, $\widehat{ab}$ are not possible).

Leader dots in tables.

Straddle rules in tables.

More than 1 justified column in a table.

Special fractions (½). We use case ($\frac{1}{2}$) or shilling (1/2).

3rd order inferiors (subs and supers).

Indices in root signs (e.g. $\sqrt[2]{}$ $\sqrt[3]{}$)

Column heads in tables set at right angles to the table body, or in a different point size than table.

Characters that are constructed by superimposing one over another are available only in one point size.

Composition Standards

French spacing (single word space after terminal period of a sentence).

Subscripts and superscripts align.

Text is not run around narrow figures, but captions are positioned to right or left of figure with baselines aligning.

Vectors are set in boldface roman type unless it is requested to set boldface italic or lightface italic with an arrow above.

Virtually anything can be done by hand. Some things, like straddle rules in tables, are relatively simple. But other things, like indices in roots, third order subs, etc., can be a nightmare, particularly if they occur often. High quality is difficult to maintain in such cases.

The designer must become acquainted with the special needs of the manuscript to be set in relation to the conventions of the field. Not all problems occur in any one manuscript, but each one needs to be matched against the capabilities of the compositor. The designer is the only one, usually, who is in a position to do this.

If, after careful consideration of the problems in the manuscript, it appears that the wrong compositor has been selected, the designer should consult the production person and make clear the reasons for thinking so. To help in making such a judgment, the systematic collecting of relevant documentation is important, but it is also necessary for designers to have personal contacts at the composition house, to whom they can turn for answers to technical questions. The questions should be accurately put and not wasteful of an informant's time, but the contact person should not respond with vague assurances or technical double-talk.

Sources of information about technical style

Designers should become as familiar as possible with the editorial structures in technical fields for which they design, but beyond this they need to have at their disposal detailed reference materials on specific fields of technical composition.

A Manual of Style (University of Chicago) has good treatments of tables, foreign languages, and mathematics in type. It also has a good general bibliography that includes the style manuals for professional societies, such as the American Institute of Physics, the American Mathematical Society, the American Medical Association, the Conference of Biological Editors, the Modern Language Association, as well as *The Handbook of Physics and Chemistry, Setting Mathematics* (an excellent guide to the Monotype system by Arthur Phillips), and *A Handbook of Biological Illustration* (a valuable guide to various kinds of scientific illustration for nonscientists by Frances W. Zweifel).

The United States Government Printing Office *Style Manual* can often be useful to the designer of difficult composition. Its sections on tabular work and foreign languages are especially detailed. The set-up of the *Congressional Record* may be less than enthralling to the designer, but the absence of any "design" or original styling can help the designer to see the editorial structures in their undisguised states.

Style manuals from experienced compositors and publishers can be especially valuable, but they are still too rare. The best of these for technical composition is probably the booklet *McGraw-Hill Technical Composition Standards,* given by the McGraw-Hill Book Company to its authors of technical books.

With reference books such as these available to provide information on traditional and accepted usage in various fields, the designer has a place to start and the benefit of ready-made experience. In discussions with author, editor, and compositor, the designer can refer to such materials as authorities, but, more importantly, a familiarity with accepted usages will secure the designer a measure of trust that may make it possible to propose changes in traditional usage.

Tables

Tables of numbers, with horizontal rules only, are relatively easy to typeset, but the more words, vertical rules, heads, mixed entry styles, etc. there are, the more difficult the setting becomes. This is especially true if spanner (multicolumn) heads, split or merged columns, or horizontal alignments of multiline entries are also required. (For the terminology of tables, see Figure 7–5.) In many subject areas tabular markup can be very complex, and it is different for almost every composing system. Fortunately, it is not necessary for the designer to understand all the markup and keying strategies, but because systems vary so much in their capacities, it is desirable to understand the general options provided by a given typesetter, especially one who supplies much tabular composition.

In general:

1. In the simplest systems, only tab-setting capacity is provided for, with quad left, quad center, and quad right alignments to the tab positions. Lines are always keyed across, and justified or leadered column entries are not usually possible. Arrangements for centering or indenting the table, spaces between columns, alignments of items, the breaking of word-block entries, as well as almost everything else, are left to markup or operator strategies. Vertical rules are not provided for.

2. In more sophisticated systems, most normal text modes or codings are permitted in tab columns, e.g., autoleadering. Less often, nontypeset test lines may also be provided for. The test lines can establish tab locations for the specific needs of columns by test-setting the long items of each column and setting tabs accordingly. This is especially useful for tables with word entries and to establish specified spaces between long items of adjacent columns (by keying the spaces as part of the test line). Justified entries, "reverse leading," and vertical positioning of entries in relation to other entries that are to align across may be possible, and nontypeset test lines can redefine the tabs for the needs of split or merged columns. Vertical rules usually cannot be set. Indenting or centering of the entire table can seldom be done automatically.

3. In the most sophisticated systems, column widths may be established by the system automatically. After the entire table has been keyed, system (or user) defined spaces may be set between columns, and the table can be centered or indented automatically. Also, a variety of other automatic logic may be provided, enabling justified or unjustified word entries, horizontal top align-

ments of multiline entries, multiline mathematical entries, alignment of columns on any indicated alignment character, such as a period or a dash, rather than simple left, right, or center alignment. Vertical rules are provided, and a variety of spaces may be set automatically, as for example spaces above and below horizontal rules, above footnotes, and above and below the entire table. The logical tabular routines of automatic systems can be extremely involved, and they are being evolved continuously.

Obviously it helps for the designer to know, at the least, whether vertical rules can be set economically. In general, the more sophisticated the system, the more necessary it is for the designer to know its capacities in considerable detail. A careful designer will cooperate with an automatic system and can usually gain many design advantages thereby, without arbitrarily interfering with its automatic features. The simpler systems require less understanding, but less can be required of them.

Unless the Test-line feature is available, one common specification of designers, an em- or point-designated space between long items of adjacent columns, is one of the most difficult specifications to implement in many systems (even some very sophisticated ones), except in very simple tables. Such specifications may often be treated as general indications only, and this should be understood by the designer.

The fitting of tables to text measure and text page is tricky business. The table size that the designer specifies in the composition order is in effect a maximum size, and the common qualifying phrase "or to fit" means that this size may be reduced as necessary to fit the table to the page. To set a minimum size is risky and may result in accidentally overset tables. The order in which the available fitting options are exercised is usually left to the typesetter, but designers may wish to specify their own preferences. One common order of fitting is: (a) reduce leading, (b) reduce size, (c) reduce leading of the reduced size, (d) reduce size of boxheads separately from the table size, if this will help, (e) reduce set size of the type, if this is available and will help, (f) turn the table on the page, or break over onto the next page, or both, (g) use a larger area than the normal text page, and (h) overset the table and reduce it photographically to fit (this often provides the maximum type size possible, but makes it very difficult to correct the table in later editions).

In some automatic systems the philosophy allows for a trial setting for tables, which may sometimes overset the page. If there is doubt about how to resolve the fitting problem, the customer (designer or author) is shown this trial setting and is allowed to express a preference as to how to solve the problem. There is usually no penalty for the reset.

The matter of internal table alignments is most often, but not always, an editorial problem, since they affect interpretation of table content. Boxheads may align at the bottom, center, or top, at left, right, or center (usually a design

DEFINITION AND PARTS OF A TABLE

To define and describe fully all of the many parts, terms, and details which enter into tabular presentation is difficult to explain in a few words or to understand readily without an accompanying visual example. The example shown is directed at those concerned with the construction and makeup of tables, with guidelines identifying tabular terms and details. Many of the terms can be applied to any form of tabular matter.

TABLE 10.—*Heading or headline*

[Headnote or bracket line]

	Stubhead	Column head	Spanner head [1]				Standard date column head	Reading column head
			Runup column head over 12 ems deep [1]	Runup column head making more than 2 lines	Subspanner head			
					Runup column head 12 ems or less	Runup column head		
	CENTERHEAD	*Millions of dollars*	*Tons*	*Tons*	*Number*	*Thousands of pounds*		
1	Lead or caption line [2]	[3] 900	150	191	246	1, 987	Feb. 12, 1958 [4]	Reading column.[5]
2	Wheat and other grains	189	257	250	379	1, 235	May 9, 1957	
3	Lumber and millwork	326	382	177	584	1, 742	Dec. 31, 1957	
4	do.[6]	573	176	263	129	1, 963	do.	Do.[7]
5	Total line	1, 988	965	881	1, 338	6, 927		([8]).
	CENTERHEAD							
6	Lead or caption line	1, 057	([9])	286	2, 673	1, 891	July 19, 1958	Same reading column.
7	Mining equipment	-321	156	112	1, 114	3, 821	May 3, 1958	Do.
8	do.	769						
9	([10])	258	387	596	342	2, 297	June 15, 1958	Reading column.
10	Total line	2, 405	543	994	4, 129	8, 009		

The panel
Head rule—usually single
Boxhead
Boxhead cutoff rule—usually inferior dashes
Centerline in stub column
The line
Ditto or "do." line
Single dashline
Parallel dashline
Block or group
Total line
Quadline
Cutoff rule
Stub column
Figures bear off
Figures against
Reading column
Units of quantity over figure columns—italic
Clear
Field or body
Leader line

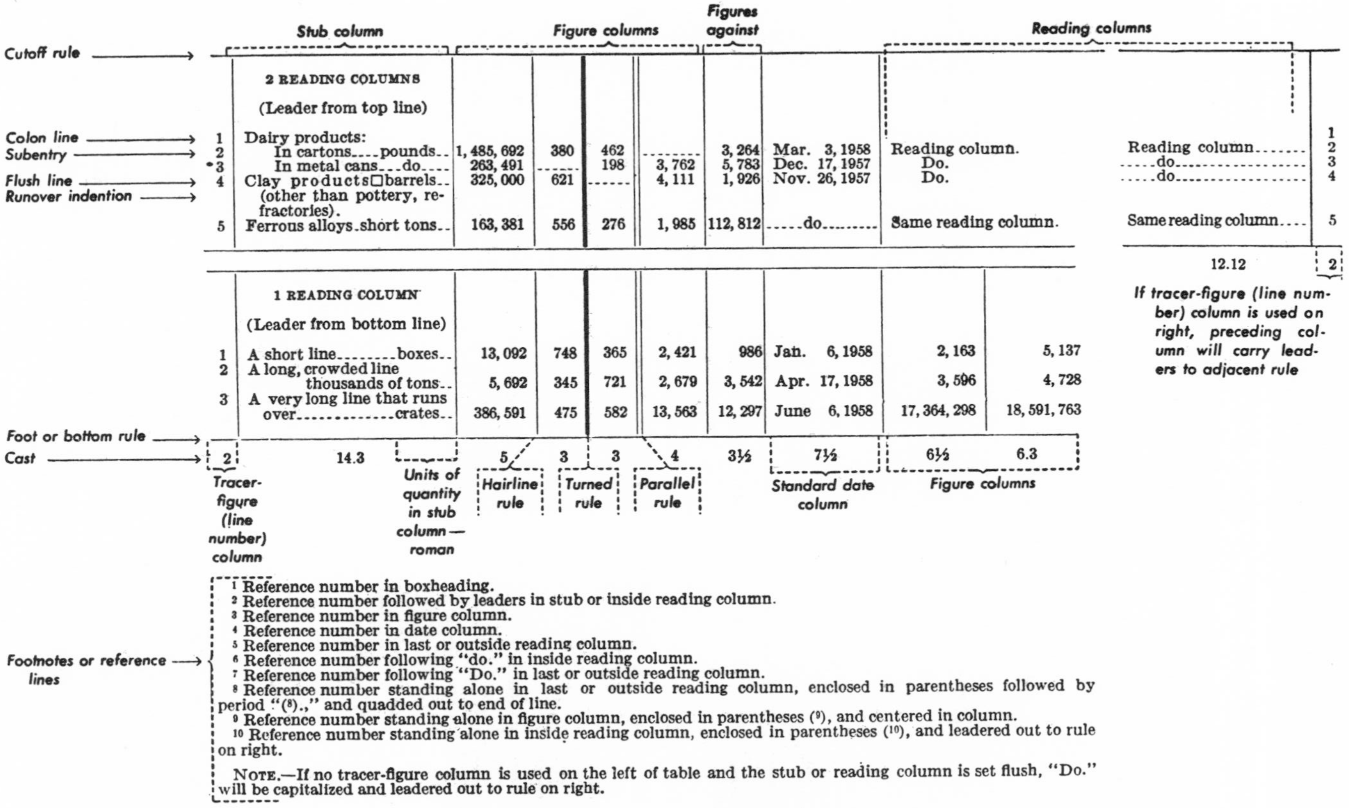

	Stub column	Figure columns				Figures against		Reading columns
	2 READING COLUMNS (Leader from top line)							
1	Dairy products:							
2	In cartons....pounds..	1,485,692	380	462	....	3,264	Mar. 3, 1958	Reading column.
•3	In metal cans...do....	263,491	------	198	3,762	5,783	Dec. 17, 1957	Do.
4	Clay products□barrels.. (other than pottery, refractories).	325,000	621	------	4,111	1,926	Nov. 26, 1957	Do.
5	Ferrous alloys.short tons..	163,381	556	276	1,985	112,812	....do........	Same reading column.

Reading columns	
	1
Reading column.......	2
....do................	3
....do................	4
Same reading column....	5
12.12	2

If tracer-figure (line number) column is used on right, preceding column will carry leaders to adjacent rule

	1 READING COLUMN (Leader from bottom line)								
1	A short line........boxes..	13,092	748	365	2,421	986	Jan. 6, 1958	2,163	5,137
2	A long, crowded line thousands of tons..	5,692	345	721	2,679	3,542	Apr. 17, 1958	3,596	4,728
3	A very long line that runs over.............crates..	386,591	475	582	13,563	12,297	June 6, 1958	17,364,298	18,591,763
2	14.3	5	3	3	4	3½	7½	6½	6.3

Cutoff rule
Colon line
Subentry
Flush line
Runover indention
Foot or bottom rule
Cast
Tracer-figure (line number) column
Units of quantity in stub column—roman
Hairline rule
Turned rule
Parallel rule
Standard date column
Figure columns
Footnotes or reference lines

[1] Reference number in boxheading.
[2] Reference number followed by leaders in stub or inside reading column.
[3] Reference number in figure column.
[4] Reference number in date column.
[5] Reference number in last or outside reading column.
[6] Reference number following "do." in inside reading column.
[7] Reference number following "Do." in last or outside reading column.
[8] Reference number standing alone in last or outside reading column, enclosed in parentheses followed by period "(8).," and quadded out to end of line.
[9] Reference number standing alone in figure column, enclosed in parentheses (9), and centered in column.
[10] Reference number standing alone in inside reading column, enclosed in parentheses (10), and leadered out to rule on right.

NOTE.—If no tracer-figure column is used on the left of table and the stub or reading column is set flush, "Do." will be capitalized and leadered out to rule on right.

7-5 *Terminology used for tabular work by the U.S. Government Printing Office (from the GPO* Style Manual).

option). Items in the column may center, align left or right, or align vertically on a specified character in the column, such as a decimal point (though it may not always be such an obvious alignment character). Left-most and right-most columns may be flush left and right with the ends of horizontal rules, or they may be indented somewhat (a design decision too).

Spanner heads, end rules, text blocks in tables, mathematics in tables, and special characters in table type sizes may or may not be practical without handwork. "Word" tables with unpredictable column and line breaks may be handled somewhat differently from tables with numbers, or others with predictable line breaks.

Special tabular problems do not arise with every book, but if designers leave such problems to the typesetter, they should at least know generally what to expect. It is obvious that a good working relationship with a competent typesetter, whose system the designer comes to know in detail, is of great value to the designer, especially the technical book designer.

Mathematics

A few mathematical expressions may occur in almost any book and do not present much of a problem to unspecialized typesetters. They can usually handle them when the expressions are not over two levels and do not include multilevel signs of aggregation, such as brackets or parentheses, assuming that the necessary characters are available. Really complex mathematical setting is quite another affair and can only be handled by the specialized typesetter.

Mathematical expressions may run into text lines or appear as centered "displays." When the centering of mathematical expressions is not separately specified, it is normal practice for the compositor to follow the manuscript, although the breaking of these expressions is much easier to control when they are centered. Centering also avoids having to increase the leading between text lines to accommodate oversized mathematical signs or expressions. It is usually simpler, and clearer for the reader, to center all expressions that would spread the normally leaded line if they were run into text; and this is sometimes specified (with the author's consent, but not without it), even when the manuscript runs much of the mathematics into the text lines. But the designer should not undertake to specify in this way without consulting the editor.

It is usual for the designer to specify not only the type size of math displays (almost always text size), but the spaces above and below (usually one text line), whether the displays are to be centered horizontally (centering is usual, even for most off-center books) or flush, and the position and style of the equation numbers (if the composition system affords a choice in this regard). It should be kept in mind that the displayed expressions are not separate from the text. The mathematician reads them as continuous with the text. That is why a period is placed by some authors (not all) at the end of each display that completes a sentence started in the text.

Traditional mathematical texts and journals often follow these heading conventions: "theorem," "lemma," "corollary," and "proposition" have the heading in caps and small caps and the text in italic. "Proof," "definition," "example," "case," "note," and "remark" have the heading in cap and lowercase italic, and the text in roman. The above headings are usually run in, with period and em quad following and with one line space above. In less traditional usage the style of headings varies, of course.

In most mathematical typesetting systems the sizing and positioning of the mathematical characters is determined in some respects by house style, but also in more basic ways by the mechanics of the system in use. In fully automatic systems it is determined by system definitions and logic. In any case, the exact sizing and positioning of mathematical characters are not specified by the publisher, except occasionally when the grade level of elementary mathematics books may make small modifications desirable. For example, an editor or author may want larger than normal superiors and inferiors. When second-order superiors and inferiors are not required, those of the first order can sometimes be made larger than would otherwise be practical. However, usually the six superior and inferior orders, limits and aggregation signs, radicals, accents, operators, and signs of relationship are all sized and positioned in relation to each other according to very carefully worked out schemes (mechanical and logical) that are the rules of each system.

Authors, who write most difficult mathematical expressions in longhand, are seldom familiar with system limits, and if they have not published books before may chafe somewhat at the restrictions imposed by any system. The designer should understand each system well enough not to be irritated by it.

Two instructional samples of mathematical composition are shown in Figure 7–6 to illustrate two types of spacing and sizing problems: operator spacing and fraction style.* The system represented is traditional Monotype. One sample shows 5/18-em (5 Monotype units) spaces as the vertical black bars beside the mathematical operators (such as $+$, $-$, $\times$, $\div$, etc.) and in other positions where extra space is required. Other symbols and signs are set close up, and the general spacing is normal for adult mathematics. The designer will note, however, that all characters also carry variable side-bearing spaces that are built into the Monotype system of casting, thus the visual or white space is a good deal more in many cases than just the added space. For this reason spacings, such as those illustrated here, are hard to specify for systems whose side-bearing spaces are unknown. The usual solution is to specify "wide" or "tight" operator spacing, when specification is necessary. The usual interpretation of these vague terms is in relation to traditional Monotype spacing, pretty much as illustrated in the sample shown. Some automatic systems allow publisher control of these spaces with less trouble than traditional systems, but the

*From documentation of The Quinn & Boden Company, Inc.

In the following example | is used to designate a 5 unit space; all other symbols and signs are set close up.

$$b_xa|\lim_{i\to 0}|a|dx|+\int^{2\pi}\int^{\beta}_{\alpha+b|}|\int\left(\frac{b|+|1}{a}\right)^2+|a|\cos|b_x(y|+|1)(x|-|m)$$

$$\cdot\sum_i|g^2|\cdots|h\cdot b|=|a_{ij}|^2|+|a|+|b|\int^{\pi\beta}\frac{1}{x|+|y|}|\int\frac{|z|-|x}{a}$$

$$=|\tan^{-1}|+|\sqrt{1|+|\dot{a}}|dx|dy|-|\sqrt{2}|\pi|\prod_i^N|\alpha|\frac{a|+|b}{1}$$

$$-|2|\sqrt{\frac{b}{\alpha|-|\beta y}}|\left(\frac{1|+|4}{a}\right)^2+|\left(\frac{a|+|c}{b}\right)|=\int^{a+\beta}2\pi a|\left(\sum|\frac{1}{s|+|\beta}\right)$$

$$\times|\left(\frac{1}{2}|\sum_b^a|\frac{a\cdot b}{x}\right)|=|d(\sin|\theta)|+|\sin|(d|+|\theta)$$

$$=|-|\sin^2|\theta|=|\sum|\left(\frac{a|-|1}{b}\right)$$

Also:

$(\sqrt{1|+|a})$ *but* $(2|+|a|=|2\sqrt{1|+|a|+|b|})$

$\|\;|a|+|b|\|\;|=|-x$ $\int_C f\int_V$ $\left(\frac{a}{b}\right)|\left(\frac{b}{x}\right)$

$\oint\left(\frac{a}{b}\right)$ $\int_A|\left(\frac{a}{b}\right)$ $(f)|\left(1|-|\frac{d}{b}\right)$

The size of a *numerical* fraction is to be governed usually by that of the symbol immediately following. When fractions are formed with italic or Greek letters, always use built-up or bar fractions.

Examples:

$\tfrac{1}{2}\beta\,\frac{\partial\phi}{\partial x}$ *not* $\frac{1}{2}\,\beta\,\frac{\partial\phi}{\partial x}$

$\tfrac{1}{2}\log\frac{\partial\phi(a+1)}{\partial x(b+1)}$ *not* $\frac{1}{2}\log\frac{\partial\phi(a+1)}{\partial x(b+1)}$

$\frac{1}{2}\sum\frac{1}{a+b}$ *not* $\tfrac{1}{2}\sum\frac{1}{a+b}$

$\tfrac{1}{2}\int y\,dx$ *not* $\frac{1}{2}\int y\,dx$ *but* $\frac{1}{2}\int\frac{a}{a+b}$ *not* $\tfrac{1}{2}\int\frac{a}{a+b}$

$\frac{1}{4}\sqrt{\left(\frac{2}{\pi}\right)^{1/2}}$ *not* $\tfrac{1}{4}\sqrt{\left(\frac{2}{\pi}\right)^{1/2}}$

$\frac{1}{2}\frac{a+b}{b-1}$ *not* $\tfrac{1}{2}\frac{a+b}{b-1}$

$\frac{1}{2}-\frac{x}{a}$ *not* $\tfrac{1}{2}-\frac{x}{a}$

Miscellaneous examples:

$\frac{2}{\pi}\int^{a+b}J\,dx$ $\frac{1}{\pi a}\sum\frac{1}{m+1}$

$$\sqrt{\left(\frac{2}{\pi}\right)}\,\beta(\tfrac{1}{2}+t)\cos(\tfrac{1}{4}\pi+\tfrac{1}{2}r)$$

controllable spaces have to be modified as groups rather than individually, if economy is not to suffer. For example, for lower grades the spaces around operators might be increased to the equivalent of 7 or 8 units. Justifying spaces, of course, are never used in mathematical expressions, because the spaces must be consistent.

The right half of Figure 7–6 shows the compositor's rules for the treatment of fractions. Fractions are referred to differently in different systems. Usually the style 1/25 is called the "shilling" or "solidus" or "slant" style, while $\frac{1}{25}$ is called the "en" or "nut" or "case" style, and ¹⁄₂₅ is called the "em" or "piece" or "special" style. In some systems the special style is not available, with the shilling style substituting for the special. In text matter, fractions that contain no decimal, comma, or letter are usually set special style, if it is available. But in displayed matter, fractions are usually set en or case, except for superiors or inferiors, which are set em (or shilling, where em is not available). The reason for not using case fractions in superior or inferior positions may be obvious. They are so small, even in text size, that they are all but illegible in such positions. (Only very common fractions are available as "font" fractions, e.g., ¼.)

The designer should be aware that mathematical expressions in text or display should be broken only if necessary, and then only on "verbs" or signs of relation ($=$, $>$, $\geq$, $\subsetneq$, $\equiv$, $\backsim$, $\cong$, $\gg$, $\neq$, etc.), or when absolutely necessary on "conjunctions" or signs of operations ($+$, $-$, $\cdot$, $\times$, $\div$). When a multiplication sign is understood in an expression, and the equation must be broken at that point, it is supplied explicitly ($\times$) to begin the runover. All such matters are under editorial control, but it is well for the designer to know something of what is going on.

Even the placement of equation numbers is not entirely a design decision, because many authors and editors have definite opinions. (Some mathematicians seem to prefer them on the left, other scientists on the right.) But not all systems can set equation numbers in both positions.

Foreign languages

There is little that need be said about the design of foreign-language books, except that the accent and special character capacity of not only the text type, but the display type as well, must generally be considered. The editorial structures of language instruction books may be complicated, but they are about the same as those encountered in English grammar books. As for the more advanced texts, it is often worthwhile to review the typography of books set in the native country. Sometimes these can provide appropriate ideas and starting points for design.

7-6 (Left) *Traditional spacing of Monotype mathematical work, using the 5-unit space.* (Right) *Sizing and usages of fractions in mathematical expressions. These are from the style manual of a traditional and experienced mathematics compositor.*

Chemistry

Almost all aspects of chemical formulas and equations are matters of author and editor control. For example, compositors follow copy on the placement of chemical symbols in relation to the points of the hexagon or bond. It is generally up to authors to make their intentions clear, and designers do not get involved. The designer should consult the editor if there is reason to question the normal usage of the typesetter, or, for example, when, because of grade-level consideration, it is necessary to modify the normal size for the notation used above and below arrows (sometimes referred to as "arrow matter"), for glossed explanations, or perhaps the spacing to be used around operators. In fact, only two mathematical operators appear regularly in chemical formulas, the plus and the equals sign. If the designer considers the advisability of setting formulas in a sans-serif face, this decision should not be taken without consulting the editor.

Other difficult composition

There are many areas of difficult composition that have not been touched upon. School workbooks, for example, are a class of difficult composition all by themselves, even though most of the problems simply involve different ways of setting lists, allowing for fill-in blanks, and making pages come out even. Dictionaries are also a very specialized problem, but one that few designers face. Catalogs are a category that includes a great many variations, only one of which most book designers see, the book catalog.

The handling of catalogs by computerized typesetting systems that are able to sort the basic catalog file and produce not only several types of catalogs, but various other information as well, is a special problem that relates in part to the designer, in part to the editor, and in part to the data processor (who, in many cases, is also the typesetter). A computerized system can accomplish a great variety of selection, retrieval, sorting, and typesetting functions, including a number of specialized listings, but the basic problem is one of imposing a file structure on the basic information to make it optimally useful. While a good deal can be done with a typesetting file, a great deal more can be done with a rigorous, bibliographically oriented data-processing file.

The file structuring, encoding, editing, and control of catalog composition are processes too detailed and individualized to enter into here. But the designer who becomes involved with a computer-sorted book catalog should consult with the data-processing contact on the general problems of design. The restrictions on the usual typographic parameters (size, typeface, leading, page size, and indentions) are not severe, but the basic styling of entries almost always needs to remain the same (especially cap, cap and lowercase, and small cap) for all catalogs made from the same file.

The solution of all problems of difficult composition is dependent upon having the right kind of information: (1) know the conventions of the special field of the book, (2) know the needs of the manuscript in relation to the conventions, (3) know the compositor's capabilities, and (4) know enough not to specify needlessly or inconsistently.

CHAPTER 8
Design Processing of Complex Texts

Of the many kinds of complex texts, the one on which we shall focus in this chapter is the nontechnical or semitechnical illustrated high school or college textbook for a market of considerable size. Such a book would employ at least one extra color and perhaps some four-color process; it would probably have "satellite" materials, such as a workbook, tests, and a teachers' manual or teachers' edition. A book of this type is usually a large project and one of a very cooperative nature. It represents a large capital investment and may take several years to develop and produce. It may or may not be part of a graded series, but it will almost certainly be revised, and if it is successful, it may go on to wear out a number of art directors, editors, and even authors.

The design of such books may often be of crucial importance to their success, at least initially, for other publishing houses are most certainly competing for the same market and publishing their own books covering nearly identical areas. Since the design and production phases of such books are very long, it is particularly important that the structure within which design takes place is understood and well organized. If the design work is begun intelligently and organized competently, the later phases of the work can be taken over, as necessary, by assistant designers without the project suffering unduly.

Design work on such major publishing projects is under the general direction of one designer (who may be called an art director), but it is very much a team effort. The other members of the team are: assistant designers, art editors, researchers, dummiers, and either an art department and photo department or free-lance people functioning in those capacities. The number of people working on the project varies, depending on the size of the project. In any case, the art team works with members of the editorial team (editors, copy editors, supervising editors) and the production team (project production control, and estimating, as well as overall production supervision).

In terms of responsibility and reporting, the designer or art director and those in the design group may be a part of the editorial department, part of the production department, or an independent department reporting to a senior executive. It is perhaps most usual for design to be under production, but a very good case may be made that design is more an editorial function than a production function.

People work best when they know *what* they are supposed to be doing and know *how* to go about doing it. It is unfortunately true that time seldom seems to be available for proper training, and we may observe new people put into jobs for which they have had no adequate training. It is not only unfair to such people, but the projects on which they are working also may suffer quite unnecessarily, as may other members of the team. All members of the design group should know (1) what their responsibilities are, (2) how to go about fulfilling those responsibilities, (3) to whom they should report their progress and difficulties, and (4) what remedies are available when they encounter difficulties.

Responsibilities of the art director

The art director has many other responsibilities in addition to the typography and design of books. Some of these relate to job training, but most of them relate to art procurement and handling, or to production costs and schedules in the art department. These general, or nondesign, functions are particularly numerous for complex texts, such as those we are now considering. We may list some of these areas of responsibility that are not, strictly speaking, designing at all.

1. Length of the book
2. Illustration space requirements and allocations
3. Illustration types (proportions of line and halftone)
   Line (black, nonprocess color, 4/C process color)
   Halftone (black, nonprocess color, 4/C process color)
4. Illustration placement in relation to color availability on press and practical positioning on press (avoidance of bleeds on the gripper edge, especially)
5. Illustration costs in relation to costs budgeted
   Artists' fees and photographers' fees
   Photo research permissions fees
   Art correction and retouching costs
   Photocopying, photostats, and miscellaneous similar costs

6. Schedule dates
   Art, rough sketches, and finals
   Photo research completed
   Illustration camera copy to production
   Dummy (predummy plan, start dummy, finish dummy, to printer)

The scheduling of design operations is to be taken up in the next chapter. Let it suffice here to say that the scheduling of the entire project is most easily related to: (1) the start date, or the date the manuscript is "transmitted" to design and production from editorial, (2) the date the manuscript is delivered to the compositor for composition, (3) the date galleys or "first pass" is complete, (4) the date paging is complete, (5) the date final costs are completely accounted for, and (6) the bound-book date.

The delegation of design work

In the processing of complex books it is obvious that work is divided and delegated in various ways. How this is done depends on the way in which the publisher is organized, the size of the project, and the size of the department. Job descriptions and job titles may vary somewhat from publisher to publisher, but the same tasks need to be done. In some publishing houses and for some projects, designers/art directors may do nothing but delegate and supervise others, while in other situations they may do a great many tasks themselves. In any event there are four main areas in which work must be done: (1) typography and basic project design, (2) picture research and records, (3) art editing and dealing with artists, and (4) dummying and related records.

We shall not assume that we have a different person for each function, and we shall not assume any particular division of these tasks, because the variety in projects and publishers is too great to make this realistic. We shall simply list the various jobs that need to be done over and above the basic work of typography and basic design. These tasks are the ones the designer most often delegates, in one way or another, whether the team consists of many people or perhaps only one design assistant.

Design responsibilities often delegated

- Read manuscript and work out illustration program (of nontechnical books) with designer and editor.
- Plan picture research from author's and/or editor's notes.
- Do the picture research.
- Check accuracy of research information, when possible, and check on legality, permissions, and such negative indicators as invasion of privacy, bad taste, advertising, and so on.
- Keep an illustration list showing the current status of all illustrations (see form on page 132).

- Obtain permissions for photos and other pictures, pay for them, and return those not used.
- Record relevant information on illustrations and supply this to the editor as a basis for captions (in nontechnical books).
- Compile credit copy for the editor.
- Draw up artists' contracts and route them as necessary.
- Assign the artwork and give specific details to artists.
- Handle traffic on illustrations (from artist, through the designer, to editorial and author, and back to artist).
- Check accuracy of artwork against specifications.
- Pay the artists after work is received and approved.
- Prepare necessary copy for reproduction (scaling, cropping, retouching, obtaining color assemblies, mechanicals, keeping records of work sent).
- Check illustration blues or proofs and make sure all necessary persons do so as well, before they are released.
- Prepare storage package of art and photos used, after book goes to press.
- *Keep production control informed concerning:*

  Manuscript castoff in relation to the production plan

  Galley castoff in relation to manuscript castoff

  Predummy plan in relation to color usage in text and production plan

  Dummy length in relation to the production plan

  Color-use adjustments in relation to press form plan

  Cost of artwork and research permissions in relation to budgeted costs

  The number of each class of color illustration in relation to the plan

  Any changes considered desirable in the press form plan

  Any problems relating to the design part of the schedule (artists' schedules, research schedules, missing elements, etc.)

As may easily be appreciated, these responsibilities add up to a considerable amount of detail and require a great amount of coordination. It is quite understandable that what is required (even ahead of design and visual ability) is the ability to keep orderly track of all design-related activities. The design housekeeping function is of paramount importance, and therefore this is often delegated to one person who has few, if any, other responsibilities outside the one complex book. Designers and researchers very often are required to work on a number of concurrent projects, the number varying greatly depending on the complexity of the projects. A designer (in one year) may work equally hard on 60 relatively uncomplicated trade books or one complex text series. Researchers can work on a number of projects at the same time. At one agency or picture source they can look for many different subjects at the same time.

Often the person who has primary responsibility for keeping track of the detail on one book is the person who handles the dummy (the most detailed record of what is going into each book) and the relations with artists. If these two functions are handled by the same person, he or she may be called an "art editor," or an assistant designer. In any case, it is this function that needs to be described in more detail in order to understand the processing of the complex textbook.

Functions of the art editor

In relation to the design and art editing functions, textbooks can usefully be separated into three categories: (a) nontechnical books, including most books for lower grade levels, reading and literature books, language books, and most nonscientific books, (b) technical or scientific books, including the more advanced social sciences and mathematics, and (c) semitechnical books, including such fields as history, psychology, and economics.

This distinction is useful here mainly in respect to the illustration programs. In the lower grades, and generally for nontechnical books, the actual development of the illustration program is often in large part the responsibility of the publisher. For the more advanced educational levels and generally for technical and scientific books this is not true. There the author is the only person capable of developing and judging the illustration program, perhaps with some help from the technical editor. The publisher's responsibility for technical and scientific illustrations is one of general styling and handling only, not one of choice and development. Some semitechnical books have very few technical illustrations and therefore resemble the nontechnical book, while others have many technical illustrations.

In practice, when technical illustrations are *not* supplied by the author, they must be assigned to an artist as early as possible, so that the illustrations can be submitted, corrected, and finished before the dummy is started. Also, picture research for semitechnical books may have been largely done by the author, but when it has not, it too should be completed before the dummy is started. The reason for these requirements is obvious. Since technical illustrations are not under the control of the publisher, detailed plans (such as the dummy) cannot be made for the book until such illustrations have been completed.

This is not true for nontechnical illustrations in either nontechnical or semitechnical books. Nontechnical illustrations are in large part specified and controlled by the publisher, and detailed plans (such as the dummy) may be safely laid for the book before the illustrations are completed. Thus, illustration space may be used as a controllable and variable element in book-length planning for books with nontechnical illustrations. This is not possible for most technical and scientific books.

Planning the illustration program

Since illustrations for technical books are usually developed by the author, the art editor's functions, at least in the planning and developmental phases, apply chiefly to nontechnical books or semitechnical books with nontechnical illustrations. The functions described below are those that apply whether the illustration program is large or small, and regardless of how the work is divided. Once illustrations are in hand, both technical and nontechnical illustrations are handled in similar ways.

The illustration lists, suggestions, and notes from author and editor should be carefully considered first. Then the manuscript should be read, making notes of new ideas and adding suggestions or criticism to the lists already considered. If galleys are available, there may be a set on which illustration notes can be written.

When the illustration program is considerable, at least one meeting should be arranged with editor and designer (and author, if practical) to consider details and exchange views, using the approved production plan as a guide to the type and number of illustrations allowed for the book. Choice of artists may be discussed. The designer may take this occasion to propose methods of grouping illustrations to achieve a coherent arrangement of visual subject matter or to deal with paging problems created by too many illustrations for a small amount of covering text. The use of illustrations as design features may be discussed, and any questions of editorial policy can be clarified.

If some pieces of technical art are required, any remaining questions relating to them should be cleared up first, so that work on them can begin immediately. If artists have been located for these, samples of the artists' work should be shown to the editor and author for their approval. But if artists have not been selected, ways of finding such artists can be discussed, prices decided upon, and examples chosen for sample sketches (see Chapter 3).

Following this policy meeting, the location of artists for the nontechnical art can proceed. Agents, as well as individual artists, may be called in, and after weighing all aspects of price, suitability, and quality, suitable artists should be chosen and artists' contracts drawn up.

At this point, a tentative illustration list should also be drawn up on the basis of information available, and preliminary picture research can be started on the basis of pictures known to be definitely needed.

Next, an estimate of book length should be made from the manuscript, based on approved sample pages, the illustration program, and the specifications of the composition order (see Chapter 6). The art editor will normally assist the designer.

An essential information folder

If the art editor is to do the dummying on the book, it is desirable that he or she keep a folder of basic information relative to the book. This folder should have the latest information and records of how the book is being put together. Only the person in charge of the dummy is in a position to keep this information fully up to date. The folder should be available to all concerned, but it should be kept intact; that is, no one should remove material from it, even when it is being consulted. The folder should contain nothing more than: (a) the press form plan for the book, (b) approved sample pages, (c) the latest schedule, (d) the composition order, (e) the illustration list, and (f) the production plan. It should not become a file for miscellaneous information.

Predummy planning for nontechnical books

The length of complex nontechnical books can be controlled by modifications to the illustration spaces allowed. In the original production plan, the illustration program is allotted a "reasonable" proportion of space, based on the illustration needs of the subject, the amount of space allowed in competitive books, and so on. Estimated text, illustration space, front and back matter are added, and a corresponding number of press forms assigned, usually to the nearest 32 or 64 pages. The economic plans for the book are based on this number of pages, and the designer attempts to tailor the space required for text to fit the plan. However, the designer may not be completely successful in this, and, in any case, the illustration space in the original plan is simply a rough figure allowing a lump number of pages. Before starting to dummy, it is desirable to refine this projection so that the actual dummying can proceed as efficiently as possible. This refinement may be called the "predummy plan" and is usually done after the galleys are received, by the person who will later do the dummy. The procedure is as follows:

1. Cast off the galleys to determine the pages required for text. This is done by marking the galley number found at the top of the galley four or five times across the face of the galley to identify it. The set of galleys on which this is done can be cut up for dummying after editorial changes affecting space have been noted on it by the copy editor.
2. Check the number of illustration pages allowed in the production plan. To do this, first add the text pages required to the estimated number of pages for front and back matter and any other special features not counted in the galley castoff. This gives total pages of text. Next subtract the total pages of text from total pages planned, giving illustration pages allowed by the production plan. If this figure is either too large or too small, editorial, design, and production control should confer on possible solutions before deciding to propose a change in the production plan. (*Note:* In computerized composition, text setting, and therefore text length, can be adjusted by the designer at this stage without penalty.)
3. Make a plan for the approximate placement of text and illustrations, based on the galley castoff, the illustration pages allowed, the tentative illustration list, and the press form plan for the book, showing length, available color, and so on. To do this, make a copy of the table of contents, adding any items that may not be listed, such as special features and picture sections. Rule five

columns down the page beside the contents. As space is allocated for each subdivision of the book (part, chapter, selection, etc.), these columns will be filled in as follows:

a. Number of pages of text
b. Number of pages of introductory or study aid material
c. Number of pages remaining for illustration space
d. Total number of pages in the subdivision
e. Running total of pages (add the total of all subdivisions calculated thus far)

All figures entered are estimated to the nearest tenth of a page. Illustration space is allowed by referring to the tentative illustration list, the pages on the press form plan, and estimating the amount of the total space allowed that should be devoted to the subdivision under consideration. The type and number of illustrations allowed in the plan for the book must also be taken into account.

It is to be expected that problems will arise and that consultation with designer and production control will be necessary. This, in fact, is the main reason for making a predummy plan. For example, four-color illustrations may be required for a specific section of the book, but the press form plan may show that four color has been allocated too early in the book. Design and editorial problems, too, will arise at this time and require space adjustments. In every case, the art editor must consult with all the people involved. No changes to any plan in the basic book folder should be undertaken without consultation. When the predummy plan is complete, it should be approved by the designer, production control, and the editor. If all need to meet together to make adjustments, this should be arranged.

When it is finished, the predummy plan gives approximate information concerning the size, placement, colors, and distribution of illustrations, the placement of special features, and the length of each subdivision of the book. (Content and number of pieces has not yet been considered, except in the case of technical pieces already available.)

When the predummy plan has been approved, the art editor can start to work out the details of illustration content and determine the number of illustrations in any given section, referring to the predummy plan for the total space available. Obviously, at this stage, too, a considerable amount of adjustment will take place.

When the predummy plan is accomplished, a realistic scheduling of the various elements in the art and design functions can take place: (a) dummy to start, (b) art sketches, (c) art finishes, (d) picture research to finish, (e) editorial approval to be received, (f) completed revisions, and (g) final dummy approved for the printer. It may be desirable to schedule major parts of the book separately.

It should be noted that technical books occasionally also have either flexible illustration programs or illustrations that can be sized flexibly. In such cases, a predummy plan may be useful, and a dummy can help control book length.

The dummy

The person making the dummy is making a detailed plan for the compositor, which shows the exact arrangement of all elements on each page: text, illustrations, heads, captions, footnotes, etc. This gives the publisher complete control over the way the book is arranged, and for complex books that can be of great advantage to the editor, the designer, and even the author. Readers can only see two pages of a book at a time, and the manner in which material is arranged can critically affect their experience of a book in relation, say, to a competitive book. In other words, dummying is designing and, as such, it affects the sale of the book.

A dummy need not be made for every complex book, of course. Sometimes only an especially difficult or heavily illustrated part of a book needs to be dummied. When many illustrations are bunched in relation to covering text, a dummy is called for, at least for the section involved. This is the basic problem that dummies are called upon to solve in all books, technical and nontechnical, but not the only problem. As we have noted, in nontechnical books the dummy also allocates and distributes a calculated amount of illustration space and hence aids in planning and adjusting book length, while technical illustrations are seldom very flexible.

As a rule of thumb, a complete dummy may be indicated simply to solve awkward paging problems in books (that are not modular) when more than one sizable illustration is likely to occur per page in more than 30 percent of the text pages. For modular books the figure might be raised to about 50 percent of text pages.

A dummy may be unnecessary even in complex and somewhat heavily illustrated books when illustrations are well distributed. It is sometimes possible for the designer to group illustrations on separate pages or in separate sections where they do not pose paging problems. The remaining illustrations may be handled by giving the compositor general instructions for placement. Modular design planning can make dummying much less necessary, even when complex text and numerous illustrations would normally suggest it.

Books with few illustrations but with complex editorial structures, such as grammer books or really complex mathematics, may suggest a dummy just to simplify the making of page mechanicals. A dummy is just a plan; and, when in doubt, it is better to plan.

To make a dummy for a book, after a predummy plan (if any) has been approved, proceed as follows:

1. (If a predummy plan exists.) On prepared dummy sheets, printed for the book, lay out the beginning of each subdivision of the book, on the pages

assigned in the predummy plan. In other words lay out the book in skeleton, not forgetting the front and back matter, and observing the design rules as to the way each subdivision is to open (left- or right-hand page, or either one). Once this skeleton is in hand, if it appears necessary to make a rush schedule, the work of dummying may even be divided among several people, provided they maintain close coordination and review each other's sections.

2. (Whether or not a predummy plan exists.) The marked set of galleys to be used for the dummy is cut up and taped into position on the dummy sheets, proceeding from the front of the book (page 1 of text) to the back, or from the beginning of each subdivision, when there is more than one dummier. All the decisions concerning paging and illustration spaces are made as the work proceeds.

The dummier should always remember that the greatest danger is the accidental loss or omission of any element. This can sometimes mean a great deal of redummying and, obviously, can be very annoying. Precautions can be taken to avoid it. A clean desk and orderly habits are great assets. A breeze is a great enemy. The pieces of cut-up galley should be lightly taped in place until it is certain that the arrangement will not have to be revised.

3. The first 40–50 pages of the dummy should be shown to the designer and production control for suggestions and technical approval. Also, if the dummy is long, major sections should be approved before going ahead with the entire project. The dummier should ask questions of designer and production control whenever doubtful situations arise, and should maintain communication at all times. This is far preferable to redummying long sections because of a misunderstanding that was not cleared up.

4. As the work progresses, the dummy is marked clearly to indicate any deviations from the predummy plan (if any) that affect space or the illustrations. These should be discussed with designer, editor, or production control, depending on who is involved. The dummy should carry exact notes on the number of lines to be added or subtracted as a result of editorial changes. (Actual changes of wording are made on the master set of galleys, not on the dummy. Both editor and copy editor should know this.) The higher the educational level, and the more technical the book, the fewer are the changes that can be permitted, even of an apparently trivial nature, without consulting the author.

Information about illustrations in color, bleed pages, pages starting major book divisions, etc. is entered on the press form plan. Any technical art supplied by the author, or already done, is placed in position.

5. After the designer, editor, and production control have approved the first version of the dummy, detailed specifications for all remaining (nontechnical) art should be agreed upon and the work assigned to specific artists.

6. Assignment, checking, and clearing of artwork and picture research proceeds. Photostats, blues, or proofs are put in position when it is necessary to visualize pages and spreads.

On the important and carefully worked out book, all illustrations should be represented visually in the dummy before it is approved. On less important books, it may be sufficient to have only grouped illustrations represented, so that unfortunate pictorial relations can be eliminated. When all necessary illustrations are in the dummy, it is sent to editorial (on schedule, hopefully) for editorial adjustments and legend writing. The dummy is then checked by the copy editor against the master set of galleys.

A summary of information and materials necessary for dummying a typical nontechnical complex book, with color, may prove useful:

Information needed: (a) press form plan, complete with color breakdown and gripper information; (b) the predummy plan; (c) a tentative cut list (see below); (d) sample pages and composition order; (e) the rules to be followed in dummying, such as those given in the list at the beginning of Chapter 5; (f) information on how captions are to be handled, i.e., whether they are to be cast off or written to fit, or whether arbitrary lengths are to be decided on by the editor; and (g) a list giving the space requirements for any elements not represented in galleys, to be added later.

Materials needed: (a) set of galleys (to be cut up for dummying), numbered in red and marked by the copy editor for any editorial changes that affect space; (b) dummy sheets printed for the job in two-page spreads, which (if a predummy plan exists) should be marked, before the dummying starts, for folios, color, grippers on press, and major division openings; (c) gauges made for the job, showing standard page depth, lines of footnotes (which should not be cut apart for dummying, just line counted), caption lines, etc.; and (d) blueprints or proofs of all technical art, and any other art that has been completed. On the face of each such illustration should be clearly noted its number and what type of color it will have, if any.

The master illustration list

The tentative illustration list already mentioned, illustration notes, and preliminary research all form the basis for the master illustration list, which is drawn up as the book is dummied. This master list may be corrected, but it will remain the complete and up-to-date guide to projected illustrations and their actual status. The art editor must keep it current and accurate. The master illustration list form shown in Figure 8–1 indicates the elements of information that are required.

A numbering scheme should be established with the editor for identifying illustrations. This is usually not the final numbering, but it should be easy to use, and everyone working on the book should be familiar with it. Numbering within subdivisions is suggested, the first digit being the number of the subdivision (such as the chapter number) and the second, the number of the illustration within that subdivision (e.g., 5–12 for Illustration 12 in Chapter 5). No

ILLUSTRATION LIST: TITLE________ AUTHOR________ ART EDITOR________ SHEET________

KEY: P = photo, L = line illustration, C = color (flat), T = transparency, PU = pick-up

Working Fig No / Final No	Subject / Credit	Size / Type	Color	Bleed	OK Edit / OK Design	Order / Sketch	Skch out / Final in	Shot / Blues	OK Blues	Amt pd / Date pd

8-1 *A typical illustration list, to be filled in by an art editor. A form such as this is the basic record of illustration status.*

distinction is made in numbering for any particular class of illustration, *and in no case is an illustration number changed during the course of work on the book.*

When an illustration is dropped, this is noted on the list and the number crossed off. No deleted number should be reused, except when a simple substitution is made. New illustrations simply may be added at the bottom of the list and given new numbers. It is not to be expected that numbers will always be consecutive throughout the dummy; they are used only for purposes of identification. These illustration-list numbers are used to identify all camera copy and, in general, are used to identify illustrations during the various working stages of the book—by artists, researchers, design, production, and the compositor.

After the dummy has been approved, the final consecutive figure numbers (if any are to be used in the legends) are written in the lower part of the box in the first column of the list. These numbers are added to legend copy by the copy editor, but the legend is also identified by the old working number, because the working number is the one that appears on all illustration copy and proofs or blues.

Receipt of illustration sketches, finals, and blues or proofs is noted on the master illustration list in the appropriate columns.

Illustrations not supplied by the author

A list of standard design, production, and editorial specifications applying to all the illustrations not already supplied should be drawn up, specifying method of sizing, labeling and numbering, handling of color, description of the intended reader, and so on. Artists' contracts should be drawn up and signed, as necessary, before work is started. Each artist should receive full instructions, including research notes and the due dates for roughs and final art, together with any research materials needed to do the job. Both artist and agent (if any) should be fully aware of the prices being paid; ill feeling may result if prices are not clearly defined before work is done.

Picture research

When artwork has been assigned, the art editor is free to turn to picture research. For large jobs a separate researcher may often be assigned. There should be some indication, usually from editorial or design, as to the relative importance of the various subjects for research; otherwise, a great deal of time may be spent on getting "just the right picture" when the place or manner in which it will be used may make this rather unnecessary. A review should be made of any legal aspects that may be encountered in the field being researched (see Appendix A). The researcher should remember that the responsibility for permissions, as well as the legal aspects of use, belong for the most part to the researcher. For each required subject a fair

PICTURE RESEARCH TRANSMITTAL SLIP

RECEIVED FROM ______

No. ______ Date ______

Description ______

Book ______

Art editor ______

RETURN OR PURCHASE

TO ______ DATE ______

Address ______

Returning (no.) ______

Description ______

Holding (no.) ______

Bill us for (no.) ______

Description ______

selection of good material should be submitted, not a single possibility or too much unwinnowed material.

Of course, a first check of existing house visual files should be made (photos, clippings, tear sheets, etc.). Other researchers should be consulted; someone may have been working in a similar area recently. The editor, the author, and the local library may have books and magazines that provide clues to promising picture sources, or to existing pictures that could be used.

But most importantly, *Picture Sources-3,* edited by Ann Novotny, or *Stock Photo and Assignment Source Book,* edited by Fred W. McDarrah (see Bibliography) should be considered, and a list of agencies, museums, companies, etc., known to be at least somewhat specialized or generally promising in the subject area, should be drawn up. Competing books also should be reviewed in order not to copy the selections of pictures.

Free sources should be explored first, public relations departments of large companies, federal, state, and local government agencies, and picture collections of some libraries. Sources at a distance and those known to be slow in responding should be contacted early, to allow time for reply.

Commercial picture agencies may be telephoned when the request is simple, but when the quality and mood of the picture is important, the art editor should go in person to look at the material available nearby.

Commercial picture agencies normally lend pictures on consignment, charges being made only for pictures actually used. However, some agencies may charge research or holding fees. When a good deal of borrowed material is held for a long time, as is the case in some book programs, it must be admitted that some such charges are justified. No more than a reasonable amount of material should be requested, and it should not be held longer than necessary, in any case.

Material obtained from agencies should be signed out under the researcher's name *and* the name of the book. Information, such as date received, date returned, and when and if a bill was requested for the material, should be recorded immediately in a research log book. Research transmittal slips may take the place of the log for simple jobs, but for jobs of any size these slips (shown opposite) can serve as entry to the log book. Where a considerable amount of picture research is done, as is the case with most publishers handling the kind of complex books under discussion, it will be economical and advisable to have one clerk handle all research traffic with respect to the research log, for all art editors.

The importance of picture traffic records is hard to overstate. Some agencies do not keep very accurate records of their own picture traffic, and if questions arise as to the whereabouts of pictures lent, as does happen all too frequently, accurate records are important not only to prevent charges for pictures not used, or returned, but to maintain good relations with the agency for the future.

The left side of the slip is filled in when the pictures are received, after which it is filed or given to the clerk together with the agency packing slip (if any) to be entered in the research log and filed. As pictures are returned, the right side of the slip is filled in, noting the number still being held, if any. Send a copy of this slip with the photos that are returned to the agency. As each picture is chosen for the book, note this on the right side of the slip and in the log and write the agency to request a bill.

It is not the purpose of this chapter to go into the details of picture research, but only to indicate the steps that must be followed in the orderly handling of the illustration program. If the project is small, the designer who has little help may end up doing some of this personally. However, this is normally an uneconomical use of the designer's time, and we shall assume, as we have heretofore, that the services of an art editor are available.

Unless a separate researcher has been assigned, the art editor is simultaneously handling two aspects of illustration procurement, assigned art and research. As rough sketches of the assigned art are received, they are checked for scaling, color use, and editorial accuracy. Approval is obtained from the designer and editor, together with any corrections. The final artwork is checked in the same way. Picture research continues, staying within the budget, with the same checks as for the assigned art. Rejected pictures are returned as soon as possible, and bills for both assigned art and researched pictures that are definitely accepted should be approved by the art editor and passed on for payment the day they are received.

An illustration file for nondummied books

It is advisable for books that are not dummied to have a separate illustration file that contains proofs or blues of all illustrations, with the working illustration number, final figure number (if any), and final legend copy. The compositor can use this file in the makeup of pages with the master set of galleys.

A proof or blueprint of each illustration, marked for correct cropping, is pasted on a separate sheet of 8½" × 11" paper that is stamped with the name of the book. This sheet carries both the working and final figure number (if any), and the galley number on which the illustration reference occurs. The reference on the galley should indicate the point after which the illustration should be placed (that is, as soon as is practical after that point).

This illustration file should be approved by the editor and by the designer.

Legends (captions) and credits

Unless the illustrations are supplied with the manuscript, legends and credits often cannot be handled with the rest of the text, since they depend on the illustrations and on the information available with the illustrations. Nevertheless, art editors and designers do not write legends; editors or authors do. Art editors are responsible for proper identification of researched pictures and for other appropriate information available from the picture sources. The designer simply sets up rules for styling, width of legends, and placement of legends and credits.

The author normally writes legends for any technical artwork or photos, no matter when or how they are obtained. Such legends should be written at least by the time final art is received, or in the case of researched photographs, when they are received by the author for approval. For researched pictures, necessary information should be available from the art editor's legend information list. The legends for nondummied books are typed or pasted in the illustration file recommended above. Nontechnical legends may often be written by editors.

For dummied books, legends must be included in the planned picture spaces. As they are written, they should be typed to measure; that is, typed so that each line has the same number of characters as there will be in the typeset line. When legends are to be set to a great number of different measures, they are more difficult to fit properly, and this is to be avoided unless it is really necessary to the design.

The designer marks the legend copy, after it has been copy edited, and it is sent (preferably in one batch) to the compositor. Whenever possible, this should be done before a book is dummied, so that legend proofs can be put into the dummy. At the latest, the legend copy should accompany corrected galleys when they go to the compositor for paging.

Sometimes optional words, which can be deleted to fit the legend to a given number of lines, or to ensure full last lines, are circled in color, and the compositor is allowed to use personal discretion. The number of lines the legend is to make is marked beside the legend.

The position of each legend is marked on the dummy sheets, and the legend manuscript is keyed to page and illustration number (the working number that appears on the proof or blue).

Credits, unlike legends, are usually written by the art editor, who also decides on the form of credit to be used. This is so because the art editor is responsible to, and is in most direct contact with, the owner of the rights to the picture. The credits may go with individual pictures or be grouped as a list in front or back matter. Unless credits appear with the pictures page numbers should appear for each credit.

Free picture sources should be credited in full whenever possible, and for photographs the photographer, as well as the agency, should be credited. Credits for reproductions of fine art must read exactly as specified, unless permission has been obtained to make changes. Artwork picked up from other books of the same publisher should also be credited in full to the other book.

Credits for copyrighted pictures and for some fine art must appear with the picture, unless written permission is obtained to place it elsewhere. Some agencies charge extra if the credit does not go on the same page. Otherwise the placement of the credit is up to designer and editor, either just below the picture (or in some other proximate position if the designer prefers) or in a separate list in the front or back matter. It is common in trade books for the credit to be run in at the end of the caption, but far less common in textbooks, since it is not part of the educational material, after all.

Sending the dummy to the compositor

The dummy and the master set of galleys, having been checked and approved by editor and copy editor, should receive a final check by the art editor and designer. Any late proofs or blues are marked with number and color information, folded to size and taped in position. Photostats are used if nothing else is available on the occasional late illustration. Any recently received legend or credit copy is taped in position, and editorial changes made to permit pages to fit are checked. All new editorial copy is keyed into the dummy and checked for proper fit. When credits are to appear on the page with the illustration, the art editor (or the designer) should indicate exact positioning.

All unnecessary notes and instructions should be erased or crossed out on the dummy, and a final check made against the press form plan, especially for color. After the designer and production control have given final approval, the master galleys and the dummy go to the compositor for paging, along with instructions for running titles and edited copy, if this is necessary. In due time pages are the result, which must be checked against the dummy.

Occasionally it is worthwhile to prepare a second and more finished dummy, made from copies of the finished pages. This is mainly desirable when the pages from the compositor do not show halftone illustrations in position, as is usually the case when composition systems deliver photo paper composition output rather than film. To make this finished dummy, trim illustration proofs or blues carefully and position them precisely on copies of the correct pages. Write the cut number on the face of each illustration, with an indication of color, if any. The designer should check this dummy, noting carefully wherever type is to be separated for color.

Folded blues for simpler books, and registered film contact imaging sheets in color for complex books, are the final checkpoint before the book goes to press. Look especially for consistency of spacing and completeness in all respects (missing credits, etc.).

Final steps in the art-editing function

Page proof is checked (with a transparent page-plan overlay) for completeness, consistency, color usage, page length, and so on, by art editor, editor, designer, copy editor, and production control, and returned to the printer. But even then the art editor's work is by no means done.

The master illustration list must be checked to be sure that all pictures (including late ones, cover, front matter, etc.) have been paid for. Unused pictures that may be kept should be filed, and those that may not be kept should be returned. All relevant data should be written (lightly) on the back of any pictures filed, including a note if it was paid for but not used.

A storage package should be made containing all artwork and photographs used in the book, but this should normally not be sent to storage until bound books are received. All correspondence of value should be filed in a permanent file (e.g., relating to permissions, payments, return of photos, legend data, etc.). The art editor's folder of essential production information should be filed with permanent production information on the book.

When bound copies of the book are available, the art editor should go through one copy, page by page, making note of any errors while the book is fresh in memory. All errors should be noted for correction in the next printing through the use of standard correction forms provided by the editorial department.

Correspondence should be checked for promised or requested free books or tearsheets, and a list should be made of all who should receive these. After getting necessary approval, these materials should be sent out as promptly as possible, with a personal note.

After bound books are in the warehouse, the art editor can clean house: throw out dummy, galleys, page proof, illustration proof, reproduction proofs, and all other unwanted material. The art storage package can be sent to its resting place.

The final step is to compile a list of sources for the illustrations in the book. This list gives all information concerning ownership, rights, crediting, source, and re-use. All drawings should be identified as to artist, with names and addresses, and notes as to the form of contract concerning rights and re-use. Total number of pictures on which fees were paid, total amount paid, and any restrictions on rights should be noted. This list is for the benefit of the permissions department as well as other art editors and researchers. Copies should be filed in the permanent production file for the book and sent to permissions.

Checklist of art-editor/assistant-designer functions

1. Count manuscript and estimate book length
2. Cast off galleys
3. Write individual illustration specifications
4. Make a predummy plan
5. Prepare artists' contracts and art schedules
6. Obtain dummy forms and consult with designer on dummy
7. Dummy the book
8. Handle art assignments and traffic

9. Do picture research
10. Keep master illustration list
11. Prepare copy for camera
12. Handle art corrections and retouching of photos
13. Make all necessary adjustments to dummy
14. Check page proof
15. Compile credit list
16. Check final blues (or other contact images) and press sheets
17. Return and file photos; pay photo bills; prepare photos for storage
18. Prepare original art for storage; pay final art bills
19. When books are available: examine for corrections, send complimentary copies and tear sheets
20. Compile list of sources of illustrations

Art and design pricing

Artists, designers, and the buyers of freelance art and design are interested in the prices of these services. A great deal of art must be bought for complex books, and, while single freelance designers are seldom practical for really large projects, design studios are frequently employed. The books, and the artwork, may be in black only or in two, three, or four colors. Artwork may be for an entire book, a cover, major opening, a text spread, a page, or a fraction of a page. Design work may be for books of all degrees of complexity, and the books may be of great or little importance to the publisher from the point of view of expected sale, subsidiary rights, and so on. The amount of work or number of units may be large or small; research may or may not be required; the artist or designer may or may not be experienced and may or may not be the only person for the job. All of the above factors, together with the uniqueness of the product, are what make the pricing of art and design work so difficult. Art prices are those that a particular artist or designer can negotiate in a particular situation, for a particular book, with a particular client.

It is quite unlikely that art and design services ever can have really representative or standardized ("going") prices. Artists decide what they think they can get and then try to get it. Quite a number, in effect, leave it up to the publisher to set prices. Even if artists work out an hourly, or weekly, or yearly rate that they consider fair or necessary compensation for their services, and then apportion charges based on this, the prices charged by competitors cannot be ignored.

Artists traditionally have found it difficult to cooperate or bargain collectively in any way, but there has lately been more effort to give publicity, at least, to standards of fair practice and to current price structures. The Graphic Artists Guild publishes and revises a helpful booklet entitled *Pricing and Ethical Guidelines* (see Bibliography). In addition to pricing guidelines, it contains sections on trade practices in book design, book-jacket design, and book illustration, as well as various other related graphic fields. This is a worthy effort to give publicity to professional standards in an area that, without question, has been subjected to more than occasional exploitation owing to lack of cooperation and information. The time is not long past, for example, when artists often were invited to submit sketches on a speculative basis, and payment for sketches rejected, whatever the reason, was not always forthcoming.

Art directors or art buyers in publishing houses have, in fact, a complex responsibility in relation to artists and freelance designers. Their job is to get the best work available for the least money. Economy, of course, is not simply buying cheaply, but is rather obtaining the best value in relation to real need. The amount budgeted for art and design services should be fixed with all considerations in mind, and this requires a great deal of experience and current awareness. If the art budget is carefully arrived at, it can properly be revealed to the artist and serve either as the fixed price or at least the basis for negotiation. Unfortunately, the "budget" has often been used as a figure of speech to justify a low price offer, and it is perhaps rightly suspected by many artists.

Ultimately, the success of an art or design program depends mainly on mutual trust and respect between artist and buyer. This should be supplemented, not impeded, by proper formal contract. The most successful relationships are based on considerations of trust, rather than on hardnosed bargaining between strangers. Successful art directors sincerely try to treat their artists well, and vice versa. The relationship is entirely symbiotic, and neither will function well without sympathetic cooperation. A great deal is lost if this is forgotten.

In summary

The designer should know what steps are necessary for the design processing of complex books, even though the more complex the project is, and the more projects there are, the more such work will be delegated to others, such as art editors, researchers, and assistant designers. In their nonvisual aspects, many of the steps outlined above may come under the general supervision of production supervisors, supervisors of art editors and researchers, or art buyers. In any case, designers should take care not to be so caught up in the details of the system in which they work that they lose sight of their primary function —seeing to it that the design of each book has visual quality that sets it apart from its competition. One well-known president of a house that publishes many complex texts has often referred to this as "the old pizzazz."

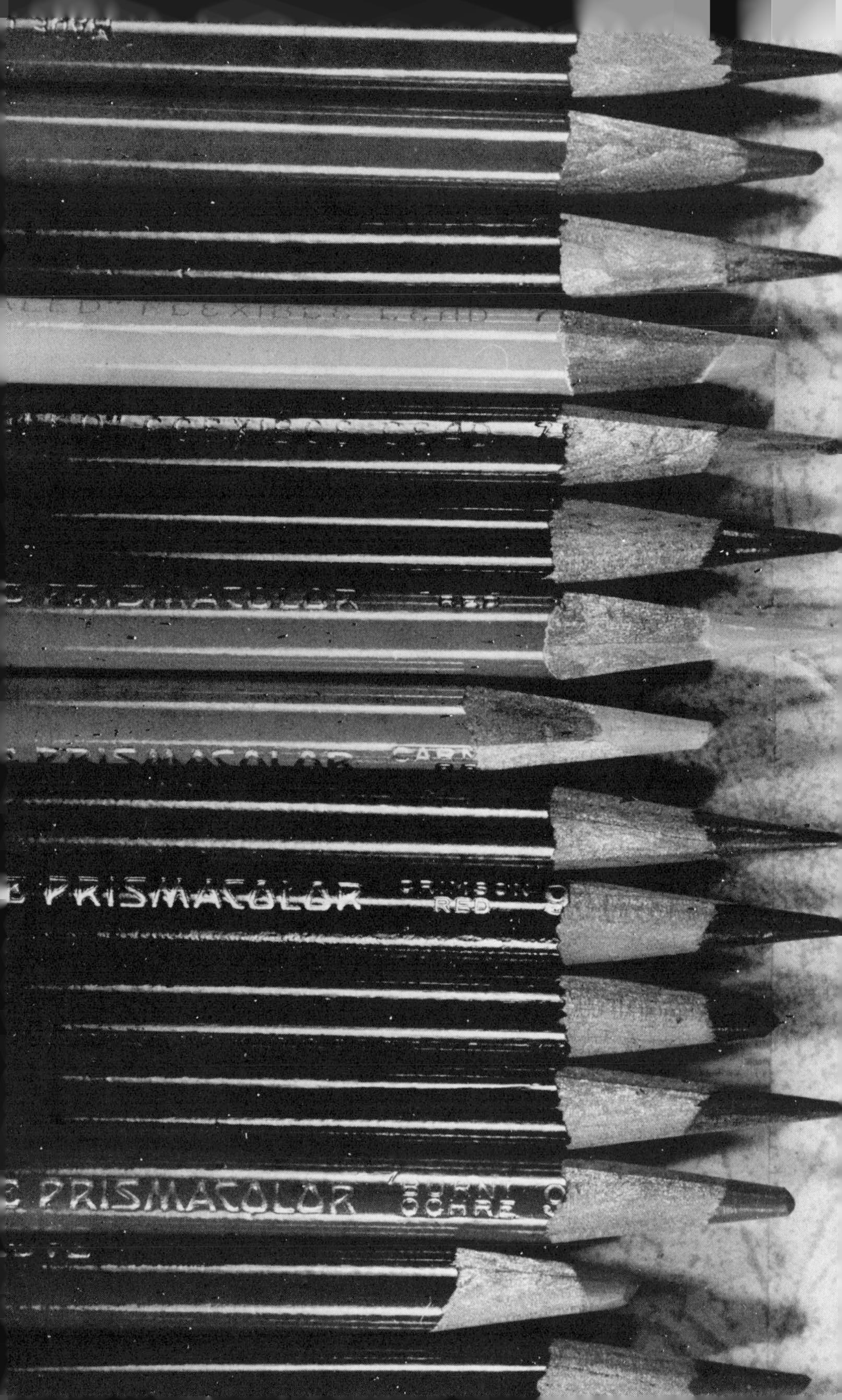
PRISMACOLOR
CRIMSON RED
PRISMACOLOR
OCHRE

CHAPTER 9
Scheduling Art Activities

The scheduling of interdependent activities such as those of an art and design department is a problematic affair. At one extreme it is trying to shuffle current staff to keep them reasonably busy with current work flow. At the other extreme it is scheduling and rescheduling in ways that not only set goals of accomplishment but also attempt to coordinate the various tasks by means of schedule. In the latter instance, schedule is conceived as a means of enabling events to fit together efficiently. Publishing is somewhat seasonal, which poses other problems, because permanent staff should not be large enough to cover the peak loads.

Systematic scheduling is difficult to apply to most art/design/production problems in books because (1) books are one-time, nonstandardized products that are, in fact, planned to be unique in most respects; (2) they depend heavily on a key creative factor, authorship, which is not under the publisher's effective schedule control; and (3) while most books are detailed and unique, they are not large projects in the design/production sense. Manufacturing people unacquainted with the special needs of book manufacture are often appalled at the amount of essentially unschedulable activity and detail that is involved.

Scheduling simple books

This study is about complex books, but as an example let us simplify for a moment. How many average books can an average designer handle in a year? The simpler and more homogeneous the books, the easier the question is to answer, but even for these books there must be some refinement if there is to be a meaningful answer.

We may try to formulate an answer for relatively simple books under streamlined art/design conditions. Consider trade books, averaging about 320 pages, black only, having about 25 illustrations, with the following simplifying conditions:

1. Books designed as complete packages, and not in pieces (jackets not included in the design job)
2. Minimal or no sample pages
3. Minimal or no sketches or editorial approval
4. Character counts of manuscripts done by persons other than the designer
5. Standardized papers, trims, dummy sheets, and binding materials
6. Well-tested arrangements and few suppliers
7. Art detail taken care of by persons other than the designer (retouching, labeling, mounting, repro corrections, mechanicals, dummies, and so on)
8. Scheduling and traffic done by production control, with minimal design responsibility
9. Minimal editorial changes during production phase
10. No final or revised page proof or blueprint check
11. No group meetings and conferences
12. Adequate and quiet work space

Naturally the books of this description may vary considerably, especially as to typographic complexity and number of illustrations. An experienced designer, however, can design such books under the conditions listed above at a rate of about 60 books each year, or 1.2 each week for 50 weeks. Designing any more than that is simply standardized processing, not designing, and the product will reflect this. An occasional book may be designed in a day or so, or a composition order written in an hour or so, but these are isolated events.

The simplifying conditions listed above are not met by most publishing operations, and the less such conditions are met, the longer the design times will be. In the long run, trying to force too much work through a design department results in less efficiency rather than more, and in costly mistakes by suppliers because the design department is the interface between publisher and printer. Individual publishers may work out their own average design times based on their own types of work, bearing in mind the above factors.

It is true that most books are not simple enough to fit into the above pattern —and yet not really sizable enough to be scheduled in the manner to be proposed below for large projects. In other words, it is assumed that most books must be design scheduled as they now are, pretty much by experienced intuition and by suppliers' schedules, which will come as no surprise to the art scheduler.

But when a considerable number of complex books are to be scheduled through a large art department, there are some specialized methods that can be considered. Even where traditional and less analytical methods are preferred in practice, the following analysis may be useful simply as a study tool that presents a relatively accurate idea of how the interdependent activities of art, design, and production relate to each other. In other words, the analysis is useful even when the projects are not big enough to make the method practical as a working tool.

Scheduling multiple large design/art projects

The aims of this type of scheduling are smooth flow, cooperative and efficient allocation of work, flexibility in the face of the unexpected, and overall economy of time and money. When these aims can be realized in reasonable degree, the results should be better books and happier people, with a minimum of "hurry up and wait."

The large art department producing complex books, such as those described in the previous chapter, is not an independent entity. Its activities, like those of the editorial department, are often not even scheduled separately during the production phase. They are simply included in the overall production schedule. But for the complex book, the schedule often depends so heavily on art and design functions that these functions largely determine the overall schedule—the editorial work having been in large part completed before the production schedule is started, and the purely production functions consisting largely of the combined schedules of outside suppliers. The design schedule, then, constitutes a major and critical part of the overall production schedule. It can, in fact, be plugged into that schedule.

In Chapter 1, art and design activities were broken down into 30 separate steps, or "events." A summary version of these events is given below for use as a framework in scheduling these activities. It will be remembered, however, that this list poses two problems with respect to the scheduling of individual books: (1) not all of the events listed apply to every book, and (2) the events do not occur neatly, in sequence, but rather overlap in ways that are difficult to describe, although not impossible to anticipate in a general way. For example, design work, artwork, picture research, and dummying may all be going on at the same time. They do not happen one after the other, for most books. The events would not proceed linearly, end to end, even if all events were to occur in one book.

In order to clarify this overlapping sequence in the summary that follows, art and design activities are listed at the left. To the right of each activity is the number of any event that *necessarily* and *immediately* precedes it. Parentheses enclose the numbers of events that may or may not be required for any given book.

Art and design activities	*Preceding events*
1. Transmittal (start) meeting	0
2. Conference and planning and text study	1
3. Text design	2
4. Sample pages and OKs	3
5. Manuscript castoff	4
6. Manuscript design markup	5
7. *Galleys**	6
8. Galley design corrections	7
9. Galley castoff	8
10. Predummy plan/picture specs review	9
11. Dummy	9(10,13,18)**
12. Art sketches	4(10,11)
13. Correct art sketches	12
14. Art finishes	13(11)
15. Correct art finishes	14
16. *Art blues or proofs*	15
17. Picture research and photography	4(10,11)
18. Decisions on researched pictures	17
19. Cropping and retouching researched pictures	18(11)
20. *Researched-picture blues or proofs*	19
21. Adjust dummy (or ready to page)	11,15,19
22. *Page make-up*	9(21)
23. Review and correct pages for design	16,20,22
24. Cover design (OK and mechanical)	4
25. Credit list and caption check	23
26. Back matter design	23(25)
27. Front matter design and OK	23
28. Pay art bills and store art	15
29. Pay photo bills, return, and file photos	19
30. Check final revises	24,26,27

*Italicized activities are production-oriented activities.
**Numbered activities in parentheses may or may not be required for a given book.

In using this list of events to plan an overall schedule for a particular book, it is necessary to determine which events are critical to the schedule and how coordination among critical elements can best be maintained, or reestablished if lost.

Recent techniques in the art of scheduling can help to describe how overlapping functions affect overall schedule and work coordination. In general, these new methods treat any schedule as a network of interconnected events, a network that is traversed from start to finish on lines connecting the events. More specifically, a technique called the "Critical Path Method" (CPM) of scheduling can help one visualize the problem. The "critical path" in any schedule network includes only those events that are "critical" to the overall schedule. This path is the sequence of dependent events *that requires the longest time to complete,* from the first step to the end of the project. It is called "critical" because the overall schedule cannot be any shorter than the combined times on that path.

Using the "Critical Path Method" to schedule books

A simple application of the Critical Path Method, as required by the 30 art activities listed, can be comprehended rather easily in visual form. This form is seen to be a specialized flow chart showing the dependencies and the flow from one event to another. It will have been noted that the list of events, while it represents many items of an overall book schedule, is actually only a departmental list of art activities. The italicized events in the list are the only production-oriented events, and these are included only because art activities depend on them: galleys, art blues or proofs, researched-picture blues or proofs, and pages.

On the CPM charts that follow, the larger circled numbers represent the 30 art and design events listed above, and the connecting lines are activities leading up to these events. The events, represented by numbers, are always understood to mean the *completion* of the activity, and the lines leading up to any event represent the activities required for its completion. Numbers on the lines in Figure 9–1 represent the number of working days necessary to complete the activities for a hypothetical book, and many possible schedule paths can be followed sequentially from one event to another. But it will be readily apparent that not all the activities scheduled for any given book can be on the critical path. All events can be scheduled, but the critical path makes clear which events are crucial to the overall schedule. The overall schedule is based on the number of working days necessary to complete the activities on the critical path.

Sometimes the critical path through the network may be guessed rather easily from the nature of the book and the character of its illustration program, as is intuitively done in traditional scheduling. But this is not always easy or possible. As we have observed, the illustration program (whether nontechnical, semitechnical, or technical) is an important factor in how the book is handled in design and art editing. In general, the critical path for scheduling will go through the events of dummying, *or* of the art program, *or* of the picture research program, depending on which of these requires the most time after the schedule is put into operation.

1. If the book has a large art program and a small picture research program, the critical path will go through the art-handling events—unless much of the art has been completed before the schedule starts. Then, usually, it will go through dummying, unless that takes less time than the picture research.
2. If the book has a large picture research program and a small art program,

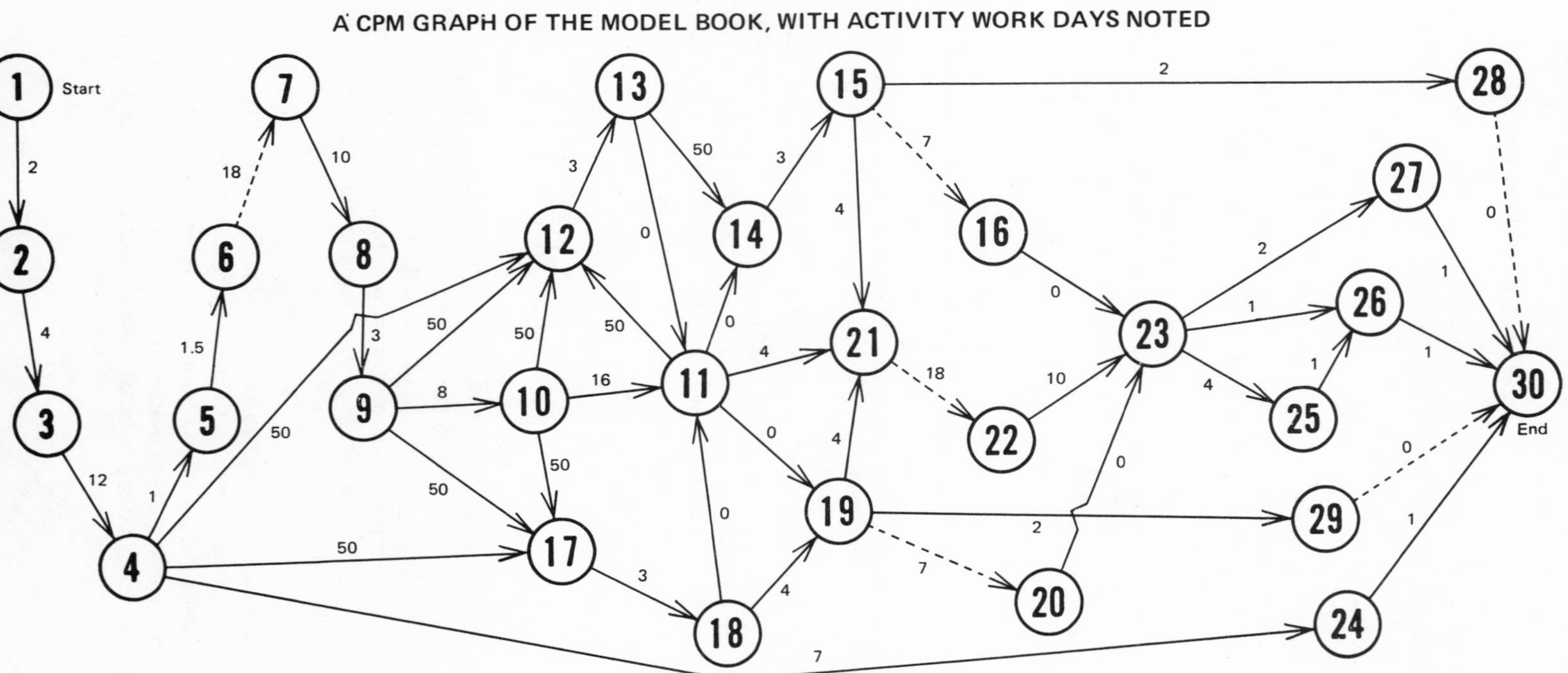

9-1 *A Critical Path Method (CPM) chart for a model book (as described in the text). The numbers in the circles correspond to the numbers in the list of numbered art/design activities on page 146. The numbers on the lines stand for* working days. *Certain assumptions have been made about work rates, as described in the text. Dashed lines are not art department activities. (No critical path has been identified on this chart.)*

the critical path will go through the research events—unless the research has been completed, for the most part, before the schedule starts. Then, usually, it will go through dummying, unless that takes less time than the art.

3. If the art and picture research programs are large and nearly equal in terms of estimated time, both paths should be calculated to see which is longer, that is, which is more critical to the schedule.

4. If both art and picture research programs are small, or largely completed before the schedule starts, but the book nevertheless needs dummying, the critical path will go through the dummying.

5. If the book does not require dummying and has small art and picture-research programs, the schedule is mainly determined by supplier scheduling. The critical path for art activities, however, still goes through the activities that require the most time.

In any case, the critical path is not chosen arbitrarily but is determined by adding up the estimated times noted on the lines by the person doing the scheduling. The suggestions above concerning the probable location of the path are offered only for purposes of clarification.

First, then, work days are estimated for all events required for a specific book, and these are noted on the lines of a chart such as that in Figure 9–1. In that example all the activities have been estimated for a rather common type of book that might have these characteristics:

- one column
- average typographic complexity
- black only
- 448 pages
- 100 halftones (research cannot start until after event 9, galley castoff)
- 100 pieces of art (sketches cannot start until after event 11, completion of dummy)
- predummy plan and dummy are required
- reasonably experienced editor, designer, and art editor

Of the simplifying conditions listed for trade books under "Scheduling simple books" above, only adequate work space and help with art details can be counted on by the designer.

It will be noted that certain assumptions have been made about work rates that involve specifiable units of work.

Event No.	*Rates per Working Day*
7	Galleys come in at the rate of 25 book pages (this information would come from production or be checked there).
9	Galley castoff is at the rate of 150 book pages.
10	Predummy planning is at the rate of 80 divided into the total

units on line 3 of the form shown as Figure 9–3 (text pages + art units + research units), which we'll call PAR.

11 Dummy is at the rate of 40 divided into PAR.
12 Art sketches are at the rate of two each day.
14 Art finishes are at the rate of two each day.
17 Research acceptances are at two each day.
21 Dummy adjustments are at the rate of 160 divided into PAR.
22 Pages are made up at a rate of 25 pages each day (this would come from production or be checked by them).
25 Credit and caption check is at the rate of 50 divided into art units plus research units.
16 & 20 Receipt of blues or proof on artwork and photos is allowed an additional seven days to clear the last batch.
8 & 23 Final batches of galleys and pages are allowed ten days to clear editorial, although design corrections at this stage would not require so long.

Estimated rates such as these are based on certain assumptions about the work and the workers. They are based on experience and are modifiable for all sorts of reasons in regard to an individual project. They are given here as illustrations of a basic book, a kind of benchmark model. The reader may want to make a similar model reflecting other needs. Such a model can be used, modified by appropriate "difficulty factors," to produce quick rough schedules.

There are three types of events that should be distinguished: (1) those that do not vary according to the number of unit pieces in the book (for example: cover design, front and back matter design); (2) those that do vary according to numbers of units involved (for example: art, picture research, and dummying); and (3) those that should not take any extra time, that will go on while some other necessary activities are taking place. These are called "zero time activities." These make the chart more flexible in use. For example, after technical art sketches have been completed in event 13, it may be desirable that

9-2 (Opposite page, top) *The path, through art preparation events, is shown by the heavy lines. Below the chart the* elapsed *times have been added and recalculated in months and days to schedule the numbered events. (The first numeral is the event number. In parentheses are months and days.) A revision of the schedule is also given (for a revision of art piece rate estimates as described in the text).*

(Middle) *The path is through research events (i.e., photo research). Below the chart the elapsed times are added and recalculated to schedule the key events in months and days.*

(Bottom) *The path is through the dummying events. Elapsed times are added and recalculated to schedule key events in months and days.*

Comparing total times for the three paths we see that the path through art preparation events is critical to the overall schedule because it is the longest.

E PATH THROUGH ART PREPARATION EVENTS

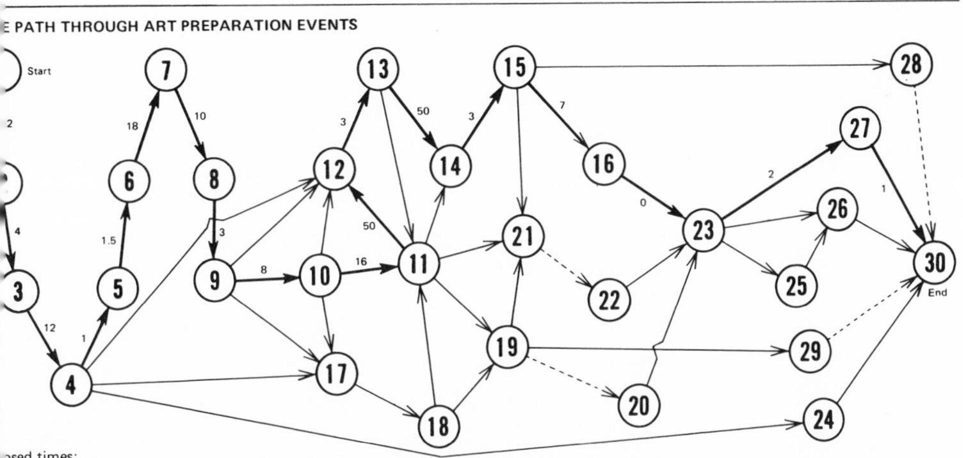

ɔsed times:

nths and days total for events: 7 (1+23), 11 (3+14), 15 (8+11), 23 (8+21), 30 (8+25)

ised times with art rate of 5 per day: 11 (3+14), 15 (5+18), 23 (5+28), 30 (6+2)

E PATH THROUGH RESEARCH EVENTS

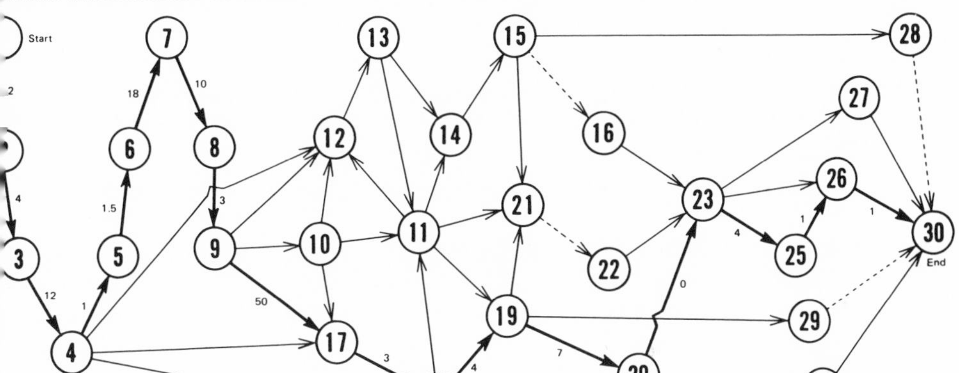

psed times:

nths and days total for events: 7 (1+23), 19 (4+30), 23 (5+10), 30 (5+18)

E PATH THROUGH DUMMY EVENTS

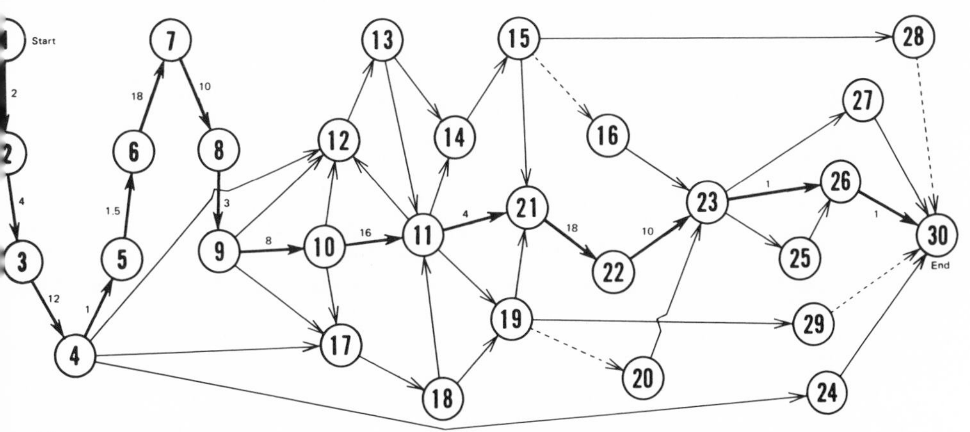

ɪpsed times:

ɔnths and days total for events: 7 (1+23), 23 (4+29), 30 (5+1)

the path return to the dummy at event 11. This does not require time and is labeled "0." (See Figure 9–3.)

To illustrate how the cumulative times on typical paths may be compared, the art, dummy, and picture research paths have been shown on three separate charts (Figure 9–2). The critical path through the model book can be found by adding up the working days on the art path (192 days), the picture research path (121 days), and the dummy path (110 days). The art path is by far the longest, which makes it the critical path. The book will require about 192 working days to complete—*unless* some of the conditions on the art path can be changed. To finish the art at the same time as the picture research, 71 working days must be saved in the art schedule. (This would also save 71 days in the overall schedule, whereas saving time in research will not affect the overall schedule at all.)

These facts suggest courses of action, and we can consider alternatives, such as giving the art to a studio that can put several artists to work on it instead of one. Or perhaps the artist already chosen might employ assistants. Some art might be started before the dummy is fully complete, and some of the pieces might even be dropped.

We are actually concerned only with events 12 and 14, the art sketches and finishes. A production rate of 2 each day has been assumed for both, so that 100 illustrations now require 50 days to sketch and 50 to finish. In order to save 71 days, the production rate would have to be 7 pieces each day for both sketches and finishes (provided that no pieces are eliminated or started early). With this saving of time, 100 sketches and 100 finishes will be completed in 29 days. That much efficiency may not be possible, but if the rate can be 5 each day, we shall save 60 days, without eliminating art or starting it before the dummy is approved.

Let us assume that we settle for a rate of 5 each day, and that the overall working days on the art path are reduced to 132. Some other option might be taken, but the foregoing illustrates the general method of use for the chart. It not only serves as a schedule, but also clarifies the need for adjustments and helps to coordinate tasks.

We want to schedule calendar dates, not working days, and to do this the working days need to be divided by 5 and multiplied by 7 to get elapsed days. The elapsed days are then added cumulatively throughout a chosen path, and at each step where a calendar date is wanted they can be divided by 30.4 to get months and days left over. These in turn are added to the start date to obtain desired calendar dates for any event.

In the chart above (Figure 9–2) the number of work days originally noted has been cumulatively converted to the number of elapsed months and additional days required for the critical events numbered 7, 11, 15, 23, and 30. (For example, 5 + 12 = five months and 12 days.) These times may, of course, be added to any given start date.

Naturally, very few people will be enthusiastic about going through this

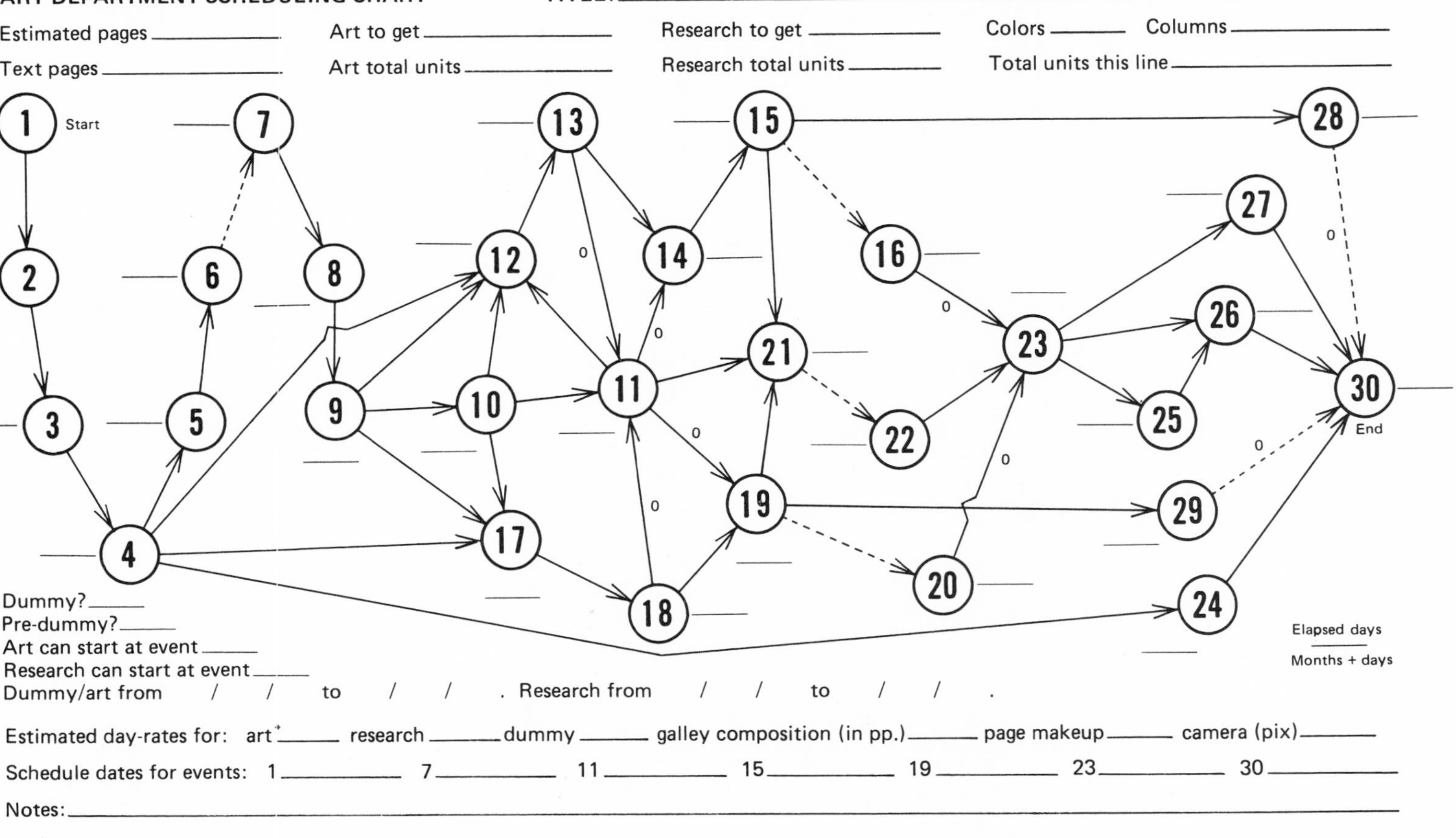

9-3 *A Critical Path Method chart adaptable for possible use with many books. See Figure 9-4.*

ART DEPARTMENT SCHEDULING CHART **TITLE:** SAMPLE SCHEDULE **DATE:** 5/5/78

Estimated pages 576 Art to get 49 Research to get 92 Colors 1 Columns 1

Text pages 550 Art total units 64 Research total units 110 Total units this line 724 ('PAR')

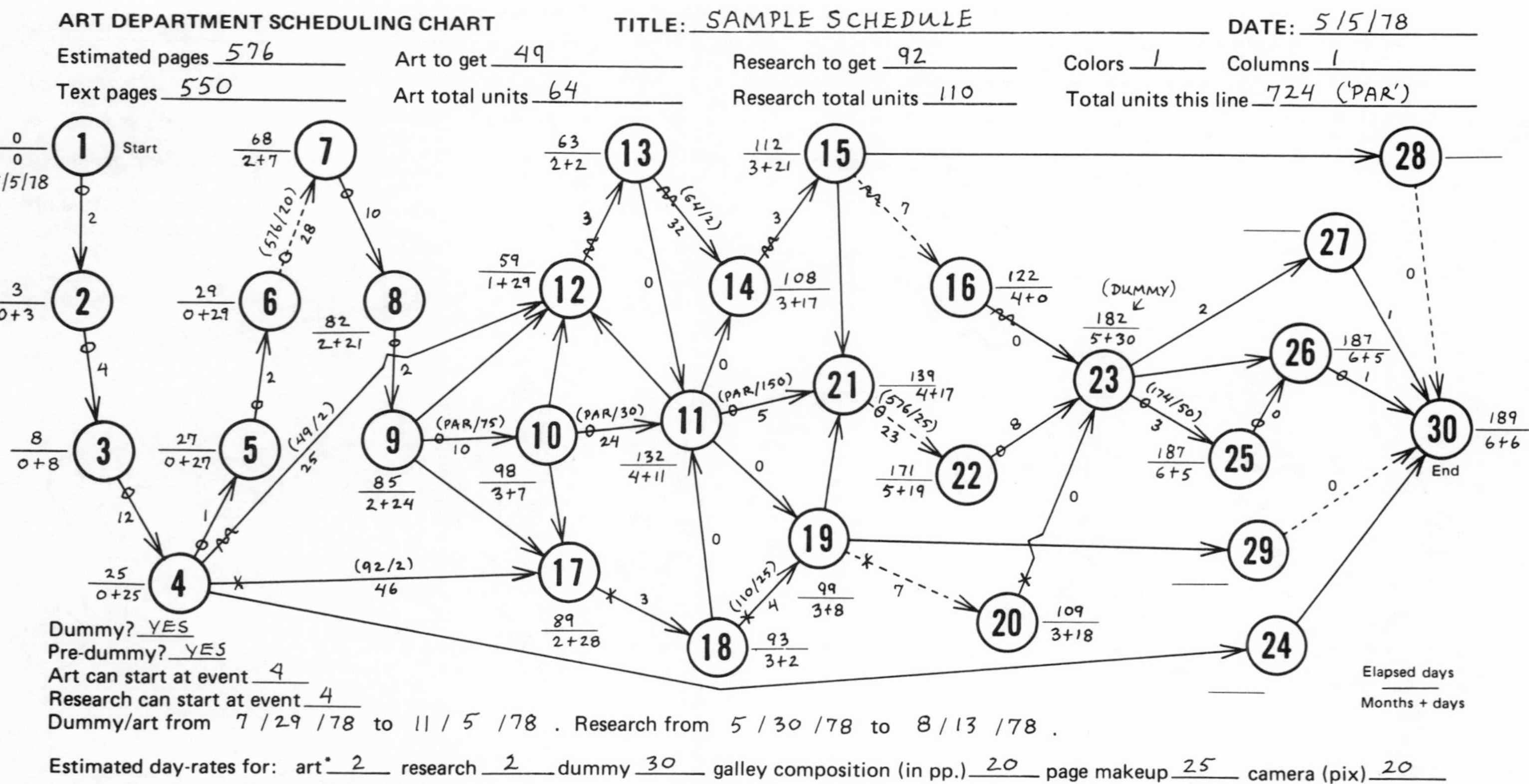

Dummy? YES

Pre-dummy? YES

Art can start at event 4

Research can start at event 4

Dummy/art from 7/29/78 to 11/5/78. Research from 5/30/78 to 8/13/78.

Estimated day-rates for: art* 2 research 2 dummy 30 galley composition (in pp.) 20 page makeup 25 camera (pix) 20

Schedule dates for events: 1 5/5/78 7 7/12/78 11 9/16/78 15 8/26/78 19 8/13/78 23 11/5/78 30 11/11/78

Notes: DUMMY IS THE CRITICAL PATH. AT STEP 23 (CORRECTED PAGES) RESEARCH HAS 10 WEEKS SLACK, ART HANDLING HAS 9 WEEKS SLACK. RESEARCH CAN BE COMPLETED BEFORE PRE-DUMMY PLAN. RE-ASSIGN RESEARCHER TO DUMMY PART 2.

*Sketches or finishes

CUT TIMES FOR #11 AND #21 BY 50%. REVISED DATE #23: 10/15, REVISED #30: 10/21/78, IF RESEARCH IS ON SCHEDULE.

procedure for many events, either with pencil or simple calculator. The procedure is presented here because (1) the network method is the only one that shows clearly and visually the actual interrelationships of art and design functions, and (2) the calculation can, if it is desirable, be put on an inexpensive programmable pocket calculator, allowing the scheduler to calculate elapsed times and calendar dates from raw work days about as fast as they can be written down.

The method, of course, is generalized so that occasionally the scheduled dates may fall on weekends or on the 31st of a month with only 30 days. These errors are of no consequence, however, and can be corrected by calendar inspection.

* * *

The above is a simplified description of the use of CPM for one defined book, or type of book. Some possible paths are not even shown on the foregoing charts. If practical use is to be made of this method, a working chart such as the one shown in Figure 9–3 can be devised. All the relevant information can be entered on one sheet, as shown in Figure 9–4 and explained in the legend.

Before leaving this topic, some general observations on CPM scheduling may be of interest.

1. Any delay in critical path activities will mean a delay in completion of the overall project. On the other hand, all activities not on the critical path can be delayed in varying degrees without affecting the overall schedule; that is, those participating in these activities have some "slack" time, or time to spare. From a practical point of view slack time means not only more time to complete an activity, but also an option to transfer people from a noncritical activity to a critical activity (when this is practical), thereby shortening the overall schedule and making it unnecessary for people to have nothing to do.

9-4 *The general procedure for using the chart on the opposite page is: (1) Fill out as much information as possible at the top and bottom of the chart, obtaining production information as required; (2) trace the paths through dummy, art, and picture research, or as required for the particular book (colored pencils are handy, but in the sample the small circles (dummy), crosses (art), and waves (picture research) identify the lines); (3) estimate the number of work days on the paths, using appropriate work rates (these have been noted for the sample at the bottom of the chart); (4) calculate the elapsed days, and months + days, from work days; (5) observe which path is critical and note the relevant schedule dates (translated from the months + days); (6) note whether slack times in noncritical activities can be utilized to shorten the times of critical path activities, and recalculate some critical path times as may seem desirable. With a programmed calculator and a little practice with the method, a chart such as this should require only a few minutes to prepare.*

For example, if the critical path is through research activities and the art editor has slack time in artist supervision and dummying, extra help may be given by the art editor to an assigned picture researcher. (Normally, changes in work assignment will happen only if the person assigning work tasks is *aware* that there is slack time in a noncritical task.)

2. If time can be saved on the critical path, then this directly affects the final date. On the other hand, time saved in noncritical activities will have no effect on the final date, unless this allows help to be transferred to activities on the critical path, shortening the time necessary to perform tasks there.

3. Any event preceding (necessary to) a critical path event may cause a delay in the critical path if it is late. Step 23, the design correction of pages, depends on the preceding events of art and researched picture proofs or blues, as well as on page proofs having been received. (In the last chapter it was mentioned that a dummy can seldom be started without necessary technical art.) There are many examples of such event dependence; in fact, that is what the chart is constructed to show. Sometimes the dependence is obvious, like manuscript castoff dependence upon sample page approval, but sometimes it is not so obvious. Technical art progress would be represented on the graph by events on the path 4–12–13–10 (see Figure 9–3), showing that such art could be undertaken early, proceeding from sketches to revised sketches. At this point the final sizes would be known and the dummy could be started. (A line from 13 to 10 could be added to the chart for that book.)

It will be obvious by now that network charting of this type is simply making explicit and orderly what every person who makes a schedule is in fact trying to do intuitively. Critical paths are not always obvious, and slack time is often hard to anticipate. Moreover, activities preceding critical path events constantly create delays because they have been overlooked. The visual and graphic Critical Path Method (CPM), presented here in barest outline, suggests that an orderly notation can be an aid to intuition and a valuable tool in solving scheduling problems.

A "Books-in-Work" chart

The 30 events taken as the basis for individual book scheduling by CPM also may form the basis for a "Books-in-Work" chart (Figure 9–5), showing all books currently being worked on by the art department. It is shown here, with the names of events shortened. Each book in work is allowed one line across, and the dates for scheduled events are written in the squares below the event numbers. The narrow spaces above the lines are filled in only when the event is on the critical path, thus showing at a glance which activities and dates are most important to the overall schedule. When any event is completed, the square below it will be dated and colored or shaded in. Events that do not apply to the book in question may be crossed out or shaded in with another color.

BOOKS-IN-WORK CHART: ART DEPARTMENT

AUTHOR	1 Start	2 Plan	3 Design	4 Samples	5 Castoff	6 Markup	7 Galleys	8 G/correct	9 G/castoff	10 Pre-dummy	11 Dummy	12 Art sketch	13 A/S correct	14 Art finish	15 A/F correct	16 Art blues	17 Research	18 R/evaluate	19 R/size etc.	20 R/blues	21 Dummy adjust	22 Pages	23 P/correct	24 Cover design	25 Credit list	26 Back design	27 Front design	28 Art pay etc.	29 Research pay	30 Last check

9-5 *On this Books-in-Work chart the numbers correspond to the 30 art/design department activities listed on page 146. The small space above each date rectangle is filled in only if the event is on the critical path. Every third line may be used, to allow for revisions.*

Thus, although the chart does not show overlapping relationships, it can function like the traditional Gantt milestone chart, or "progress chart." Scheduled dates may be written in pencil, so that the schedule can be revised without damaging the chart; or only every third line may be used for original schedules, thus leaving room for two revises and/or keeping the chart uncluttered.

Obviously the Books-in-Work chart is in no way dependent upon the method of scheduling, whether network scheduling or some other method is used. If the events comprising the critical path have not been accurately determined, they can at least be guessed at, as suggested above, which can be of some help.

On the other hand, the form does require accurate current information on as many books as are in work and in respect to as many activities as are in work. If the art department is sizable, this information is not easy to obtain without regular reporting by all key people.

Weekly job-status report

Regular weekly reporting of job status is greatly facilitated by a regular report form to be filled out by as many key people as may seem necessary. (See the sample form that follows.) As will be obvious, the use of the same 30 steps we have been considering in relation to other scheduling forms can make the form easy to fill out, and also easy to correlate with individual schedules and the Books-in-Work chart. The steps being worked on can easily be checked with the Books-in-Work chart and the latter kept up to date. Jobs falling behind are separately listed and thus can be easily checked as to whether the steps are on the critical path or precede an event on that path. The amount of slack available can be calculated, if that is desirable. Each report lists the kinds of help that can be used in areas falling behind in schedule and also asks whether any slack time is anticipated during the coming week ("time to help others"). Such information is often difficult to obtain and is useful only when it is correlated with other information regarding help needed or wanted.

There is more feasible job interchangeability and mutual help potential in the average art department than is often realized. Mutual help is particularly practical among assistant designers, art editors, and researchers. If such interchange is properly organized and encouraged there are many people who welcome the opportunity to help others as an alternative to boredom when they have nothing they can do on their own projects. This is especially true when they later enjoy reciprocal benefits.

Work standards file

It is useful to keep a file of past work performances for various kinds of art jobs, both for jobs that are done in the publishing house and those that are done by outside agencies.

It is important to keep in such a file estimates and bills of various kinds to

ART DEPARTMENT WEEKLY JOB STATUS REPORT

Date: ____________________

Name ______________________________________ **Job title** ____________________

List all the jobs on which you are now working regularly, in the order of priority. Give the step number you are working on, and the approximate percentage of that step completed. (See list of steps, 1–30)

	Step #	% Done
A. ______________________________	____	____
B. ______________________________	____	____
C. ______________________________	____	____
D. ______________________________	____	____
E. ______________________________	____	____
Misc ______________________________	____	____

List jobs falling behind schedule in your area. (Refer to letters above, and be as specific as you can about the problem.)

____

____

____

____

____

What kind of help can you use in the areas of schedule trouble? (Refer to numbers above.)

____

____

____

What tools or materials do you need that you don't have?

____

Are you likely to have time to help others this week? *Hours?*

Other suggestions ____

____

____

be used in estimating future work, provided that they are submitted by competent professionals. These are most useful when unit time and cost rates are given; in fact it is a good idea to request that bills and estimates be submitted in this form. For example: "100 two-color graphs and charts for high school history book @ $45, scheduled for production at a rate of 2 sketches or 2 finishes per working day." Since any other information is usually irrelevant to permanent records, either this information should be circled when it is present or it should be roughly calculated if it is not. If a typical finished item can be filed with the record, so much the better. It is less useful to include in such a file the overall time taken to perform complex jobs, because the figures may be distorted due to miscellaneous delays.

Records of in-house unit production rates should be kept for typical jobs and typical workers. A separate record sheet (such as the one shown below) for jobs

WORK RATE EXPERIENCE SHEET

General task definition ____________________

Work unit__________ Time unit__________ Average rate* this sheet ______

Book title ____________________

Task particulars ____________________

____________________ Work rate__________

Book title ____________________

Task particulars ____________________

____________________ Work rate__________

Book title ____________________

Task particulars ____________________

____________________ Work rate__________

Book title ____________________

Task particulars ____________________

____________________ Work rate__________

Book title ____________________

Task particulars ____________________

____________________ Work rate__________

*Work rate = time unit divided by work units

like dummying can record what the dummiers think are typical rates for various kinds of jobs, exclusive of any major kinds of interruptions. These rates can simply be listed by book titles: "Such and such a book, basic average dummying rate 30 pages per day for text," and so on. Such records can be useful for scheduling day rates and for establishing the "difficulty factors" for various kinds of books in relation to a basic "benchmark" schedule. These can be useful when rough schedules are needed. For in-house jobs there is likely to be some resistance to the establishing of "standards," but it can be made plain that these records are not, in fact, work standards and may more often be used to make sure that enough time is allowed in schedules.

CHAPTER 10
Paper, Printing, and Binding: The Design Aspects

When it comes to paper, printing, and binding, it is not feasible for designers to become too involved with specific or comparative technologies, which are now so highly complex. They need only a basic knowledge of available methods, a working knowledge of where the options and problems lie, and a knack for asking meaningful and practical questions. This will enable them to deal with technological change, without having to wrestle with it. Instead of giving technical recommendations to suppliers, designers should give a clear description of the intended visual result, leaving it to the supplier to work out the technical requirements. If the intended result is not attainable within a given set of conditions, it is up to the supplier to consult with the designer as to the adjustments that may be practical.

Text paper

Modern papers are of remarkably good quality and uniformity. In general, text-paper buying in the medium or large publishing house is a matter of economics, availability, established paper-buying policies, general editorial and sales expectations, the requirements of the printing process, and the specific presses at the printer. Very often paper is bought in large lots, even freight car loads, or on consignment from the paper merchant (shipped to the printer in large lots and paid for by publishers as it is used).

For all these reasons, papers for individual books are seldom specified arbitrarily by the designer. Apart from very unusual design requirements, which would need approval from editorial as well as production, the design paper requirements of various classes of books are well understood and taken care of without the designer playing much of a part in the specification process.

Nevertheless, the designer needs to be aware of the paper being used for each job. The author recalls some paper and presswork combinations where bold type looked as though it had been, in the traditional figure of speech, "printed with apple butter on a hay press." Unfortunate results can sometimes be avoided if the designer bears in mind the following factors as they may affect design of typography and illustration.

1. *Finish.*
   a. For letterpress (seldom used for book work any more), the paper finish is of critical importance to the printability of halftones and screen tints (Benday). Lines per inch for mechanical screens cannot, in commercial letterpress, safely exceed the following degrees of fineness for the paper finishes indicated:

Uncoated antique (or eggshell)	85 line screen
Uncoated machine finish	100 " "
Uncoated English finish	110 " "
Plate (or "super") finish	120 " "
Coated (dull finish)	133 " "
Coated (gloss finish)	150 " "

   b. For offset the finish of the paper does not control the fineness of mechanical screens that can be used—at least not to the extent that it does in letterpress. This is, of course, because the rubber blanket from which the ink is transferred to paper conforms quite easily to the surfaces of papers, even when they are somewhat irregular. Screens as high as 300 lines can be printed on vellum-finish offset papers for special jobs, although in commercial sheet-fed printing screens do not normally exceed 150 lines per inch. In web work, 120–133 is the norm.

      Offset papers are traditionally available in finishes often described as: antique, eggshell, vellum, regular, satin, gloss, and high gloss.
2. *Surface characteristics.* For both offset and letterpress, these include surface sizing, no surface sizing, "beater" sizing, film coating (or pigmenting), machine coating, and off-machine coating. Most offset papers today, especially those intended for multicolor printing, are at least surface sized. In general, of course, the more important the halftone detail, the smoother the paper needs to be, even in offset.
3. *Compressibility.* More compressibility often makes letterpress papers more printable, but is seldom a factor in offset printing.
4. *Ink receptivity and penetration.* Letterpress has more penetration.
5. *Bonding.* High bond is necessary in offset papers to prevent "picking" due

to the pull of tacky inks used in the offset process. High water resistance is necessary to prevent excessive water absorption during offset printing. This high bond is what makes most offset papers seem "harder" than letterpress papers.

6. *Color (or shade).* For text papers this means a range of subtle shades of cool whites and warm whites, not strongly colored papers. This is of real concern to the designer since it affects the appearance of illustrations and printed colors. For example, a designer who feels that a few four-color illustrations should not necessarily dictate a flat white sheet for an entire job should say so. The shades of text papers are not adequately described by names such as "off-white," "natural," "blue-white," or "ivory." The color must be examined under appropriate light conditions to be properly evaluated. (Cool white fluorescent lighting is often used in school classrooms and so is appropriate for examining schoolbook text papers. See the discussion below under four-color process printing.)
7. *Weight and bulk.* Weight is customarily expressed in pounds per ream (500 sheets) or per 1000 sheets of a given size (25″ × 38″ is the standard or "basis" size for book papers, to which all other weights refer). Bulk indicates the thickness of the paper, which does not necessarily vary in relation to weight. It is either expressed in thousandths of an inch, or in pages per inch.
8. *Various other characteristics* may be considered, such as opacity (resistance of the paper to the transmission of light, particularly as regards "show through" from printed areas on the backs of pages), "brightness" (the amount of light reflected from the surface of the sheet, called "glare" when it is felt to be excessive), grain and foldability, fiber composition, filler content, "hand" (feel), and so on.

It is very rare for designers to need estimates of text paper quantities, costs, spoilages, weights, reams, and rolls, and these will not even be discussed here. Colored papers will be discussed under "Bindings" below. Paper companies put out samples and informational literature about their own papers that the designer should study.

Standard paper sizes and press sizes affect the standard trimmed sizes with which the designer works. The following sheet, web, and trimmed sizes are typical for books at major publishers. They are used unless unusual sales or design situations dictate otherwise, and any change is made only after due consideration is given to all the production and cost factors involved. Before final plans are made on any book the desired trimmed size should be checked for availability, for web- or sheet-fed press. Colors, bleed page problems, paper finish, bulk, weight, etc. should also be cleared.

SOME TRIMMED SIZES, FROM STANDARD SHEET SIZES

Sheet size	Untrimmed size*	Common full trimmed size
44 × 66	5.50 × 8.25	5 3/8 × 8
45 × 68	5.62 × 8.50	5 1/2 × 8 1/4
46 × 69	5.75 × 8.62	5 5/8 × 8 3/8
49 × 74	6.12 × 9.25	6 × 9
42 × 76	6.25 × 9.50	6 1/4 × 9 1/4
46 ½ × 76	6.50 × 9.50	6 3/8 × 9 1/4
50 × 76	6.50 × 9.25	6 3/8 × 9
52 × 76	7.00 × 9.5 (48s)	6 7/8 × 9 1/4
52 × 74	7.75 × 9.50 (48s)	7 1/2 × 9 1/4

*Untrimmed front and foot, or foot only, may be used in traditional trade books.

WEB OFFSET AND CONVERTING ROLLS AND TRIMMED SIZES*

Roll Width (")	Trimmed Size(")
22 1/2	5 3/8 × 8
23 1/4	5 1/2 × 8 1/4; 5 5/8 × 8 1/2
23 1/2	5 1/2 × 8 7/16
25 1/2	6 × 9
26	6 1/8 × 9 1/4
33 (very common)	5 5/16 × 8; 5 7/16 × 8; 8 × 11
34 (very common)	5 1/2 × 8 1/4; 8 1/4 × 11
44 (rather rare)	5 5/16 × 8; 5 3/8 × 8
45 (rather rare)	5 3/8 × 8; 5 1/2 × 8 1/4
50	6 × 9; 6 1/8 × 9 1/4

*Rolls are typical of consignment papers available at large manufacturers.
Roll widths of 22 1/2"–26" are mostly for the so-called half-size webs.

Printing

Since 1970 the web-fed rotary offset printing process has progressively become dominant for book work of long or moderate runs. As a result, the survival of letterpress in its traditional forms has become questionable, even for the shorter runs where it was once assumed to be most viable. Sheet-fed presses, with their start and stop operations and consequent problems of registration and transfer, have been on the way out for most book work. The offset web process is now the "big daddy" of all printing processes.

Web printing will not be described in any detail here, for although designers may occasionally ride quality control on the web press, they will be concerned with the design acceptability of colors, completeness of the project, and so on, not with the process itself, which is for all practical purposes an automated black box. Modern webs deliver 16-, 24-, 32-, or 48- page signatures (folded sheets), have in-line folding, and on-run computer monitored register control and color control.

Owing to the great increase in the uses of the approximate 6" × 9" trimmed size during recent years, and in order to compete favorably with letterpress even for shorter runs, the so-called quarter sized web has recently appeared.

This is primarily geared for the 7½″ × 9¼″ or 9½″, 6½″ × 9″, and 5″ × 8¼″ trims. It delivers untrimmed 32-page signatures of from 4½″ to 7¾″ × 9 11/16″ at about 30,000 impressions per hour. It can also deal successfully with the increasingly lightweight papers that are becoming practical.

Web technology is impressive, but it concerns the designer hardly at all, if the end product is good—which it generally is, provided that adequate preparatory steps have been taken. The relationships of ink and paper chemistry, of presses, folders, and so on, are about as comprehensible to the nontechnical student as the workings of the TV tube. The designer is advised to relax and enjoy them, while at the same time keeping an eye on the final product. The designer who is called upon to exercise quality control should not be intimidated, although the web should not be required to wait idly while the designer tries to make a decision.

The "Cameron" process is a special type of letterpress printing, using a web of 38″, 44″, or 62″ width. It is used to print all pages of a book sequentially, in one pass, from flexible relief-type photopolymer plates mounted on two printing belts. The paper web is slit and cut into a stream of 4-page signatures that are continuously collated into books, for adhesive binding. The process can deliver over 200 finished books per minute.

As, perhaps, may be guessed from this description, for the most part it has been used for lower quality single-color books without halftones, although it is sometimes claimed that halftones up to 110-line screen can run successfully. The process is mentioned here mainly so that the designer may be aware that it is a high speed letterpress process in which quality is not high, and in which the use of halftones is still very limited. The design use of solid blacks is not recommended.

Color planning for press forms

Color planning must obviously be undertaken early in the planning of the book, and to do this the printing and folding operations must be taken into account. Color flexibility and handling vary considerably among the various presses, delivery systems, and folding systems used by offset and letterpress printers. Production control at the publisher's end should consult early with the designer, and a representative of the press, on the plan for each book using color.

The actual planning instrument used by the publisher to coordinate color use is usually called a "press form plan" or "pages on press plan" (see Figure 10–1). It shows the detailed color plan of the book, indicating what pages and what press forms have what colors (black, nonprocess color, process color), which pages are on which forms, which pages fall on press gripper edges, and so on. This form should be checked with the representative of the press, but it is initiated by production control at the publisher's end.

10-1 *A press form plan or "pages on press" plan. It can be used to keep track of the physical plan of the book in terms of press sheets, colors, illustrations, bleeds, inserts, oversized pages, book divisions, and so on.*

TITLE .... This form prepared by .... Approved by Printer (   ) Date (   )

Pages of Front matter....................(   )
Pages of Back matter....................(   )
Pages of Inserts.........................(   )
Pages of Text............................(   )
Pages of Bleeds (marked   )..........(   )
Pages oversize (not bleed) (marked   ).....(   )
Unit Openings (marked   )..........(   )
........halftones (total) ....bleed halftones
........oversize halftones ....line cuts (total)
........bleed line cuts ....oversize line cuts

Trimmed size............
Total Pages in Book......................
Number of Sheets (total)..................
Sheet size...........
Margins (after trim)
Head....... Back.......

Number of colors	Keyed below	Colors
( )............/..........	....	....
( )............/..........	....	....
( )............/..........	....	....
( )............/..........	....	....
( )............/..........	....	....
( )............/..........	....	....
( )............/..........	....	....
( )............/..........	....	....
( )............/..........	....	....

( )		( )		( )		( )		( )		( )		( )		( )		( )		( )		( )		( )		( )		( )		( )		( )		( )	
i	ii	1	2	33	34	65	66	97	98	129	130	161	162	193	194	225	226	257	258	289	290	321	322	353	354	385	386	417	418	449	450	481	482
iv	iii	4	3	36	35	68	67	100	99	132	131	164	163	196	195	228	227	260	259	292	291	324	323	356	355	388	387	420	419	452	451	484	483
v	vi	5	6	37	38	69	70	101	102	133	134	165	166	197	198	229	230	261	262	293	294	325	326	357	358	389	390	421	422	453	454	485	486
viii	vii	8	7	40	39	72	71	104	103	136	135	168	167	200	199	232	231	264	263	296	295	328	327	360	359	392	391	424	423	456	455	488	487
ix	x	9	10	41	42	73	74	105	106	137	138	169	170	201	202	233	234	265	266	297	298	329	330	361	362	393	394	425	426	457	458	489	490
xii	xi	12	11	44	43	76	75	108	107	140	139	172	171	204	203	236	235	268	267	300	299	332	331	364	363	396	395	428	427	460	459	492	491
xiii	xiv	13	14	45	46	77	78	109	110	141	142	173	174	205	206	237	238	269	270	301	302	333	334	365	366	397	398	429	430	461	462	493	494
xvi	xv	16	15	48	47	80	79	112	111	144	143	176	175	208	207	240	239	272	271	304	303	336	335	368	367	400	399	432	431	464	463	496	495
xvii	xviii	17	18	49	50	81	82	113	114	145	146	177	178	209	210	241	242	273	274	305	306	337	338	369	370	401	402	433	434	465	466	497	498
xx	xix	20	19	52	51	84	83	116	115	148	147	180	179	212	211	244	243	276	275	308	307	340	339	372	371	404	403	436	435	468	467	500	499
xxi	xxii	21	22	53	54	85	86	117	118	149	150	181	182	213	214	245	246	277	278	309	310	341	342	373	374	405	406	437	438	469	470	501	502
xxiv	xxiii	24	23	56	55	88	87	120	119	152	151	184	183	216	215	248	247	280	279	312	311	334	343	376	375	408	407	440	439	472	471	504	503
xxv	xxvi	25	26	57	58	89	90	121	122	153	154	185	186	217	218	249	250	281	282	313	314	345	346	377	378	409	410	441	442	473	474	505	506
xxviii	xxvii	28	27	60	59	92	91	124	123	156	155	188	187	220	219	252	251	284	283	316	315	348	347	380	379	412	411	444	443	476	475	508	507
xxix	xxx	29	30	61	62	93	94	125	126	157	158	189	190	221	222	253	254	285	286	317	318	349	350	381	382	413	414	445	446	477	478	509	510
xxxii	xxxi	32	31	64	63	96	95	128	127	160	159	192	191	224	223	256	255	288	287	320	319	352	351	384	383	416	415	448	447	480	479	512	511
( )		( )		( )		( )		( )		( )		( )		( )		( )		( )		( )		( )		( )		( )		( )		( )		( )	

The following typical outline of considerations in regard to the press form plan is given so that the designer may be aware of the kinds of factors involved, the possible adjustments and, in general, the way in which adjustments are made. The designer should not make adjustments to the plan, even when design requirements make the changes necessary (during the dummying phase particularly). In fact, the press form should *never* be changed except by the person originating it. The following are typical descriptions and general considerations in regard to the press form plan, but they should not be expected to apply to any one system in complete detail.

1. The basic physical unit of the book is the "signature," or folded sheet of paper, whether this is a separate sheet going into the press or cut from a web. The basic printing unit is one side of the signature, one "form," or half the number of pages in the signature, even when the sheet is "perfected" or printed on both sides at once. A 64-page signature has one 32-page form printed on each side; a 128-page signature has one 64-page form printed on each side. A binding unit may be part of a larger printed signature, but is delivered separately for binding. For 64- or 128-page signatures, the binding unit is often 32 pages, but not always. As noted above, modern webs can deliver binding units of 16, 24, 32, or 48 pages. (These binding units are often loosely referred to as signatures, too.) For most books, 32 pages is still the most usual and economical minimum binding unit.

2. For long-run work, and especially color work (for 6½″ × 9¼″ trim or under, only), the most desirable printing unit is the 128-page signature (one 64-page form printed on each side). However, this sheet is slit on press and delivered as two 64-page binding units, which are slit again on the folder and need not necessarily be utilized sequentially in the book. This provides flexibility in the placement of color in the book, but makes it desirable to plan color overall in 128-page groupings of four 32-page units.

3. Each side of the press sheet (signature) can be printed with a different color or combination of colors. Therefore, each 64 pages of a 128-page signature can be two 32-page binding units of one color and two of another color, but these must overall be in balanced pairs of 32s.

4. Press ink fountains can sometimes be split to print half in one color set and half in another (although oversized paper may be required for this). If one side of a 128-page signature is printed in black and one extra color (the split colors being blue and red, say), with the back of the sheet in black only, the effect will be to create 4 binding units of 32 pages, half of which have alternating spreads of red and black or black only, and half of which have alternating spreads of blue and black or black only. These binding units need not, of course, be utilized sequentially in the book. The lesson in all this is that on press many things are possible, and the designer should consult with a specialist when special color-use problems arise in dummying a complex book.

5. If an odd 16 pages must be accommodated, it is often printed on a separate single-color press and utilized at the end of the book, as index or other back matter not requiring color. If it is introduced earlier in the book, it may have unused potential to be printed in two or more colors, and the effect on the press form plan is to push all subsequent binding units ahead 16 pages.

6. Actual sheet impositions for the press in question must be worked out so that press gripper edges can be located, and undesirable groupings of pages requiring heavy inking can be avoided, if possible. Groupings that make for difficult ink distribution are four adjacent pages, triangles, or long pairs. Bleeds usually should not occur on the gripper edge, and should be avoided if possible in press "tape lanes." Gripper edges and groupings can only be located on press impositions.

PRESS FORMS

Pages	*64s*	*32s*	*Pages*	*64s*	*32s*
32	½	1	416	6 ½	13
64	1	2	448	7	14
96	1 ½	3	480	7 ½	15
128	2	4	512	8	16
160	2 ½	5	544	8 ½	17
192	3	6	576	9	18
224	3 ½	7	608	9 ½	19
256	4	8	640	10	20
288	4 ½	9	672	10 ½	21
320	5	10	704	11	22
352	5 ½	11	736	11 ½	23
384	6	12	768	12	24

Four-color process printing

General descriptions of halftone and line reproduction, color, offset, letterpress, and gravure printing are readily available. They will not be treated here because the working book designer seldom has any problem with straight halftone or line reproduction, or much practical need for letterpress or gravure. The designer's main concern is with offset lithography, and four-color process reproduction is the greatest problem in relation to printing. If this can be dealt with properly, the other problems of printing seem minor.

With regard to actual press runs, the designer's job occasionally may include some color quality control. But modern web presses with computer-monitored register and color controls do a much better job of controlling register and color than a designer sitting at the end of the press. Most of the quality in color printing is determined long before press time and depends on: (a) good copy preparation, (b) careful planning of the color separations (screening for the exact combination of inks and paper planned for the job), and (c) careful correction of color proofs—or contact color images when proofs are not provided.

Copy preparation will be discussed in greater detail later on. As to the planning of separations, the offset-separation department of the printer (or the independent separators) should be made aware of the choice of paper before separations or screenings are done. The exact paper color (shade), surface gloss, and water absorptivity are important to color separating. The inks are generally not under publisher control except, perhaps, in regard to their general quality or cost. (The cost may somewhat affect the range they can cover, their brilliance, and their permanence.) But whether inks are expensive or inexpensive, they should be taken into account along with paper stock in matching the separations to the requirements of the job. All proofs, of course, should be pulled with the correct inks on the correct stock for the job, even though not usually on a production press. Production control may wish to specify recommended densitometer readings for the four process colors: wet (15 seconds), set (30 minutes), and dry (24 hours).

In spite of recent advances in color technology (scanners, computer-generated halftones, direct screening, and so on), color matching remains the art of adjusting separations and screening to the job conditions, especially the paper. There are mainly two distortions for which adjustment may be necessary, "hue error" and "grayness factor." These are present in almost any ink/paper combination. However, it is possible to evaluate paper shade, gloss, and water absorptivity and then to use this information in formulas that can predict the effect of the specific paper/ink combination during the press run.

Thus, the designer should realize that not all color problems can be solved by good copy preparation and proof correction. The printer needs to know the paper that will be used, and needs to *use* this knowledge properly. It is true that most book publishers do not pay top dollar for color separations, and often do not really expect high quality color work, except perhaps in art books. But there are several conditions that, if met, can ensure better quality than is generally seen, even for economical budgets.

1. Inform the printer of the paper choice early
2. Use the same lighting at publisher and printer to view both transparencies and reflected copy (reflected art and proofs)
3. Use care and system in marking corrections at proof stage, and *get* proofs whenever possible, rather than contact images.

The interdependency of the three process colors (not counting black) is greatest in the reproduction of grays. Muddy brown or blue grays, where copy shows neutral gray, is an immediate indication of the need for color adjustment. This is why a gray scale is often processed with proofs as a test. An unsatisfactory gray factor adjustment is commonly solved by actually screening the separations out of normal balance to compensate. In fact, if the screens are not shot to achieve proper adjustment for the ink/paper combination, no amount of adjustment of color strength on press is likely to be successful. Even if balance can be temporarily achieved with ink strength on press for the first run (under constant supervision for all forms), it is not likely to be duplicated successfully on subsequent printings.

The diagram of the standard Graphic Arts Technical Foundation color circle (Figure 10–2) shows the basic spectrum colors: red, blue, and green; and midway between these, the theoretically perfect process colors: cyan, magenta, and yellow. (The perfect cyan, for example, is halfway between green and blue.) Actual commercial inks, however, do not match these perfect process ideals. Approximately 90% of these inks fall in the shaded areas instead. This is the so-called hue error, least in the case of process yellows and greatest for the magentas. (As mentioned above, hue error and grayness factor can be compensated for by screening separations out of balance, if paper and ink combinations are known.)

Some four-color contact imaging systems compensate for hue error by providing several alternative cyans and magentas, as shown by the inner dots in the shaded areas. The figures indicate percentages of hue variance from the

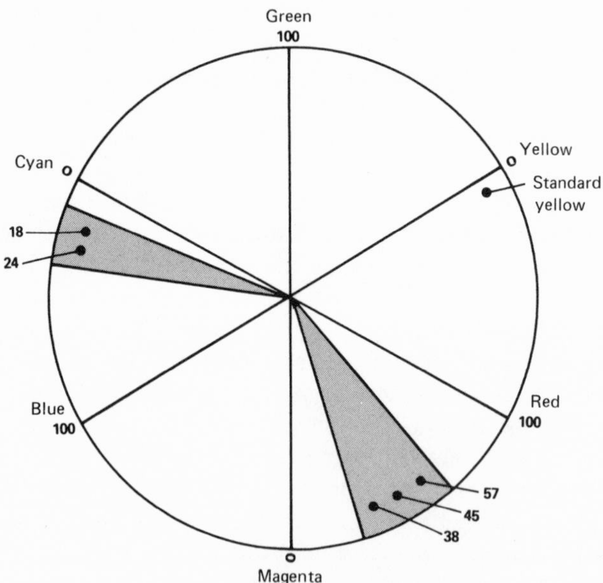

10-2 *A "color circle," showing spectrum colors, process ink colors, variances from ideal colors, and approximate placement of colors in a contact imaging color simulation system.*

perfect colors (5% variance is undetectable). These film magentas and cyans are matched to the inks to be used (when the contact images are made), thus providing an approximate indication of on-press result.

The proper evaluation of progressive proofs, particularly when neutral grays and color bars are included, can usually clear up problems of hue, overprint hue, and the gray balance so that the final balance needs little correction on press.

All color proofs, but particularly four-color process proofs, should be completely standardized for paper, inks, and the order and manner of proofing. Corrections to unstandard proofs (that cannot be closely duplicated on press) are of little value. But beyond that, the light conditions under which proofs are viewed must be standard at both printer and publisher. The conditions affecting the viewing of color copy and color proofs are these:

1. The publisher and printer should use the same controlled light sources for viewing transparent copy as are used for viewing reflected copy and proofs. The kind of light used for viewing affects the color. Other factors that affect the color are light intensity, reflectiveness of the viewed surface, evenness of illumination, and the surrounding room colors. Small, moderately priced, backlit, professional viewers with color temperature of 5000 degrees Kelvin are handy for transparencies. But standard viewing is also necessary for reflected copy and proofs. This is not so easily arranged, short of a standardized viewing system, which, while commercially obtainable, is not inexpensive. In any case even if standard lighting conditions are not available, viewing should still be, as nearly as possible, the *same* at both printer and publisher—under the same type of fluorescent bulbs, for example, in a darkened, neutral-colored room. Ordinary incandescent lamps should never be used. (See the table that follows on the appearance of colors under fluorescent lamps.)

2. The conditions under which publisher and printer view the book should be, as nearly as possible, the same as those under which the reader will view the book, especially in the case of schoolbooks. There are many fluorescent bulbs that can be used in classrooms, but probably the most common one in schools is the so-called cool white bulb with a Kelvin temperature of about 4200 degrees. The ANSI standard for graphic arts viewing is now 5000 degrees Kelvin, which is close to daylight but not an entirely satisfactory light in which to view schoolbook color. There are no completely satisfactory lighting conditions, of course, but some consideration can be given to using the cool white bulbs at printer and publisher, at least for schoolbooks, and especially if a standardized system is not available.

Correcting color proofs

Assuming the rare circumstance in which the printer has adjusted for hue error and gray factor in the ink/paper combination, the proofing has been done

APPEARANCE OF COLORS UNDER FLUORESCENT LAMPS

Color	Type of Lamp					
	Daylight	*Standard Cool White*	*Deluxe Cool White*	*Standard Warm White*	*Deluxe Warm White*	*Incan-descent Lamps*
Maroon	Dull	Dull	Dull	Dull	Fair	Good
Red	Fair	Dull	Dull	Fair	Good	Good
Pink	Fair	Fair	Fair	Fair	Good	Good
Rust	Dull	Fair	Fair	Fair	Fair	Good
Orange	Dull	Dull	Fair	Fair	Fair	Good
Brown	Dull	Fair	Good	Good	Fair	Good
Tan	Dull	Fair	Good	Good	Fair	Good
Golden yellow	Dull	Fair	Fair	Good	Fair	Good
Yellow	Dull	Fair	Good	Good	Dull	Fair
Olive	Good	Fair	Fair	Fair	Brown	Brown
Chartreuse	Good	Good	Good	Good	Yellowed	Yellowed
Dark green	Good	Good	Good	Fair	Dull	Dull
Light green	Good	Good	Good	Fair	Dull	Dull
Peacock blue	Good	Good	Dull	Dull	Dull	Dull
Turquoise	Good	Fair	Dull	Dull	Dull	Dull
Royal blue	Good	Fair	Dull	Dull	Dull	Dull
Light blue	Good	Fair	Dull	Dull	Dull	Dull
Purple	Good	Fair	Dull	Dull	Good	Dull
Lavender	Good	Good	Dull	Dull	Good	Dull
Magenta	Good	Good	Fair	Dull	Good	Dull
Gray	Good	Good	Fair	Soft	Soft	Dull

(From NAVDOCKS, DM-1, Feb. 1962.)

correctly, and both printer and publisher are viewing the proofs under the same lighting conditions, the designer still has to correct the color proofs (or color contact images). How does one go about this?

First of all, the designer looks for gross patterns of color shift; next, for subtle patterns of color shift; and lastly, for local colors that need correction. The designer does not rush in and start marking local corrections to individual pieces right away. Gross patterns of color imbalance are most easily spotted in color bars and gray scales that printers usually include on color proof sheets (particularly in the color overprint patches). If these tests are acceptable, the designer next compares all the original copy with the proof, under the correct lighting, before marking any of them, looking for any consistent pattern of color shift.

Almost always the color shift will be in the direction of cyan or magenta in combination with yellow. Yellow is too weak a color to be a danger, except in combination with one of the others. Black is neutral as far as color goes, but it can be too weak or too strong, too flat or too contrasty. In fact, black is not theoretically necessary when the other colors are in really good balance. Its main function is to correct or mask the gray-factor error, and to provide snap to the darker values of gray.

Only when an apparent color shift overall has been identified, or the balance has been approved overall, should more local corrections be undertaken. If this rule is not observed, the local color corrections may be ill-advised, as will be obvious.

In general, the designer should use visual language in ways that make corrections as clear as possible, rather than using technical language. The colors are referred to separately, and such requests as "+ 20% red" or "– 10% blue" are used to indicate added magenta or less cyan. Percentages are, however, somewhat tricky unless an exact area of approximately even color is specifically referred to. A 70 percent tone increased by 20 percent becomes an 84 percent tone, while a 20 percent tone increased by 20 percent becomes only a 24 percent tone. This is not always what is intended by this language, even though such usages are generally understood to be very approximate figures of speech. It is usually better to say something like "+ a little red" or "too much blue" or "solid yellow here." "Compare with the original again" is always understood.

The printer then corrects the screened separations by chemically reducing the size of positive dots to be made lighter, and by enlarging dots to be made darker (actually by reducing the dots in a negative and making a positive). After this, the work is re-proved, and the correction process continues, for as long as is practical for the desired result. The judgment and skill that the dot etcher can bring to the work are partially wasted unless the designer's intentions are made clear. If the copy has been properly prepared, the above steps adhered to, and revised proofs corrected until they are acceptable, then the designer is doing what is necessary and the color printing should be quite acceptable on the press.

But a further note is perhaps in order. No color reproduction is "correct," even though very careful reproduction of flat artwork done on white surfaces (such as water color) can come close. The most we are usually justified in saying is that it should be a reasonably satisfactory interpretation for the purpose. Some of the most admired color "reproduction" is a long way from the original, especially when color film originals are involved. To the objective eye, almost any transparency is a long way from its subject, even though the result may be an "improvement" on the original subject from some points of view. The designer's judgment (or that of the person at the color separation camera) is what represents these "other points of view."

What is most usually wanted is "more" than nature provides—more colorful effects than were present in real life, bluer blues, redder reds, and the like. Most color separators supply some of this "more" without being asked, as do the manufacturers of most color films. Kodachrome, for example, is a more colorful film than Anscochrome, and more successful. However, more of everything is apt to look cheap, which is not always desirable. The judgment of the designer should play a role in the somewhat selective search for "more" color. This will happen if the designer keeps in mind that the way in which natural colors are interpreted through film is somewhat arbitrary anyhow. The effect (what ends up in the book) is the proof of the pudding.

The general "philosophy" or approach to color separation should be discussed with the printer in relation to each set of color copy. This is entirely apart from all questions of fidelity to the originals and any adjustments. In a sense, this seems to prejudice all that we have been considering in the way of careful reproduction. This arbitrary modification of color is probably the least understood and least exercised area of color control, yet one of the most obvious and necessary. If the designer can afford the time, and the book can afford the expense, the designer can, in effect, modify the color reproduction as a painter modifies colors. For most books this is not called for, of course, and it can be costly. But a general discussion of the approach to each *set* of color copy with a knowledgable person close to the work of separating can sometimes produce dramatic improvements. The designer, in this way, sometimes may be able to use photographs that are unsatisfactory from the point of view of color, simply by modifying the color balance as necessary.

Rules of thumb for color copy

1. Use transparencies, when possible, rather than reflected art copy, but remember that the contrast range of transparencies cannot be reproduced in print. The contrast range of the transparency is often 1000 to 1, whereas that of the printed reproduction is seldom more than 60 to 1. The eye sees much more highlight and shadow detail in the transparency on the light box than can be held in print.

2. The transparency should be flatter, less contrasty than it should appear in reproduction, because reproduction increases contrast. For example, a 1:3 light-to-shadow contrast range in the transparency may often be increased to 1:4, 1:5, or 1:6 in reproduction. The black ink contributes a lot to this. The 1:3 range is a good safe range with which to start.

3. Avoid contrasty transparencies that have both highlight and shadow areas that should show detail in print. Reproduction cannot hold both, and one must be sacrificed at the expense of the other. (If the copy must be used, the designer can specify which detail is to be held.)

4. Use one method for communicating color matches or color changes. For example, a set of Kodak color-correction filters can be used in specification (e.g., "Sky to be transparency plus CC10 cyan filter"). All color changes in transparencies should be made by a competent professional working with 5000 Kelvin light, using retouching dyes compatible with the transparency dyes.

5. Nothing beats a proper exposure. The old adage "underexpose for repro-

duction" is no longer true, especially with electronic scanners. While underexposure may help some highlight details, it muddies the shadows.

Bindings

The designer is not concerned with most actual bookbinding operations. But modern bindings are primary sales tools, and are very much part of the designer's job in respect to their visual characteristics, which, in some cases, may depend heavily on some of their physical characteristics. Binding designs, of course, are: (a) preprinted on paper for "softbound" books, whether these are adhesive ("perfect") bound or Smyth-sewn; (b) preprinted on cloth or nonwoven synthetic material, which is wrapped around boards for "hardbound" books; and (c) stamped on cloth, paper, synthetic nonwoven material, or any combination of these.

Preprinted paper

Paper bindings are increasingly taking the place of hard bindings for educational books at many levels, especially the college level, and the design of these bindings is very important to the publisher. Major books often use full process color—the less important books, two or three flat colors. They are printed on cover-weight stocks, usually white. They may be press varnished, use high-gloss inks, or simply be of antique finish.

The designer allows the trimmed size, plus ⅛" all around, for the mechanical, and the bulk of the book is allowed for the spine (sometimes plus 1/16" for the rounding of the corners). The aesthetics of cover design are not the concern of this discussion. Let it suffice to say that paper bindings are generally more conservative than trade jackets, because their function is permanent rather than ephemeral. The book titles can be in smaller type, because these bindings will be lived with, but the overall impact is extremely important, even in traditionally conservative subject areas.

Preprinted cloth or nonwoven synthetic material

These are used mainly for hardbound schoolbooks and basic college books. If the material is cloth, it is usually white pyroxylin-impregnated cloth, especially finished for offset printing, although other colors and finishes are occasionally used. The printing characteristics of the white cloth are not greatly different from paper, and many of the same design considerations apply.

However, most of these hardbound books are intended to last far longer than paperbound books, whether the material used is cloth or one of the great variety of nonwoven synthetics. The wear and abuse to which schoolbooks are often subjected is a design consideration of real importance in relation to preprinted covers, in spite of the protective coating that is given the printed surface. The designer can minimize the apparent wear on corners and edges in various ways, especially by avoiding dark colors on maximum wear areas,

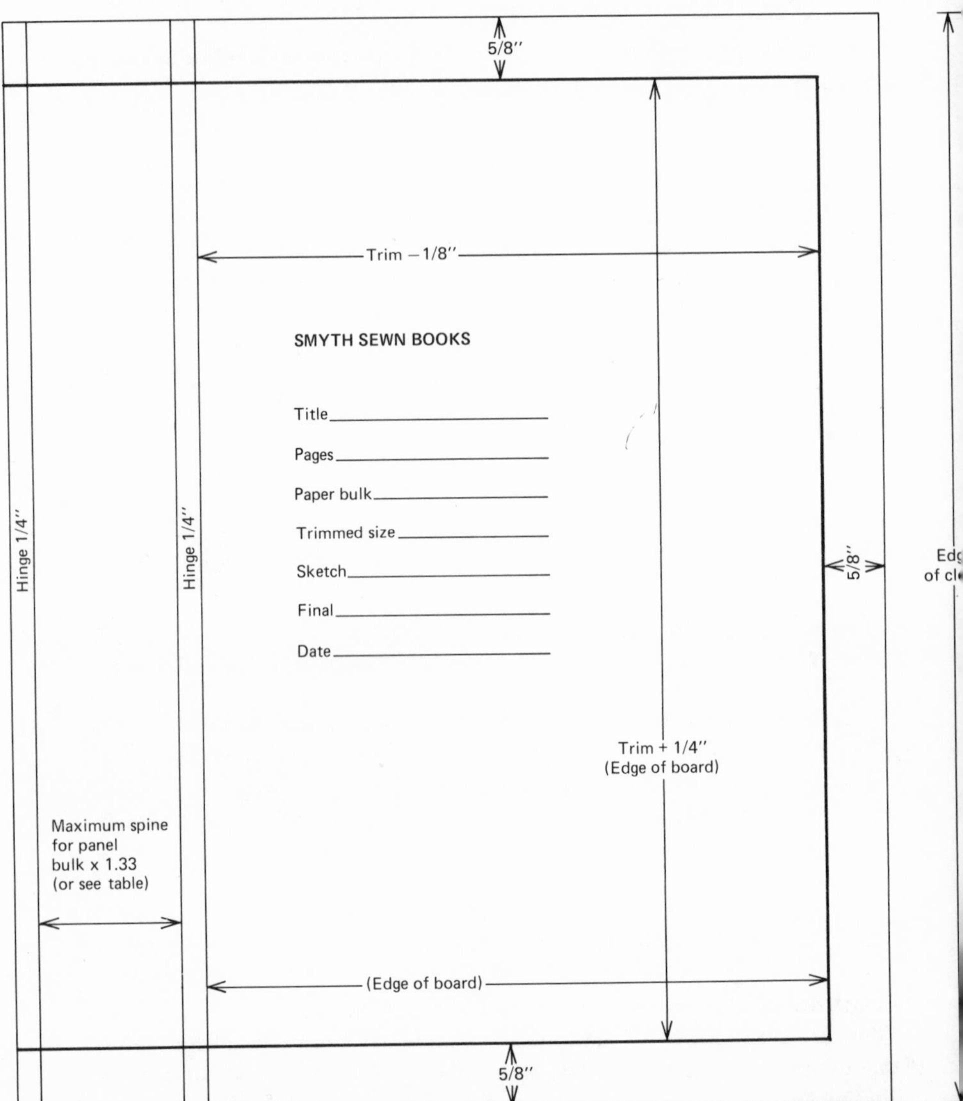

10-3 *A sizing guide for preprinted covers of Smyth-sewn books.*

and occasionally by the use of pattern, visual variety, or some other form of camouflage.

If the printed base material is a synthetic plasticized material, it is often possible to use almost any color, and to bond especially prepared inks to it chemically. This bonding is more of a production problem than a design problem. There are few restrictions on the design. Usually a considerable number of surface textures are available for synthetic materials, which the designer may specify. But the designer should bear in mind the wear problem

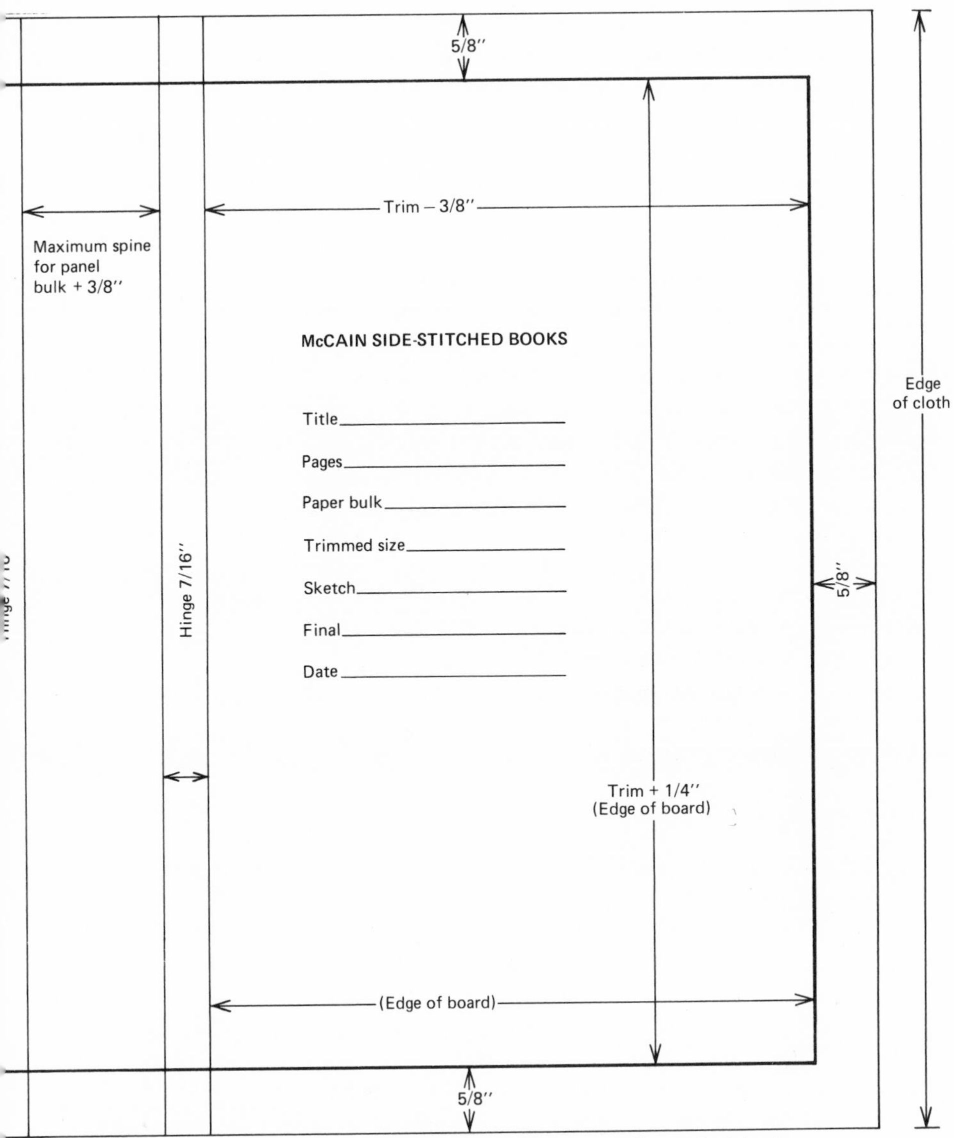

10-4 *A sizing guide for preprinted covers of McCain side-stitched books.*

inherent in surfaces that are too smooth, with or without bonding inks, and accept a surface with at least a minimum texturing to provide good wear characteristics.

For preprinted covers the cloth must be planned to wrap around the boards in the casemaking operation, prior to actual casing in. Layout plans are shown in Figures 10–3 and 10–4 for both Smyth-sewn and McCain-stitched (side-sewn) bindings.

The new binding process, known as "welding," does not greatly affect design considerations. "Side welding" corresponds to McCain side sewing, "saddle welding" to Smyth or saddle sewing, and "signature welding" to perfect binding. However, gutter margins and cross-gutter bleed allowances should be checked with the binder if welded binding is to be used.

Stamped covers

This is the traditional way of binding books. While preprinted covers usually derive their effects from the uses of printed color, typography, and design on a white base, stamped covers derive their effects from the color, texture, and surface of the base material, as well as from whatever stamped type and designs may be added to it. Colored and/or textured cloths, papers, and nonwoven synthetics may be used. Although the variety of book cloths has, in fact, been reduced in recent years, it is still considerable, and the number of synthetic materials, colors, and textures has greatly increased.

There is no point in attempting here to describe the various styles of cloth colors (traditionally "vellum" or solid colors, and "linen" or surface-textured colors), impregnation (traditionally "starch" or "pyroxylin"), surface (traditionally "natural," or rough, and "finished," or smooth), and weights (traditionally "A," or light, to "C," or heavier, plus "novel" cloths, "buckrams," etc.). The designer working on a stamped cover usually starts by consulting the sample books of suppliers of book covering materials (in the cost categories approved in the book budget). Finding some base material suitable for the book in question, the designer then decides what to put on it, and possibly some other material to combine with it. The covering may be only cloth, cloth and paper, only nonwoven, nonwoven and paper, cloth and nonwoven, or only paper (if it is especially prepared to bind books).

When paper is used with either cloth or nonwoven material, it is usually used for side panels (front and back). The width of the paper on the side may be discretionary, provided the pasted joint with the spine material is actually over the side board. These combination cases are termed "three-piece covers," and they must be manufactured on a special kind of binding equipment that feeds the strips for spine and sides onto boards during the casemaking process. Not all binders have this equipment, hence this point needs to be cleared ahead of time. Naturally, the three-piece cases must be manufactured before they can be stamped, as opposed to preprinted covers, which must be printed before the cases can be made.

The stamping of cases may be done with inks or foils, and while there is no restriction on the colors of ink that may be used, the designer is limited in foil colors to those that are manufactured by the suppliers of foil. For ink stamping the limits are rather those of ink coverage and the degree of detail practically obtainable. A light color of ink will not cover a dark color of cloth in one impression. Blind stamping may be used to smooth the cloth for color application, but for economy's sake, the designer is usually restricted to a limited number of "hits" or impressions per book cover. Inks have been used, traditionally, for color panels or areas upon which to stamp foil, either on spine or on the front cover.

Ink stamping of type is a cruder process than printing on paper. The designer should not attempt to stamp small type sizes in ink when there are small interior "counters" to the letters that may fill up on the stamping press, such as in the lowercase "e" or "a." Small sizes are especially undesirable when more than one hit may be required. The registration of successive hits of ink is often not perfect because the entire cover is fed into the press. It is more awkward than paper to feed, and its edges are not as perfect.

Unlike ink stamping, which is done cold and in the manner of regular letterpress printing, foil colors must be stamped under heat to enable them to release properly from the foil backing and bond to the stamped surface. Stamping is usually done with brass dies to resist the heat, pressure, and wear. Foil may be stamped on any base, on ink, or on other foil (heavy foils called "panel foils"). Second impressions of foil are not required to secure good coverage.

Foils are available in a variety of metallic and pigmented colors and surfaces. The sample books of foil suppliers must be consulted and an exact product description given. For example, there are many "colors" and kinds of "gold" foil, "bronze," and aluminum ("silver"). It is not sufficient to specify "gold" or "aluminum" or "bronze." The maker and number must be specified. (Note: The plastic foils often shown in manufacturer's specimens are made to bond with plastics, usually in various packaging applications. Some of these may bond with nonwoven plastic book covering materials. The plastic foils usually stamp at considerably higher temperatures than most other foils.) Different foil manufacturers make their foils to stamp at somewhat different temperatures, but normal range is often about 210–250 degrees, with plastic foils nearer 300 degrees.

Each separate impression of ink or foil means an extra pass through a press, which is expensive.* But while each impression of ink must be made separately, several colors of foil may often be combined into one impression, thus maintaining economy. To combine foil colors, the designer must plan the way in which they are to be used, according to the general rules of stamping. Foil is charged for by the square inch, and the amount of foil and the cost per impression can be roughly calculated. The following factors are to be kept in mind when planning foil stamping:

*There are "multiple head" stamping presses, but these are essentially multiple presses mounted in a line.

1. Covers can be fed into the stamping press in either direction, that is, endwise or sidewise. The foils are fed onto the stamping surface from rolls mounted in parallel above the stamping press. Usually rolls are fed only in one direction, but sometimes they can be fed in two directions at right angles to each other.
2. Several different foils may be stamped at the same time, provided the elements to be stamped are at least 3/16″ apart. Very occasionally problems may arise in combining foils that stamp at different temperatures. (Bronze, for example, stamps at rather higher temperatures than most other metallic foils.)
3. The length of foil from each roll that is required to stamp each cover is termed a "pull," and while the designer is quite unlikely to be limited as to the total number of foil rolls that can be used (up to 7 or 8), there is usually a limit of 3 pulls. In the unlikely event that the designer wants six colors of foil, several of them may need to utilize the same length pull that is used by other foils.
4. If separate design elements can be designed to stamp from separate foil rolls, then economy and color flexibility is maintained. But if they must stamp from the same roll, then they must, of course, be the same color—and also (usually) be reasonably close together if they are not to waste excessive foil between them on the pull. The pull must be long enough to include them both.

   The exception to this rule is that "skips" can sometimes be arranged so that a shorter pull can stamp a "forward" design element, while the "following" design element is skipped into a blank area in the stamping foil left by the pull length (see Figure 10–5). The designer can roughly plan skips by using tracing paper, making trial pull diagrams, and moving the tracing paper the length of the pull over the design elements, to see whether a skip can be utilized with any given length of pull and positioning of the elements. This planning of skips is tricky unless the designer is familiar with the stamping press to be used, and any skip plan is subject to approval by the binder.

The most common way of using foils is to make a relatively simple scheme for the spine, in which 2 or 3 parallel color rolls are utilized economically by the design. For example, the title may be in one color, author in another,

10-5 (Top) *A generalized diagram of the foil stamping operation showing foil rolls feeding down over brass dies on the press bed. The cover will be stamped onto the brass dies, transferring the foil from the rolls to the cover.* (Below) *Diagrammatic representation of the economical use of foil, utilizing a "skip" pattern and a short "pull" to avoid wasting foil between stamped elements.*

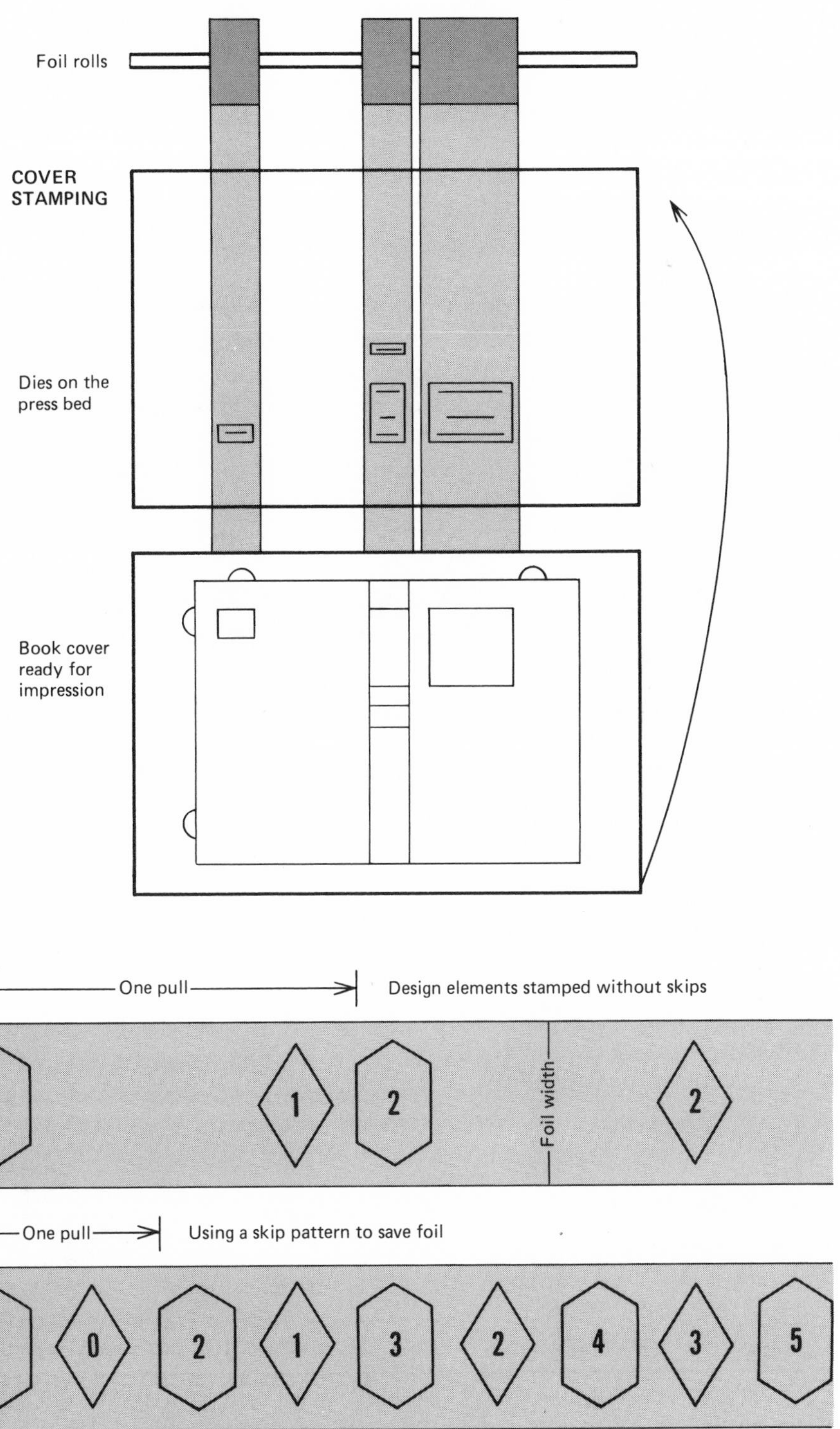

Foil rolls
COVER STAMPING
Dies on the press bed
Book cover ready for impression
One pull
Design elements stamped without skips
Foil width
1
1
2
2
One pull
Using a skip pattern to save foil
1
0
2
1
3
2
4
3
5

and publisher in a third. The case is fed into the press sideways. (If there is a design on the front cover, it may be positioned close to the spine in order not to waste foil.) Alternatively, the spine stamping may be all in one color and the side in another color, in which case the cover would be fed endwise. (See Figure 10–5.)

For stamped books the mechanics of fitting are as follows:

a) The front and back panel is the size of the boards, which are usually ¼" longer than the height of the trim (⅛" top and bottom), and ⅛" less than the trim in width. These are the maximum side panel dimensions for stamping. It is not advisable to run either ink or foil stamping off the edge of the board.

b) If there are panel dies for the spine, the maximum width for these on Smyth-sewn books is given by the formula (use 1/16" for convenience):

$$\text{Spine panel width} = \text{bulk} \times 1.33$$

c) Maximum width of spine lettering is panel width minus ⅛", or 1/16" each side for safety.

d) If there are "fillet lines" running across the spine, these will be the same width, approximately, as the panel die. However, for safety's sake, they are usually made a little longer, and the binder cuts them down if

RELATION OF MAXIMUM SPINE WIDTH TO BULK (SMYTH-SEWN BOOKS)*

Bulk (in.)	*Spine width (in.)*	*Bulk (in.)*	*Spine width (in.)*
1/4	3/8	1–11/16	2–3/16
5/16	1/2	1–3/4	2–5/16
3/8	9/16	1–13/16	2–3/8
7/16	5/8	1–7/8	2–7/16
1/2	11/16	1–15/16	2–1/2
9/16	3/4	2	2–5/8
5/8	7/8	2–1/16	2–11/16
11/16	15/16	2–1/8	2–3/4
3/4	1	2–3/16	2–13/16
13/16	1–1/8	2–1/4	2–15/16
7/8	1–3/16	2–5/16	3
15/16	1–1/4	2–3/8	3–1/16
1	1–5/16	2–7/16	3–1/8
1–1/16	1–7/16	2–1/2	3–1/4
1–1/8	1–1/2	2–9/16	3–5/16
1–3/16	1–9/16	2–5/8	3–3/8
1–1/4	1–11/16	2–11/16	3–7/16
1–5/16	1–5/8	2–3/4	3–9/16
1–3/8	1–13/16	2–13/16	3–5/8
1–7/16	1–7/8	2–7/8	3–11/16
1–1/2	2	2–15/16	3–3/4
1–9/16	2–1/16	3	3–13/16
1–5/8	2–1/8		

*Maximum spine width on side-stitched books is, for practical purposes, simply bulk plus 3/8".

necessary. They can be made the width of the panel plus ⅛″ (1/16″ extra each side).

The formula, bulk times 1.33, is accurate for practical purposes, for books bulking ½″ to 2½″. But to cover extremes of bulk, and to make calculation unnecessary, the table opposite may be used for panel width. (Note: In practice, binders differ in the amount of "round" they put on spines, which may result in variations of as much as 1/16″ or even ⅛″ in maximum spine width.)

Paper manufacturers provide tables that give bulks for their papers, for books of various lengths. However, even though the designer may seldom have occasion to figure bulks, it is well to know how this is done if no tables or other sources of information are available.

1. Measure four thicknesses of paper with a caliper. One point is 1/1000 inch. (Surely everyone carries a caliper!)
2. 8000 / caliper points = pages per inch
3. Bulk (sixteenths of an inch) $= \dfrac{\text{(Book pages / pages per inch)}}{.0625}$

BINDING SPECIFICATIONS
FOR HARDBOUND STAMPED COVERS Date________

Publisher ____________________________ Designer__________

Binder____

Title_____________________________ Author________________

____One-piece ____Two-piece ____Three-piece ____Other

____

Spine material____

Front material ____________________________ Back__________

Spine stamping ____

____

Front stamping ____

____

Endpapers____

Head and footbands _______________________ Top stain_________

Head and footbands, endpapers, and top stain complete the binding specifications picture for trade books that are hardbound. Softbound books use none of these. Textbooks almost never use top stain, though they may use head and footbands and endpapers.

Obviously all elements of the binding are coordinated by the designer. To find out what head and footband materials are available, the designer must consult the manufacturer's list. To specify top stain, the designer provides a color swatch or a color-system number, or both. The specifications for binding materials go to the binder along with reproduction copy for dies, pasted up accurately to show position of the design elements on the spine and side panels. Binding Specifications for Hardbound Stamped Covers is a typical memo form to the binder.

BMI specifications

Since the 1930s, BMI (Book Manufacturers Institute) specifications have controlled many of the physical materials and some of the typography used in elementary and high school textbooks planned for sale in states having statewide textbook buying or "adoption" agencies. Texas alone, for example, has such a buying system and is reputed to spend over $25,000,000 annually on statewide adoption materials.

These BMI specifications affect chiefly paper, printing, and binding material specifications: paper permanence, strength, opacity, gloss, color, and weight; endpapers, reinforcements, sewing, stitching, adhesives, binders' board weights, the acceptability of cover materials; inks and foils for stamping; thread strength, etc., together with methods of testing and means of standards maintenance.

The only such specifications that affect the designer directly are the book margin requirements and those concerning cover materials, inks, and foils. Margin specifications (like most BMI specifications) are different for different classes and sizes of books, and they apply to the normal text-page margins, rather than to illustrations or to occasional marginal elements, folios, and so on. Nonbleed pictures are required to have at least ¼″ net margins.

BMI specifications change from time to time, and the latest information should be consulted. For example, nonwoven cover materials were not allowed for a long time, but now they are allowed. The production department of a textbook publisher will have the latest set of specifications.

It should be noted that BMI specifications are more properly referred to as NASTA specifications (National Association of State Textbook Administrators). The Book Manufacturers Institute is one of four other industry and educational groups cooperating in maintaining the specifications, which are indeed useful, both in maintaining good manufacturing standards and in preventing conflict and fragmentation in state specifications that could result, as it did in the past, in confused and inefficient manufacturing requirements for publishers and manufacturers.

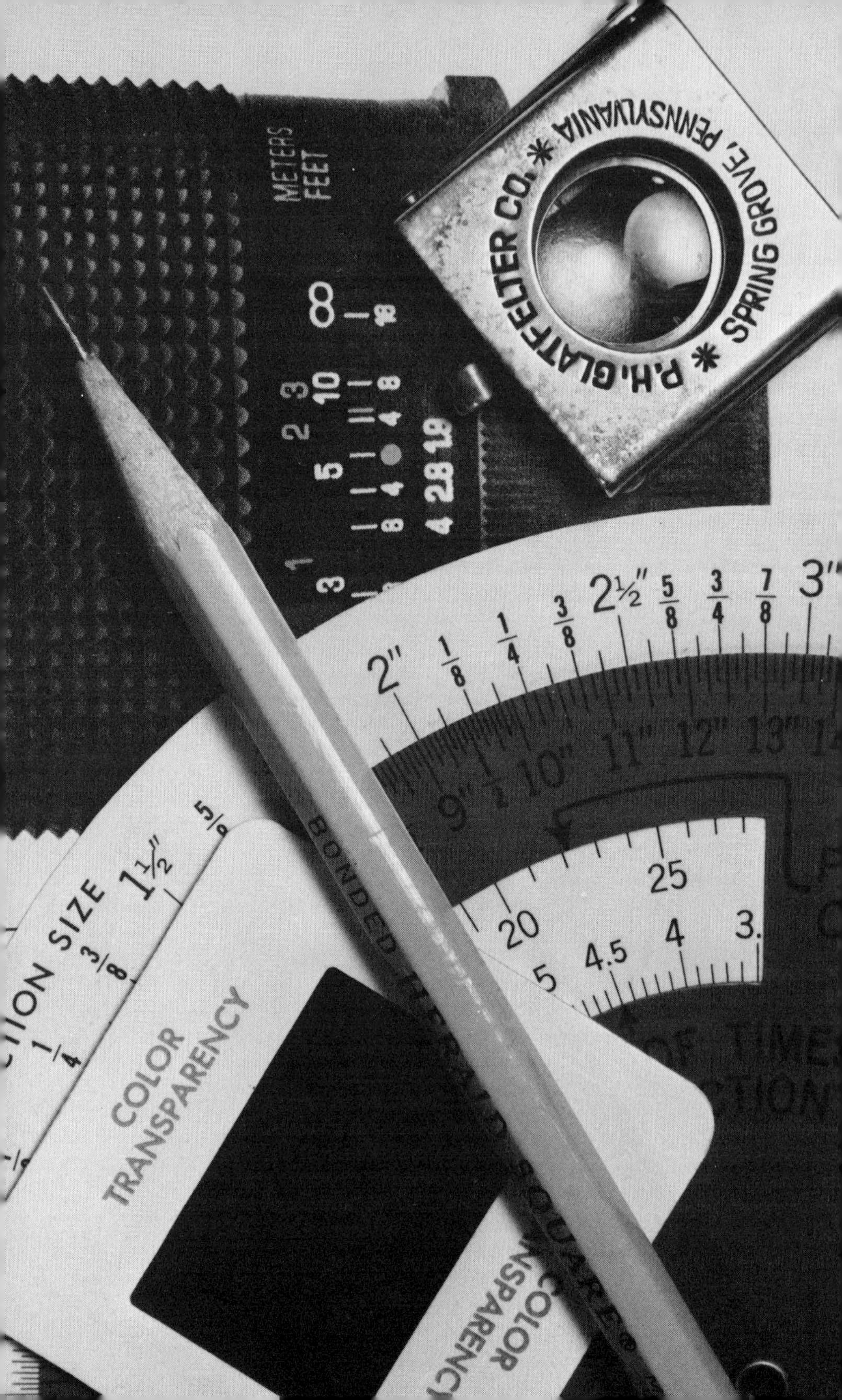

METERS
FEET
P.H. GLATFELTER CO. * SPRING GROVE, PENNSYLVANIA *
2" 1/8 1/4 3/8 2½" 5/8 3/4 7/8 3"
9" 10" 11" 12" 13"
20 25
5 4.5 4 3.
SIZE 1½"
COLOR TRANSPARENCY
COLOR TRANSPARENCY
BONDED

CHAPTER 11
The Processing of Illustrations

The processing of illustrations is one of the major responsibilities of the designer and the art department. For the complex book it is full of details and must be well planned and orderly at every stage in order not to get out of hand. Losing so much as a 35mm transparency can be very expensive both in time and money. Orderly work habits are invaluable, and a clear idea of work flow and supplier requirements is essential.

Before going on to discuss the more technical aspects of the processing of pictures, we may briefly review typical steps in working with artwork and artists. (Some of these were described in a different context in Chapter 8, "Design Processing of Complex Texts," as part of the duties of the art editor or assistant designer.)

Artists and artwork

1. The designer reviews possible artists and finds one, or as many as needed, who is suitable for the job and acceptable both to the designer and to the editor.

2. A meeting is arranged with the artist, designer, editor, and art editor during which the general needs and philosophy of the book are conveyed.

3. A general memo is drawn up by the designer and production control covering technical aspects of the work to be done: printing process, illustration numbering method (to be used also by the artists), scale for reduction of originals to reproduction size, allowances for bleeds and gutter, overlay materials and inks, nonprocess color separation and tint laying (by an artist or offset

camera), registration marks and their placement, artistic medium, labeling or other type (who supplies it and who pays for it), who is to do any necessary research, and so on. Some aspects of this memo are also covered by the artist's contract, but not all—and artists often do not read contracts very carefully.

4. The artist's contract is drawn up and signed before the work is started. (See the sample contract at the end of this chapter.) This establishes the anticipated number of pieces, payment, responsibilities, rights, schedules, and so on. It should be approved as necessary and a copy made for each of the following: the artist, the editorial department, the book file, and the contracts supervision department, if any. Total contracts should be within the book's art budget.

5. For each illustration basic specifications are supplied covering: size, in inches, after reduction; color availability, with swatches, or color-system number for nonprocess colors; and illustration number, as per the illustration list.

6. Subject matter and editorial/artistic specifications are often given somewhat differently for technical and for nontechnical books:

a. *Technical books.* Specifications are usually written on separate sheets as concisely as possible. All notes and specifications from author or editor are included. Reference sources are cited if they are needed. Label copy is given exactly and is copy edited and generally styled for typography before going to the artist. The designer may add notes on matters of design concern (see Chapter 2). When a part of the manuscript is relevant to the illustration, it may be copied and included, but this usually is not necessary for technical art.

b. *Nontechnical books.* Specifications may be partly oral, but it is the job of the person assigning the work to get the information across. The essentials of subject matter, tone, emphasis, and so on, should be noted in writing. The artist should have a copy of the dummy page or galley to be illustrated and access to the entire chapter, selection, or book, in some form. On the dummy page key words or passages relating to the illustration may be circled or underlined, and additional notes can be added, references cited, dangers or taboos clarified, and so on.

7. When a sizable batch of artwork is assigned, it is often a good idea to make a brief list of illustrations for the artist and to make a copy for the files. The date the work is assigned should be noted, as well as the dates that sketches and finished art are due. The list should bear the name and telephone number of the person assigning the art.

8. As the art is assigned, the person assigning it should go over the details verbally to clear up any ambiguities.

9. Style samples, in rough and finish, are usually submitted by the artist for approval on the first four or five pieces before going ahead with the entire job.

10. The art traffic of sketches, finishes, and approval by designer, editor, and sometimes author (especially if any technical work is involved) is all handled by the person keeping the illustration list, usually the art editor.

11. If plans change and a new artist's contract is necessary, one should be drawn up. This is usually not necessary for changes in schedule but only for substantial changes in the number of units or unit payment, artist default, reassignment of work, and so on. Usually pro rata adjustment suffices without a new contract.

12. As rough and final art is processed (as in Item 10) it is turned over to production control, in batches. All pieces of art and all overlays should bear the correct illustration number, and the name of the book should be written or stamped on the back of each piece of art.

13. Contact images (blues, etc.) or illustration proofs are checked as they come from the separator or from the printer's camera department. (For aspects of process-color work see Chapter 10.)

14. Late changes and repairs are made, as necessary, either by the artist or by an in-house art department.

15. At the end of the job, or as agreed upon, payments are made to artists; an artists' acknowledgment list is compiled, copy edited, and submitted to editorial; and all original art is collected and prepared for storage.

Illustrations in the offset process

Various aspects of the offset process relevant to the processing of illustrations also may be summarized, as follows:

1. Sample pages may be required in multiple copies, and with printed illustrations if they are important to the design of an important book. Otherwise a set or two of photostats may be pasted in spaces allowed. (Note: If only photocopied black samples are required, 100-line screened stats or Veloxes will duplicate fairly well. If, at the other extreme, full color is required, a nonrepro-quality Kodak type C print can be used for critical large sizes; for small sizes, even ordinary drugstore color prints can be pasted up for one or two sets. If nonprocess color is important to the illustrations or to display type, it can be incorporated into sample pages by means of one of the systems of contact color imaging (see Item 6 below). If the samples are sufficiently important they can be press proved. Even if this is not resorted to, it should be remembered that the samples for important books and series are, in fact, rather elaborate concoctions best handled by an art department or studio having access to color keying, overlay film colors, matting, and the variety of presentation techniques now available.

2. If book composition is being done on a film composition system (or one that may optionally produce film), the illustrations may appear in page proofs —or even in galleys—if they are ready. If composition is done on a paper base or via reproduction proofs on paper, the illustrations are stripped in after the page makeup is completed and then photographed. A film compositor who regularly incorporates illustrations into pages may do the illustration camera

work, but more often it is done by a lithographic camera or separation company and then supplied to the compositor (or supplied directly to the printer if the compositor is not the printer). Occasionally continuous tone or screened film separations may be supplied from another job or from another source of illustration, such as advertisements. The film should be checked for condition and compatibility of screening when it is received.

3. Considerably more latitude is present in the treatment of illustrations for offset than for letterpress. In particular, the edges of halftones are not subject to the same wear and damage on press. Silhouettes and vignettes are practical as well as drop-out halftones, in which the highlight dots are dropped entirely. Combination effects, using type with halftones, color, and line art, are more easily achieved. The result of this increased flexibility in offset is that more visually complex work tends to be planned and executed for offset than for letterpress, and more mechanicals are done in the publishing house, or at least under the designer's control and supervision. Offset contact imaging, such as blues, brown lines, and so on, are usually provided sized, but without the film having been cut to size. (Four-color process images may be masked to size, but the film is not cut.) Thus, in offset the cropping (but not the scaling) can be changed without remaking the illustration, at the time proofs are checked. This provides an extra element of control and adjustment that is not present in letterpress, where cuts can only be trimmed if adjustment is needed.

4. For the preparation of mechanicals see the Standard Instructions for Handling Picture Sections and Mechanicals on page 205.

5. Color composites for offset (to save money and sometimes to correct color) may be obtained when several pieces of color appear on the same page. A layout of the page, on an accurate dummy sheet, is made, showing the exact positions of all the illustrations and indicating sizes, spaces between, and so on. Individual transparencies (or reflective copy) are cropped, scaled, and usually stats to size are pasted into the layout, in position, or keyed to it. Stats, copy, and layouts are given to a color lab, with general instructions concerning color compensations, balance, retouching, and so on. The lab makes corrected color-transparency copies to scale and masks them into one composite color assembly, which is eventually shot as one piece by the lithographer or separator.

6. Contact-imaging processes provide checks on the assembly stages of book production. Throughout this book the traditional term "blues" is often used for any form of contact imaging. But the more general term "contact imaging" refers not only to blues, silver prints, brown-line prints, Van Dykes, and so on, but to any system of providing a contact proof from positive or negative film, to show any and all colors in proper register and placement—whether or not the particular system attempts to show "true" or process colors.

The term "blues" is perhaps the simplest shorthand for this process because of the variety of privately owned trade names that now exist for contact imaging, and the continued change and development that may be expected in these methods. In fact, because blues are the most traditional, cheapest, and easiest form of contact imaging, they are usually requested, particularly in the form of "folded blues" for press forms, even when one of the film contact imaging systems is also used for color breakdown.

As has been mentioned, offset color work is often separated, and sometimes stripped to forms, by an independent color separator, and then shipped to the printer. Production control requires checks, in some form of contact images, at each step along the route from compositor to press.

7. In regard to full process color contact imaging, there are several systems that can provide the first stage of "proof" in color—which sometimes may be the only stage, when time is short. The images simulate full color either by film process color overlays or by color transfers to a base. (The reader is reminded of the discussion of color and color correcting, and the color circle, in the last chapter.) It may not be economically justifiable to color prove a small number of relatively noncritical color pieces, but color imaging is not the equivalent of press proving with correct inks and paper, even when the system offers several magenta and cyan choices.

Two- and three-color art is seldom color proved. On the other hand, composite paper contact images showing color and black on one sheet are hard to read and seldom satisfactory. If film contact imaging is not used because of the expense, at least the paper contacts should be separated for color. They can be checked on a light table, although registration of paper contacts will not be as accurate as film contacts because of paper distortion. Film contact imaging should always be requested for complex mechanicals, with colors as accurate as is practical.

8. If the compositor is a film compositor, page blues are supplied with illustrations and tints in place—or if color is involved and the job can stand the expense, separated and near-correct color imaging can be supplied.

If the compositor is a paper-base compositor and not a film compositor, spaces are left for illustrations in page makeup. Tints to be laid, illustrations to come, and typographic color breakup are noted in the master set, and scaled blues of the illustrations are supplied. After pages are approved editorially, blues of the illustrations are cropped exactly and may, if necessary, be pasted into a duplicate set of pages by the publisher's art editor or designer. If the illustrations are not critical, they may be cropped and keyed for the compositor and general instructions for placement given. Mechanicals are made for any pages not covered by page proof and for pages altered considerably from repros. All pages are checked for color breaks, tints to be added are carefully indicated, and each page is marked with all necessary instructions. Blanket instructions are risky.

As may be appreciated, film composition has real advantages during the paging stages of complex books. In combination with film contact imaging in near-correct colors (over 50 colors are often available), this is the most luxurious way to go. But not often the cheapest.

Composite contact images (paper or film) are the final check stage for offset, prior to platemaking and press sheets. All marked pages and other mechanicals supplied by the publisher should be returned by the separator and printer for checking. Everything must be marked that does not appear as it should appear in the book, as to position, size, color, completeness, and so on. There is no plate proof in offset as there is in letterpress. The next step is the printed sheet.

9. Approximate comparative costs are given below for various types of artwork and photographs of comparable size, including *all* costs for the original copy, the camera work, corrections, and press plates. (The costs for black and white halftone are used as a base of 1.0.)

Black only	
Halftone photo	1.0
Artwork line cut	1.4
Artwork halftone	1.8
Two-color	
Halftone (flat color tint)	1.7
Artwork line cut	2.1
Artwork halftone	2.6
Duotone photo	4.2
Four-color process	
Artwork (preseparated)	12.0
Artwork (not preseparated)	12.5
Halftone (from photo transparency)	12.5*

These indexes are, of course, merely representative, and actual costs may vary widely owing to many factors. Sometimes premium prices are paid for originals, while at other times they are obtained free; in-house photography can greatly alter the price of transparencies or black and white photos, and so on.

Further notes on the handling of illustrations

As noted before, the number given to the illustration on the illustration list is the identifying number used for all stages of processing and by all people, up to the time the illustration appears in page proof with its final number (if any). Artwork, photos, galley references, page references, any contact images, correspondence, payments, and so on all use the illustration list number.

All illustrations with overlays, combinations, surprints, and two-color mechanicals of any kind must have registration marks or corner marks. These

*No retouching is allowed for on transparencies.

should not be far outside the area of the art, but should be clearly identifiable as register marks. Printed-tape register marks are available. Artists should be required to put on their own register marks.

Scaling and cropping

The art editor or assistant designer usually scales and crops illustration material, unless the designer prefers to do it. All dimensions are given in inches. When a specific space in a layout is to be filled with a photograph, the easiest way to accomplish this is to take the diagonal of the rectangle available (allowing space for the caption, if any, and spaces around the photo) using tracing paper. Transfer this visually variable proportion to the photograph and crop to best advantage, marking the critical dimension as invariable and the less critical dimension as variable in one direction (see Figure 11-1).

When the space has not been determined by the layout or dummy, reverse this process: crop the photograph to best advantage first, then take the diagonal of the cropping, using tracing paper, and transfer this to the layout or dummy sheet (marking the critical dimension as invariable and the less critical dimension as variable in one direction). The proportional scale of inches can be used, if necessary, to check the dimensions. The circular plastic scale is handy.

For most pictures that can be cropped at all, there is one dimension that is critical, usually a dimension that should match something else, column or page width, another picture width (as when two pictures appear one above the other), and so on. As noted above, it is usually safest to specify both dimensions, but owing to the rules of proportion it is not usually possible to specify both with perfect accuracy to an even sixteenth of an inch. One of them usually has to vary slightly, and if any scaling error exists, perhaps a bit more than slightly. The error, if any, should be assignable only to the noncritical dimension, and to the side of that dimension on which it will have the least critical effect. The best way of indicating all this is simply to specify both dimensions as accurately as possible and then say "crop top" or "crop bottom" if the noncritical dimension is the depth; or "crop left" or "crop right" if the noncritical dimension is the width.

In laying out a number of pictures on a page, it is worthwhile, after having determined the general sizing and positioning, to find out which overall dimension is critical. If the pictures in the widest row add up to being tighter in relation to the available width than the pictures in the deepest column in relation to the available depth, then the width is the critical dimension. Otherwise it is the depth. Once the critical dimension is known the available space for that dimension is divided appropriately first. Then the other croppings can be done.

Laying out a page of many pictures can usually be best accomplished by deciding: (1) which subjects are most important, (2) what relationships other less important subjects should have to the most important ones, (3) which

CROPPING PHOTOGRAPHS TO SCALE

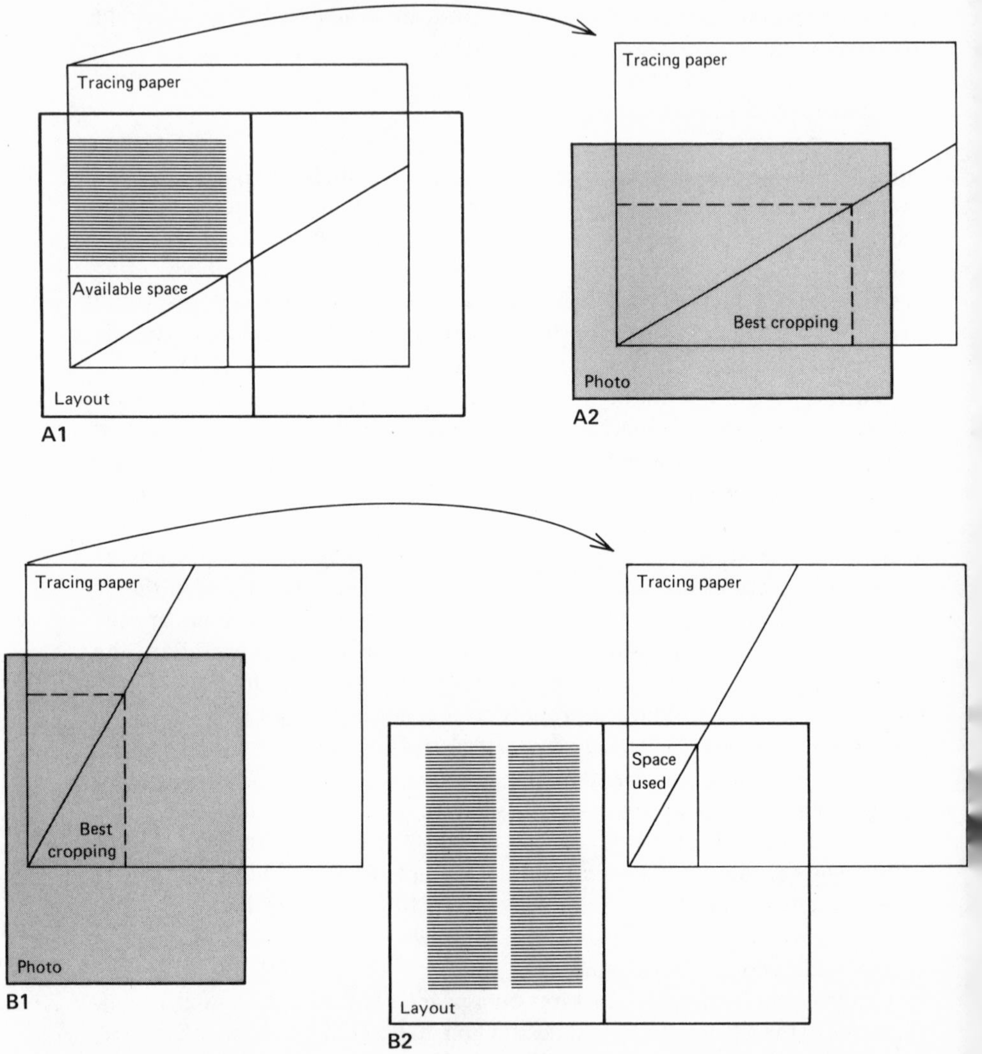

11-1 *The sizing of photographs: (A) the diagonal of the available space is transferred to the photograph, where the best same-proportional cropping is found, and (B) the best cropping is found on the photograph, and its diagonal then defines the as-yet unspecified space in the layout.*

dimension is critical (unless that is obvious on the face of it), (4) how to divide up the critical dimension, (5) how to divide up the noncritical dimension, and (6) what alignments to create. Legend space, of course, must be allowed. If each legend is always below the photograph it can be counted as part of it; if not, space must be reserved appropriately elsewhere.

Black and white photographic prints are scaled by marking on the borders with Stabilo or grease pencil. (The Stabilo is less easily rubbed off.) Photographs should not be covered with tracing paper to show cropping or squaring because there is a temptation to write on the overlay with the photo underneath, thus damaging it. It is also hard to register and is easily lost. If there is no border on the photo, fasten strips of paper to the back with masking tape, letting the strip show along the edges of the copy. Mark croppings on that. If cropping, squaring, or other instructions are complicated, make a photocopy on an office copier and mark all instructions carefully on that.

Color transparencies are marked with temporary scaling, for a photostat, with grease pencil on the sleeve of the transparency. The photostat is marked for sizing, cropping, and any other instructions concerning reproduction. (Note: All 35mm transparencies selected for use should be provided with an acetate sleeve, which should be taped to a larger piece of stiff paper. Other sizes of transparencies come from color-lab processing with sleeves of their own). The 35 mm transparency mounts should not be marked unless the transparencies are company property. (When more than one transparency is to go on one page, consider having color composites made, as explained above.)

Artwork scaling is put on by the artist and checked by the designer or art editor. For letterpress engravers, but seldom for offset camera, "flats" are sometimes prepared of grouped line illustrations to be reduced in the same scale. The grouped illustrations are shot at one time, and this can result in savings to the publisher. Photographs should be grouped for camera only when they are of the same tonality.

In sizing illustrations (or flats), the actual long dimension of a drawing is used. It is marked in inches. This is usually less likely to be misunderstood than saying "1/3 off" or "reduce 25%," and so on. If percentage terminology is to be used at all, it is much clearer to say "66% of copy" or "50% of copy." If a flat is made, it is important that all illustrations be the same reduction and have the same weight board so that they can go into a camera vacuum frame properly.

Bleed allowances

In sizing photos or art, ⅛″ trim is allowed for bleed. Thus a full page bleed measures trimmed size plus ¼″ deep and trimmed size plus ⅛″ wide. Gutter "bleeds," however, require varying allowances depending on the type of binding used for the book. Most hardbound trade, high school, and college books are Smyth sewn, while many elementary books are McCain or side stitched.

An increasing number of trade and college books are "perfect" (adhesive) bound.

For Smyth-sewn books, gutter bleeds on one page only need no additional allowance for the gutter. Cross-gutter bleeds need no additional space unless the illustration contains type or important detail that might be hard to read in the gutter (e.g., maps). To allow for some loss in the gutter, an allowance of ⅛″ on each side (¼″ total) is made by splitting the illustration and moving it into the page on each side.

For side-stitched books, gutter bleeds on one page only lose 5/16″ under the stitching, and no important details should appear within ¾″ of the fold. Cross-gutter bleeds should be split and made narrower by 5/16″ on each side (⅝″ total). A photostat of an illustration that crosses a gutter should be split, cropped, and properly positioned in the dummy as a guide to the printer in making up pages.

Perfect-bound books lose 3/16″ in the gutter, ⅜″ cross-gutter.

Artists should be advised of these adjustments.

Mounting and retouching photos

When original photos or photo prints are ordered they should be specified double-weight glossy with borders, usually "full-negative." It is much easier to crop than to have to get a new photo because you need a little more copy on one side.

Photos should not be mounted, unless absolutely necessary for extensive retouching (e.g., airbrushing), or because the print is cracked and liable to further damage. If mounting is necessary, mount photos only on a dry mount press, unless they are relatively expendable. Mounting with rubber cement will in time discolor and damage the photo. In any case, *always* copy all information on the back of the photo onto the mount *before* mounting!

Retouching of black and white prints is often desirable. Few prints do not, at least, need spotting. This should be done with retouching colors to match the color tone of the print. Opaque whites or blacks that do not match the reflectivity of the print surface should be avoided, if possible, because they may pick up in reproduction.

Retouching of color transparencies is very critical and should only be done by a specialist working on a *duplicate* transparency with proper dyes. Color labs will make duplicate transparencies and retouch them. Scratches and damage can be repaired, but if a specific overall color shift is wanted it will usually be better for the color separator to do it. Carefully masked color duplicates are expensive, and every time copy goes through another set of lenses and another film stage there is some loss, distortion, and possibly unpleasant surprises. If color composites are being made for the sake of economy, retouching can be done on the duplicates at that time.

Handling photographic prints

Photographic prints are delicate and often quite valuable. They must be handled with care and stored with care. The surface of a print is easily damaged. Scratches, abrasions, and cracks in the emulsion are likely to show up in reproduction, sometimes even when they may not be obvious to the eye. Take the following precautions:

1. When writing on the back of a print, use a soft pencil and write lightly, on a hard surface. Normal pressure with a #2 pencil, especially on a soft surface, will press through and imprint the writing on the print surface. Write close to the edges rather than in the middle. *Never* use a ball point pen. If a rubber stamp is used, stamp lightly with light-colored ink, such as green or blue, rather than using red or black. Be sure that offsetting does not take place. (The author once had to work on a whole batch of invaluable original photos that had been nearly ruined by overinked stamping in black, with offsetting caused by stacking.)
2. Do not fasten regular size paper clips directly over a photo. Fold a piece of stiff paper or a file card around the print under the clip to prevent its leaving an impression, or use large paper clips.
3. Do not write on an overlay or any other paper when a print is underneath, either purposely or accidentally!
4. Prints often curl if left exposed to dry air, which can often result in damage when they are flattened again. Keep them flat whether they are in a file or loose, and do not attempt to straighten a curled print by curling it the other way. Just put it under a gentle weight, in a humid place if possible.
5. When mailing photos, use more than one thickness of heavy corrugated or pressed board, a bold stamp saying "PHOTOS: DO NOT BEND," and first class mail (when messenger delivery is not practical).
6. Do not use Scotch tape, masking tape, or any other kind of tape unless really necessary—and then only temporarily. Tapes disintegrate, stain, and stick to other prints if left on for a period of time. Overlays put on prints to protect retouched surfaces should be attached by the least sticky tape available, usually the so-called Magic Tape.

Handling color transparencies

Color transparencies are more valuable and more delicate than prints, and in the case of 35mm transparencies they are also small, easily lost, difficult to view, difficult to handle, and too numerous! The 35mm transparency is by far the most common size transparency in book work, and it is usually much enlarged in reproduction, making any scratch or abrasion very visible. The first requisite for working with 35mm transparencies, or in fact any transparencies, is a good viewing magnifier of at least 5× power. Publishers who do not provide glasses like this for those who work with transparencies are likely to regret it. Note also:

1. When transparencies are sent from agencies on approval, the publisher is responsible for their return in the same condition they were received. For this reason they should be examined with a glass when received, any damage noted, and the source notified of it immediately and in writing (see Appendix A).

2. Transparencies should be kept in transparent sleeves. The 35mm slides often do not have sleeves when submitted, but if they are selected for reproduction, or kept and circulated for approval, they should be supplied with sleeves. Larger transparencies usually have sleeves, but if these are open at both ends, as is common, the ends should be closed with masking tape so that the transparency cannot slide out and get underfoot. Fingers should not touch the surface of a transparency. (If it is necessary to clean transparencies, use film cleaner only, *never alcohol.*)

3. Because of the value of color transparencies, they should be stored in special envelopes stamped clearly "COLOR COPY, DO NOT BEND," whether the copy is being stored or sent elsewhere, either in the publishing office or out. Always use envelope stiffeners. Put individual transparencies in a plastic filing sheet, or tape them by the sleeves to a piece of stiff paper. Records of the number of transparencies should always accompany them. When mailing, insure transparencies and send first class.*

4. Cropping and sizing of transparencies should, whenever possible, be done on photostats. Sizing and cropping on acetate sleeves or on 35mm mounts is not really satisfactory. (Mounts must be removed by the color separator, who slits the ends of the mount, removes the transparency, and then replaces it and tapes the mount when finished.)

5. Various semi-permanent filing systems are available for transparencies and slides. For slides the easiest and cheapest is probably 8½″ × 11″ plastic file sheets, with pockets for slides. These can be viewed easily, and can be stored easily. Ownership of all slides filed should be indicated right on the mount.

Reproduction quality photostats and Veloxes

Reproduction-quality photostats (stats) are usually adequate camera copy for line work of ordinary degrees of fineness and detail—either direct positives, or glossy negatives and positives when work needs to be done on the negative stage to obtain a clean positive. Direct positive stats are often obtained from messy pasteups just to eliminate the cut paper lines and reduce the chances of

*If a photographic contract specifies a loss or damage value for the photographs, that value should be used for insurance purposes.

small pieces coming off and being lost. Fine lines, however, are often weakened in any photostats, to the point where they are actually lost in reproduction. There is always some loss, and, of course, any black that is less than 50% will not pick up at all. If the stat is made just to drop the pasteup shadow lines, some thin lines in the copy may also be dropped.

Nonrepro quality stats have been proposed for comprehensive layouts to show detailed cropping instructions and to put in dummy when no proof or blue is available, as with late illustrations. If these need to be duplicated for any reason (e.g., layouts) the stats may be ordered as 85-line screened direct positives, which duplicate reasonably well on office duplicators, at least better than unscreened. But these stats should be clearly marked to indicate that they are not camera copy!

When line copy contains very fine detail that may be dropped in ordinary photostats, "fine line" photo prints may be ordered. These are more expensive than ordinary repro stats, but they hold detail extremely well.

Screened photo prints, known as Veloxes, are available in rather coarse screens, which may be useful on occasion for special effects (50-, 55-, 60-, 65-, 75-, 85-, and 100-line screens). These may be ordered either from art or from photos, either square or dropout, and in combination with line.

Special line "conversion screens" (to convert continuous tone copy to line copy) are available in several patterns, such as granular "mezzotint," linear, circle, and cross-hatch (see Figure 11–2). Line conversions and Veloxes must usually be ordered from specialty photoprint houses, whose product lists should be consulted for exact services and prices. Special screens and coarse halftone screens such as Veloxes are normally not used in books, except for special effects. The designer will know whether they suit some special purpose. If they do, they can usually be pasted directly into paper repro pages, to be used as line repro copy. Where fine flat-tint screens are wanted, they should be laid by the printer in the form of Benday tints. Some special effects screens, such as mezzotint, are available in finer versions than conversion prints, in the printer's camera department.

Handling of late illustrations

When galleys go to the printer for paging, sized illustration copy should accompany them (if not already sent). However, in the case of late illustrations, the following is good procedure: (1) on galleys and/or dummy (or pages, if necessary) note "illustration to come," giving illustration list number, dimensions, a note indicating whether it is to be captioned or not, and whether it should bleed or not, if these factors are known; (2) as soon as the illustration becomes available, the editor and designer should okay it; (3) it is sized, cropped, and identified by illustration list number (if it is a replacement for one previously sent, it should be so marked, and if a copy for the one it replaces is available, it should be marked "kill" and sent with the new illustration); and

Mezzotint

Linear

Cross-hatch

(4) the late illustration and any relevant material should be given immediately to production control for the book.

Handling letterpress illustrations

Illustrated books are almost never printed by letterpress today. Nevertheless, the designer who is asked to handle an illustrated book that is being printed by letterpress should be at least generally aware of the major differences between letterpress and offset methods of handling. Most differences arise from the interposition of another supplier, the letterpress engraver, between publisher and printer. Additional production checks are necessary to keep track of the flow of engravings, especially since the finished cuts are shipped directly to the printer rather than going through the publisher's office. One person is usually in charge of this checking procedure, and the check point is traditionally called the "engraving desk." This is the only point of contact with engravers. The "engraving desk" checks out all copy, checks all proofs for quality, identification, and price, and distributes proofs.

The operation of obtaining proofs is automatic in letterpress engraving, even for black-and-white line or halftone cuts, whereas for offset there may be no real proofs at all until press sheets, except for critical full-color work and very critical black and nonprocess color. Often only blues may provide the check. Thus in letterpress, unlike offset, proofs are always available as soon as cuts are made, to be corrected, pasted into the dummy, and so on. Traditionally a number of proof copies are distributed, to designer and art editor, to artist, editor, author (for technical art), production file, and engraving-desk file. When revised and corrected proofs are available, these are distributed in the same way. Thus a lot of proofs are floating about and have to be kept track of, filed, correlated, and so on, usually by the art editor. For offset, two sets of blues often suffice, one to be circulated as necessary and to bear all corrections, and one to be cut up for dummy or mechanicals.

It has already been pointed out that, in offset, blues are sized but not actually cropped, and that this gives additional flexibility since the cropping can be changed up until the last moment, whereas letterpress cuts can only be trimmed if a change in space makes a change in the illustration necessary. In four-color process, the costs of a mistake in sizing are so considerable that letterpress engravers are often asked to submit a blueprint of the black plate only, for checking, before they go ahead with making the complete cut.

For all these reasons the handling of letterpress illustrations is more complicated than offset handling, even though the actual letterpress cuts are usually simpler in design conception than offset illustrations, with fewer complex mechanicals and so on. In letterpress work complex illustrations require a great deal of additional work, and the penalties are higher for small mistakes.

Forms useful in dealing with illustration processing

Five forms are shown. The first is a standard set of instructions for handling mechanicals and picture sections. It is self-explanatory and can be useful in assigning work packages either to outside free-lance design and pasteup people, or in-house to persons not fully familiar with the job at hand, such as trainees. This form can serve as a checklist and enable several people to work separately on parts of a job, using the same general procedures.

The second form is a checklist for offset dummies prior to release to the offset printer. This form is intended for books of moderate complexity, such as illustrated trade books, for which pictures are sized at the same time that the book is designed. Thus the designer receives galleys and at the same time receives blues for the illustrations. The dummy can then proceed with all necessary materials present. Of course, owing to the difficulties of anticipating exact page makeup problems, some remakes of illustrations are to be anticipated (see the heading "Illustrations" on the form). Where the illustration program is almost entirely decided before the book is designed, as is often the case with heavily illustrated trade books for which the author supplies the complete illustration program, this method of handling the illustrations speeds up the production cycle. Its only drawback is a few remade illustrations.

The third form is useful for books having only a few illustrations, whether a dummy is to be made or perhaps only mechanicals for separate inserts. Such a book has comparatively simple requirements in respect to illustrations. At least two sets of blues should be requested, so that one set can be circulated and marked for corrections, while another can be cut up as necessary for mechanicals or dummy. Illustrations are broken down as to type and as to focus. The breakdown as to focus is optional, but it can result in savings at the camera stage. Depending on the number of illustrations (and their diversity of copy from a reproduction point of view), an effort is made to reduce to a minimum the number of focuses required, so that groups of photos can be shot together. This should not be attempted when copy differences of detail or contrast are very marked, or when really critical reproduction is required.

Grouping for focus is usually not as difficult as it sounds, and the designer will find that copy often falls naturally into several grouped focuses. Exceptions may be made as required, of course, but money can usually be saved with a little thought. The groups are written on the form. For example: 40 percent of copy (to left of the line) and a list of illustration numbers opposite.

The fourth form is simply an art or photo transmittal form suitable for offset or any other process. The designer or art editor would use such a form to accompany sets of artwork ready for production control and the camera.

The fifth form is an illustration information sheet on which it is convenient to record information relevant to typesetting and the allowance of picture spaces. This is particularly useful in dealing with automatic systems that can allow picture spaces as early as "first pass" (galley) stage.

STANDARD INSTRUCTIONS FOR HANDLING PICTURE SECTIONS AND MECHANICALS

Title ______________________ **Designer**________**Pages**________**Date**________

☐ Picture placement and pagination guide supplied ☐ Sketches wanted

Please read these instructions. Let us know if there are any that you want to depart from. If you want to bleed please request an imposition, for gripper restrictions.

1. Page dimension. A form is given herewith. (If an oversized page is given it is for oversized nonbleed pictures, and can be used wherever desirable.) Note that in any case, pictures should not come closer than 1/4″ to the trimmed edge, unless they actually bleed. Bleed allowance is 1/8″. Avoid bleeds across the gutter fold, because of line-up problems and loss at the fold. If you must bleed across the fold, indicate exactly where the split comes on the copy, and whether the film must be spread to avoid loss of copy (usually 1/16″ each side of fold).

2. Camera. Please indicate on all doubtful copy whether line or halftone process is to be used. Standard screen is 133 line, normal dot. Note any other needed.

3. Retouching. Spot and retouch only as necessary and in relation to the size to be reproduced. Minimum on anything historical. Flag major repairs necessary (e.g., air-brushing, etc.). Mount and flap retouched or fragile copy—*after* transferring all information on back of the photo to the mount. Silhouette with opaque white where necessary, if copy is not valuable. If valuable, mark for the printer to do the silhouetting. Note: do not use paper clips on photos, write over photos, or use ball point pens.

4. Sizing. If pictures are to be fully cropped when the mechanical is made, put both sets of crop marks on the face of the copy in red grease pencil, so that they can be picked up by the camera (also illustration number). Put paper backing or strips on edges, as necessary. Indicate the size for one dimension, or for both if you wish (if you indicate which dimension can vary, and in which direction). Indicate the size in inches, or as a percentage of the size of the original. When the blues are ready they can be fitted into your mechanical by the printer if both dimensions are shown, or by you or us if only one is shown. Normal procedure is uncropped blues to be fitted later. Photostats should be used only for special mechanicals, for small jobs, to save time, and when OKed for larger jobs. Use screened stats (85 line) if available. Cropping: Please do not crop too tightly, especially heads, hands, and essential features. Watch horizon lines; and watch for flopped copy (letters reversed, etc.).

5. Type. Reproduction proof will be supplied from the OKed copy marked by you for type. Please mark all measures. The typeface is______. Caption size and leading is____/____. Credits are ____/____. Captions are usually to be set justified, and picture width or slightly less. *But note . . .* do not set captions closer than 3/8″ to gutter or fore-edge, or closer than 1/2″ to bottom trim. Do not justify captions set at the sides of pictures. Set flush at the picture side and ragged at the other side. Often you will need to break such captions for the compositor, for sense and appearance.

6. Mechanicals. Please indicate untrimmed, trimmed and center-fold lines in black, treating each two-page unit as a spread. Indicate halftones in one of two ways: (1) a red ink outline, or (2) by a "window" cut to size from Letrafilm 151 M. Same for line copy unless a same size repro stat is placed in position. Space between closely adjoining pictures should be about 1/4″. Captions should be placed 1/8″ or slightly less from the picture, whether at side or underneath. This is adjusted as seems best if there is a credit under the picture. Normal credit position is flush right under picture, 2 points space above. Captions of less than one line are to be centered ☐; or flush at left with other captions ☐. Captions at side should be aligned consistently.

7. Misc. Do not mark on 35mm transparency mounts. Avoid picture sizes and alignments that are "almost but not quite" matched. Extra space is better on the outsides of the page than in the center. Introduce contrasts when consistent with editorial use. Put all color copy on a separate overlay unless it can be simply marked for separation.

8. NOTES:

CHECKLIST FOR OFFSET DUMMIES

From ______________________________ **Date**________

Title ____

____Note outline of complete pagination, for forms of________pages.
____Note all design corrections for master galleys. Check copy editor and editor.
____Note all caption revisions made necessary because of placement, etc., for master galleys. Check copy editor and editor.
____Note on dummy any abnormal usages or positions of running titles.
____Note positions for normal and drop folios, and any pages that are to have no running title or folio.
____Mark all outside bleed illustrations, and all cross-gutter positions and allowances.
____Check press imposition and eliminate any conflicts of bleeds with gripper edges.
____Mark all illustrations using color (if available), and all typography in color.
____Supply a marked master layout sheet or dummy form, showing type areas, running titles and folios, and guidelines for standard picture positions.
____Note standard spaces between picture and caption (and around credit lines, if necessary).
____Indicate any doubtful picture sizes in inches, on dummy. Mark any necessary alignments.
____Note status of (and pages allowed for) front and back matter.

ILLUSTRATIONS

____A. *When shot before dummying, and blues are available.* Note all reshoots in dummy and supply corrected copy to return with dummy. Note all deletions; return the blue, marked "kill." Mark replacements in dummy and on replaced blue, and supply marked copy.

____B. *When illustrations are supplied for the first time with the dummy.* List all those supplied for the first time, by focus if possible. (See separate sheet "Illustrations to Offset Camera".)

ILLUSTRATIONS TO OFFSET CAMERA*

To ______________________________

From ______________________ **Date** __________

Book title ______________________ **Author** __________

Please supply____sets of blues (or other:__________)

To be used for:_____full dummy,_____partial dummy,_____insert mechanical

Information for imposition check:

Trimmed size________×________

Front-matter pages (roman)________to________

Arabic text folios________to________

Total pages________(even forms: ______________________)

Color usage ______________________________

Insert positioning ______________________________

Total pieces of art herewith________To come________.

Total pieces of art in book________.

Line art, total________(Color: ______________________)

Photographs, total________(Color: ______________________)

BREAKDOWN BY FOCUS

Percent of copy	*Illustration numbers*

*Primarily for books with limited color usage.

ART/PHOTO TRANSMITTAL*

To ________________________________ From __________ Date ______

Book title ________________________________ Author ______________

For: Offset camera and separations ☐ Letterpress engravings ☐ Other ☐ ________

________ pieces 1-color art

________ pieces 2-color art

________ pieces 3-color art

________ pieces 4-color art

________ charts (base and ____ overlays)

________ maps (base and ____ overlays)

________ mechanicals for pages

________ B & W photos

________ B & W photos for duotones or 2-color

________ Color transparencies for camera

________ Color assemblies for camera

________ Transparencies for color assemblies

Figure numbers (group by focus percentages)	*Figure numbers (group by color / B & W)*
Comments	Comments

*Primarily for books with complex color usage.

ILLUSTRATION INFORMATION SHEET: TITLE ______________________________

STANDARD SPACES FOR THIS TITLE: Above and below pix (or below legend) ______ **pts. Pix to legend** ______ **pts.**

LEGEND TYPE: Size and body ______ / ______ **. Face** ______________ **Legend width** ______________

PIX # ________ SUBJECT ______________________________ MS. PAGE

POSITION: [ ] AFTER REFERENCE, [ ] **DIRECTLY** AFTER REFERENCE, [ ] SEE LAYOUT, [ ] SIDE BY SIDE WITH PIX # ____

ILLUSTRATION SIZE: WIDTH (MAY BE OMITTED) ________ , DEPTH ______________

LEGEND: [ ] AT SIDE (DEPTH = 0), ESTIM. LINES ______ × BODY ______ = PTS DEPTH ______________

PIX # ________ SUBJECT ______________________________ MS. PAGE

POSITION: [ ] AFTER REFERENCE, [ ] **DIRECTLY** AFTER REFERENCE, [ ] SEE LAYOUT, [ ] SIDE BY SIDE WITH PIX # ____

ILLUSTRATION SIZE: WIDTH (MAY BE OMITTED) ________ , DEPTH ______________

LEGEND: [ ] AT SIDE (DEPTH = 0), ESTIM. LINES ______ × BODY ______ = PTS DEPTH ______________

PIX # ________ SUBJECT ______________________________ MS. PAGE

POSITION: [ ] AFTER REFERENCE, [ ] **DIRECTLY** AFTER REFERENCE, [ ] SEE LAYOUT, [ ] SIDE BY SIDE WITH PIX # ____

ILLUSTRATION SIZE: WIDTH (MAY BE OMITTED) ________ , DEPTH ______________

LEGEND: [ ] AT SIDE (DEPTH = 0), ESTIM. LINES ______ × BODY ______ = PTS DEPTH ______________

PIX # ________ SUBJECT ______________________________ MS. PAGE

POSITION: [ ] AFTER REFERENCE, [ ] **DIRECTLY** AFTER REFERENCE, [ ] SEE LAYOUT, [ ] SIDE BY SIDE WITH PIX # ____

ILLUSTRATION SIZE: WIDTH (MAY BE OMITTED) ________ , DEPTH ______________

LEGEND: [ ] AT SIDE (DEPTH = 0), ESTIM. LINES ______ × BODY ______ = PTS DEPTH ______________

PIX # ________ SUBJECT ______________________________ MS. PAGE

POSITION: [ ] AFTER REFERENCE, [ ] **DIRECTLY** AFTER REFERENCE, [ ] SEE LAYOUT, [ ] SIDE BY SIDE WITH PIX # ____

ILLUSTRATION SIZE: WIDTH (MAY BE OMITTED) ________ , DEPTH ______________

LEGEND: [ ] AT SIDE (DEPTH = 0), ESTIM. LINES ______ × BODY ______ = PTS DEPTH ______________

PIX # ________ SUBJECT ______________________________ MS. PAGE

POSITION: [ ] AFTER REFERENCE, [ ] **DIRECTLY** AFTER REFERENCE, [ ] SEE LAYOUT, [ ] SIDE BY SIDE WITH PIX # ____

ILLUSTRATION SIZE: WIDTH (MAY BE OMITTED) ________ , DEPTH ______________

LEGEND: [ ] AT SIDE (DEPTH = 0), ESTIM. LINES ______ × BODY ______ = PTS DEPTH ______________

Forms for artists

The forms at the end of this chapter are typical of those needed to deal with various aspects of illustrations. They are relatively self-explanatory. The contract forms for artists and photographers are examples of forms drawn to protect the publisher. Any contract is an agreement resulting from negotiation, even if negotiation is minimal. (See Appendix A for more analysis of details involved in such agreements.) The reason for having printed contracts is to make lengthy and detailed negotiation unnecessary, and to suggest a form of agreement advantageous to the party proposing the contractual terms. For this reason publisher and artist or photographer may have their own contract forms, proposing rather different terms. All parties should remember that mutually beneficial collaboration is the object. Grossly one-sided agreements do not serve this purpose and build ill will even when they are agreed to. Printed contracts should be revised occasionally to reflect the actual state of trade customs.

The "Code of Ethics and Standards of Fair Practice" of the Graphic Artists Guild is included even though it does not apply specifically to books. It is useful for the book designer to understand the point of view of artists, who may work in several media at once, including books.

Any contract can be modified during negotiations by modifications signed by both parties (for example, by additions or deletions on the face or on the back of the printed contract). The fact that it is printed should not be taken as a sign that a contract form is in any sense "correct," or unalterable, or the law of the land.

The forms that follow are for:

Artist Contract
Photographer Contract
Map Specifications
Chart Notes
Art Department Work Sheet

ARTIST CONTRACT

Publisher ________________________________ Date____________
Address ________________________________
The Artist ________________________________ agrees to make for the Publisher ________________________________the following original artwork, which shall be satisfactory to the Publisher, for the work provisionally titled: ________________________________ (hereinafter called the Work).
DESCRIPTION: ________________________________
____

____pieces of art in____color(s),____in line,____halftone,____pre-sep.
____pieces of art in____color(s),____in line,____halftone,____pre-sep.
____pieces of art in____color(s),____in line,____halftone,____pre-sep.
____pieces of art in____color(s),____in line,____halftone,____pre-sep.
____pieces of art total

Reduction or scale: ________________________________
____

Labeling to be done by________________. Labeling costs to be paid by__________ .
Research to be done by ________________________________ .
The artist shall deliver said artwork to the Publisher starting__________and ending__________provided the Publisher supplies adequate information from which the artwork is to be made on or before__________.
The last assignments to be given by__________. On delivery and acceptance of said artwork as satisfactory, the Publisher shall pay the Artist the sum of $ __________ . To be paid as:
____
________________________________ .

If requested by the Publisher, the Artist agrees to prepare additional drawings for the Work and the Publisher shall compensate the Artist proportionately. Such additional drawings shall be covered under the terms of this Agreement.

The Artist represents and warrants that all artwork prepared under the terms of this Agreement shall be original and shall not violate any copyright, proprietary right or other right.

All artwork prepared under this Agreement shall be work-for-hire of which the Publisher is author-at-law and the Publisher shall be the exclusive owner of all rights in the original artwork and reproductions thereof, including all copyrights, extensions of copyright, and renewals. The Publisher shall, at its sole discretion, have the right to use the artwork in the Work and in any other materials or publications, including but not limited to the exclusive right to print, publish, film, display, record, broadcast, transmit, and otherwise reproduce and exploit the Work in its original or adapted form in all languages and formats, in audio-visual form and in all other forms, media and systems, including information storage and retrieval systems, or by any other process now known or hereafter developed.

This instrument, which shall be construed and governed by the laws of the State of ________________, constitutes the whole Agreement between the Artist and the Publisher and any variations therefrom shall be valid only if incorporated on the reverse hereof and signed by both parties. The Artist acknowledges that the Publisher may publish works and materials dealing with subject matter similar to that contained in the Work, and nothing contained in this Agreement shall bar the Publisher from publishing such other works and materials. Nothing in this Agreement shall be construed to require the Publisher to act as a trustee for the benefit of the Artist or otherwise to act as a fiduciary.

Initialed by production:____________editor:____________Artist: ____________

For the Publisher:____________ Tax number: ____________

PHOTOGRAPHER CONTRACT

Publisher ______________________________ Date __________

Address ______________________________

The Photographer, ______________________________, agrees to execute for ______________________________, the Publisher, the following photographic assignment, which shall be satisfactory to the Publisher:

(hereinafter called the Material) for the sum of $ ______________________________

(______________________________dollars) plus the cost of the following: color film, contact prints of all negatives for the Publisher, travel expenses, model fees; this Material to be incorporated in the work provisionally entitled:

____

(hereinafter called the Work).

The Photographer agrees to furnish the black-and-white film at his own expense.

In consideration of the Publisher's obligation hereunder, the Photographer grants to the Publisher, its successors, assigns and/or licensees, first book reproduction rights in the Material in the Work named above and the right to reproduce the Material thereafter in any and all of the Publisher's other publications, or in any supplementary or advertising Material in connection therewith, without any further payment.

All color transparencies shall be the property of the Photographer, but the Publisher may retain indefinitely as many of the color transparencies as it deems desirable. The Photographer may borrow said color transparencies for the use of purchasers of other reproduction rights (except that the Photographer agrees that no reproduction rights shall be granted to any book publisher without the written approval of the Publisher), subject to possible delays due to the Publisher's use, and the Photographer agrees to return all borrowed transparencies to the Publisher in good condition within two (2) months. The Publisher shall take such care of the transparencies in its possession as if they were its own, but in the case of loss or damage, the Publisher's responsibility shall not exceed $1.00 (one dollar) per frame.

The Photographer agrees to retain one set of black-and-white contact prints and the negatives for all photographs he takes under this agreement so that the Publisher may order further enlargements if needed.

The Photographer agrees to obtain model releases from persons appearing in the photographs or, in the case of minors, from their parents as follows:

This agreement constitutes the whole agreement, and any variations shall be valid only if incorporated on the reverse hereof and signed by both parties.

Initialed by production:__________ editor:__________ Photographer: __________

For the Publisher:__________ Tax number: __________

MAP SPECIFICATIONS

Book title ______________________ Author ______________ Date ________

Map number _____ Chapter number _____ Ms. page _____ Specs by __________

Size after reduction ________ Colors ______________ Line/halftone ________

Subject and purpose:

Area (approximate):

Projection:

Categories to show and label (see separate list of labels):

Categories to show but not label:

References:

Attached copy:

Color usage:

Label types and sizes:

Grid ______________________ Mile scale __________ North sign ________

NOTES:

CHART NOTES

Title: ______________________ Author ______________ Date __________

Chart no. ______ Chapter no. ______ Ms. page ______ Specs by __________

Size after reduction ______________________ Colors ______

Purpose of the chart:

Contents of chart (give statistics):

References:

Labels:

Special considerations:

Legend:

ART DEPARTMENT WORK SHEET

Book ______________________________

From ______________________ Date ________

Dept. ______________________ Designer ________

Date needed ________________ Drawing Nos. ________

Production manager ________________ Tel. no. ________

CHECK LIST

FOLLOW:		WORK ON:	
Manuscript	________	New sketch	________
Sketches	________	New mechanical	________
Sample pages	________	Repro proof	________
Dummy	________	Color overlays	________
Foul proof	________	Illustrations	________
Flags	________	Cover mechanical	________
Tissue overlays	________	Other?	________

General instructions

ART DEPARTMENT

Author/title ______________________________

Department ______________________ Date ________

Production manager: ______________________________

Received from: ______________________________

Artist	Hours	Date	Artist	Hours	Date	Artist	Hours	Date

Charge to:

Approved by: ______________________________

Art department ______________________________

Total charge $ ________ Total hours ________

Code of ethics and standards of fair practice*

1. Orders to graphic artists or their agents shall be executed on a standard purchase order form including price, fee, or rate and special compensation when required, due date and a summarized description of the work and the use for which it is ordered. When no price, fee or rate can be established at the time the order is issued, a guarantee shall be given that no artist involved shall be paid less than his established fee or rate.

2. All changes not due to the fault of the artist or representative shall require a supplementary order form and shall be billed to the purchaser as an additional or separate charge.

3. There shall be no fee for revisions made necessary by errors on the part of the artist or his representative.

4. Alterations to artwork shall not be made without consulting the originating artist, when possible, and the artist shall be allowed the first option to make all alterations.

5. A review board consisting of agreed upon representatives of the Graphic Artists Guild and clients shall arbitrate disputes.

6. Work, in progress, cancelled by a buyer shall be delivered immediately and billed according to the time, effort and expense incurred. Work temporarily stopped by a buyer shall be considered cancelled after a reasonable period of time.

7. Payment is considered due the artist and/or his representative within 30 days from the date of receipt of invoice. An invoice to the buyer unpaid after 40 days from receipt shall be increased a given percentage and increased monthly thereafter. Where extended assignments are involved, partial invoicing shall be honored.

8. Nonconformance with agreed upon standards of performance or failure by the artist to deliver the contracted work when due, without prior consent by the buyer, shall be considered a breach of contract and shall release the buyer from obligation.

9. An artist should not be asked to work on speculation. Work originating with the artist may be marketed on its merit and, of course, remains the property of the artist until purchased and paid for. Art contests, except for educational or charitable purposes, are not approved because of their speculative nature.

10. There shall be no rebates, discounts, gifts or bonuses to buyers by artists or their representatives.

*From "Pricing and Ethical Guidelines," 2nd Edition, 1975, Graphic Artists Guild.

11. Wherever the original graphic art is purchased for reproduction rights only, the original work shall remain the property of the artist and may be sold by special agreement only. The reproduction rights and any other rights purchased must be stated in the purchase agreement. If the purchase price of artwork is based on specific use or uses and later the material is used more extensively than originally planned, the artist is to receive adequate additional remuneration.

12. A question of plagiarism shall be taken upon request to the review board for arbitration and recommendation prior to action by due process of law.

13. Name credit shall be given the artist for all editorial work. The right of name credit on advertising work shall be by agreement between the artist and buyer and shall be indicated in the purchase agreement.

14. Any business agreement between an artist and representative shall be in writing and may take any form agreed to provided that it does not violate the Constitution and By-Laws, Rules and Regulations, and this Code of the Graphic Artists Guild.

15. The graphic artist shall always have the prerogative to decide when and where his samples are to be shown and no work may be shown by a representative anonymously or without expressed agreement and authority to do so.

16. Upon termination of a business agreement between an artist and representative, any work under contract shall continue under the terms of the agreement until the existing contracts or purchase agreement are fulfilled.

17. Minimum fees, prices, or rates are the standard bases upon which assignments are to be negotiated.

18. Interpretation of this Code shall be the prerogative of the Board of Directors of the Graphic Artists Guild which shall have the authority to make alterations or additions at its discretion.

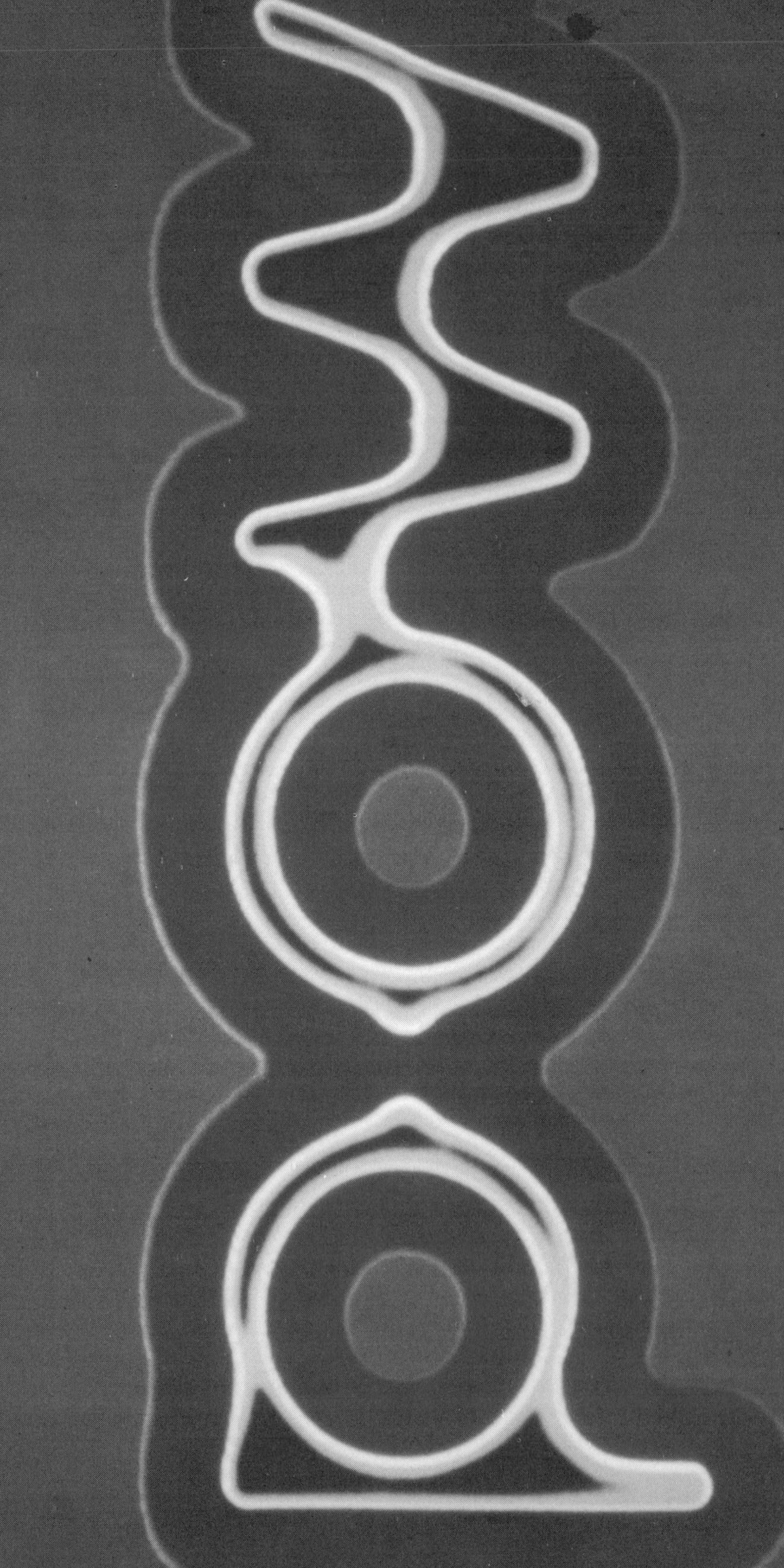

CHAPTER 12
New Directions in Design

Since this book is about the systematic aspects of design, not about aesthetics and style, the new directions to be discussed here are systematic directions, not stylistic directions, although they may not be entirely disassociated.

More offset printing is a trend. Thinner papers is a trend. More, and more flexible, web-press technology is a trend. Paper book covers and perfect bindings are trends. More trimmed sizes approximately 6″ × 9″ is a trend. Greatly increased variety in handset, optically spaced, condensable and slantable, Typositor-style display type is a trend. Color-system specification for ink colors is a trend. Fancier presentation methods for comprehensive sketches and more complex mechanicals are trends. More prepress four-color simulation by contact imaging is a trend. Computer-controlled complex text setting is a trend. Information storage and retrieval of updatable and alternative form materials for a variety of publishing uses is a trend. (Development of short-run to-order publishing and printing is still only a small trend.) Cheaper information storage with greater speed in handling, though a big trend in some industries, is a small trend in publishing. More sophisticated controls for all information processing is a trend, and the refinement of graphic arts controls is part of this.

The explosive proliferation of electronic typesetting devices and systems is a trend of unprecedented energy—from relatively inexpensive machines (both "direct-entry" and tape-operated), roughly comparable in terms of complexity of operation to that of the old Linotype machine, to systems with extremely sophisticated logical controls, hardware subtleties, speeds of typesetting, and text storage capacities. Microprocessor technology will play a big role.

We could add that the feeling of confusion about so many options and trends is a trend, and resentment at feeling confused is also a trend. Perhaps the desire to get away from it all is a trend evident in design as in other fields, for although there is no discernible trend towards real simplification, there is a very discernible one towards more desire for simplification.

What do these trends, and others, add up to for the designer? Chiefly, and especially in the big company, there is much more to keep track of than even a few years ago, and often things that promise to help may end up complicating life. The changes of scene are too swift.

Most of the trends noted above are trends towards new systems and ways of using them. They all affect design in one way or another, but probably the most basic set of trends affects how text itself is stored, changed, and controlled in typesetting, and how design is actually carried out. Electronic storage, automatic format controls stored in the system, and variable output design formats will most basically affect the way the designer works.

Designing by exception

Design always means the specification of something. Traditional design is considered to start with the edited manuscript, some typesetting machine and its limitations, and forms on which to specify. As we have seen, the designer learns not to specify everything, but even if the designer specifies very little, a great many options may have to be considered. (Remember the discussion of design options for setting lists?) The more active the designer, the greater the number of options that are likely to be considered.

In any case, considering all the options is not the only method available. Another is the use of so-called "standard formats," which has been recommended by production people, probably, since the time of Gutenberg. Standard formats never have been used much, other than for series, because author, editor, designer, salesman, and reader have small enthusiasm for standardized books.

Let us assume that cover, front matter, part and chapter openings, and illustration programs always will remain completely open to design interpretation. That still leaves text-setting decisions of all kinds for the various basic editorial structures that occur in all books. It is quite plain that most designers do not really like this aspect of their work, because it is frightfully repetitious and is usually conspicuous when it is badly done. The design of a variety of text structures requires that a great many options be considered, marked up, *and* followed up. It is the design follow-up time that is generally underestimated, together with the other costs of follow-up all along the line. This load of specification is undertaken, not because designers really want to "design" most of these structures, but simply because decisions have to be made by someone, so that setting can proceed. What designers really want is for most editorial text structures to be set the way they are *usually* set by professional designers—and to be left alone to do the more important jobs of design. If designers could simply request "the usual solution," instead of having to specify and mark, they would. In fact, this is now possible with automatic systems, but it takes a bit of initial arranging.

"Design by exception" is a method that experienced designers use all the time in an intuitive way. At every text design decision point, the designer thinks in these terms: "This text structure is *usually* specified in this way. Shall I specify that way, or shall I make an *exception?*" This is the essence of designing by exception, but in this loose intuitive form it is just taking advantage of habit, and no matter what decision is made all the same specifications and follow-up steps have to be taken anyhow.

In systematic design by exception, a certain class of work is supplied with a full set of specifications for "what I want to do unless I make an exception and specify otherwise." Then, for any design in that class, only the exceptions to the model need to be specified. This method can be useful whenever editorial structure design problems have a basically repetitive pattern, as they have in most books. Trade books have one set of common structures, school workbooks have another, book catalogs another, research math and physics another, chemistry another, standardized tests another, complex tabular presentation another, and so on. As a guess, 80 to 90 percent of text composition is done with 15 or 20 editorial structures (counting all separate line heads as one type of structure and run-in heads as another).

Design by exception can be most useful to the designer when it is conscious, systematic, and implemented by computer-controlled composition using stored format controls. For perfectly consistent and effortless control of complex processes, nothing like computer control of format has ever been available to the designer before. But it should be clear that sets of automatic text formats are not standard formats in any sense that would make the designer apprehensive; this is because the basic parameters of text composition are always variable and job-specifiable. Typeface, point size, leading, paragraph indent, measure, special indents, ragged settings and centerings are always reset on a job basis, as they are for traditional systems. Further, the sets of design formats that may be thought desirable can be very flexible, and can include much or little, from a few specifications up to what amounts to complete format control, with variability retained only for the basic parameters just mentioned. After all, any "standard" instructions function in the absence of any other specifications, as for example: "Please set all our indexes per specs below, unless otherwise marked." What has undergone great change recently is the capacity to carry out specifications accurately and consistently, under computer control.

Computer control and composition

We are going to discuss the concept of "stored formats," and for this reason we shall consider only composition control capable of utilizing stored formats automatically—not smaller specialized computers handling only such matters as hyphenation and justification. Computer-controlled composition is not necessarily difficult composition, of course, even though some of the most difficult composition is now computer controlled.

In any case, it is worthwhile for the designer to have at least a general idea of how this control is exercised. Even a superficial analysis can convey the general idea, and although there are quite a number of different systems, they all operate in much the same way. Understanding something of the general logic by which they operate will convince the designer that design itself, the logic of format in all books, is in fact the subject of any graphic-arts-oriented computer language. The exact "words" used for computer control of composition look somewhat strange at first, because the language they comprise is so much abbreviated and regularized; yet, it is nothing more than designers' language. With a little patience, the designer may find it quite fascinating, and it is much easier than the languages studied in school.

Like any language, a graphic arts computer language is composed of words and sentences, various kinds of statements, and even implied questions. In a graphic arts language the "words" are mostly abbreviations for graphic arts terms. (For our examples we shall use the PAGE-1 language developed to control the VideoComp CRT typesetting system used to set this book. Others are rather similar.) In practice, format-control statements to effect the specified formats are written by the compositor's format markup person and inserted into the manuscript at a point where the control is to take effect. Format statements are separated from the words of the manuscript itself only by so-called delimiters, such as brackets. These delimiters cause the typesetting device to recognize controls as controls, rather than set them as text characters.

The main elements of the language are (a) the words; (b) the punctuation; (c) the numerical values, called "parameters," that may be associated with certain words; and (d) the syntax or rules by which the other elements may be controlled and combined. For example, some noun-type words are tf, ps, bl, sw, pi, and gv—meaning typeface, point size, body-leaded, set width, paragraph indent, and general variable (like *x* or *y* in algebra). Some verb-type words are ql, qr, and cv—meaning to quad (move) flush left, quad flush right, and center vertically. Some marks of punctuation are semicolon, comma, and brackets. The semicolon means the end of a separate statement, the comma separates a control word from a value associated with it (the parameter), and the brackets are delimiters.

To put these things together, we may write a simple control statement and then translate it:

[ps,10;sw,11;bl,12]

Translation: "Control statements follow. For text following the controls, put these specifications into effect: point size to have a value of 10 points; set width to have a value of 11 points; body-leaded to have a value of 12 points. End control statements." Such simple shorthand tricks are not very impressive, but neither is the simple substitution of + for "added to" or × for "multiplied by." But as A. N. Whitehead observed, "By relieving the brain of all unnecessary work, a good notation sets it free to concentrate on more advanced problems, and in effect increases the mental power of the human race." This may be more obvious in the instances that follow.

An important concept is the programmer-defined "variable," like the "x" in algebra. In the PAGE-1 language, such a variable is called a "general variable" or "gv." For example, [gv10,12] defines general variable number 10 to be equivalent to 12. This concept will take us in an interesting direction that relates closely to design and composition control. For instance, if we say [gv2,10], and later say [ps,gv2], what value will ps (point size) have then? It will have the value that gv2 has, namely 10.

This concept of the variable, shared by all computer languages, allows the writing of very generalized control statements, which may be redefined easily and as often as necessary just by the substitution of new values for the general variables. This has powerful implications for the consistent control of editorial structure design with little effort. Control routines that are general in form but variable in execution are familiar to the data processor but not to most designers and editors, for whom the potential is only now becoming interesting.

Stored control formats

The basic concept we shall deal with here is one that greatly simplifies the execution of design details, once some initial work has been done. It is known as the "stored control format routine," or (in PAGE-1) simply a "format." Control statements for complex text can be, naturally, very complex themselves, and it would be intolerable if they had to be written out every time they were needed. Fortunately this is not necessary. They can be given a name, stored in locations that are instantly accessible, and then are on instant call whenever the name is used in any control situation. A "name" such as F5 might be used for a simple set of changes involved in switching from text setting to a side head setting, or it might stand for a short, but more sophisticated, statement, such as [eq,gv10,0[[ig]]], which could mean "If general variable number 10 has a current value of 0, then ignore completely and do not set the text that follows. Otherwise, set what follows without any change in format." (The gv10 might have been set to zero, or to something else, in preparation for some optional text, such as enrichment or study materials.) Thus, these general purpose controls may apply both to the functions of the designer and those of the editor. In both cases a stored format (that has been properly tested) is like a good habit that can be used any time with no strain.

Let us consider one relatively simple instance, putting together the concepts of word, statement, punctuation, delimiter, general variable, and stored format. A chapter opening may be coded as follows by the compositor's markup person:

[C1] 5 (Chapter number)
[C2]Chaptertitle
[C3]Startofchaptertext

C1, C2, C3 are stored format names. The actual format statements that are equivalent to C1 might be:

[dn,gv107;ps,gv17;bl,gv32;tf,gv47;lb,gv71;ql]

This may be translated: "Space down the points specified in gv107; set the point size to the value in gv17; set the body leaded (total body) to the number of points in gv32; use the typeface whose system number is given in gv47; reset the left indention to the right of the original page definition by the number of points in gv71; and quad left to that point."

Format statements for C2 and C3 would be handled similarly.

With each change of editorial structure, a certain set of factors has to be changed. The transitions from Structure 1 to Structure 2 potentially involve the same factors every time, not only in the same book, but in almost all books; only the values associated with them change. That is why the generalized stored-control format is so useful. All that is required is to plug in a different set of variables at the start of each new job. Then minimal marking, such as C1, C2, etc., can produce all sorts of different formats. Format statements can become very complex indeed, but they can be constructed so that only the general variable parameters need be changed.

Designers need not concern themselves with the writing of format statements, but they may want to take advantage of the consistency and subtlety of stored formats in ways similar to some suggested below. This will be the biggest trend in the way design of text is executed. This type of format control is so generalized that it cannot go out of date with any machine or system, and it is essentially the same wherever storage of control formats is possible. Only the details differ, and these are really not the concern of the designer.

It is perhaps a somewhat novel idea to most designers that a standard method of handling does not necessarily need to produce a standard typographic output. Let us consider again the completed mathematical and technical composition order shown in Figure 4–2. The specifications as filled in indicate what will be done unless something else is specified. This allows for design by exception. For example the text typeface noted is Times Roman set 10/12. If a blank form were sent in with only "Format specifications #1" as noted, with 10/13 specified for main text, the leading would be the only design exception and all the rest would not need to be specified at all. Any number of such exceptions could be made on the order, but *only* the exceptions would need to be written in. The rest would be automatic.

Catalogs of designed formats

One obvious difficulty with standard text format control is that editors, authors, and designers do not want to *read* specifications and composition orders. They really want to know how proposed text formats* will *look.* If there are a dozen or more ways to set lists automatically, they want to be able to point to a visual example and say "Let's use *that* solution." To make this practical, "that solution" should show the basic structure of the text, but without any commitment to text face, size, leading, measure, paragraph indents, special indents, or quadding. This kind of format shopping is not impractical and calls for a kind of buyer's catalog of common text formats from which a considerable variety of solutions can be specified and ordered "off the shelf," but not sight unseen. A companion to this volume, *Book Design: Text Format Models,* by this author, is such a catalog. It visually presents structures in common use for trade and textbooks.

In fact, many catalogs of structures may eventually cover many different areas of publishing. Some of these catalogs would be generally useful, while others might be very specialized. These catalogs are primarily worked out by the publisher and the designer, but they are, nonetheless, generalized control instruments. Any compositor with any degree of automatic control can offer any part of such a catalog on an automatic basis. The rest of the catalog can still be very useful as a means of specifying, even though it is not all offered under automatic control.

This catalog method of text structure specification is described simply as one possible trend in design work. One function of design may turn out to be the designing of cataloged systems of automatic format controls for various classes of text composition. The catalogs should be flexible, open-ended, and useful to both publisher and compositor, but they can be highly designed, as well as specialized. Each catalog would have, approximately, the following characteristics:

1. It would describe one set of common text structures needed by one publisher, and/or one required by a subset of text composition, such as trade, mathematics, workbook, or tabular.
2. It would be generalized as to the basic typographic parameters. That is, the typeface, size, leading, measure, paragraph indent, special indents, set size, quaddings, etc. would not be specified.

*The design aspect of any definable editorial structure, such as a footnote, table, heading, list, index, bibliography, and so on.

3. The standard formats covered would be presented visually as models in the catalog, and there would be an appropriate variety of solutions for each format, rather than just one solution. Each solution would have a name tag or key that would stand for all specifications related to it.

4. Any composition house could implement the models in the catalog according to the capacity of its available controls, and in its own ways. Each compositor would simply inform publishers of the degree of automation provided, or perhaps simply the price of composition would be enough in some cases. The publisher would not have to be tied to one compositor or composition system to get automated format controls, and the compositor could offer the same system to any publisher, thus extending the market for services provided.

5. Various individual composition orders (based on visual catalogs) could be made available by different composition sources. These could offer various "design by exception" packages. They could, of course, be worked out for individual publishers, or for generalized subsets of publishing. No design flexibility would be lost thereby, since any part of format control would be subject to override specification by the designer at any time.

6. The name tags or keys from the catalog would be used to mark the manuscripts, wherever the named structure models were accepted. When a structure model is not accepted, normal specifications and manuscript marks would be used.

7. Paging would be a separate problem. Any page makeup rules (and special character use conventions) would actually be unrelated to the text format models, but could profitably be documented to aid overall system performance. (See below for special character usages, and see Chapter 5 under "Typical rules for automatic paging.")

The text structure matrix

In text settings, changes in design specifications control the transfer from one structure to another. Obviously only certain kinds of transfers occur in any one book. There is an easy and orderly way of noting just which transfers, in fact, do occur, so that the designer can specify for them all (sometimes necessary when working closely with an automatic system).

1. List all text structures A . . . B . . . C . . . down the left of a grid, such as the one shown opposite. Label these "preceding."

2. List the same structures in the same order across the top of the grid (or simply use the letters). These are labeled "succeeding."

3. Make a check in the intersection box whenever a preceding structure is actually followed (at least once in the manuscript) by the specific succeeding structure. Obviously a structure does not usually follow itself, so the diagonal row showing such transfers is seldom required. (There are exceptions, such as tables that follow tables.)

4. Design the checked transfers by providing necessary specifications.

Figure 12–1 shows the grid for a relatively simple and typical book having 10 text structures. As an example, the circled check indicates that heading B is followed, at least once in the manuscript, by a table. Format specifications for this transfer are thus required. A table-to-table transfer is also required (see box F-F).

Succeeding text structures

Preceding text structures

		A	B	C	D	E	F	G	H	I	J	K	L	M	N	O	P
MAIN TEXT	A		✓	✓	✓	✓	✓		✓	✓	✓						
EXTRACT	B	✓		✓	✓				✓								
HEADING A	C	✓			✓												
〃 B	D	✓				✓	(✓)		✓								
〃 C	E	✓									✓						
TABLE	F	✓			✓	✓	✓										
BIBLIOGRAPHY	G			✓							✓						
LIST	H	✓	✓			✓					✓						
OUTLINE	I	✓				✓											
STUDY AIDS	J			✓	✓												
	K																
	L																
	M																
	N																
	O																
	P																

TEXT STRUCTURE TRANSFERS TITLE:

12-1 *An example of the "grid" method of identifying transfers from one typographic structure to another (in any given manuscript or class of work). A check is made in the appropriate square of the grid whenever any given structure listed at the left is followed at least once in the manuscript by another listed at the top. (The letters at the top identify the same structures as they do at the left.)*

Note that, in automatic systems with stored format control capability, each checked transfer will have one control routine that may be automatically utilized every time its name is encountered in the keyed text stream. The grid method is appropriate as an aid to developing format libraries for different areas of publishing having different sets of structures.

A publisher-compositor interface for noncomplex work

As has been mentioned, publishers do not wish to tie themselves down to one source of composition, unless it is absolutely necessary to do so in order to solve specific complex problems such as catalog work, encyclopedia work, or other projects that are suitable for computer-controlled updating, sorting, and reformatting. In other words, publishers have no wish to commit themselves to one system of composition just to be able to do complex work, when most of their work is not complex. They would like to do more OCR (Optical Character Recognition) work, and perhaps some forms of in-house keyboarding, but not at the cost of tying down much of their work to one system.

Cooperation between publishers and the various compositors capable of electronically controlled typesetting is still very difficult, mainly because scarcely two such compositors use the same combination of input and processing systems, character coding, control formats, fonts, and special (nontypewriter) character identifications. In order not to be tied down to one system, the publisher may still avoid them all, whenever possible.

Industry-wide standards in coding and text format controls, especially for complex materials, are in all probability impossible to achieve, but a very practical degree of marketplace or de facto compatibility could be achieved by a few publishers and compositors, at least for reasonably simple materials. This compatibility could spread to others and to more complex materials, because of its simplicity and desirability. It may be recalled that electricity never got off the ground until manufacturers decided to standardize the socket size. The catalog of structure models is one kind of a standard socket, and so also is a standard set of "look-up" conventions for special characters and situations that cannot be covered by standard codes. For those designers who are not familiar with how such coding conventions work, one such set of conventions is proposed below, partly to show how simply it can work, and partly to provide a generalized model of how special character calls and format transfers are arranged.†

1. Only two machine-readable input systems would be standard: (a) one OCR system, to be decided upon, and (b) industry standard 9-track magnetic tape, using *only* the same characters used in the chosen OCR system.

2. One basic look-up scheme is proposed for special characters not represented in Item 1, and one scheme for format identification. These basic schemes would be implemented in different ways, depending on the needs of various types of composition, but for *all* levels these conventions are suggested: Three characters from the set in Item 1 would be reserved for look-up flags (e.g., *, @, #). All other characters would be equal to the typeset character. The flag characters would have the following translations assigned to them by cooperating compositors and publishers:

a) One flag (e.g., *) is reserved to indicate that the compositor is to refer to special instructions, such as a style sheet, hard copy, or an instruction list. In

†Adapted from Paul Hoffman, "$S^2P^2N^n$," in the *Seybold Report* (October 25, 1976).

other words, the compositor's translation may be anything that can be looked up in job specifications.

b) Another flag (e.g., @) is always followed by two standard keyboard characters (per Item 1) that identify one nonstandard or special character. This would allow, with shift and unshift, some 7310 definitions (permutations of 86 characters taken two at a time). The compositor is provided with a list of translations to settable characters and arranges for automatic translation to the intended character whenever an @ code is encountered.

c) The other flag (e.g., #) is always followed by two standard characters that can potentially identify some 7310 optional publisher-defined typographic formats, a list of which would accompany each job. (Such a list might be associated with the formats in a typographic format-model catalog.) Format changes are transfers from one structure or substructure to another. Thus, for example, the change from text to extract might be signaled by #ex, and from extract to text by #tx. The name tags in any format catalog could easily be translated to appropriate two-character codes. The number of different format transfers would vary greatly depending on the complexity level of the text being set, from a dozen or so to several hundred.

These conventions, or similar "marketplace standards," would be essentially nonrestrictive to publishers and compositors alike, but would enable them to deal with each other on a basis of mutual intelligibility and healthy competition that would benefit all. A great deal more composition would be done by systems with automatic controls, a trend that is currently held up by lack of easy communication and by the compositor's desires to lock in publishers who don't want to be locked in.

All this will affect the work of the designer, because the text formats required are the designer's concern. These can be worked out for required areas of composition, or simply chosen from a suitable format catalog. They would be automatically available at various compositors as capabilities allowed. This would give the designer and the publisher freedom of movement and allow the designer to specify by exception. With automatic controls that have been properly tested there is no worry about consistent follow-through, even for the most complex specifications.

Stored automatic text-format controls seem to be the most potent single instrument for change in the methodology of design. They should be much more of a benefit than a threat to the design function and the designer.

Automatic electronic page makeup and layout

For years the making of pages in electronic typesetting systems has been subjected to experiment, for various kinds of printed materials (especially newspapers and magazines) and with varying degrees of success. The following observations can be made relative to the application of automatic paging to books:

1. No paging system comes very close to dealing successfully with the full variety of paging problems common to most textbook publishers. In other words, these systems are not, in any sense, "general purpose" to the publisher who produces a range of relatively complex books.

2. There have been almost no systematic descriptions of the exact kinds of paging problems each system can handle routinely. The publisher is accustomed to overseeing such problems in detail, and is reluctant to deal with systems that do not document themselves.

3. There has been no serious effort on the part of designers or editors to adapt the traditional handcraft methods and rules of page makeup to more logical methods that could be better dealt with automatically.

4. The needs and potentials of noninteractive (i.e., not providing for designer direction or intervention) paging or layout systems have not been sufficiently distinguished from the needs and potentials of designer-interactive systems. In use, these systems require separate development and are aimed at separate classes of materials.

5. Using the traditional rules of page makeup, the paging of text with even modest admixtures of headings and non-main-text editorial structures can present enormous logical problems requiring the simultaneous consideration of many pages—even without the additional problem of significant numbers of illustrations. Automatic paging programs have usually been either for highly simplified materials or for highly predictable materials (i.e., special formats with needs that do not generalize to the problems of most books).

6. Interactive page layout, based on manipulation of design element images on CRT terminals, is still (1978) primitive in terms of the range of design decision and the variety of text presented (though it is very ingenious). It is also unavailable commercially, awkward in use, lacking in the ability to produce hard-copy layouts for cooperative consideration, and basically suited only to essentially simple or repetitive requirements, such as relatively fixed-format magazines and directories. Costs may be expected to be greater than paper and scissors.

7. In normal use, noninteractive paging of relatively simple text still requires occasional human intervention. The designer-interactive paging system is the only one that can approach the page variety of traditional layout involving significant numbers of illustrations. But since the designer must still make the judgments and operate the interactive system, we are justified in asking whether (regardless of the expense) it is, in fact, a superior tool to layout paper and scissors. It will, indeed (at least theoretically), produce information to control output of made-up pages, without requiring the traditional galley stage. To regard this as an advantage for books, however, makes the almost

certainly unwarranted assumption that the galley stage can, in fact, be dispensed with in relation to layout. The designer does not make layout decisions in isolation; nor is the most responsible designer likely to do the detailed layout on the electronic system, the manipulation of which is necessarily akin to elementary dummying.

8. In the analysis of electronic typesetting, page makeup (whether interactive or noninteractive) should be considered as a problem essentially separate from basic composition. The nature of the problem is entirely different, related simply to the codex form of the book and not to information as such. The various specialized kinds of paging and layout problems should be separately analyzed and solved as their requirements dictate rather than being treated as one amorphous "paging" problem attached to text composition. Text is information; paging is the breaking up of the information, following the requirements of the codex form.

Electronically generated color

Ways of obtaining "correct" color reproduction have been discussed in Chapter 10, and it has been noted that the new methods of obtaining correct color, such as electronic scanning, do not materially affect the designer's role in color use.

However, color can be synthesized electronically, arbitrarily. Such color can be specified with great flexibility, and thus the process by which this happens is of great interest to the designer. We may consider the most general case and allow the reader to investigate more particular applications.

In general: (1) Copy of any type, having any gradation of gray value, is put before a black and white television camera. (2) The video signal is analyzed by an analog computer, which measures the black and white tonal value of the image at every point. (3) These tonal values are then arbitrarily divided by the designer into segments or ranges; that is, the image is "posterized," in the traditional term. Each of these ranges can be rendered into any of the additive mixtures of primary colors. That is, each range or segment can be treated independently of its relative values in the original copy. There may typically be from 2 to 40 possible ranges defined, and the discrimination may be so acute that a sheet of white paper can be divided into several distinct values. (4) When a desirable combination of colorized segments is seen by the designer on a TV monitor, the same image is photographed elsewhere from a fine grain TV image.

The illustration facing the opening of this chapter was made in this manner—from a defocused image of the sans-serif letters "pow." (The original is in startling shades of red, yellow, green, and black.) Figure 12-2 shows the separation of color ranges. This type of process can be seen to be close to the logical ultimate in design control of color. Although at first glance the necessity for arbitrary division of the gray values of the copy

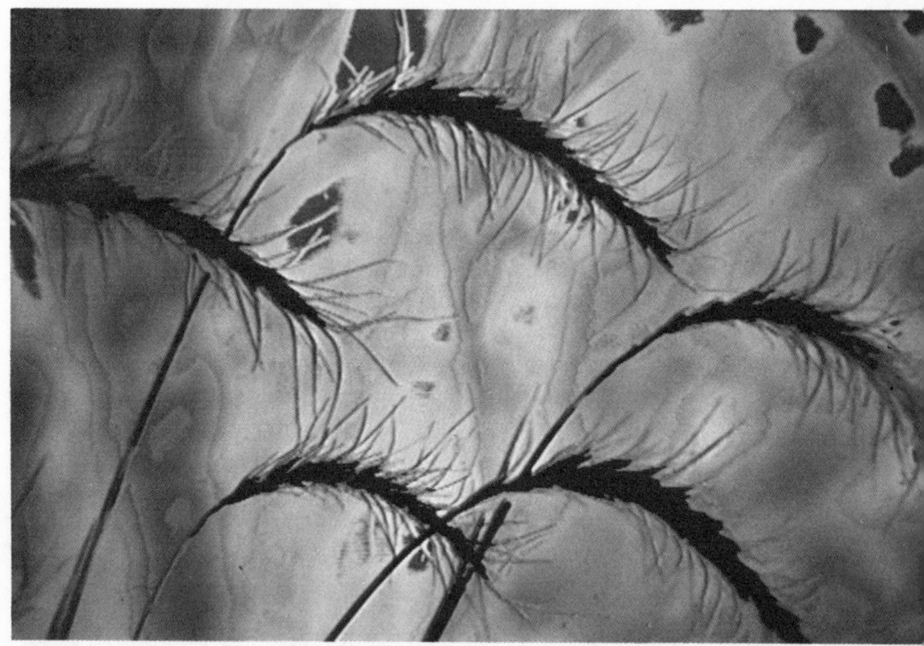

12-2 *These electronically posterized photographs have been divided into a number of grey value ranges, each of which may be assigned an arbitrary synthesized additive color mix. Although these reproductions give only a rough idea of the way the subject appears to the scanning black and white TV camera, the final colors can be mixed at will, to be photographed from a fine grain color TV tube. (Courtesy of Metacolor Inc., San Francisco.)*

into the "posterized" segments might seem a limitation, on second thought it might be obvious that there are only two other paths available: (a) the choice of color for *every* individual point in the image (the method of the painter, but generally impractical for the working designer); or (b) the choice of color for *all* points at once (the limited method of adding a single color to a black and white image, or the method of obtaining a single type of analog, essentially the method of color photography). Case (a) is impractical, and case (b), while now available, affords the designer minimal controls over color. The only practical alternative is the division of the image into tonal ranges, as described.

It will be noticed that there is almost no theoretical restriction on the additive color mixtures, or on the discrimination in the defined gray-value segments. Nor is there much restriction on the kinds of copy acceptable: black and white, color, opaque, transparent, negative, positive, printed, drawn, painted, two-dimensional, three-dimensional (consistent with focus and sharpness requirements), size typically 1 square inch to at least 11″ × 14″, and so on. A somewhat greater limitation is in the fineness possible in the TV screen, which limits the sharpness of edges.

It is convenient for the designer to operate a process such as this in real time; that is, to supervise the modification of the image as necessary until a satisfactory result is obtained. But when the designer cannot be present in the studio, appropriately simplified specifications can be worked out. The results may be as realistic or as wild as may seem desirable. The amount of control afforded the designer may perhaps best be described as an embarrassment of riches.

The end product of such a process is typically a 35mm slide, but any form of photographic recording, preseparation, and so on, can be used simply by setting it up before the TV image.

Public Law 94-553
94th Congress

An Act

For the general revision of the Copyright Law, title 17 of the United States Code, and for other purposes.

Oct. 19, 1976
[S. 22]

Be it enacted by the Senate and House of Representatives of the United States of America in Congress assembled,

Title 17, USC, Copyrights.

TITLE I—GENERAL REVISION OF COPYRIGHT LAW

SEC. 101. Title 17 of the United States Code, entitled "Copyrights", is hereby amended in its entirety to read as follows:

TITLE 17—COPYRIGHTS

CHAPTER	Sec.
1. SUBJECT MATTER AND SCOPE OF COPYRIGHT	101
2. COPYRIGHT OWNERSHIP AND TRANSFER	201
3. DURATION OF COPYRIGHT	301
4. COPYRIGHT NOTICE, DEPOSIT, AND REGISTRATION	401
5. COPYRIGHT INFRINGEMENT AND REMEDIES	501
6. MANUFACTURING REQUIREMENT AND IMPORTATION	601
7. COPYRIGHT OFFICE	701
8. COPYRIGHT ROYALTY TRIBUNAL	801

Chapter 1.—SUBJECT MATTER AND SCOPE OF COPYRIGHT

Sec.
101. Definitions.
102. Subject matter of copyright: In general.
103. Subject matter of copyright: Compilations and derivative works.
104. Subject matter of copyright: National origin.
105. Subject matter of copyright: United States Government works.
106. Exclusive rights in copyrighted works.
107. Limitations on exclusive rights: Fair use.
108. Limitations on exclusive rights: Reproduction by libraries and archives.
109. Limitations on exclusive rights: Effect of transfer of particular copy or phonorecord.
110. Limitations on exclusive rights: Exemption of certain performances and displays.
111. Limitations on exclusive rights: Secondary transmissions.
112. Limitations on exclusive rights: Ephemeral recordings.
113. Scope of exclusive rights in pictorial, graphic, and sculptural works.
114. Scope of exclusive rights in sound recordings.
115. Scope of exclusive rights in nondramatic musical works: Compulsory license for making and distributing phonorecords.
116. Scope of exclusive rights in nondramatic musical works: Public performances by means of coin-operated phonorecord players.
117. Scope of exclusive rights: Use in conjunction with computers and similar information systems.
118. Scope of exclusive rights: Use of certain works in connection with noncommercial broadcasting.

§ 101. Definitions

17 USC 101.

As used in this title, the following terms and their variant forms mean the following:

An "anonymous work" is a work on the copies or phonorecords of which no natural person is identified as author.

"Audiovisual works" are works that consist of a series of related images which are intrinsically intended to be shown by the use of machines or devices such as projectors, viewers, or electronic equipment, together with accompanying sounds, if any, regardless

APPENDIX A
Legal aspects of illustration and design use

It is the purpose of this section to give the art director, designer, editor, and art buyer some understanding of the legal use of illustrations and designs in books, so that misunderstandings are avoided, litigation is unnecessary, and relations with artists, designers, and photographic sources may be as uncomplicated and productive as possible. The general revision of the Copyright Law, Title 17, of the United States Code, effective January 1, 1978, the first general revision since 1909, gives added incentive for a review by art and design people of legal considerations in relation to their jobs. There is a new law, but there are also many interpretations from older law that are still relevant.

The following is intended as an informal presentation of some of the considerations most relevant to art and design in the particular area of books, but it should by no means be regarded as a full legal treatment of the subject. The law is rich in problematic interpretations and exceptions to general rules, and short treatments must necessarily omit most of these. This can, at best, permit the reader to judge better as to when and where care and attention should be exercised, what some of the critical factors and changes are, and when legal advice may perhaps be desirable. Copyright law in relation to art and design for books has never been a field with a great deal of litigation, and hence a great deal of its interpretation rests on legal opinion rather than on case law.

Acquisition of rights and the new copyright law

When the old copyright law was in effect, the legal relationships between publishers and artists often were informal but, nonetheless, legally adequate. It is hoped that the informality will continue under the new law, but all the parties—publishers, artists, designers, and photographers—need to give special attention to the new law's provisions, since they sometimes require signed agreements for an effective transfer of rights.

The art director is interested mainly in the quality and suitability of the work, but there must be an awareness, too, of the legal standards by which the rights to it are affected. These six aspects of the new law should be kept in mind:

1. The initial ownership of copyright belongs to the "author." (The "author" of art, photograph, or design is the artist, photographer, or designer.)

2. The author, ordinarily, is the one who created the work. However, in the case of a work made for hire, the one who commissioned the work is considered to be the "author" and thus the initial owner of copyright. (The term "for hire" is discussed in greater detail below.)

3. When someone wishes to acquire a right of copyright from the initial owner on an exclusive basis, a transfer of copyright ownership is involved. The new law provides that a transfer of copyright ownership is not valid unless there is a document reflecting the transfer, which is signed by the owner of the rights conveyed or by the owner's agent.

4. Generally speaking, there are five rights of copyright—the rights to do or to authorize any of the following: (1) to reproduce the copyrighted work, (2) to distribute copies to the public, (3) to prepare derivative works based on the copyrighted work, (4) to perform the copyrighted work publicly, and (5) to display the copyrighted work publicly. Any of these rights may be transferred and owned separately, and there can be a transfer of copyright ownership (and thus the need for a signed document) even if only one or two of the rights is transferred on an exclusive basis and even if the transfer is for a limited time.

5. When a right of copyright is acquired on a *nonexclusive* basis, the new copyright law does not require a signed document, although it is desirable to have one in order to avoid misunderstandings that might otherwise arise.

6. There is a special rule relating to separate contributions to a collective work. (A collective work is defined as a work, such as an anthology, in which a number of contributions that are separate and independent works are assembled into a collective whole. But it should be understood that artist, photographer, and designer also are contributors to the collective work of a book, with the author or authors, and are thus legally the "authors" of their contributions.) The "author" of each separate contribution is the initial owner of copyright in it. Unless there is an express transfer of the copyright or any rights under it, the owner of the copyright in the collective work as a whole is presumed to have acquired, with respect to the separate contribution, only the privilege of reproducing and distributing the contribution as part of that particular collective work, any revision of that collective work, and any later collective work in the same series. (The old law was often interpreted to mean that the owner of the collective work acquired all rights unless there was a demonstrable understanding to the contrary.)

Taking the above six rules into account, the art director or art buyer has to keep in mind these questions with respect to art, design, and photography: Who is the initial owner of copyright? If it is the artist, designer, or photographer, what exclusive rights (that is, what signed documents) need be acquired from him or her? Even if only nonexclusive rights are wanted, does the artist's work fall into a category of a separate contribution to a collective work? If so, as is usually the case, are temporary rights in trust sufficient, or should an express agreement be obtained covering broader rights?

Another category of art, design, and photography to be considered is works made for hire. Here the employer, or the one who commissioned the work, is considered to be the initial owner of copyright.

A work made "for hire" may be a work prepared by an employee within the scope of his or her employment. The employer owns all the rights of copyright unless the parties have expressly agreed otherwise in a written instrument signed by them.

But a work also will be a work made for hire if two conditions are met. *First,* the parties must expressly agree, in a written instrument signed by them, that the work shall be considered a work made "for hire." *Second,* the work must be specially ordered or commissioned for use as a supplementary work; an instructional text; a contribution to a collective work; a compilation; an atlas; as a part of an audiovisual work; or as a translation, a test, or answer material for a test. A supplementary work is defined as a work prepared as a secondary adjunct to a work by another author for the purpose of introducing, concluding, illustrating, explaining, revising, commenting upon, or assisting in the use of the other work, such as pictorial illustrations, maps, charts, and tables. Art and design work for books may usually be described as supplementary work.

As a general rule, the broader the rights acquired by the publisher, the higher the fee paid with respect to the work, since the artist's rights to use the work are being restricted. However, even when the art director is in a bargaining position to obtain broad rights without paying "extra," he or she may find it fairer not to seek rights that are not really needed. Of course, in judging what rights are really needed, the publisher should keep in mind more than just the immediate uses planned for the art. The publisher should also be aware of possible future uses and of the desirability, in some circumstances, of having the art used exclusively in the publisher's work.

As for the formalities to be followed, lengthy agreements often are not necessary. However, when transfers of exclusive rights are involved (or when there is to be a work for hire which requires a signed agreement), a statement on a purchase order will not suffice unless it is correctly worded and also signed by both parties.

Types of artwork

Several kinds of "art" may be distinguished: (1) original artwork done to the publisher's specifications; (2) "fine art" of various kinds, not done to the publisher's specifications but useful in books for various reasons; (3) "commercial art," also not done to the publisher's specifications but seen to be useful and "picked up" from other sources; (4) art from other sources that is adapted, redrawn, or otherwise "borrowed" in part or in whole; and (5) art in the public domain.

In all cases the publisher wishes to use an image that someone else supplies. How is this brought about? In simplest form, when a written or oral request is made for an illustration or design, stating the use to which it is to be put, the receipt of that illustration from artist or owner ordinarily constitutes permission for the use stated. However, as explained above, this permission would only cover a *nonexclusive* right (unless a work made for hire was being created), and a signed document would be needed to obtain exclusive rights.

Ordinarily, a credit to the source of a picture is expected by the artist unless otherwise discussed. It should be at least informally agreed upon as to where within the book the credit is to appear, whether on the page with the picture or elsewhere.

Artwork done to the publisher's specifications

Here the right to reproduce is established through some form of agreement between publisher and artist. Even a verbal agreement is often legally valid, but such an agreement encourages misunderstanding as to the exact terms agreed to—and it is not sufficient when the publisher wishes to obtain a transfer of exclusive rights.

Aside from these considerations, there is no set or standard form for the artist-publisher agreement. The requirements and circumstances of both publishers and artists may differ widely, and thus the artist contract shown in Chapter 11 is merely suggestive. The publisher should evolve a form or forms suitable to the publisher's needs and the needs of the artists normally dealt with, remembering that all such agreements are, in fact, open to negotiation. In practice, any parts of a standard form that are not agreed to or applicable may be struck out and other provisions added as necessary. Changes should be initialed by both parties and the form signed by the artist and by a person capable of acting legally for the publishing company. Contracts are, of course, something that few people like to take time for, but from the publisher's point of view they are more necessary under the revised law than under the old.

As a practical matter, it is not always required that both parties sign an agreement for it to have effect. For example, if the publisher sends a proper contract to an artist, and the artist has agreed to the arrangement and has started the job but keeps forgetting to sign the contract and return it, what should be done? It is not always necessary to hold up the job. If the parties have, in fact, agreed to terms (and if a signed agreement is not required because exclusive rights are not being sought, or because the work is being done by an employee), the agreement may be considered binding. Indeed, it can be binding even if the publisher doesn't want it to be. If the publisher wants a binding agreement to exist *only* if the document is appropriately signed, this should be made clear in advance.

Fine art, not done to the publisher's specifications

Under the old law it was often assumed that the right to reproduce fine art was vested in the current owner of the work, unless the owner's purchase agreement with the artist contained restrictions. As an example of such restrictions, the estate of Grandma Moses holds copyright to all her paintings, but such a situation was relatively rare. The old law may, in fact, still be important in relation to artwork sold before 1978. But under the revised law the assumption is that all rights remain with the creator of the work unless otherwise conveyed, and thus the publisher who wishes to acquire reproduction rights to fine art must now more often seek permission from the original artist, or from the artist's estate, or establish, to the publisher's satisfaction, that someone else has acquired the right to grant the necessary permission.

In practice, the publisher often deals with a museum, gallery, or other agency, and has traditionally followed the advice received from them in regard to what permissions, if any, needed to be obtained. If such advice is followed, the publisher may still be presumed to be acting in good faith and, in case of error, will most probably be able to reach a reasonable agreement, but the publisher is not automatically shielded. If private owners of artwork are dealt with directly, then there should be reasonable assurance that the owner of the art is also the owner of the required reproduction rights.

In obtaining permission to reproduce fine art there may be a permission fee and/or a reproduction fee involved. Also, some museums do not give final permission to reproduce until a satisfactory proof has been submitted, thus acting as responsible agents for the works entrusted to them. Artists may now decide to adopt a similar attitude. In some cases three separate permissions may be necessary to reproduce a work of fine art: that of the artist, the owner, and the photographer who takes the photograph of the work, for reproduction.

The art director should be particularly aware that cropping works of fine art is often questionable practice, as is the superimposition of type, retouching, and deliberate changes of color balance. Some artists or museums may require that no cropping or altering be done, other than creating labeled "details" which are almost always permitted. On the other hand, if permission has been given to reproduce without qualifications as to the manner, the agency granting the permission has no "moral right" to protest cropping, overlaying, or even retouching, although in gross cases action might be possible if the use went beyond implied or customary limitations. The good will of artists and museums can be important to the publisher, and it is to be hoped that design uses of fine art would not be such as to provoke artistic outrage.

Commercial art and reference art

These may be considered together since they both may, on occasion, be reproduced from another publication of some kind, or redrawn from such a source. Copyright applies to these works of art as well as to other types, and the legal standards previously discussed are applicable. Even when adapting a work, permission may be necessary, since the right to prepare derivative works is one of the rights of copyright. It should be noted, however, that not everything about a work of art is always protected by copyright. The artist's copyright protects his or her form of expression but not the underlying idea.

Art in the public domain

In the "public domain" means simply that ownership of rights in the work belong to the public rather than to any individual or organization. Once anything is in the public domain it remains so indefinitely. All fine art, commercial art, or reference art that is clearly in the public domain may be copied and reproduced directly, or redrawn as necessary, without permission from anyone.

Works of the U.S. Government are in the public domain in the United States, as are all works whose copyrights have lapsed (see below, under "Further considerations . . ."). Copy photographs of historical prints in the public domain are often considered *not* to be in the public domain themselves; at least it has been so assumed by agencies dealing in such materials. But take note of this from Circular 40j, "Copyright for Photographs," from the U.S. Copyright Office: "*Uncopyrightable works.* A work that merely reproduces images through the operation of mechanical or photomechanical processes, with no appreciable element of original pictorial expression, is not registerable as a photograph. Thus, a reproduction of textual material alone is generally not registerable. . . ." The choice of example and the use of the word "generally" introduce elements of uncertainty, but in any case, those who provide the results of research to the publisher in convenient form are entitled to be paid for their efforts.

It is well known to graphic designers that typeface designs are widely and rather closely copied and that such copying has been very difficult to control. The revised law apparently still does not recognize typeface design as a copyrightable category, although Congress has expressed some willingness to consider authorizing legislation. The absence of specific legislation at present is unfortunate and may, in part, result from legislative insensitivity to the small but distinct and unique factors that render typeface designs successful or unsuccessful. Yet it is plain to any observer that these small distinctions are fully appreciated in the marketplace of graphic usage.

Further considerations of the revised copyright law

Artists and art buyers may still be most familiar with the old law. Under the old law as amended, that is until 1978, there were two kinds of copyright, common law copyright and statutory copyright. After the creation of an illustration of any kind, but before its publication, the work was automatically protected by "common law copyright" without any action on the part of the creator. When and if the work was published in any form bearing a notice of copyright, the work automatically acquired statutory copyright, no separate form of copyright being required.

As of January 1, 1978, by terms of the new Copyright Law, statutory copyright covers all works, both before and after publication. Common-law copyright was largely abolished, and works are protected from the original act of creation. Before the revised law, publication of visual material in an uncopyrighted publication ordinarily meant loss of copyright, for the document and its visual materials together, and reversion to the public domain. The revised law is more lenient in this respect, as will be more fully explained below, but copyright may still be lost through publication in an uncopyrighted publication.

In general, the copyright on a book or similar printed form is sufficient to prevent any illustrations therein from going into the public domain, and in this respect therefore no separate action is required on the part of artist or designer. Nevertheless, it may be desirable in certain cases for the artist to have a separate copyright notice and/or registry, even though it is not ordinarily necessary for protection; at the very least, notice and information is thereby given to other potential users of the art as to ownership of copyright. Artists who have not conveyed exclusive rights to the publisher retain rights of their own, but this is not readily apparent to a reader unless there is some notice of this fact. The additional notice must, of course, be agreed to by the publisher as to form and placement. Such notice will ordinarily appear on the same page with the illustration, or on the copyright page of the book or close to it. The name of the artist should be given in "recognizable" form, with the copyright symbol or the word "copyright" and the year of the copyright.

Various other aspects of the revised copyright law should be mentioned:

1. The duration of copyright has been changed. For works already under statutory protection the new law retains the old copyright term of 28 years from first publication (or from registration in some cases), renewable for a second term of protection. However, the new law increases the length of the second period to 47 years. Copyrights in their first term must still be renewed to receive the full new maximum protection of 75 years. Copyrights already in their second term automatically are extended to the maximum of 75 years without the need for further renewal.

2. For works created after January 1, 1978, the new law provides a term lasting for the author's lifetime plus an additional 50 years. For works made "for hire," and for anonymous and pseudonymous works, the new term will be 75 years from publication or 100 years from creation, whichever is shorter. As noted above, works produced under contract may or may not always be considered "made for hire."

For unpublished works that are already in existence on January 1, 1978, but are not protected by pre-1978 statutory copyright and have not gone into the public domain, the new law will generally provide automatic copyright protection for the lifetime of the artist plus 50 years, or the 75- or 100-year terms prescribed for new works. Special dates of termination are provided for copyrights in older works of this sort.

The new act does not, of course, restore copyright protection for any work that went into the public domain under the old law.

3. The new law continues the prohibition in the former law against U.S. copyright in works of the United States Government but clarifies its scope by defining works covered by this prohibition as those prepared by an officer or employee of the U.S. Government as part of that person's official duties.

4. The old law required as a mandatory condition of copyright protection that the published copies of a work bear a copyright notice. The new law also calls for a notice on published copies, but omission of the notice or errors in its form will not immediately result in forfeit of the copyright, and such conditions can be corrected within certain time limits (usually five years). Innocent infringers who have been misled by the omission of the notice, or by errors in it, will be shielded from liability.

Types of reproduction rights in art and design

Mutual agreements and contracts, copyright law, the legal rights of subjects and the public, and court decisions interpreting all these are the main instruments governing the extent, nature, and duration of reproduction rights. Copyright law, the rights of subjects and the public, and legal interpretations are relatively fixed at any given time and not subject to negotiation and control by the publisher, but contractual agreements are quite flexible. Agreements securing ownership or permission to reproduce artwork or photography are the result of negotiation and the basis of contracts and "quasi-contracts" describing the exact extent of rights being purchased.

In book work most art has traditionally been sold for a specific book, with exclusive and unrestricted rights conveyed via the artist's contract or, under the old copyright law, without it by means of the publisher's implied exclusive rights in work purchased, if not otherwise limited by agreement. Many more restrictions have usually been placed upon photographs, which are usually easier to market to more than one publication. There is no intrinsic difference between the two classes as to the ways they may be sold. It is to be expected in either case that when exclusive rights are conveyed, the price may well be higher, and when restrictions are placed on rights, the price may be lower. Thus the sale of only restricted rights may not necessarily be to the artist's or photographer's or designer's advantage, unless it is in fact likely that the work may be sold to more than one customer.

The factors through which restrictions on rights may operate often include the following:

1. Number of times the illustration is to be reproduced (e.g., one time under one copyright)
2. Placement in the publication (e.g., cover, part opening, etc.)
3. Languages in which publication is to appear (e.g., English)
4. Area of distribution (e.g., U.S.)
5. Size of the reproduction (e.g., ¼ page)
6. Time limit on reproducing the illustration (e.g., 7 years)
7. Name of one publication, and date, if applicable
8. Edition (e.g., hard or soft cover, book-club edition, etc.)
9. Limit on number of insertions in one publication (e.g., one insertion)
10. Size of printing for which rights are conveyed (e.g., under 10,000)
11. Special limitations (e.g., book rights, textbook rights, first rights, and so on; see below)

We shall attempt to discuss only certain important aspects of the many possible combinations.

One-time rights

Most picture agencies and photographers sell their pictures with one-time rights stipulated, all additional rights being reserved. If other rights are needed, these are subject to negotiation and, usually, extra fees. One-time rights are also called "one-time use," or "one use only," or "one-time reproduction." The publisher has the right to reproduce the picture in multiple printings of one edition of the book for which it is purchased. A separate edition, such as an edition in a different language, usually is not covered by the agreement, but the form of specific agreement controls in each particular case. Prints, negatives, contacts, transparencies, and any other physical representation of the illustration remain the property of the artist or photographer under a contract for one-time rights. They must be returned after reproduction. The book copyright gives the publisher only rights "in trust" for the one-time use.

First rights

This restriction conveys the right to reproduce an illustration for its first reproduction only. Such rights may also be limited as to the length of time they are valid, or as to the type of publication in which they may appear. For example, first rights may be granted for a year and for books only, thus allowing the photographer or artist to sell the illustration immediately to a magazine, and to other books after a year.

In the making of complex textbooks, more than a year may pass between the purchase of a photograph and the actual publication date of the book. Thus, any time restriction should be carefully calculated. (In practice, first rights are often obtained for photography done on specific assignment, when other uses for the photos are not anticipated by the publisher.)

Exclusive rights

If an assignment involves pictures of general usefulness, a photographer may often ask a higher price for exclusive rights (either explicitly conveyed or done "for hire") than when the pictures are thought to have little general usefulness.

Advertising or promotion rights

First, it should be noted that, entirely apart from the rights a photographer or artist may be willing to sell, it is unlawful to use any person's photograph in most advertising without their written consent, as will be more fully explained below. The same prohibition applies to portrait artwork, but in practice such use is rarer.

In regard to permission for advertising, when one-time rights are acquired for editorial use of a picture, ordinarily that picture also may be used in the promotion of that book only, unless the agreement stipulates otherwise. (See below, under "The use of photographs—legal aspects.")

Photographic agency rates for pictures used simply for advertising, promotion, or "trade" are usually a great deal higher than for use in the text of a book.

U.S. rights, world rights, etc.

U.S. rights enable publication and distribution in the United States and its possessions. World rights enable publication in the entire world and, if the contract provides, also may make it possible for the publisher to license others to publish the work in any other country. World rights, of course, cost more than U.S. rights, so it is advisable to check ahead of time with the sales department or editor to make sure which books are planned for world sale. This is far easier than renegotiating art and photo fees or contracts.

In many combinations of the above, restrictions may be placed on rights conveyed to the publisher by suppliers of art, photographs, and design. Contracts can be drawn or tailored to fit many kinds of requirements. Restrictions on exclusive rights can operate to the publisher's benefit as well as to the benefit of the artist, since more restrictions may commonly mean lower price. The real point of negotiation and carefully made contracts is to enable the publisher to buy whatever rights may be required and, at the same time, to enable the artist to retain rights that are useful to him or her and not to the publisher.

The use of photographs—legal aspects

There are a number of considerations that apply to photographs that seldom apply to artwork. We shall note some of these informally here, but for a more extended treatment of these topics, the designer may wish to consult pertinent books on the subject, special circulars of the U.S. Copyright Office (Library of Congress, Washington, D.C. 20559), and, of course, the new Copyright Law (Public Law 94–553).

It should be stressed that court interpretations in respect to a changing field such as photography do not by any means settle all possible questions in regard to legal problems that may arise.

The following observations are intended to have special relevance to the work of the designer, or art editor, or anyone else charged with buying photographs for the publisher.

- When exclusive rights are required the usual contractual agreement between publisher and an assigned photographer usually has been one of employment. The work is done or supplied specifically "for hire." Otherwise, the most common arrangement is to buy "one-time" rights. Other rights, described above, are arranged for as required.
- Even when the publisher engages a photographer to take pictures "for hire," any negatives produced belong, by trade custom, to the photographer, in the absence of any other agreement. But the right to *print* anything from the negatives belongs to the hiring publisher. (Photographers who clearly understand this may not be anxious to store the negatives for the publisher, since this implies responsibility for the virtual property of another.) All transparencies also belong to the publisher, in the absence

of any other agreement, but trade practice has often been to return unwanted transparencies to the photographer, who may sell them again. In the absence of a contract formalizing this practice, it would appear contradictory. In fact, there may even be an implied contract returning rights to the photographer when the publisher returns unwanted transparencies. In that case it is not clear whether the publisher can later decide to repossess any or all of the transparencies. In fact, a case involving transparencies lost during return to the photographer was settled out of court in favor of the photographer, who claimed that the admitted attempt to return the transparencies implied a contract to return them, even though there was no written or oral contract. (The publisher had claimed that the transparencies did not belong to the photographer and that therefore he could collect no damages.) Publishers may yet decide that it is safer not to return unwanted transparencies unless this is stipulated in a contract.

- People who are the subjects of photographs have rights, and if these rights are infringed they may sue for damages and injunctive relief. Chiefly these rights are: (a) the right not to be falsely injured in reputation, to be free from "libel"; and (b) the right not to have their private lives unfairly invaded, to be free from "invasion of privacy."
- Six states have statutory right of privacy laws, among them New York State. Most of the decisions developing the concept stem from New York, but many other states have developed privacy law through interpretations.
- The New York Civil Rights Law says that *written* consent to the use of any person's name or photograph is required for any purpose of advertising or "trade." "Trade" may be described as any commercialized use other than advertising, but this law is not intended to restrict publication and sale of books. Thus, the use of a person's picture in informative nonfiction is not a violation merely because it helps to sell a book. But the unauthorized use of a person's photograph with fiction, or to promote a book with which it has no factual connection, would ordinarily be a violation.
- Four basic guidelines relate to whether a person's privacy has been unlawfully invaded, proper permission not having been granted:

  a. If the photograph is part of an advertisement, there is a violation.
  b. If it is used in a work of fiction, there is a violation.
  c. If it is used in connection with current news of immediate public interest, there is no violation.
  d. If it is used in an educational or informative publication, there is no violation.

  These are only general guidelines, since exceptions are possible. For example, a photograph of the subject of a biography used in advertising the book ordinarily would not require permission.
- Violations in areas of libel and invasion of privacy allow the injured party to sue the publisher for money damages and injunctive relief. Therefore the publisher should take care that necessary permissions are obtained; usually these are safest

when they run to the publisher rather than to the photographer.

- To avoid possible actions for invasion of privacy in states not having statutes relating to invasion of privacy, a good rule (when in doubt and no permission has been granted) is to avoid using any person's picture in a way that might shock average sensibilities.
- A "public person" (in general, an eminent or newsworthy person) has very little right of privacy concerning his or her public life. In other words, the right of privacy ceases to the extent the life ceases to be private. A public figure ordinarily must prove reckless disregard of truth in order to claim invasion of privacy in reports about his or her public life.
- Protection against invasion of privacy does not prevent pictures that satirize, exaggerate, and so on, as long as the pictures are truthful (e.g., unretouched) and as long as they do not "shock the sensibilities" of the average person in relation to the person depicted (permission not having been granted).
- It is better to be safe than sorry, and the safest rule is to obtain releases whenever possible, at least from the main subjects of photographs. It is not always possible to foresee how pictures may be used in the future. The very fact of having obtained some kind of release greatly decreases the chances of suit. It is particularly important to obtain releases from parent or guardian in the case of minors.
- Pictures that are not in themselves in violation of the rights of individuals may become in violation if they are miscaptioned or used with text that creates an impression that violates such rights. The courts consider the use of pictures, in conjunction with any accompanying captions, legends, or text, a practice that can scarcely be quarreled with.
- Consent forms (so-called "model releases") to be signed by the subjects of photographs are of various kinds. (See the suggested form opposite.) There is no standard form, and, no matter what the form says, any consent obtained does not, generally, apply to a photograph that is, in fact, used libelously or in such a way as to invade privacy. It should be well noted that consent also may not operate if there is no real connection between the release signed and the photograph to which it is to apply. If the consenting model thinks the photograph is for one purpose and then it is used for another purpose the release may be valueless. The form should be signed at the *end* of the photographic session and dated. Negatives should be datable in some way to establish a connection with the release date. Many a release carelessly obtained might not stand up to a court test in every context, but, essentially, consent forms simply make it much less likely that the subject will sue, unless there is serious cause.
- As has been noted, the revised copyright law is more lenient than the previous law in regard to accidental publication without copyright notice or with errors in the notice. The copyright is not automatically lost, as could happen under the old law. Thus, even though innocent infringers are protected from liability, designers and picture editors may wish to be more cautious about assuming that photographs have lost copyright protection through accidental error or omission of the notice.

STANDARD MODEL RELEASE FORM

I hereby consent to the reproduction, sale, and/or use of photographs of myself, for all purposes, with or without the use of my name, by the publisher

____

and by any nominee or designee of the publisher, including any agency, client, or other publication, in all forms and media and in all manners, including advertising, trade, display editorial, and exhibition.

In giving this consent I release the publisher, his nominees and designees, from liability for any violation of any personal or proprietary right that I may have in connection with sale, reproduction, or use of such photographs in any medium.

I am more than twenty one years of age.

Signed________________________________

Address ________________________________

Witness ________________________________

Date ________________________________

Parent or guardian's consent:

I am the parent or guardian of the minor named above, and possessed of the legal authority to execute the above consent and release. I approve the foregoing and waive any rights in the premises.

Signed________________________________

Address ________________________________

Witness ________________________________

Date ________________________________

- Separate copyright notices on photographs are the business of the photographer. The publisher is concerned only because the copyright notice, if one is agreed to, must be included on the same page with the reproduction, or somewhere else, as agreed upon. If a supplied photograph itself bears a separate copyright notice it often appears on the back of the print or on the face of the transparency.
- In cases of loss of, or damage to, photographic copy, the absence of an establishable market value does not limit the owner to nominal damages when the holder is liable. The cost of replacement may be used, together with other circumstances, as a measure of recoverable damages (i.e., in the establishment of an "intrinsic value"). Loss of, or damage to, a single transparency may be valued in the neighborhood of $15,000 and that of a single black and white print in the neighborhood of $100! Thus, it is obviously prudent to establish more modest loss or damage replacement values in contractual agreements. The fact that a photograph may be part of a series of similar shots that are not lost or damaged is not a complete defense.
- For many reasons it is obviously important for the publisher to check all delivery memos and all invoices to be sure that they are accurate in terms of (a) what is delivered, (b) its condition, and (c) the terms of sale. Unacceptable terms and/or damaged or incomplete delivery should be promptly objected to in writing.
- Standard contracts for photographers on assignment work should be drawn up in form acceptable to the publisher. The photographers may, of course, have ideas and forms of their own, and some compromise may need to be worked out. However, constant bargaining is time consuming, and for this reason it is recommended that the publisher's contract forms should reflect a fair arrangement. Some forms might well explicitly recognize rights to be retained by the photographer. Fair contracts result in less friction and wasted time and enable the publisher to deal more easily with competent professionals who know the legal aspects of their craft.
- All contracts should be signed before work is started. The publisher does not benefit in the long run from law suits or ill will, no matter what the results of litigation may be.
- As an example of terms that reflect the desires of photographers, the Society of Photographers in Communications (formerly the American Society of Magazine Photographers [ASMP]) suggests a form to appear on the reverse side of photographers' invoices (see the *ASMP Guide to Business Practices in Photography.* New York: ASMP, 1973). Some of its terms, such as the short holding period, are clearly intended for advertising and are impractical for book publishers.

The copyright of design

Complete book designs, including the interior design, have been copyrighted by designers, and many book jackets are copyrighted separately, even when they do not contain traditionally defined "artwork." In other words, copyrightable artwork is not confined to traditional "art."

The first designer to copyright a complete book design was Joan Stoliar, designer of

Illusions by Richard Bach (Delacorte Press/Eleanor Fried). Notice on the copyright page of the book reads "Design copyright © by Joan Stoliar." (See Paul Doebler, "Copyright for Book Designs?" *Publishers Weekly* [July 4, 1977]: 59.)

The design for *Illusions* was registered under the old "Class G," as a "Graphic Design Collection." This terminology may seem odd, but the reasoning apparently was that the design was in fact a collection of arrangements (i.e., layouts involving choice and placement of elements) that is in toto a "contribution to a collective work." At least that was judged the most likely category in which to apply, and it was proven successful. The arrangements were original as such, even though the elements they contained were for the most part not original in the sense that artwork is original.

While design may be copyrightable just as any other original work of authorship, a design often is not thought of in copyright terms, and thus it sometimes is appropriate, through the use of specific copyright statements, to call attention to the copyright claim even when a separate copyright notice for the design is not required. Since the focus on copyrights for design is more or less just emerging, new contractual patterns may come forth between publisher and designers. As with other transactions involving copyrights, all parties must consider what rights they really want, what they can get as a practical matter and at what cost, and, not least, what is fair.

It should, of course, be borne in mind that "quality" is not a criterion of originality in respect to the copyright law. A work of art does not require to be judged "great," or even to be well regarded by any judge whatever, to be original and therefore copyrightable.

"View of Utopia," a woodcut in the 1578 Basel edition of Sir Thomas More's Utopia. *A description of this picture is entered on the card shown in Figure B-2.*

APPENDIX B
The attributes of pictures

Deciding how to use pictures is one problem, but finding pictures is quite another, whether the pictures are fine art, historical records, commercial art, clippings, photography, or pictures reproduced in books. It is difficult enough sometimes to find a particular photograph you have taken yourself, but to find a picture in the sea of art and picture archives, one needs to be a specialist. Picture research is a specialty chiefly concerned with locating and dealing with agencies or other sources that may have collections of pictures in the areas of interest. It is assumed that these agencies can find pictures within their own collections. However, in working with them it becomes quite obvious that this assumption is not true for a great part of the extensive collections they may supervise.

The method for finding pictures with specific attributes that will be discussed in this appendix is intended for use in relatively modest collections of a few thousand important and usable pictures, which are in considerable demand. The method is not intended for use in very large or relatively unimportant or inactive collections.

The discussion of the attributes of pictures, hopefully, will give designers new insights into how pictures can be used for editorial purposes and how research can be logically carried on when done carefully, even when the means employed is not nearly as systematic as the one suggested. The system described may sound rather complicated, but in use it is simple. Physically it is similar to that used for artists' cards in Chapter 3 (see Figure 3–1). For larger collections computerization is practical.

Picture retrieval by concept coordination*

There are no good dictionaries of visual language, no neatly organized parcels of visual concepts like books of verbal concepts—with indexing by contents, glossaries, descriptive titles, classification schemes, heading schemes, catalogs, bibliographies, and

*Adapted from Stanley Rice, "Picture Retrieval by Concept Coordination," *Special Libraries* (December 1969).

all the apparatus that constitutes the traditional filing and retrieval apparatus of verbal collections.

Pictures are, on the surface, comparatively simple, but so far it has been difficult to classify them by any system that allows for general or complex file interrogation. Usually pictures have been filed by job numbers, by the name of the photographer or artist, by job titles, or by an alphabetical accumulation of subject headings.

Most frequently pictures are used in ways that are complementary to words—with a speech or in one form of publication or another. Consequently, teachers, authors, editors, and others who wish to write or speak (and have images to supplement their words) would like to be able to *find* pictures in their area of interest. They need to interrogate picture files and to direct questions of precision and complexity to collections to which they may have access. This interrogation is not now possible, and it is to this problem that we address ourselves here.

Picture researchers may be frustrated occasionally by not being able to locate pictures that are known to exist, but that have been misplaced or indexed with different concepts in mind. However, they are far more often frustrated by knowing *what* they want but not knowing *how* to search for a pictorial representation of it.

If they do not have a job number, an artist's name, or a photographer's name, they are usually reduced to using whatever heading schemes and file folder names have taken root in the picture collections that they query. These schemes generally follow the traditional schemes for verbal subject heading indexing—if they follow anything at all. Most of them are arranged alphabetically by subject, and any guide or thesaurus–dictionary is rudimentary, if extant.

Some larger collections use two or three Dewey classification numbers in combination with assigned subject headings, but most picture classification schedules are simply of the grow-it-yourself variety. Such files acquire folders for whatever may happen along, and such schedules very quickly become highly idiosyncratic. The chief saving grace is that the librarian who has a long tenure will learn to locate the items that are most in demand. Then the folders will acquire names important to the local needs, but such files tend to be dormant except for the simple and repetitious demands. Duplicated use of the same pictures by many publications is by no means attributable only to the excellence or uniqueness of the pictures. Idiosyncratic files cannot be interrogated; they can only be browsed. Browsing is valuable but so is interrogation.

Concept coordination

The concept-coordinated system of record filing and retrieval has apparently been applied to picture retrieval only in a few sophisticated, mechanized and scientifically oriented collections. Sophisticated and mechanized indexing systems are clearly not the answer for very many picture collections; yet, so far they appear to be the only use of concept coordination in picture filing.

Our purpose here is to discuss concept coordination in nonscientific, relatively unspecialized, small or medium collections, with correspondingly modest budgets. The aim is a generalized example, easy to modify for specific uses or to use in its present form for the humanities or social studies, and especially for the fine arts.

Let us think in terms of a few thousand valuable pictures that we wish to coordinate conceptually for serious interrogation. We shall want to ask the file some really discriminating and hard questions, not just: "Do you have a picture of the *Lusitania?*" or "How about a picture of Ulysses S. Grant?"

Let us consider a typically "difficult" request:

> "May I please see your 15th century and 18th century Italian and French and your late 20th century American paintings and drawings that show the spirit of revolt in society as opposed to political acquiescence? We want these pictures in order to compare the art with the literary and philosophical writings of those periods and places. We want only color subjects. We also want to show poor people as well as rich, and we don't want all the virtue on the side of revolt or all the passivity on the side of the conservatives."

If the file being interrogated contains any real quantity of paintings and drawings of the countries and time periods in question, such a request is within the possible useful scope of the file. As with any file, of course, a fully specific question may produce a disappointment (an empty set), but this disappointment is also useful information. Other files may be more useful, and most questions can be generalized intelligently with increased chances for favorable findings.

If the file is a concept-coordinated file (in which "items" are coordinated with their associated "features" or "characteristics"), we can question it in terms of the features, characteristics, or attributes of the items we seek, rather than seeking the items directly by name. We may not know any name for the combination of characteristics we seek, let alone a name that might have been anticipated by the collection. What name would we give to the items sought in our "difficult" request?

We ask a concept-coordinated file, serially, for a series of features, embodied in the items they represent: *(1)* paintings; *(2)* Italian and French, and *(3)* 15th and 18th centuries; *(4)* American, and *(5)* late 20th century; *(6)* people, and *(7)* groups of more than two; *(8)* protesting or in revolt; *(9)* active or heroic, or *(10)* passive or static; *(11)* affluent, or *(12)* not affluent; *(13)* powerful, or *(14)* not powerful; and *(15)* conflict-related. This is the combination of features or attributes we seek.

There are a number of ways that this search could be carried out and listed, depending upon the particulars of the file and its handling system. This example is based, generally, upon the model described in this discussion. The handling will be described in its simplest terms.

A picture may be of some assistance in describing a search for pictures. Through Item 8 above, the relations between the sets of features requested can be pictured in a Venn diagram (Figure B-1) showing the "intersections" of the sets.

The strength of the concept-coordinated file idea, in appropriate contexts, is difficult to appreciate with any exactness. The number of separate "file folders" created by a

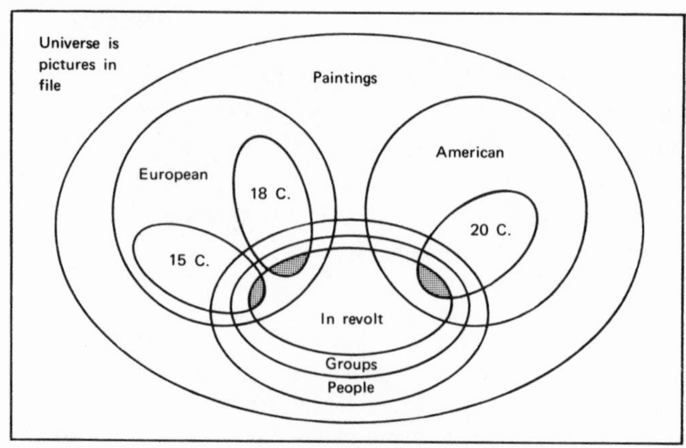

B-1 *A Venn or "circle" diagram illustrating the relationships of the "difficult problem" of picture research, as described in the text. The outer rectangle includes all the pictures in the file. The shaded portions are the pictures actually sought.*

modest concept-coordinated file, such as will be proposed here, becomes almost astronomical, especially when some of the schedules are composed of nonmutually exclusive features.

The file structure

We will need some definitions and classifications.

Picture. Any fixed image.

Universe of discourse. Entities (considered only in respect to the main picture subject) of which pictured representations exist in file.

Item. A picture, represented for classification purposes by an edge-notched card (or other vehicle) in file.

Feature. An attribute or characteristic of the main subject of the picture.

Vehicle. The edge-notched card (in this simple model application) with schedules and other information as listed below.

A concrete example may be helpful. Edge-notched cards are one possible vehicle whose use is widely understood. The complete classification of a picture ("View of Utopia," the frontispiece to this appendix) is shown as a typical notched card (Figure B-2). In this case a few words and 20 notches represent: place, famous, complex, man-controlled, relief print, 1500–1800, fine art original, letter U (subject: Utopia), innocent, good, optimistic, social, urban, for approval, mythical, letter S (origin: Switzerland), and a B artistic rating. These serve to classify a woodcut of More's *Utopia* (Basel edition, 1518), file accession No. 1002W.

Non-punches (complements) also supply information: artist unknown (or unimportant), more than two main elements, *not* conflict-related (here peaceful), *not* work-related definitely, *not* realistic, *not* aggressive, *not* protesting. Any combination of these concepts (either positive or negative) will produce this card as evidence that this picture possesses each of these features. Likewise these features possess this embodiment, the picture.

The form of the parallel picture file (the pictures that are symbolically represented by the cards) need not be specified here. Such a file could be a file of negatives, master prints, miscellaneous clippings, or in fact any collection that can be numbered and whose members can be located again as necessary. However, it is essential that the file be properly maintained and not be carelessly added to or subtracted from without adding or subtracting cards.

The classification scheme is printed on the back of a McBee Keysort Card. This provides an inexpensive way to test an application for a particular collection. Categories are as follows:

1. Subject classifications. Two Dewey Decimal digits usually (class and division) with third digit optional (section).

2. Names. Common names of main subjects or artists' last names. If the artist is known and important, the artist's name should be listed and an additional position punched to indicate that the name *is* an artist. Some photographers can be treated as artists if desirable. But for most subjects the names stand for our old friends, the alphabetical subject heads for file folders. We can look for cats under C and Ulysses S. Grant under G. If it is important to do so, we can make a thesaurus–dictionary to regularize usage for those who wish to look in this way for items instead of features. We cannot do any more with this alphabetical file alone than we can with any other such file, but it should make many people more comfortable just to know that it is there. Synonyms may also be punched.

3. Dates. These indicate the main *subject* reference, except where the "artist" position is punched, in which case the date refers to the artist's dates, and the name is the artist's name. By appropriate date ranges, for example: before 1 AD, 1 AD–800, 800–1500, 1500–1800, 1800–1900, 1900–1939, 1939–1960, and after 1960.

4. Classes of picturable entities. These classes are intended to be almost mutually exclusive and collectively exhaustive for the universe of picturable entities:

Person	Process
Thing	Place
Animal	Relationship
Plant	No definable class

Obviously these terms are to be understood in certain broad senses. "Animal" includes all live creatures except man. "Thing" includes substances as well as objects and constructs. "Process" stands for identifiable complex progressions and makes one moment stand for the whole time sequence of the process—as when the subject is "storm" or "assembly line" or "crop dusting." The process itself must be the *main* subject and more important than anything else in the picture. "Relationship" refers to abstract relationships when they are the main subjects (maps, charts, diagrams, etc.). Examples of "no definable class" are an abstract painting, music notation, perhaps news clippings, etc.

5. Generic features. These apply to almost all classes listed above. Of 84 possibilities

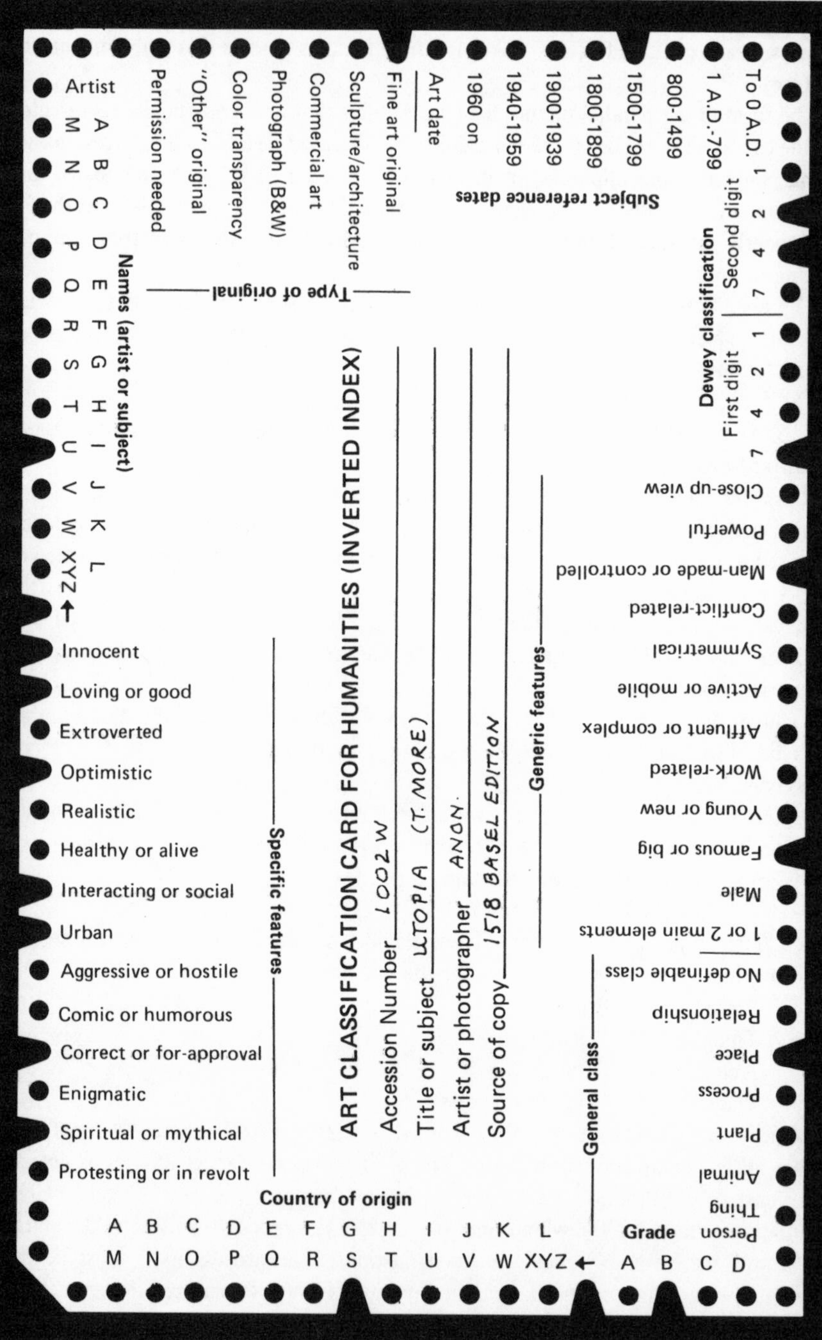

B-2 *An edge-notched card describes the "View of Utopia" in terms of its attributes or characteristics, which can be used to search the file. This illustration can be duplicated on cards, or other variations can be created to test applications of the indexing method described, technically known as "inverted indexing," or concept coordination. (The card shown is the McBee Keysort card #W11749ER.)*

(excluding "No definable class"), these terms are in significant degree applicable to 75. The complement of each is at the right.

Male	Female
Famous or big	Not famous or not big
Young or new	Not young or not new
Work-related	Not work-related
Affluent or complex	Not affluent or not complex
Active or mobile	Not active or not mobile
Symmetrical	Not symmetrical
Conflict-related	Not conflict-related
Man-made or controlled	Not man-made or controlled
Powerful	Not powerful
"Close-up" view	Not "close-up" view
1 or 2 main elements in picture	3 or more main elements

These terms are applied to the *main* subject of the picture. In any pair of terms that occurs in the left column either member of the pair may apply to the subject, but both need not. The terms by which the items are classified (by the person coding the picture) are in the left column. Each feature is coded if it is present in the main subject. If it is not present, it is not coded. Thus, if we want items with the feature "male" we search for "male." But suppose we want items with the feature "female"? It cannot have been coded; *but* we can search for "male" and then take all the items that do *not* respond. Those will be the women—if we have sorted for the "person" class first. If not, we may also get some female "animals" like vixens, or some "things" associated with females.

The terms in the right column are the complements of those in the left column. All that is *not* included on the left *is* included on the right, for each feature. The complement of "work-related" is "not work-related." We cannot say that its complement is "leisure-related" because that would leave too many conditions that are in between work and leisure unclassified and irretrievable. This reflects something of a lack of discrimination in the complementary list terms, which could be remedied by defining many more terms in the left column. This might be done in a computer application, but when a computer is not used it is more practical to have a relatively simple classification system—and live with the lack of discrimination. Greater item recall will result, even if it is with less precision; and with less work.

This compromise seems to work well in practice for this model application—especially if the file interrogator keeps in mind some of the common uses for the complementary terms. For example, "not work-related" is *often* "leisure-related"; "not conflict-related" *can* be "peace-related"; "not powerful" is *sometimes* "weak"; "not close-up" view is *sometimes* "distant" view, etc.—*but not always,* by any means.

The true complement of "work-related" *must* be "not work-related"—a broad concept with a certain lack of discrimination that could include a lunch counter scene (unless the main subject is the counterman). Is climbing a mountain on vacation "work-related"? This is a typical question, which might be decided in several ways. Descriptive scope notes to generic and special feature lists should be elaborated to meet the felt needs of any particular collection on the basis of experience, e.g., "Work means related to performing a regular job for pay," or "Use physical definition of work."

These generic terms are not at all mutually exclusive and cannot pretend to be collectively exhaustive for classes. Normally they will be sorted *after* one of the first eight classes has been chosen, and the classes will have been sorted by the classification selected. The sorting may be carried out in any order and using any features, either present or absent. The use of the absent features (set complementation) needs to be kept in mind when interrogating the file.

6. Specific features. The list below *best* fits the arts, but the social studies, literature, and history can be generally served by it as well. (The pure sciences and technical subjects will need other lists of specific features.)

Innocent	Not innocent
Loving or good	Not loving or good
Extroverted	Not extroverted
Optimistic	Not optimistic
Realistic	Not realistic
Healthy or alive	Not healthy or dead
Interacting or social	Not interacting or not social
Urban	Not urban
Aggressive or hostile	Not aggressive or not hostile
Comic or humorous	Not comic or not humorous
Correct or for approval	Not correct or not for approval
Enigmatic	Not enigmatic
Spiritual or mythical	Not spiritual or not mythical
Protesting or in revolt	Not protesting or not in revolt

Only one term of any pair in the left column need apply. Classification is on the basis of the left column only. The right column is to aid interrogation. (It may be supplemented by a list of appropriate complement synonyms.)

Sorting can be in any order. Usually any "specific" sort follows a "generic" sort, but not necessarily. Many strategies will intuitively suggest themselves as the most direct route in particular cases.

This set of specific features applies to "people-oriented" pictures for the most part. Other sets of features can be elaborated for other subject areas. When the subject area has already been carefully classified, for example biology, such classifications will naturally serve as the basis for a feature code.

7. Countries of origin (of pictures). Alphabetical by name of country. The arrow punch indicates the lower row of letters—as, in the illustration, "S" is punched for Switzerland.

8. Information about the picture represented. These items, or a similar list, are punched only when they apply to the picture:

Fine art original (painting, drawing, etc.)
Sculptural original
Commercial art original (include maps, diagrams, etc.)
Photo original—black and white
Color transparency original
Other type of picture (clippings, etc.)
Permission needed

An optional piece of information about the picture is a subjective artistic rating that can be given by the classifier. People who work with pictures very often like to make subjective judgments of artistic merit, and sometimes such judgments are helpful even though there is little possibility of any objective standards. At most, however, this will save looking at some of the pictures, or it will encourage the inspection of others.

9. Information to appear on the face of the card:

Accession or list number of item
Title or subject
Artist's or photographer's name
Source of reproducible copy

Notes (miscellaneous information) can be written on the back of the card.

General suggestions

When translating the visual language into words, by means of which we can discuss, interrogate, relate, and so on, we *must* rely in part upon subjective judgments. This is especially true in the fine arts where much of the effect and communication depend upon the viewer's willingness to project subjective feelings. Thoughtful subjective classifications are to be encouraged. The pictures must be "read" and interpreted intelligently but not speculated upon wildly. In assigning specific features it is preferable to err on the side of greater "recall" from the file rather than greater "precision." This means freedom to express subjective feelings. Unwanted pictures, or those with the wrong interpretation for the searcher, are rejected on inspection.

One person should be trained and put in charge of the use of the file. On the other hand, a short instruction in classification, subject to the rules of the person in charge, is all that is usually necessary to prepare someone to interrogate the file. Learning to paraphrase general vocabulary questions in the file's terms and learning to evolve search strategies are not difficult skills. It is mostly common sense, but one must think of the file categories and make these the terms of the search definition.

For example, in searching for the specific features it is hardly necessary to sort for "people" first, because the specific features apply almost exclusively to people. We could narrow the search by a generic feature sort either before or after a specific feature sort. Several alternative search strategies are possible for many ideas; this can provide a pleasant and often surprising form of browsing. In fact, for most types of search there is almost no way to make a mistake in using the file, and the method of use is quickly learned. However, as mentioned before the *complements* of the generic and specific lists should be used imaginatively, and when sorting for them, one must remember to take the cards that do *not* respond.

Mistakes, of course, are quite possible in some types of classifying for the file. Care should be exercised to classify items by the search categories. For example, visual representations such as paintings, drawings, and photographs almost always should be classified by the subject they represent. An important exception (in this model) is fine art by well known artists which should be alphabetically filed in the "names" section by the artist's name, instead of by subject.

In this case the "artist" position is punched, as well as the first letter of the artist's last name. When the artist is *not* well known, the classification may be by the name of a person who is the subject of the picture or just the "name" of the subject, in which case the "artist" position is not punched, but only the first letter of the subject name. (In the example "U" is punched for Utopia.)

File maintenance is accomplished in two ways: a periodic check can be made on the consecutively ordered master *picture* file. We hope, for the sake of retrieval, that this file can be inviolate. If numbers are missing and the picture must be presumed lost and irreplaceable, the corresponding cards are removed from the card file and a list of missing numbers kept.

The greatest precautions should be taken to prevent deterioration and losses from the master file. Current usage is often so irregular that even the idea of an inviolate master file may sound strange and unlikely to many picture librarians, but without it there can be no standard of maintenance and no structure to permit retrieval. The master file must be quite *selective,* of course; there are oceans of pictures in the universe of picturable subjects. For most collections the first question will be what to include, or which part of a large collection to classify for retrieval.

Scope of the system

A complete rationale for any set of schedules and descriptors for the features of the picture could be quite an undertaking. In trying to embrace, descriptively, whatever can be pictured, a considerable amount of intuition is necessarily operative.

Somewhat theoretically, the descriptors can be thought of as a loose approximation to Bertrand Russell's "minimum vocabulary"* of description, in which every part of a given body of knowledge can be expressed by means of words belonging to that "minimum vocabulary," and no word in the vocabulary can be defined in terms of other words in it.

In regard to the choice of a minimum vocabulary, the visual aspect of the descriptive continuum has certain special characteristics that come to our aid. For example, as we

*Bertrand, Russell, *Human Knowledge—Its Scope and Limits.* (New York: Simon and Schuster), p. 257.

have noted, there are only about seven classes of entities that can be pictured at all, as contrasted with the many more classes that can be thought of and written about.

We simplify further by considering each picture, for classification purposes, only in relation to its main subject, and this subject chiefly in relation to the aspect actually pictured. In the case of still pictures, which we consider here exclusively, time shrinks to a fraction of a second, usually.

As with any concept-coordinated file a reasonable compromise is sought between adequate *recall* (getting everything that may be relevant) and *precision* (not getting too much of the irrelevant with the relevant). This compromise is always a somewhat generalized operation, one that cannot designate the specific picture. The last stage is, properly, visual screening of a reasonable number of possibilities.

A natural reaction of some researchers to a filing system such as this may be that it is too complex, and every detail a likely subject for debate. It may be felt that people without library training will be unable to operate such a system. A modest trial soon dispels this feeling, however. Unlike books, pictures are "all on the surface"; and it is possible for persons of average intelligence to classify them with considerable subtlety after a short acquaintance with the classification schedules. Of course, the classifications must be done conscientiously or there is no true file, but four or five minutes per picture is not excessive for most valuable files or for most classifiers. It is quite unnecessary for those using the system to understand the reasons for its structure, or even the nature of filing by concept coordination. But regardless of who does the classification, an adequate initial instruction *and continuing spot checking* is essential to maintain the integrity of the file. The test is whether classifiers and searchers understand each other in practice, and whether the sensitivity and pertinency of the day-to-day performance makes the construction of the file worthwhile.

The system is, in an important respect, fail-safe. For those who wish only to find a picture of Ulysses S. Grant, or to see some Gauguin drawings, and have no use for concept coordination, Grant is still under G (with the "artist" position *un*punched), and so is Gauguin (with the "artist" position punched), no matter where the originals are located. And where would Grant be in the typical direct subject-heading file? "People–Famous–Dead," perhaps? Never to be seen again, perhaps.

Selected Bibliography

American Institute of Physics. *Style Manual for Guidance in the Preparation of Papers.* New York: American Institute of Physics, 1967.

American Medical Association. *Style Book and Editorial Manual.* 3rd edition. Chicago: American Medical Association, 1965.

American Society of Magazine Photographers/Society of Photographers in Communications. *ASMP Guide to Business Practices in Photography.* New York: ASMP, 1973.

Ballinger, Raymond A. *Graphic Reproduction Techniques.* New York: Van Nostrand Reinhold, 1976.

Billmeyer, F. W., Jr., and Saltzman, M. *Principles of Color Technology.* New York: John Wiley & Sons, 1966.

Byrd, William, Press. *Mathematics in Type.* Richmond, Va.: The William Byrd Press, 1954.

Cavallo, R. M., and Kahan, S. *Photography: What's the Law?* New York: Crown Publishers, 1976.

Conference of Biological Editors. *Style Manual for Biological Journals.* 2nd edition. Washington, D.C.: American Institute of Biological Sciences, 1964.

Crawford, Tad. *Legal Guide for the Visual Artist.* New York: Hawthorne Books, 1977.

Croy, O. R. *Camera Copying and Reproduction.* New York: Hastings House, 1964.

DeVinne, Theodore Low. *The Practice of Typography: Plain Printing Types* and *Correct Composition*. 2 vols. New York: The Century Co., 1900.

Durrant, W. R.; Meacock, C. W.; and Whitworth, R. E. *Machine Printing.* New York: Hastings House, 1973.

Graphic Artists Guild. *Pricing and Ethical Guidelines.* New York: Graphic Artists Guild, 1975.

Graphic Arts Technical Foundation (Pittsburgh, Pa.) publications:

- #1509 *Color Separation Photography: With an Introduction to Masking* (Erwin Jaffe, Edward Brody, and others, 1959)
- #1520 *Electronic Composition: A Guide to the Revolution in Typesetting* (N. Edward Berg, 1975)
- #6051 *How to Test the Effect of Paper Color on Process Color Reproduction* (Frank M. Preucil, undated)
- #7213 *Copy Preparation for Phototypesetting* (Daniel J. Makuta, 1971)
- #7219 *The Multi-color Overlay System* (Harvey R. Levenson, 1974)
- #7222 *Typographic Production Control: A PERT Approach* (Stanford H. Rosenberg, 1975)
- #9510 *Tone and Color Correcting* (Lawrence Reichel, 1956)

Hamilton, Edward. *Graphic Design for the Computer Age.* New York: Van Nostrand Reinhold, 1974.

Herdeg, Walter, ed. *Graphis/Diagrams: The Graphic Visualization of Abstract Data.* New York: Hastings House, 1974.

Hofmann, A. *Graphic Design Manual.* New York: Van Nostrand Reinhold, 1965.

Huff, Darrell. *How to Lie with Statistics.* New York: W. W. Norton, 1954.

Hunt, R. W. G. *The Reproduction of Colour.* England: The Fountain Press, 1975.

Johnston, Edward. *Writing and Illuminating and Lettering*. London: Pitman, 1937.
Kepes, Gyorgy, ed. *Module, Proportion, Symmetry, Rhythm.* New York: George Brazillier, 1966.
Lee, Marshall. *Bookmaking: The Illustrated Guide to Design and Production.* New York: R. R. Bowker, 1965.
Levin, R. I., and Kirkpatrick, C. A. *Planning and Control with PERT/CPM.* New York: McGraw-Hill, 1966.
McDarrah, Fred W., ed. *Stock Photo and Assignment Source Book.* New York: R. R. Bowker, 1977.
McGraw-Hill Book Company. *McGraw-Hill Technical Composition Standards.* New York: McGraw-Hill, 1966.
MacKellar, Thomas. *The American Printer*. Philadelphia: MacKellar, Smiths & Jordan, 1872.
MLA Style Sheet, The. William Riley Parker, comp. New York: Modern Language Association, 1975.
Morison, Stanley. *Four Centuries of Fine Printing*. New York: Farrar Straus, 1949.
Novotny, Ann, ed. *Picture Sources 3.* New York: Special Libraries Association, 1975.
Phillips, Arthur. *Computer Peripherals and Typesetting.* London: Her Majesty's Stationery Office, 1968.
Phillips, Arthur. *Setting Mathematics: A Guide to Printers Interested in the Art.* Bristol, England: The Monotype Corp./John Wright & Sons, 1956.
Pierson, John. *Computer Typesetting Using PAGE-1.* New York: Wiley-Interscience, 1972.
Rice, Stanley. *Book Design: Text Format Models.* New York: R. R. Bowker Co., 1978.
Rosen, Ben. *Type and Typography.* New York: Van Nostrand Reinhold, 1976.
Ruder, Emil. *Typography: A Manual of Design.* New York: Hastings House, 1967.
Seybold, John W.. *Fundamentals of Modern Composition.* Media, Pa.: Seybold Publications, 1977.
Seybold Report. Media, Pa.: Seybold Publications. (A subscription periodical on composition methods.)
Shaw, Renata V., comp. *Picture Searching: Tools and Techniques.* New York: Special Libraries Association, 1973.
Simon, Oliver. *Introduction to Typography.* Cambridge, Mass.: Harvard University Press, 1945.
Skillin, Marjorie E.; Gay, Robert M.; and others. *Words into Type.* 3rd edition. New York: Meredith Publishing Company, 1974.
Swanson, Ellen. *Mathematics into Type.* Providence, R.I.: American Mathematical Society, 1971.
United States Government Printing Office. *Style Manual.* Washington, D.C.: GPO, 1967.
University of Chicago Press. *A Manual of Style.* Chicago: The University of Chicago Press, 1969.
V-I-P Tape Preparation Manual. New York: Merganthaler Linotype Company, 1976.
Zweifel, Frances W. *A Handbook of Biological Illustration.* Chicago: University of Chicago Press, 1961.

Glossary

alphabet length The length, in points, of the lowercase alphabet from *a* to *z*. When a value is given for a typeface and size, regular weight roman style is understood, unless otherwise specified.

alphanumeric A term pertaining to the roman alphabet, *a* to *z*, and the numerals 0 through 9, usually not including special characters and signs.

analog A representation of the behavior of a system by a continuously variable quantity, such as an electric current, as opposed to a discontinuous measurement, such as digital.

art editor In this book, a person functioning under the general direction of a designer, in many ways as a quasi-designer, but without specific typographic or design training. Chief duties: dummying, researching pictures, monitoring traffic, and keeping records.

ASMP American Society of Magazine Photographers, now the Society of Photographers in Communications.

"author" Under copyright law, not only the author of an original written creation, but the artist, photographer, and designer, who are the "authors" of the art, photographs, and designs they create for a book.

automatic composition system A general term meaning any typesetting system in which a significant number of decisions made by human judgment in traditional systems are made by a machine automatically following defined decision logic.

back matter Materials that follow the main text of a book, such as appendixes, glossaries, and indexes. They are numbered continuously with the main text.

band graph A graph composed of superimposed frequency polygons and developed from the basic histogram representing comparative quantities.

BMI The abbreviation for the Book Manufacturers Institute, one of several groups that oversees the manufacturing standards for school textbooks.

body Type body, or the total depth, in points, of the vertical type size plus its assigned leading.

Cameron process A letterpress printing process that employs a continuous paper "web," and is used to print, fold, and collate complete books at high speed for adhesive binding.

cap and lowercase (c&lc) A style specification meaning that all principle words are to start with a capital letter. Non-principle words are usually considered to be articles, coordinate conjunctions, and prepositions, regardless of length, and the word "to" in infinitives—except when they are the first or last words of a title. Also called "upper and lowercase" (u&lc).

caption *See* legend.

carding Traditionally, carding was the insertion of paper strips between lines of lead type to increase page depth a small amount. "Electronic carding" increases the spaces between lines, in small increments, for the same purpose. The designer may wish to allow or to disallow.

castoff The process of relating characters and pages of manuscript to book pages of a given format. Usually it does not include allowances for pictures.

characters per pica The number of characters of a defined typeface setting that fits in one linear pica, usually expressed to one or two decimal places. In normal English-language text settings, approximately 342/alphabet length (q.v.).

CIP The abbreviation for the Library of Congress Cataloging in Publication Data, printed on copyright pages.

codex The physical form of Western books, i.e., printed leaves open at the right and bound together at the back edge.

color composite A combined image of various color illustration subjects in one composite, same-size grouping that can be shot at one time to make printing plates, thus effecting economy and enabling retouching and color masking in the process of duplication of the color subjects. Done by a color laboratory.

column head The heading that appears at the top of many columns in tabular work. Sometimes called a "box head."

concept coordination The coordination and retrieval of filed items by associating their conceptual "features" or "characteristics," rather than by looking for them directly by name.

contact image A same-size image of type and/or illustration materials made by photo contact of some kind. Typically, blueprints, silver prints, brown-line prints, Van Dykes, Color-key, Poly-proof, and so on. Contact imaging is used to check various stages of bookmaking.

contrast In photography, the ratio or range of the light reflected by the light areas (or transmitted by transparency) in relation to that of the dark areas, in a single subject. The range of a color transparency may be as much as 1000 to 1, whereas the range of reproduction of the same subject may be no more than 60 to 1.

conversion screen A mechanical screen pattern that can be combined with a continuous tone photographic or art subject in such a way that the continuous gray tones are converted into black and white values only. The patterns are of various kinds.

corner quads Square corner marks, usually hollow em squares of text size, set at the top corners of those pages not full at the top (inside the regular text page dimensions). They indicate the top corners of pages such as chapter or part openings.

CPM Critical Path Method of scheduling, involving a network of interconnected activities and the events that stand for the completion of each separate activity. *See also* critical path.

critical dimension That dimension of an illustration or group of illustrations that is critical in relation to some other measurement, such as page width, or the matching dimension of another illustration.

critical path That path through a scheduling network, such as a CPM network, that requires the most time to complete. The overall schedule cannot be shorter than the combined times on the critical path. *See also* CPM.

CRT The abbreviation for cathode ray tube. In typesetting terminology this designates a very fine grain "TV" tube that is used to form the type characters, under computer control, for exposure to photographic paper or film. It allows considerable freedom of character formation, especially automatic obliquing and the expansion or condensation of horizontal set. *See also* set size.

default specification A specification that is to take effect in the absence of any other or any later specification.

delimiter In relation to text format control instructions in computer-controlled composition systems, the character(s) used to set apart (delimit) the control characters from the text characters. Brackets or angles are often used.

direct-entry typesetter A typesetting device that sets type without going through a tape (or other storage medium) stage that is subject to intermediate correction or manipulation prior to the typesetting operation.

direct positive A photographic or photostatic image that is produced in duplication of an original without going through a negative stage first.

display mathematics Mathematical expressions that occur on lines separate from the text, usually centered or flush at the left, with space above and below.

display type A somewhat indefinite term meaning type (a) of a size larger than can be set on a given typesetting device, or (b) of a size larger than is ordinarily used for text.

dummy A vehicle, usually a printed, two-page, dimensionally correct diagram of the page plan for a particular book, bearing a complete detailed physical plan for the book, including pasted up (or taped on) type proofs and illustration images to size, plus any necessary clarifying notes.

edge-notched card A card, representing an item in a file, on which the conceptual attributes of the item in question are represented by notches in the edge of the card. The cards are coordinated by means of the notches. *See also* concept coordination.

editorial structure Any definable editorial configuration in common use, such as a footnote, table, heading, list, index, or bibliography.

em A relative horizontal space measurement equal to the horizontal value of the type size being used. Thus 1 em of a 10-point size set to 9-point "set" width would be 9 points, rather than 10 points. *See also* set size.

equal area map Any map projection in which areas that are equal on the earth, or on a globe, also are represented as equal on the map. Statistical distribution should be represented only in equal area maps.

equation number The reference number of a centered mathematical equation or group of equations, usually set either flush left or flush right on the text measure opposite the last line of the equation (but centered on multiline signs of aggregation, such as brackets).

escapement In typesetting, the horizontal distance that is allowed for the setting of any particular character (or space), together with, in the case of characters, any "side-bearing" spaces.

event In CPM scheduling (q.v.), the completion of a definable stage of work.

extract *See* secondary text.

feature In concept-coordinated filing, an attribute or characteristic of an item in a file, which is used as a basis for retrieving the item. *See also* concept coordination *and* edge-notched card.

file An organized collection of records, as for example the composition file for book typesetting. Usually refers to records stored for computer utilization.

fillet line A line going across the spine of a bookbinding.

fineline print A photographic print that is made to hold very fine details of black and white copy.

first pass A term used in modern composition systems to designate the first proof or "galley" stage. "Galleys" are trays used to store lead type in traditional systems of lead composition and do not exist, of course, in most modern composition.

flat In photoengraving, a grouping of illustrations of the same form (usually supplied by the publisher), to be shot together.

floating illustration An illustration that does not have to occur at a specific point in the copy, but can position anywhere within a variable space after its text reference.

flush Aligning at left or right with something else, which must either be specified or be clear by implication. "Flush left" or "flush right" or "flush top" or "flush bottom" implies aligning with the extremities of the complete type page as defined. Any other flush condition should be made clear by specification, e.g., "flush bottom with illustration."

font A complete assortment of a given style and size of type. A traditional term usually taken to mean roman and italic caps and lowercase, small caps, common punctuation, and signs and figures. Sometimes taken to include the accompanying boldface of the style.

"for hire" If it is agreed in writing that art or photography or design is to be done "for hire" (as supplementary work for a book), then the hiring agency is legally the "author" and owns exclusive rights to the work supplied.

fore edge The margin of the type page away from the gutter and spine of the book. The area from type page to trimmed paper edge.

form In book printing, a group of pages printed at the same time, on one side of the sheet only. Usually 16 or 32 pages. Also called "press form."

format Any design, or the design aspect of any definable editorial structure, such as a footnote, table, heading, list, index, bibliography, and so on. (But note that in many automatic typesetting systems the term "format" may mean the set of automatic controls required to effect a specific repeating structure, or more precisely, to effect the transfer from one set of format controls to another.)

fractions Styles of fractions used in text composition are called (1) shilling or solidus, (2) special or em, (3) case or en, (4) built-up and (5) font. See pages 116–117.

french spacing The use of only a justifying space after periods that end sentences. The most common system of spacing in modern practice. *See also* regular spacing.

front matter The book pages occuring before the start of the main text of the book, such as title page, introduction, and contents. Also called "preliminary pages" or "prelims." Usually numbered in lowercase roman numerals.

gray scale In photo separation of color copy, a neutral scale of gray values photographed with the color copy and used as an indication of color shifts in the reproduction process.

gutter The margin of the book page next to the spine. The area from type page to spine.

hanging indent A condition of alignment in which lines subsequent to the first are indented at the left to align with the first line. Usually used for certain types of lists, and in outlines, bibliographies, and indexes.

initial cap and lowercase A style designation, often abbreviated "init. c&lc," meaning that only the first word is to be capitalized. Words normally capitalized in text, such as proper nouns, are capitalized, but not all the principal words. *See also* cap and lowercase.

interactive makeup Page makeup processes under automatic simulation (as on CRT, under computer control), which are subject to continuous designer interaction and direction.

interface A connecting channel or linkage between any two communicating systems.

interword space The space set between words, which may be a variable "justifying space" in justified composition or a fixed space (usually ¼ or 1/3 em) in unjustified composition. In many composition systems the interword space may be defined in terms of "basic" or "normal" and maximum or minimum, within rather narrow limits of tradition and justification logic.

ISBN Abbreviation for International Standard Book Numbering. This is set on the copyright page.

item identifier A numeral, letter, or ornament that identifies an item of a list, outline, or similar structure.

justify To space out lines of type to a specified measure, following specified rules of normal, minimum, and maximum word spacing, and rules of hyphenation.

Kelvin temperature A scale of temperature starting at absolute zero, used to measure light "temperature" in photography and color reproduction. A level of 5000° Kelvin has been adopted by the American National Standards Institute (ANSI) as the light temperature for comparative viewing of color reproductions and copy.

kerning Traditionally, the cutting of one lead character into an adjacent character to make them fit more tightly. In modern composition systems, it signifies the reduction of character side spaces to make typefaces fit more tightly than they are normally designed to do. This can be done on a full-text or on a selective basis and is often called "negative letterspacing." The units by which spaces are controlled vary from one composition system to another.

key An arbitrary code, used in marking an identifiable editorial structure in manuscript, that stands for the defined structure together with its associated specifications.

leaders The repetition of one or more characters, such as a period, either spaced or not spaced, to fill a line. Contents lists and stub columns in tabular work often contain leaders.

leading The vertical spacing between lines of type, formerly strips of lead introduced between the lines. This spacing may now often be either positive or negative in relation to the normal minimum body on which the typeface is designed to be set, but it is assumed to be positive unless otherwise stated. Type specified as 10/12 is set 10 point vertical size on a 12 point body, which includes two points of extra leading.

legend The two terms "legend" and "caption" are often confused, or used synonymously. They describe the explanation accompanying, usually under, an illustration. More properly, a caption is either above the illustration or is the title of a legend.

letterspacing Any adjustment, either positive or negative, in the spacing of letters that changes the "side bearings" or spaces assigned to each letter in the original design of a particular typeface. It is assumed to be positive spacing unless otherwise noted, since traditional systems could only set positive spaces. For a description of negative letterspacing *see* kerning.

libel Injury to the reputation of another through falsehood. Subjects of illustrations have the right to be free of libel.

line numbers Numbers set to identify lines, as of poetry, drama, and so on, usually set small, flush right.

line space A "1 line space" is usually assumed to be a vertical space equal to the total body size of a line of main text unless otherwise noted. The reason that it means the text line rather than a line of any other format is that, whenever possible, pages are planned to come out to even text lines in depth.

linen A type of book cloth finish that is characterized by the weave of the cloth showing lightly through applied coloration.

lining numerals Numerals that all align with capital letters: 123456789. Also called "ranging" or "modern" numerals. Lining numerals are usually used unless nonlining are specified (and available). *See also* nonlining numerals.

McCain stitching A type of bookbinding in which the sewing at the spine is done from the side, thus strongly binding the pages together. Used mainly for schoolbooks.

measure The maximum width of the normal text type line, as defined for each job.

mechanical Camera copy for any printing process, which often combines type and illustration so that it will all be shot in correct register and with correctly separated colors and tones.

model release A consent form to be signed by the subjects of photographs that may be published, indicating that the subject (and/or guardian) gives consent to the photograph and to its use as stated in the form.

module A unit of structural planning, also called "modular unit." In books, an even division of the type page, used both for the orderly sizing of illustrations and for text fitting.

name tag *See* key.

negative letterspacing *See* kerning.

nonlining numerals Numerals with ascenders and descenders: 123456789. Also called "nonranging" or "old style." Most often used in books in the humanities to harmonize with caps and lowercase or small caps. *See also* lining numerals.

oblique An electronically slanted version of a typeface, often with 11 or 17 degrees slant, but variable as a factory machine adjustment. Oblique is available only on CRT typesetting devices and is used when a true italic is not available, or as an alternative style to italic. Often it is the only "italic" available for sans serifs in CRT systems. It can be used at any time and can be specified for any characters available to the system.

OCR The abbreviation for Optical Character Recognition. An electronic pattern-recognition-based method for translating certain typewritten characters into machine-readable form for further processing.

off-center Any arrangement that is not centered in respect to separate line elements, such as headings, illustrations, tables, and so on. Often the off-center elements are flush at the left, but sometimes at the right, or in an especially quadded or indented pattern.

one-time rights The rights to reproduce and publish a picture in multiple printings of one edition of the book for which it is purchased.

operators Mathematical signs of two kinds: (1) "verbs," such as $=$, $\neq$, $< >$, $\equiv$, and so on (about 27 signs); and (2) "conjunctions," such as $+$, $-$, $\times$, and so on (about 14 signs). The spacing around operators in mathematical composition is seldom under design control.

optical centering The vertical adjustment of any element so that it appears centered to the eye. This may be different from mechanical centering, depending on the shape and balance of the element in question. This is a hand adjustment in all systems of composition, an extra cost item.

outside of page The outside edge of each page, as opposed to the "inside" or "gutter" edge.

overset A condition in which the characters to be set in one line exceed the line measure.

PAGE-1 The graphic arts computer language first evolved for the control of the VideoComp typesetting system.

PAR In this book, the number of text pages, the units of art, and the units of picture research, all added together. Used in scheduling to estimate factors such as dummying time.

parameter A variable value of control data associated with a defined item of control. In the PAGE-1 expression [ps, 10], the item is "ps" (point size) and the parameter is "10." *See also* PAGE-1.

perfect binding A bookbinding process dependent upon adhesive applied to the spine of book pages. Used almost exclusively for books with paper covers.

pica Twelve points, an absolute unit of measure approximately 1/6 of one inch, a basic unit of traditional printer's measure. Also, a size of typewriter type having 10 characters to the inch.

pictogram A chart or graph expressing comparative statistical values by means of small unitized pictures referring to the subjects of the statistics.

point An absolute unit of measure, 1/12 of one pica, approximately 1/72 of one inch, a basic unit of traditional printer's measure. The "decipoint," used in some systems, is 1/10 of one point. One point = .0138 inch, and 72 points = .9962 inch. The continental or "Didot" point = .0483 inch.

posterization The separation of continuous-tone illustration copy, such as photographs, into separate areas of equal gray value, and the subsequent treatment of these areas in some more or less arbitrary artistic fashion.

predummy plan In this book, a preliminary scheme reflecting production planning for a given book and leading to a detailed dummy for the book.

press form *See* form.

process printing A four-color (black, yellow, cyan, and magenta) printing process, involving photomechanical separation of color, used to simulate colors occurring in copy, such as color art and photographs. Also called "full color" or "4/C."

program In automatic calculation or logical manipulation of data, a set of logical sequential instructions capable of solving a given computational or logical problem.

programmable calculator A calculator capable of automatically executing a program entered by the user. *See also* program.

public domain "In the public domain" means that ownership rights belong to the public rather than to any individual or organization, as for example rights of authorship.

pull In relation to foil stamping, the length of foil necessary to apply one color of foil to one book cover.

quadding The action of filling out a line with empty spaces, or quads (originally nonprinting "quadrates"). The term "quad left" means to move the text in a line flush to the left by quadding out at the right; and "quad right" means to move the text in a line flush to the right by quadding out at the left. "Quad center" means to center a line of text by quadding out at left and right equally.

recto A right-hand page, with an odd-numbered folio.

register Two or more impressions of ink, foil, etc. (or images on a vehicle such as film) that are in correct relation to each other are "in register"; if not, they are "out of register."

regular spacing The use of a quad space, usually 1 em, after all periods that close sentences. A misnomer in modern practice since it is seldom used except in certain technical or classical texts and in some elementary grade books. *See also* French spacing.

reverse leading The operation of some typesetting machines to "go back," to reverse film movement for a specified distance, in order to start typesetting again at a specified point, e.g., to set type automatically in two or more columns.

right of privacy The legal right, enjoyed by subjects of photographs, not to have their private lives unfairly invaded, i.e., not to suffer "invasion of privacy."

run in Set on the same line, following a previous text element. Not starting a new line.

runaround An illustration set into the side or center of a type page in such a way that the type "runs around" the space occupied by the illustration.

running title The running head or running foot to each page, usually on the same line with the folio.

runover *See* turnover.

sans serif Typeface design not having the small bracketing accents at the ends of the letter strokes, often called "gothic" or "block letter." Square serif letters do not properly belong to this grouping.

secondary text Text set off from main text by distinctions of format. This is often called an "extract" because it is usually material extracted or quoted from other sources.

sentence spacing The use of a quad space, usually one em, after periods that end sentences. *See also* regular spacing.

sentence style Capitalization and sentence spacing as used in normal sentence style. Usually used as opposed to cap and lowercase in specifying heading style. It is normally equivalent to "initial cap and lowercase."

set size Also known simply as "set," the horizontal size of the type, which can be controlled and specified separately from the vertical size in computer-controlled CRT typesetting systems. The set size can be expanded or condensed within certain practical limits. The set specification must be separately designated for the typesetter, otherwise the set size will be assumed to be the same as the vertical size. The note "10/12, 9 set" means 10 point vertical size with 9 point horizontal size, leaded 2 points.

signature In printing, one printed and folded sheet ready for binding, most often 32 or 64 pages. In web press printing, in which there are no sheets, strictly speaking, the delivered binding unit may be referred to as a signature.

sinkage The vertical distance that any line or graphic element is dropped ("sunk") from the top of the normal text page, as defined. It is measured in picas and points from the top of the running head, if there is one, otherwise from the top of the first text line, or from the top of corner quads. (It should *not* be measured from the trimmed edge of the paper page.)

slack time In critical path scheduling, the amount of time "to spare," which can be used for activities not on the critical path without extending the overall schedule. *See also* critical path.

Smyth sewing A style of bookbinding in which the signatures are sewn together at the back, offering the least resistance to complete and flat opening. *See also* McCain stitching.

spanner head In a table, a column heading that applies to two or more columns. Usually it is centered over the columns to which it applies.

stat A photostat.

stored format controls In computer-controlled typesetting systems, the programmed subroutines that control the various repeating elements of format transfer. These subroutines are usually given short alpha-numeric names by which they can immediately be recalled from computer memory and utilized as required. The name need only be mentioned in the text stream, but it must be set apart from it by some recognizable "delimiter" in order not to be mistaken for actual text characters. Also called "format statements."

tape-operated typesetter A typesetting device controlled by means of a tape on which text characters and machine instructions have been stored. *See also* direct-entry typesetter.

thin space An indefinite term in typography that most commonly means horizontal spacing equivalent to about ¼ of 1 em. A more precise term is preferable.

trade book A book intended to be sold to the public through book stores, as opposed to a textbook, which is intended for quantity sale to schools or colleges.

transmittal meeting In publishing, a meeting held to "transmit" a manuscript from the editorial department to the manufacturing department, starting the manufacturing schedule. Also called a "launch meeting."

trimmed size The outside dimensions of the paper page after the book has been trimmed. Usually it is given in inches, with the horizontal dimension being given first.

turnover An unintended separate line created because the copy is too long to be contained on a previous line. If the previous line started flush left, the turnover is often, but not always, indented to show that it is a continuation line.

typositor A proprietary name of a hand-operated film typesetting device chiefly used for display typography. Often used to mean any similar device.

universal characters Characters that are not of any particular typeface design but are used "universally" with any typeface. Superior or inferior characters, mathematical signs, and most nonalpha-numeric symbols are universal characters.

upper and lowercase (u&lc) *See* cap and lowercase.

variable Any quantity whose value is free to vary under different conditions, as for example the *x* or *y* in algebra. *See also* parameter.

variant-form publishing The publishing of various selections, or text subsets, in various formats, from one basic composition file. Usually this is most economically done from a composition file under computer control.

vellum A solid-colored, smooth-finished book cloth. Also a smooth-finished paper.

velox A black-and-white photographic print capable of reproducing fine lines and mechanical screen tints up to about 100 lines per inch.

verso A left-hand page, having an even numbered folio.

vid A VideoComp unit of measurement used for horizontal spacing. There are 50 vids to 1 em.

web printing Printing done on a continuous roll or "web" of paper. The web is cut into sheets and usually slit into binding units before folding. Most large-run book printing is done on web offset presses.

widow A non-dialogue text line that is not filled to the full text measure and that begins a new page or column, or that occurs under an illustration, table, etc. It is considered poor typographic style to permit widows in final page makeup, especially when they are short. They are often allowed when they are over 2/3 or 3/4 of a line in length. Avoiding widows is one of the problems of page makeup, whether automatic or manual.

x height The height of the typeset letter *x,* as in "cap x height," or "lowercase x height."

Index

Agents for artists, 23, 216–217
Art/design activities, list of, 4–5, 146
Art/design, pricing of, 140–141
  and Graphic Artists Guild, 140
  and *Pricing and Ethical Guidelines*, 140–141
Art director/designer, function of, 1–2, 7–8, 22, 122–125
Art editor/assistant designer, function of, 125–127, 139–140
Artist contact, 211
Artists, selection of, 23–27, 126
  and agents, 23
  artist record sheet, 25 (form)
  edge-notched cards, 26 *(Fig. 3–1)*
Artwork
  assignment of, 189–190
  contact images and illustration proofs of, 191, 192
  contract for, 190
  and payment to artist, 191
  and selection of artist, 189
  sketches and finishes of, 190–191
  specifications for, 190
  style samples of, 190
  technical aspects of, 189–190

Bindings, 177–186
  cloth or nonwoven synthetic material, 177
    McCain-stitched (side-sewn), 179 *(Fig. 10–4)*, 180
    Smyth-sewn, 178 *(Fig. 10–3)*, 179–180
  paper, 177
    perfect bound, 177
    Smyth-sewn, 177
  stamped covers, 180–186
    binding specifications for, 185
    cloth, 180
    fitting, 184 (table), 186
    foil stamping of, 181–182, 183 *(Fig. 10–5)*, 184
    ink stamping of, 190
Bleeds, allowance for, 197–198
BMI (Book Manufacturers Institute) specifications, 186–187
Book Design: Text Format Models (Rice), 225
Book length, adjusting, 75–94
  and book length optimization form, 88, 89–90 (forms), 91
  and castoff
    aids to, 94, 95 *(Fig. 6–2)*, 96 *(Fig. 6–3)*, 97 *(Fig. 6–4)*
    and Castoff "Plus," 91, 92 *(Fig. 6–1)*
    and illustration program, 81
    using pocket calculator, 77, 81
    and programmable calculators, 91, 93
    and tables of castoff results, 82, 83–84 (tables), 85–86
    and text fitting, 80–82
  and character count, 75–77, 80
    separate counting of selections form, 79
    summary castoff form, 78
  and page makeup adjustment, 86–88

Castoff. *See* Book length, adjusting
Charts and graphs, 31–33, 35
  accuracy of, 35 *(Fig. 3–3)*
  checklist for, 31–32
  types of, 32, 33 *(Fig. 3–2)*, 35 *(Fig. 3–3)*
Color. *See* Four-color process reproduction; Transparencies, color
Composition, difficult
  chemistry, 118
  computer-controlled electronic composition of, 106, 107, 108 (form), 109
  foreign languages, 117
  mathematics, 114–115, 116 *(Fig. 7–6)*, 117
  and Monotype, 99–100, 101 *(Fig. 7–1)*, 102
  sources of style information for, 109
  special characters for, 102, 103 *(Fig. 7–2)*, 104 *(Fig. 7–3)*, 105 *(Fig. 7–4)*
  tables, 110–111, 112–113 *(Fig. 7–5)*, 114

Composition, display
hand composition of, 53, 56
machine setting of, 53, 56
and Typositor and similar systems, 53, 56
Composition order, 56–57, 58 *(Fig. 4–1),* 59 *(Fig. 4–2)*
Contact imaging, 191, 192
Copyright Law (revised). *See* Illustration and design use, legal aspects of
"Critical Path Method." *See* Scheduling art activities
CRT (cathode ray tube), 48–49, 57, 106, 220

Design processing, 3 *(Fig. 1–2),* 4–5, 21–23, 121–141
and art director/designer, 122–125
and art editor/assistant designer, 125, 139–140
dummying, 129–131
and illustration file, 136
and information folder, 126–127
and master illustration list, 126–127
picture research and related record keeping, 133–136
planning illustration program, 21–23, 125
predummy planning, 127–129
Design specifications as interface, 1–2
Design trends, 219–233
automatic electronic page makeup and layout, 229–231
catalogs of designed formats, 225–226
computer-controlled composition, 222–225
design by exception, 220–221
electronically generated color, 231, 232 *(Fig. 12–2),* 233
standards in coding and text-format controls, 228–229
stored automatic text-format controls, 223–225
text structure matrixes, 226, 227 *(Fig. 12–1)*
Diagrams, 38–39, 40 *(Fig. 3–6),* 41
Drawings and diagrams, science, 40–41
Dummy
and compositor, 138
information for, 126–127, 131
materials for, 131
second dummy, 138
steps in making, 129–131

Editorial structures
complexity/flexibility of, 10–14
specification of, 11–12, 14–19, 50, 52
types of, 8, 9 *(Fig. 2–1),* 17–18
typesetting options for, 51–52
Editorial substructures, 52
Ethics, Code of, and Standards of Fair Practice, 210, 216–217

Four-color process reproduction
and appearance of colors under fluorescent lamps, 174 (table)
copy preparation, 171–172
correcting proofs, 173–176
and four-color contact imaging color simulation systems, 172 *(Fig. 10–2),* 173
"grayness factor" in, 171
hue error in, 172
and process colors, 172
quality of, 170–171
selecting copy for, 176–177
viewing proofs of, 173

Graphic Artists Guild, 140
Pricing and Ethical Guidelines, 140–141
Graphic Arts Technical Foundation color circle, 172 *(Fig. 10–2). See also* Four-color process reproduction

Harris Fototronic CRT. *See* CRT
Hoffman, Paul, in the *Seybold Report,* 228–229

Illustration and design use, legal aspects of, 235–249
acquisition of rights, 236–237
provisions of new law relevant to illustration and design, 240–241
types of artwork, 237–240
art in the public domain, 239–240
artwork done to publisher's specifications, 238
commercial art and reference art, 238–239
fine art, not done to publisher's specifications, 238–239
types of reproduction rights, 242–244
advertising or promotion, 243–244
exclusive, 243
first rights, 243
one-time rights, 243
U.S., world rights, 244
Illustration forms, 210–217
art department work, 210, 215 (form)
artist's contract, 210, 211 (form)
chart specifications, 210, 214 (form)
map specifications, 210, 213
photographer's contract, 210, 212 (form)
Illustration processing forms, 205–210
art/photo transmittal, 204, 208 (form)
checklist for offset dummies, 204, 206 (form)
grouping illustrations for offset camera work, 204, 207 (form)
handling picture sections and mechanicals, 204, 205 (form)
illustration information sheet, 204, 209 (form)
Illustration programs. *See* Design processing

Illustrations
credits for, 137, 138
file for, in nondummied books, 136
legends for, 136
Illustrations, handling, 194–205
bleed allowances, 197–198
color transparencies, 199–200
late illustrations, 201, 203
line conversions, 201, 202 *(Fig. 11–2)*
mounting and retouching, 198
numbering of, 194
photographic prints, 199
register marks, 194–195
reproduction quality photostats and Veloxes, 200–201
scaling and cropping, 195, 196 *(Fig. 11–1)*, 197
Illustrations in letterpress work, 203
Illustrations in offset process, 191–194
and blues, 192–193
color composites for, 192
color proving of, 193
comparative costs of, 194
and composite contact images, 194
latitude in treatment of, 192
and pages, 191

Keying, of manuscripts, 14, 16–19

Legal aspects of illustration and design use. *See* Illustration and design use, legal aspects of
Legal aspects of photograph use. *See* Photograph use, legal aspects of
Lists, specification of, 12–14, 15 (form)

Makeup. *See* Pages, making up
Manual of Style, A (Univ. of Chicago), 2, 10, 64, 109
Maps, 33–43
analytical, 34
and cartographer, 33–34
design specifications for, 42–43
and designer, 33–34, 38
projections of, 34, 36 *(Fig. 3–4)*, 37 *(Fig. 3–5)*
reference, 34
Mathematical displays, specification of, 10–11
McDarrah, Fred W., 134
Stock Photo and Assignment Source Book, 27, 134
McGraw-Hill Technical Composition Standards, 109
Model Releases. *See* Photographic use, legal aspects of, consent forms
Modular text, 70, 71 *(Fig. 5–3)*, 72 *(Fig. 5–4)*
Monotype, 99–100, 101 *(Fig. 7–1)*, 102, 115–117

NASTA (National Association of State Textbook Administrators) specifications. *See* BMI specifications

PAGE-1 control language for VideoComp, 222–224
Pages, making up, 63–73
and dummy, 66
and illustrations, 66, 68
flow chart for, 67 *(Fig. 5–1)*
in multicolumn format, 68, 69 *(Fig. 5–2)*
instructions to compositor, 64
rules for automatic paging, 64–65
See also Modular text
Paper, text
characteristics of, 164–165
design aspects of, 163–164
and standard trimmed sizes, 165–166
Photograph use, legal aspects of, 244–249
consent forms ("model releases"), 246, 247 (form)
contracts, 248
copyright notices, 246, 248–249
invasion of privacy, 245–246
loss or damage, 248
Photographic program
checklist for, 28–29
and designer, 27–30
followup activities, 30
and location photography, 29–30
model releases, 30 (footnote)
and photographers, 28–30
planning, 28–29
processing, 30
See also Photograph use, legal aspects of
Picture research
and art editor, 133
and commercial picture agencies, 135
and free sources, 135
legal aspects of, 133
and permission, 133
and picture traffic records, 135
and publishing house files, 135
sources for, 27, 135
and transmittal slips, 134 (form), 135
See also Illustration and design use, legal aspects of; Photograph use, legal aspects of
Picture retrieval, concept coordinated system of, 251–253, 254 *(Fig. B-1)*, 255, 256 *(Fig. B-2)*, 257–261
Picture Sources (Special Libraries Association), 27, 135
Preceding events, and art and design activities, 145, 146, 156
Predummy planning, 127–128

Pricing and Ethical Guidelines (Graphic Artists Guild), 140–141
Printing
"Cameron" process, 167
and color planning for press forms, 167, 168 *(Fig. 10–1)*, 169
and signatures, 169–170
web-fed rotary offset process, 166–167

Research. *See* Picture research
Rice, Stanley, 225
Book Design: Text Format Models, 225

Sample pages, 4, 191
Scaling and cropping, 195, 196 *(Fig. 11–1)*, 197
Scheduling art activities (multiple large design art projects), 145–161
art and design activities, 146, 148
and "Books in Work" chart, 156, 157 *(Fig. 9–5)*
and the "Critical Path Method," 146, 147, 148 *(Fig. 9–1)*, 149–150, 151 *(Fig. 9–2)*, 152, 153 *(Fig. 9–2)*, 154 *(Fig. 9–4)*, 155–156
and weekly job-status reports, 158, 159 (form)
and work rate experience, 160 (form)
and work standards file, 158, 160–161
Scheduling art activities (simple books), 143–144
Special characters, 102–106 *(Figs. 7–2, 7–3, 7–4)*
Special Libraries Association, 27
Picture Sources, 27, 135
Specification
of editorial structures, 11–12, 14–19, 50–53
of "invisible" or ideal book, 60–61
and keying manuscript, 14, 16–19
of lists, 12–15
of mathematical displays, 10–11
Stock Photo and Assignment Source Book (McDarrah), 27, 135

Tabular composition, 110, 111, 112–113 *(Fig. 7–5)*
Transparencies, color
handling of, 199–200
rules of thumb for copy, 176
Typesetting
basic information for compositor, 55 (form)
composition order, 56–57, 58 *(Fig. 4–1)*, 59 *(Fig. 4–2)*
documentation from typesetter, 46–47
vertical and horizontal spacing, 47
word spacing, 47–48
See also Composition, difficult
Typesetting systems, 45–49. *See also* Composition, difficult; CRT; Monotype; Typositor; VideoComp
Typographic planning, 46, 49–50, 51 (form), 53
Typositor and similar systems, 56

U.S. Government Printing Office Style Manual, 10, 109

VideoComp, and paging, 66, 67 *(Fig. 5–1)*, 68, 222–224
See also PAGE-1 control language for VideoComp, 222–224

Zweifel, Frances W., 109
Handbook of Biological Illustration, A, 109

Set in Times Roman (VideoComp digitization)
with display in Serif Gothic Bold
Text composed on VideoComp CRT equipment
by COMCOM, a division of The Haddon Craftsmen, Inc.
Printed and bound by The Haddon Craftsmen
a division of Intext, Inc.
Paper: Lindenmeyr Sebago antique wove, cream
Cloth: Holliston Roxite B vellum
Edited by Filomena Simora
Geoffrey K. Mawby kindly read Chapter 10
Photographs by the author (except page 232)
Designed by Stanley Rice